A Practitioner's Gui
Trusts

Michael Waterworth MA (Cantab)
Barrister

Second Edition

First published in 2001

Other titles in this series:
A Practitioner's Guide to Advising Charities
A Practitioner's Guide to Beneficiaries' Actions
A Practitioner's Guide to Charity Fundraising
A Practitioner's Guide to Contentious Trusts and Estates
A Practitioner's Guide to the Court of Protection
A Practitioner's Guide to Executorship and Administration
A Practitioner's Guide to Inheritance Claims
A Practitioner's Guide to Legacies
A Practitioner's Guide to Powers and Duties of Trustees
A Practitioner's Guide to Powers of Attorney
A Practitioner's Guide to Probate
A Practitioner's Guide to Trustee Investment
A Practitioner's Guide to Trusts

A Practitioner's Guide to Drafting Trusts

Members of the LexisNexis Group worldwide

United Kingdom   LexisNexis UK, a Division of Reed Elsevier (UK) Ltd, Halsbury House, 35 Chancery Lane, LONDON, WC2A 1EL, and 4 Hill Street, EDINBURGH EH2 3JZ

Argentina	LexisNexis Argentina, BUENOS AIRES
Australia	LexisNexis Butterworths, CHATSWOOD, New South Wales
Austria	LexisNexis Verlag ARD Orac GmbH & Co KG, VIENNA
Canada	LexisNexis Butterworths, MARKHAM, Ontario
Chile	LexisNexis Chile Ltda, SANTIAGO DE CHILE
Czech Republic	Nakladatelství Orac sro, PRAGUE
France	Editions du Juris-Classeur SA, PARIS
Germany	LexisNexis Deutschland GmbH, FRANKFURT and MUNSTER
Hong Kong	LexisNexis Butterworths, HONG KONG
Hungary	HVG-Orac, BUDAPEST
India	LexisNexis Butterworths, NEW DELHI
Ireland	LexisNexis, DUBLIN
Italy	Giuffrè Editore, MILAN
Malaysia	Malayan Law Journal Sdn Bhd, KUALA LUMPUR
New Zealand	LexisNexis Butterworths, WELLINGTON
Poland	Wydawnictwo Prawnicze LexisNexis, WARSAW
Singapore	LexisNexis Butterworths, SINGAPORE
South Africa	LexisNexis Butterworths, Durban
Switzerland	Stämpfli Verlag AG, BERNE
USA	LexisNexis, DAYTON, Ohio

© Reed Elsevier (UK) Ltd 2003

A CIP Catalogue record for this book is available from the British Library.

ISBN 0 75451 914 7

Typeset by Kerrypress Ltd, Luton, Beds

Printed and bound in Great Britain by The Cromwell Press Limited, Trowbridge, Wiltshire

Visit LexisNexis UK at www.lexisnexis.co.uk

Preface

Trusts are strange creatures. They come in a variety of different forms and serve a variety of different purposes. As a result, the question what is and what is not a trust can be a difficult one to answer and many practitioners are left confused and not a little frightened by the concept.

This book is not intended as an authoritative academic treatise on trusts but as a practical account of the making and, to some extent, the managing and breaking of trusts. The emphasis is on drafting working settlements within the fiscal framework principally laid down by the Inheritance Tax Act 1984.

The book is divided into four parts. Part I is an introductory section covering the nature, uses and validity of trusts.

Part II covers the fiscal classification of trusts, a classification principally determined by the inheritance tax treatment of trusts. This part begins with the tax treatment of trusts in general terms, and then looks in turn at the most commonly used trusts – that is, interest in possession, discretionary and accumulation and maintenance trusts; before moving on to more specialised trusts such as bare and protective trusts, and trusts for the disabled and for employees. Part II also includes a discussion of charitable trusts, trusts arising on death and a brief overview of overseas trusts.

Part III is concerned with the drafting of trusts, including chapters on drafting style, the form and content of the trust deed itself, the means of constituting trusts and choice of trustees. Part III also discusses trustees' powers and duties from the drafting point of view.

Part IV includes a brief discussion of the management of a trust and a chapter covering the means of bringing trusts to an end.

Twenty-nine precedents are included in Appendix 1, ranging from complete trust deeds to useful recitals. The emphasis is on completeness and simplicity and it is hoped that from these precedents the draftsman will be able to construct his own bespoke deeds.

In addition to the precedents, the statutory materials referred to in the text are set out in full in Appendix 2.

My aim has been to include as much practical detail as possible in this book but the scope of the book is necessarily broad. Where a concept deserves further exploration, readers are referred to more academic texts such as Underhill and

Hayton, *Law Relating to Trusts and Trustees* (16th ed), *Lewin on Trusts* (17th ed) and Hanbury and Martin, *Modern Equity* (16th ed). For a more detailed discussion of the taxation issues discussed in Part II, readers are referred to *Foster's Inheritance Tax* and *Mellows: Taxation for Executors and Trustees*.

As ever, the staff of LexisNexis UK have provided excellent encouragement and assistance. I would also like to thank those colleagues and clients whose, sometimes searching, questions and informative discussions have helped me in many ways. I would also particularly like to thank my wife Caroline for her patience in the seven weeks or so since work on this book began.

The law is stated as at October 2003.

Michael Waterworth
10 Old Square
Lincoln's Inn

20 October 2003

Contents

Table of Cases

Table of Statutes

Paragraph numbers in **bold** type indicate where the legislation is set out in part or in full

Table of Statutory Instruments

Part I: Introduction to Trusts

Chapter 1

What are Trusts

What are trusts

1.1   The trust is a creation of equity and the English common law. It has passed into the use of other common law jurisdictions but has not found a home in Napoleonic or Roman civil jurisdictions. Some civil jurisdictions, such as France and Italy, have contracted to the Hague Convention on the Law Applicable to Trusts and to their Recognition but the trust remains an essentially English concept employed throughout the Commonwealth (particularly Australia, where the judiciary have made an extremely active contribution to the development of the law of trusts) and the United States.

Definitions of trust

1.2   As with any creation of the common law, there is no codified account of what is meant by a trust and no singly accepted definition. There have been a number of attempts to define what is meant by 'a trust'. One widely quoted definition, which met with the approval of Romer LJ in *Green v Russell [1959] 2 QB 226*, is that which is reproduced in Underhill and Hayton, *Law Relating to Trusts and Trustees* (16th edn):

> 'A trust is an equitable obligation, binding a person (called a trustee) to deal with property owned by him (called trust property, being distinguished from his private property) for the benefit of persons (called beneficiaries or, in old cases, *cestuis que trust*), of whom he may himself be one, and any one of whom may enforce the obligation.'

Another useful definition is that which appears in article 2 of the Hague Convention, ratified by the Recognition of Trusts Act 1987. 'Trust' is defined by the Hague Convention in the following way:

> 'For the purposes of this Convention, the term "trust" refers to the legal relationship created – *inter vivos* or on death – by a person, the settlor, when assets have been placed under the control of a trustee for the benefit of a beneficiary or for a specified purpose . . .

The reservation by the settlor of certain rights and powers, and the fact that the trustee may himself have rights as a beneficiary, are not necessarily inconsistent with the existence of a trust.'

Halsbury's Laws of England, vol 48 (reissue) para 501, includes the following:

'Where a person has property rights which he holds or is bound to exercise for or on behalf of another or others, or for the accomplishment of some particular purpose or particular purposes, he is said to hold the property in trust for that other or those others, or for that purpose or those purposes, and he is called a trustee.'

Thus, to say that something is a trust (in the sense of a private trust) is to say that there is a relationship between two persons by which one (the trustee) owes obligations to the other (the beneficiary) in respect of property over which the trustee has control and, so far as the outside world is concerned, owns. It does not matter that the trustee might be one of the beneficiaries or that he is the person who created the trust (the settlor) and might have some power over the trustees or the trust property as a result. In the case of a charitable trust (see CHAPTER 13: CHARITABLE TRUSTS) the trustee holds property for the purpose of accomplishing some purpose but there will always be somebody capable of enforcing the trustee's obligations on behalf of the beneficiaries.

As will be seen, tax statutes do not attempt to define 'a trust'. Instead, the Inheritance Tax Act 1984, Taxation of Chargeable Gains Act 1992 and Income and Corporation Taxes Act 1988 rely upon the concept of 'a settlement' which they all define in different ways by reference to trust and property held in trust without proffering a definition of the trust itself. There is a traditional distinction in the nomenclature between a trust and a settlement with the trust being set out in a document called a settlement but few practitioners employ the terms precisely and in the following chapters both terms are used. The fiscal definitions of settlements (trusts) are discussed in greater detail in CHAPTER 5: TYPES OF TRUST. Their implications are discussed in CHAPTERS 6–15.

A trust need not be an express trust made in writing but can arise as, for example, an implied, constructive or resulting trust. With the exception of the brief discussion of secret trusts in CHAPTER 14: TRUSTS ARISING ON DEATH, this book is concerned only with express trusts and their drafting.

Nature of a trust

1.3   If a trust is best defined by reference to the relationship between trustee and beneficiary, its nature is perhaps best described by reference to the obligations owed by the trustee to the beneficiary in respect of the trust property. Those are not the personal obligations of contract or of a debtor but are the proprietary obligations of a fiduciary.

Article 2 of the Hague Convention includes the following:

A trust has the following characteristics –

(a)   the assets constitute a separate fund and are not a part of the trustee's own estate;

(b)   title to the trust assets stands in the name of the trustee or in the name of another person on behalf of the trustee;

(c)   the trustee has the power and the duty, in respect of which he is account-able, to manage, employ or dispose of the assets in accordance with the terms of the trust and the special duties imposed upon him by law.

One of the most difficult points to get across to the layman is that, although a trustee owns the trust property, it is not actually his. Of course, in the case of a modern flexible trust the trustee has broad powers of investment and the like and he may have a broad discretion as to the distribution of the fund amongst the beneficiaries but the property does not belong to the trustee beneficially. It is not, as the Hague Convention puts it, part of the trustee's own estate and if he does not manage, employ or dispose of the trust property in accordance with the terms of the trust, as is his duty, he will be held accountable for breach of trust.

A trustee might also be the settlor and may be one of the beneficiaries but he cannot be the sole beneficiary. A settlor can declare that he holds property in trust to pay the income to himself for life with remainder to another but he cannot simply hold the income and capital of the property in trust for himself because he has not separated the legal and equitable (or beneficial) ownership of the property. That separation of legal and equitable title is a fundamental characteristic of the English common law trust.

Trusts which are not trusts

1.4   Not all trusts are valid trusts. Some appear to be valid but are in fact shams, others are void for illegality or for want of certainty. For further discussion of this, and of the consequences of trusts being held to be invalid, see CHAPTER 3: VALIDITY OF THE TRUST.

A trust which is a sham is not a trust at all. It is almost the opposite of a genuine trust in which property is held by a trustee on trust for a beneficiary but appears to belong to the trustee. In the case of a sham the property really does belong, not to the beneficiary, but to the trustee or settlor but things are done to give the outside world the appearance that it does not. A sham arises where the parties to 'the trust' have a common intention that acts and documents which 'create the trust' do not actually create the legal rights and obligations which they give the appearance of creating: *Snook v London and West Riding Investments Ltd [1967] 2 QB 786*. A trust which is created as a result of a mistaken understand-ing of the legal effect of a transaction or by a trustee exceeding his powers (as in the rule in *Hastings-Bass*, see CHAPTER 20: TRUSTEES' DUTIES AND POWERS) may be voidable at the behest of the parties but is not a sham.

Chapter 2

Uses of Trusts

Traditional uses

2.1   Trusts have a multiplicity of uses. Traditionally these include:

(a)   postponing the time of vesting of the trust property to avoid feckless or wayward beneficiaries wasting or dissipating it;

(b)   capital taxation planning;

(c)   allowing the settlor or testator to postpone, change or control who is to receive either the trust income or the trust capital by passing the decision over to the trustees, thus offering a wide degree of flexibility in terms of deciding who receives what and when; and

(d)   enabling the settlor or testator to choose the persons who are to ensure that his wishes in respect of the trust property are carried out, that is, the trustees.

All of the above are essentially forms of estate planning although that term is more often associated only with capital taxation planning.

A settlor can, of course, retain for himself powers to remove or dismiss trustees and to appoint new trustees in the trust instrument. These powers can be passed on by the settlor in the case of a settlement, or, in the case of a will, given to others by the testator, if the respective settlement deed or the will provides for this. The choice and control of trustees is discussed further in CHAPTER 19: CHOICE OF TRUSTEES.

This chapter aims to examine the use of trusts for those estate planning purposes in a little more detail. It is worth considering when and why a practitioner might form the judgment that a trust is more appropriate than an outright gift.

Outright or absolute gifts do, of course, have drawbacks. The recipient beneficiary may immediately sell or otherwise dispose of the property gifted, by, in the simplest case, giving away the trust property. The beneficiary may not view the trust property with the same loving fondness with which the settlor or testator and/or his family has or have nurtured it, possibly over many years or generations. Just as the settlor or testator may have fixed and definite views and intentions concerning the use of the trust property, so the recipient beneficiary may have fixed and definite views, on receiving an absolute gift of it, as to how it should be dealt with. Such views may, of course, be at a complete, or partial, divergence from one another.

Even where the beneficiary intends to preserve the property he may divorce, become bankrupt or die. In each case outside forces may deprive the beneficiary of the benefit of the gift and so defeat the settlor's intention.

Furthermore, in the absence of such a calamity, though the beneficiary might understand his duties and responsibilities in respect of the trust property, his spouse, partner or heirs may not share the same view. Nor should they be expected to. A gift is a gift after all and should not be made with conditions attached if what is really intended is best served by the use of a trust.

Flexibility

2.2   One of the main advantages of using a trust as an instrument in estate planning is the flexibility that it can offer.

The pattern of modern life is far from predictable in many ways. The course of relationships and employment is much less 'fixed' than was the case for much of the period during which the traditional settlement developed. Or so it would seem. Doubtless the traditional patriarch settlor was just as perplexed to discover his children and grandchildren choosing to marry contrary to his approval much as the modern settlor is in seeing his children and grandchildren flitting from one quasi-matrimonial relationship to another.

On any view, however, the institution of the family is now much more dynamic in conceptual terms than ever it has been in the past and the law has not always kept pace with the many and varied relationships which now exist in twenty-first century society. Divorce, bankruptcy, non-marital and same-sex relationships, second (and subsequent) marriages, family estrangement and the non-nuclear family are commonplace. It is no longer sensible to assume that a child will grow up, marry and reproduce in the traditional manner supposed by the classic nineteenth-century settlement. The pattern of the same child's life and relationships is now wholly unpredictable. In addition to these essentially personal factors are the ever-changing social and (sometimes) environmental concerns of settlors. There are, as ever, issues of death and succession but coupled with the unpredictability of family life these can lead to complex and often variable thoughts as to the proper destination of property and as to its management in the interim.

The settlor or testator can hardly be expected to reach a decision as to the appropriate age at which his bounty should vest in a child while that child is but an infant. Such decisions can often be difficult until the child is nearly an adult and the views may continue to change over time, depending upon the character of the child, its educational, physical and mental needs, emotional development and attributes. The young adult who flits from one drug-fuelled, destructive and obsessive relationship to another is hardly to be trusted as the recipient of bounty but there are a plethora of more subtle characters whose ordinary mortal failings give their benefactors cause for concern from time to time.

Taxation and legislative change may also necessitate a change of perspective, philosophy or policy concerning estate planning.

A well-drawn trust should incorporate flexibility that will enable the trustees to change course if necessary and to maintain and apply the trust property at all times for the benefit of the beneficiaries. Flexibility is an issue that will recur in CHAPTER 16: DRAFTING STYLE in the context of drafting style but it is also an important consideration in the context of the use of a trust over an absolute gift.

Managing property for old, young and disabled persons

2.3   In addition to flexibility, trusts provide a means of ensuring that gifts can be made for the benefit of those unable to manage property themselves. The elderly, the mentally ill, the physically disabled and the young are all likely to find themselves in need of financial assistance in circumstances in which they lack the wherewithal or physical ability to manage funds for themselves.

A grandparent who wishes to provide funds for the benefit of grandchildren could simply make a gift to the parents of the grandchildren and hope for the best but if there is a possibility of the parents divorcing or suffering bankruptcy then the gift might never benefit the grandchildren. In such circumstances a discretionary trust or an accumulation and maintenance trust for the benefit of the grandchildren could be usefully employed to ensure that the gift is preserved for the benefit of the intended objects. Discretionary trusts are discussed further at CHAPTER 7: DISCRETIONARY TRUSTS and accumulation and maintenance trusts at CHAPTER 8: ACCUMULATION AND MAINTENANCE TRUSTS.

A trust might be used to make provision for children and grandchildren. With independent trustees and the judicious use of a memorandum of wishes the interests of adult children should not prevail over those of the grandchildren and so some balance between the competing needs of two generations can be preserved. The use of a memorandum of wishes is discussed further at CHAPTER 16: DRAFTING STYLE while the choice of trustees is discussed at CHAPTER 19: CHOICE OF TRUSTEES.

Where the intention is to make provision for a beneficiary the management of whose own financial affairs leaves much to be desired, the settlor should consider the use of a protective trust. Protective trusts are trusts which combine an interest in favour of a person described as the principal beneficiary and a discretionary trust which arises when the interest determines if, for example, the principal beneficiary becomes bankrupt. Protective trusts are discussed further at CHAPTER 10: PROTECTIVE TRUSTS.

Where the settlor wishes to make provision for a person who is physically or mentally disabled, an outright gift is unlikely to be appropriate. The settlor will normally want to create a trust in favour of that beneficiary. Sometimes the appropriate provision should take the form of a discretionary trust and sometimes a life interest trust (discussed further at CHAPTER 6: TRUSTS WITH AN INTEREST IN POSSESSION) but there is a special tax treatment of trusts for the disabled where certain conditions are met which should affect the settlor's choice. Trusts for the disabled are discussed further at CHAPTER 11: TRUSTS FOR THE DISABLED.

Asset protection

2.4   In different legal jurisdictions this term may have different connotations, but for these purposes it is intended to mean the legitimate protection of property from creditors of beneficiaries and, to an extent, from those having influence upon the beneficiaries, their heirs, spouses or partners and, provided that appropriate avoidance is taken in time and in accordance with the statutory framework and rules, the Inland Revenue.

Of course, if engaging in asset protection by using a trust, it is important to ensure that the trust is valid in the relevant jurisdiction, that it is properly drafted to reflect the wishes of the settlor or testator and that it allows sufficient flexibility, if this is what the settlor or testator wishes, to achieve such wishes and to adapt to future circumstances and events, possibly unforeseen at the time of the establishment or drafting of the trust. This is discussed further in CHAPTER 16: DRAFTING STYLE.

The essential nature of a trust is to transfer the ownership of the trust property to trustees, chosen by the settlor or testator, to protect and manage it on behalf of the beneficiaries. The trustees will then be accountable to the beneficiaries, subject to the terms of the trust instrument and the law, for their management and application of the trust property. This is discussed further in CHAPTER 20: TRUSTEES' DUTIES AND POWERS.

The settlor may be well advised to make a letter of wishes addressed to the trustees to identify the issues that are considered to be relevant and important to him at the time of the creation or drafting of the settlement. These wishes can of course be updated by the settlor from time to time, if so desired. The letter of wishes needs to be carefully drawn to avoid it being considered to be part of the trust instrument itself and incorporated by reference. It usually takes the form of a private letter addressed to the trustees for the time being of the settlement or will from the settlor or testator. The subject of letters of wishes is covered in more detail in CHAPTER 16: DRAFTING STYLE.

Subject to the terms of the trust instrument and the law, for example the Matrimonial Causes Act 1973, the Inheritance (Provision for Family and Dependants) Act 1975 and the Debtors Acts 1869 and 1878, however, the settlement of trust property will avoid the beneficiary automatically receiving or being entitled to the trust property on the happening of events, such as the death of the settlor, and will protect the trust property from the clutches of impecunious or undesirable relatives, the bankruptcy of those who would otherwise receive the trust property, their heirs and their spouse on any divorce.

A distinction should be drawn between a trust for a beneficiary who becomes bankrupt and a trust by which the settlor intends to avoid liability to his own creditors. The former is a legitimate exercise in asset protection but the latter is not and may be set aside under sections 339 or 423 of the Insolvency Act 1986. This is discussed further in CHAPTER 3: VALIDITY OF THE TRUST.

Tax planning

2.5   Trusts can be used as vehicles for the avoidance of inheritance tax and for other capital and income taxation planning. The trust taxation regime in England and Wales, although not now as favourable in some respects as it has been in recent years, is certainly not penal and does give scope for further planning within the trust itself and flexibility in terms of deciding the terms of the ultimate vesting of the trust property.

A well-drawn trust can be used by a settlor to remove value from his estate while giving the trustees, one of whom might possibly be the settlor, control over the trust property. Essentially, on the creation of a lifetime settlement, in the case of virtually all trusts, except discretionary trusts, provided that there is no reservation of benefit in the trust property in favour of the settlor, a potentially exempt transfer will have been made by the settlor. This is subject to the availability and application of any available reliefs for inheritance tax, so that provided that the settlor survives the date of the settlement for a period of at least seven years, the value of the property settled, on the loss to the settlor's estate valuation principle for inheritance tax, will be removed from the settlor's estate. If death occurs within seven years of a potentially exempt transfer, any chargeable transfers made within fourteen years of the date of the last potentially exempt transfer will need to be taken into account to calculate the inheritance tax payable. This is discussed more fully in CHAPTER 5: TYPES OF TRUST, and the relevant taxation regimes applicable to different types of trust generally used are set out more fully in PART II.

For will planning, the most frequent uses of trusts concern the setting up of will trusts to utilise the nil rate band on the death of the first of two spouses to die; trusts to deal with the matrimonial home (or a share of the matrimonial home); and trusts to protect assets in the case of a second marriage. These aspects are dealt with in more detail in CHAPTER 14: TRUSTS ARISING ON DEATH. It is sufficient for these purposes to state that tax planning involving the matrimonial home can be difficult and complex and attempting to balance various competing interests in, for example, a second marriage situation can be difficult to achieve.

Detailed consideration of the financial needs and resources of the relevant parties needs to be undertaken in order to ensure that a proper balance is struck.

If a charitable trust is established, whether by will or during lifetime, then no inheritance tax will be payable on the establishment of the trust. Charitable trusts are considered in more detail in CHAPTER 13: CHARITABLE TRUSTS and a precedent for a charitable trust is included in APPENDIX 1 at APP1.11. Precedents for the other types of trust mentioned in PART II are also included in APPENDIX 1.

Trusts of land

2.6   Trusts most frequently occur in the case of co-ownership of land since, wherever two or more persons own land, they hold it on a trust of some sort or another. Where trusts of land are expressly declared they are often quite simple and as a result statute and the common law have intervened to provide a means of determining what is to happen in the complex circumstances which can arise when co-owners of land fall out.

Many settlors wish to provide a residence for one or more beneficiaries, for example a child who has moved away from home to university. Others see land as a sound investment and desire that their trustees invest in it. This is especially so in a rising property market at a time when interest rates are low. Either the interest in possession or the discretionary trust can provide a useful means of settling land depending upon what the settlor is trying to achieve.

Trustees' powers in relation to land, including powers in respect of property which is available for occupation by a beneficiary, are discussed more fully in CHAPTER 22: ADMINISTRATIVE PROVISIONS.

Chapter 3

Validity of the Trust

3.1   All of the issues raised in this chapter may relate to the validity of the trust itself. Clearly there is little point in drafting a trust if its validity is going to be in doubt.

Purpose trusts

3.2   Apart from charitable trusts, most purpose trusts will be invalid, since there will be nobody to enforce them. In this context purpose trusts do not include trusts for the benefit of individuals with the expressed intention of furthering specified purposes such as the payment of school fees. A purpose trust in the true sense is one which is neither for the benefit of persons nor for purposes which are charitable. In the case of a purpose trust there is nobody beneficially interested in the fulfilment of the trust capable of enforcing it. A private trust for individuals may be expressed to be intended to achieve a specified purpose but will nonetheless be enforceable by them or on their behalf.

Apart from charitable trusts there are a few exceptions to this general rule. Private purpose trusts associated with the benefit of particular animals, the maintenance of graves or tombs and the promotion of fox hunting have been accepted as valid. Even in the case of these exceptional private purpose trusts, there is no living beneficiary who can enforce the trust. They are simply anomalous and have all been accepted as a result of litigation. From time to time the modern trust draftsman will be asked to prepare an invalid purpose trust. He should be aware of difficulty and find another way of achieving the settlor's aims.

Charitable trusts are an exception to this rule since they must, by their nature, have an element of public, as opposed to private, benefit and they are able to be enforced by the Crown through the Attorney-General, or by the Charity Commissioners.

Often a distinction is made between public trusts – charitable trusts for public purposes or for certain statutory public purposes, for example education (schools or universities) or health service trusts – and private trusts. The drafting of charitable trusts is discussed further at CHAPTER 13: CHARITABLE TRUSTS.

Four other classifications of trusts can be mentioned here:

- express trusts;

- implied trusts;

- constructive trusts; and

- resulting trusts.

Express trusts

3.3   These represent the majority of trusts created and are trusts expressed by the settlor or testator usually in a settlement deed or will, but not necessarily provided that the settlor or testator has expressed his intention in such a way as to satisfy the relevant evidential requirements. In the case of a trust of land, or any interest in land, section 53(1)(b) of the Law of Property Act 1925 requires that the trust 'must be manifested and proved by some writing'. An express trust may also be imposed by statute, for example under the Administration of Estates Act 1925 on an intestacy.

Since this book is concerned with drafting trusts, it is limited in scope to the express trust. The other categories are mentioned only for completeness.

Implied trusts

3.4   It often seems that implied trusts really only exist in the minds of Parliamentary draftsmen. The concept is rather vague, since there are no formal steps to be taken in order to establish them. They can arise where an express trust is not entirely clear as to its terms and a meaning is construed from the language used in the form of constructive or resulting trusts but those are separate categories. They might also arise by operation of law but once again only the constructive and the resulting trust spring to mind. It is, perhaps, not surprising that *Halsbury's Laws of England*, vol 48 (4th edn reissue), does not attempt to define the implied trust.

Constructive trusts

3.5   These are trusts which arise from the presumed intention of the settlor or testator or are imposed where it would be unconscionable or inequitable for the person apparently entitled to property absolutely to retain it for himself. In the case of *Paragon Finance plc v DB Thakerar & Co [1999] 1 All ER 400*, Millett LJ distinguished the constructive trust proper, where equity intervenes to prevent the legal owner from unconscionably denying the beneficial interests of others, from other constructive trusts whereby equity intervenes to provide relief from fraud by rendering those implicated in the fraud accountable as if they were trustees. Estoppel claims may, if successful, result in a constructive trust being imposed. Usually an application to the court will be necessary in order to establish and confirm that such a trust exists and to clarify its particular terms.

Resulting trusts

3.6   These arise where a rebuttable presumption of intention has arisen that property held by one person is owned beneficially for another, or where, for example, the whole beneficial interest is not disposed of when settled so that part or all of the beneficial interest undisposed of actually reverts (or results) to the settlor. This will happen where, for example, on a reverter to settlor none of the beneficiaries attains a vested interest in the trust property or there are no, or no effective, ultimate default trusts specified in the trust deed. When an express trust fails because the draftsman has left loose ends untied there may be a resulting trust in favour of the settlor. This can have very damaging fiscal consequences and should be avoided.

The rule against perpetuities

3.7   The rule against perpetuities or the rule against remoteness of vesting is complex and can be subtle in its application. Failure to adhere to it is a common cause of the invalidity of the interest concerned. The rule is not easy to summarise but its purpose is to prevent settlors or testators from tying up property in settlements or will trusts indefinitely. It does not apply to a charitable trust or to gifts over from one charity to another.

A detailed account of the rule is a specialist topic in itself but what the rule does is to set out a maximum period within which the interest of a beneficiary in the trust property must vest. At common law that period must be either the duration of the lifetimes of one or more specified persons living at the date of the settlement, or the date of death of the testator in the case of a will, plus 21 years. Because the rule is in those terms, absurd permutations of interests vesting outside the period could render those interests void. The situation has been saved to an extent by the 'wait and see' provision in section 3 of the Perpetuities and Accumulations Act 1964 (reproduced in APPENDIX 2) which provides that the affected interests should be treated as valid unless, at the end of the period, it becomes clear that an interest can only vest outside a permissible perpetuity period.

In order to avoid the settlement or will trust possibly being void for perpetuity, as being outside the rule, the draftsman therefore needs to ensure that all interests under the settlement will vest within the specified perpetuity period. If the draftsman errs, so that interests under the trust may vest outside the perpetuity period, the settlement will be valid during the 'wait and see' period. The prudent draftsman will not wish to 'wait and see', but will ensure certainty in this respect.

In order to introduce certainty and to maximise the potential length of a settlement, in many older trust deeds the period is often defined by reference to what is called a 'royal lives' clause, that is, 'the period ending 21 years after the death of the last survivor of the issue living at the date hereof of His Late

Majesty King George V'. Fortunately for the modern draftsman, section 1 of the Perpetuities and Accumulations Act 1964 introduced a fixed perpetuity period of up to 80 years which applies if specified in the will or settlement creating the trusts.

The latter period is usually the one chosen for modern trust deeds and it is the perpetuity period of choice in the precedents included in this work. It is recommended that the maximum fixed period of 80 years should be chosen unless there are good reasons to adopt a shorter fixed period, except in the case of those few valid non-charitable purpose trusts where a fixed period cannot be used.

The way in which this is commonly done is that the trust deed or will specifies that 'the trust period' will be the expiry of the period of 80 years from the date of the trust (or the date of death, as applicable) or such earlier date as the trustees for the time being of the trust or will shall determine by deed and that that period will be the perpetuity period applicable to the relevant trust deed or will. The settlement or will further provides that all interests under the trust must vest within the trust period and specifies what is to happen to any property remaining in the trust at the end of the trust period.

All dispositive powers, that is, those relating to dispositions from the settlement, must be limited to being exercisable during the trust period. The same is not true of administrative provisions (Perpetuities and Accumulations Act 1964, s 8 – reproduced in APPENDIX 2).

Accumulations

3.8   The rule against excessive accumulations limits the scope of trustees to accumulate income. Any power or direction to accumulate income which infringes the rule will be invalid.

The rule provides six different permitted periods. They are:

(a)   the lifetime of the settlor;

(b)   twenty-one years from the death of the settlor;

(c)   the minorities of persons living or *en ventre sa mère* at the death of the settlor;

(d)   the minority or minorities of any person or persons who would, for the time being, if of full age, be entitled to the income directed to be accumulated;

(e)   twenty-one years from the date of the settlement; and

(f)   the minorities of persons in being at the time when the settlement is made.

The first four of these are permitted by section 164 of the Law of Property Act 1925 (reproduced in APPENDIX 2). The last two were added by section 13 of the Perpetuities and Accumulations Act 1964.

The most commonly adopted accumulation period, and the one used for the precedents included in APPENDIX 1, is twenty-one years from the date of the settlement (or twenty-one years from the death of the testator in the case of the will trust precedents).

Where the class of principal beneficiaries includes unborns, then accumulation under the statutory power set out in section 31 of the Trustee Act 1925 will need to be included as a default provision, that is, to apply after the end of the defined accumulation period specified in the settlement. The precedents set out in APPENDIX 1 include an extended statutory power.

The Law Commission, in its report No 251 *The Rules against Perpetuities and Excessive Accumulations*, has proposed a longer statutory perpetuity period of 125 years, which proposal it is hoped will be enacted into law soon. This should, however, only apply to settlements executed or for deaths occurring after the bill is enacted. The report also proposes the abolition of the rule against excessive accumulations for private individuals and it is hoped that such abolition may be effected soon.

Certainty

3.9   If the required minimum tests of certainty as to the trust, as set out below, are not met then the trust itself will not be valid. Apart from charitable trusts, all validly constituted express trusts for the benefit of persons must, in addition to avoiding falling foul of the rule against perpetuities and excessive accumulations and satisfying the required evidential requirements, satisfy the so-called 'three certainties', which are:

(a)   certainty of intention;

(b)   certainty of subject-matter; and

(c)   certainty of objects.

For charitable trusts, provided that a general charitable intention can be shown, certainty of objects only does not need to be established.

Certainty of intention

3.10   What needs to be shown under this requirement is that the settlor or testator clearly intended to create a trust. The settlement deed or will establishing the trust will usually make this clear. Problems can, however, be encountered under this heading in the case of home-made wills, badly drafted wills, or in other cases where the interpretation of the language used is unclear, or it is uncertain as to precisely what the settlor or testator intends.

Often problems will be encountered where non-technical and precatory language is used, which will result in a wish or hope being expressed rather than a formal trust being created. Clearly the particular words used will need to be carefully considered and examined to establish the precise intention of the settlor or testator. What needs to be shown in order for this test to be satisfied is that when creating the particular trust in question the settlor or testator intended to create a legally binding obligation on the trustees, enforceable by the beneficiaries (*Jones v Lock (1865) 1 Ch App 25*).

In the case of professionally drafted express trusts, the declaration of trust found in the deed should always satisfy this requirement.

Certainty of subject-matter

3.11   What is required under this test is that there is sufficient clarity as to what property is intended to be subject to the trust and that there is no uncertainty as to what particular property is intended to be settled.

Future property will not usually be capable of being settled so as to satisfy this test, for example a future hoped-for inheritance, but if valuable consideration has been given and if the property does ultimately come into the hands of the recipient of the consideration, then a constructive trust will usually arise in respect of the relevant property, the terms of which will be the terms of the trust intended by the settlor or testator.

Various forms of intellectual property and other intangible property can be sufficient to satisfy the test, provided that it can be established fairly precisely as to what particular property the settlor or testator intended to settle. For example, in *Swift v Dairywise Farms Ltd [2000] 1 All ER 320*, it was decided that milk quota was capable of satisfying this test of certainty.

An example of where problems may arise under this heading is apparent from the case of *Boyce v Boyce (1849) 16 Sim 476*, where a testator gave his four houses in Southwold to trustees in trust for his wife for life, then after her death to convey one of them, whichever she might choose, to his daughter Maria, and to convey the others to his daughter Charlotte. Maria predeceased the testator and therefore could not choose a house. It was held that due to Maria's untimely death, the whole trust was void for uncertainty after the death of the surviving widow and that a resulting trust to the testator would apply. Quite whether this case would be decided in the same way today is unclear, but a court now, given the same circumstances, might decide that the gift to Charlotte should be upheld in respect of all four houses.

Certainty of objects

3.12   This test requires that all the beneficiaries of a fixed trust can be identified, or ascertained, at the outset, or will have been identified or ascertained when the time comes to distribute the capital or income of the trust, with a sufficient degree of certainty. Problems here are usually encountered either by the particular language used being unclear, so that the persons intended to benefit from the trust cannot be identified with certainty, or by the inclusion of too wide a class of objects. A trust for 'all my relatives equally' or 'all my friends equally' would be void for uncertainty under this heading.

This problem can sometimes occur in the case of discretionary trusts – generally speaking, however, such a trust will probably be valid provided that 'a substantial number of objects' (per Megaw LJ in *Re Baden's Deed Trusts (No 2) [1973] Ch 9 at page 24*) or beneficiaries can be identified.

Problems encountered with the particular language used are often fatal to the validity of the trust whereas, provided that the trust is not administratively unworkable and can be governed and enforced by a court of equity, then the inclusion of a wide class of beneficiaries will not be fatal.

The House of Lords' decision in *McPhail v Doulton [1971] AC 424* sets out the relevant test to be applied in the case of certainty as to beneficiaries under discretionary trusts. In that case the discretionary trust provided that the trustees were to make:

> '. . . at their absolute discretion grants to or for the benefit of any of the officers and employees or ex-officers or ex-employees of the Company or to any relatives or dependants of any such persons in such amounts at such times and on such conditions (if any) as they think fit'.

At the date when the trust was established, the company in question had about 1,300 officers and employees. It was clear that the trustees could not establish the names of all of the ex-employees of the company since the company was established, and, in the same way, all of their relatives and dependants. The Court of Appeal decided that the trust was valid on the basis that the trustees could, however, decide who did or did not fall within the class by requiring sufficient evidence to be produced to them by any beneficiary claiming to be within the class, to satisfy themselves that this was indeed the case.

Where, however, a discretionary trust requires unequal division, for example at the end of the specified trust period, then the trust will be void unless a comprehensive list of all beneficiaries can be drawn up either at the outset or at the date when the trust capital falls to be distributed (*IRC v Broadway Cottages Trust [1955] Ch 20*). This is also the test which will apply in respect of a fixed trust, as mentioned above. In *McPhail v Doulton*, the House of Lords decided that in the case of a discretionary trust, in appropriate cases, the court may enforce the trust:

(a)   by appointing new trustees;

(b)   by authorising or directing representatives of the class of discretionary objects to prepare a scheme of distribution; or

(c)   if considered necessary, by directing the trustees to so distribute the trust capital.

Where one or more of the three certainties is missing, the trust will be void for uncertainty and there will usually be a resulting trust to the testator (usually creating a partial intestacy) or settlor.

Administrative workability of the trust

3.13   In order to be valid a trust must be administratively workable. Essentially the terms of the trust must be justiciable, that is, enforceable and governable by the court in accordance with legal principles. In *Morice v Bishop of Durham (1805) 10 Ves 522*, the court declared void a purported trust for 'objects of benevolence and liberality', since the court had no clear criteria to enable it to control or execute the trust.

Trusts for illegal purposes

3.14   Any trust that is established for a purpose deemed to be illegal under the law of England and Wales is void. Trusts for illegal purposes usually arise in the case of wills and very often home-made wills. Some other examples of such illegal purposes are:

(a)   trusts specifically made illegal by statute, for example, section 29 of the Exchange Control Act 1947. When exchange control restrictions were in force prior to 1979, Treasury consent was required to be obtained before interests in trust property could validly be conferred on certain persons. Similarly the Human Rights Act 1998, the Race Relations Act 1968 and the Sex Discrimination Act 1975 may have some impact in this regard, but neither the 1968 Act nor the 1975 Act invalidates provisions in private trusts;

(b)   trusts encouraging the break-up of marriages or generally militating against the institution of marriage (unless in respect of a second marriage) or in a material fashion interfering with the general duties of a parent (see *Re Caborne [1943] 2 All ER 7, Low v Peers (1770) Wilm 375, Morley v Rennoldson (1843) 2 Hare 570, Lloyd v Lloyd (1852) 2 Sim NS 255, Craven v Brady (1869) 4 Ch App 296*, and *Allen v Jackson (1875) 1 Ch D 399*);

(c)   trusts militating to or promoting or encouraging immorality, fraud, dishonesty or other matters considered to be against public policy (see *Blodwell v Edwards (1596) Cro Eliz 509*);

(d)   trusts which attempt to restrict or interfere with the power of beneficiaries to dispose of their interests given to them under the trust (see *Sykes v Sykes (1871) LR 13 Eq 56*);

(e)   trusts by which the settlor or testator attempts to change the rules concerning the devolution of property as prescribed by law, for example in the event of an intestacy or on bankruptcy (see *Re Walker [1908] 2 Ch 705* and *Re Dixon [1903] 2 Ch 458*); and

(f)   as described above, trusts which provide for the accumulation of income beyond the period allowed by law or trusts which attempt to fetter property beyond the perpetuity period allowed by law (see the Perpetuities and Accumulations Act 1964 and sections 163, 164 and 165 of the Law of Property Act 1925 – reproduced in APPENDIX 2).

In contrast, however, it should be noted that if the settlement deed contains other provisions unconnected with the illegal or impossible purpose concerned, then it will usually remain valid in respect of those unconnected provisions (see *Re Harvey (1888) 39 Ch D 289* and *Re Bence [1891] 3 Ch 242*).

Similarly it should be noted that if a term of the trust is a condition subsequent and is impossible, uncertain, contrary to public policy or illegal then the offending term is deemed to be void and the relevant interest will vest as an absolute interest, free from the relevant condition (see *Re Beard [1908] 1 Ch 383*).

If the relevant term is a condition precedent, then the position will depend upon whether the condition is attached to realty or personalty. If realty, a failure to perform the condition for any reason will result in a failure of the gift; if personalty, if the condition precedent is impossible or becomes impossible because of any act or default of the testator or is illegal, the gift will be absolute in just the same way as if the condition had been a condition subsequent. Where, however, the performance of the condition is the only *raison d'être* for the making of the gift or the impossibility concerned was unknown to the testator or where it has become impossible since the date of the gift, for example by an act of God, then both the gift and the condition will be void (see *Re Elliott [1952] Ch 217* at page 221 and *Re Wolffe [1953] 1 WLR 1211* at page 1216).

If the trust is being created by a will or codicil and the testator is domiciled abroad, then the validity of the trust may be affected by any overriding provisions applicable in the jurisdiction where the testator was domiciled.

The most common examples of illegal voidable *inter vivos* trusts are trusts created with the intention of defrauding creditors. These normally fail to achieve their objective because bankrupts tend to leave everything to the last minute.

Money laundering

3.15   Underlying the discussion of illegal purposes nowadays is the issue of money laundering. Is the trust property the proceeds of any serious criminal conduct either on the part of the settlor or testator or any other person or persons? The trust draftsman will need to take care that he is aware of the legislation and rules in this area and makes sufficient and searching enquiries of his client to ascertain the origin of the trust property and to ensure that the client is indeed the true settlor and is not a 'stooge' of another. New Money Laundering Regulations are shortly to be laid before Parliament. The consequences of getting this wrong will be severe for the draftsman; the burden of proof will be on him to show that he did not know or suspect that the trust property was the proceeds of any serious criminal conduct, including evasion of United Kingdom taxation. Under section 93A of the Criminal Justice Act 1988, the maximum penalty for assisting a money launderer is 14 years' imprisonment.

The trust draftsman will also need to ensure that he has complied with the identification requirements set out in the Money Laundering Regulations 1993, if they apply to the client in question, in order to avoid a potential criminal sanction and to ensure that the draftsman has identified the person who is his client.

It is important to note that the relevant notification procedures under the Criminal Justice Acts and the Money Laundering Regulations require disclosure of any suspicion gleaned in relevant financial business, which is likely to include all matters where trust drafting is being undertaken, whether the suspicion arises in respect of the client or any other person involved, whether directly or indirectly in the transaction. A further tightening of the law in this area is to be expected within the near future, with the likelihood that an objective standard, rather than a subjective standard as at present, will be introduced.

In view of the ease with which funds can be transferred around the world, the increasing emphasis on speed of delivery of service and the increase of globalisation (including the ease of communication), it is important to concentrate on compliance in this area and to ensure that a report to the National Criminal Intelligence Service is made in any cases where money laundering is reasonably suspected immediately the suspicion arises.

It is also important that the trust draftsman and his staff keep up-to-date with the law and regulations in this area to ensure that they are aware of what is expected of them.

Just as trusts afford a settlor or testator an opportunity to protect and ring-fence property from beneficiaries, and to an extent from the Inland Revenue (by proper and effective use of tax avoidance) and others, so in the hands of an unscrupulous or devious client they can afford opportunities to wreak havoc and to provide a smokescreen for a range of illegal or improper purposes including fraud and tax evasion.

The Law Society blue guidance card in this area provides some useful pointers in identifying where money laundering may be an issue. These are by no means exhaustive but include the following:

(a) the over-secretive client;

(b) transactions including unusual settlement requests;

(c)   transactions involving cash;

(d)   transactions with a significant foreign element; and

(e)   transactions involving unusual instructions.

While a degree of vigilance and caution is to be commended in this area, the practitioner should also be aware of his duties of client confidentiality and the consequences of failing in his obligations to the client in this regard.

Invalid trusts – consequences of invalidity (reverter to settlor)

3.16   If a declared trust is too uncertain or vague, fails to satisfy the requisite formalities, cannot be carried out or there is a complete failure of the beneficiaries, or, for example, it becomes void as a result of infringing the rules against perpetuities and excessive accumulations, then since it appears from the trust instrument that the trustees were not intended to take beneficially, there will be a resulting trust in favour of the settlor.

When a settlor or a testator has intentionally created and established a trust for an illegal consideration or purpose which fails as a result, then a resulting trust will arise in favour of the settlor or the residue of the testator's estate if:

(a)   he repented of the illegal purpose before it was carried out (see *Symes v Hughes (1870) LR 9 Eq 475*); or

(b)   he does not need to disclose the nature of the illegal purpose in order to rebut the presumption of advancement or gift but can simply rely on the presumption of resulting trust arising on the transfer or purchase of property (see *Tinsley v Milligan [1993] 3 All ER 65, [1994] 1 AC 340, HL*); or

(c)   the effect of allowing the trustee to retain the trust property might be to give effect to an unlawful object, to defeat a matter prohibited by law, or to protect a fraud (see *Ayerst v Jenkins (1873) LR 16 Eq 275* at page 283).

The case of *Tinsley v Milligan* above helps to shed some light on the matters relevant to rebut the presumption of advancement in this context. In that case two cohabiting women purchased a house jointly which they registered in the name of one of them only to enable the other, with the knowledge and approval of the registered owner, to make fraudulent social security benefit claims for the benefit of them both. When the non-registered owner cohabitee claimed a one-half share of the property, the House of Lords held, by a bare majority, that she did have an equitable interest under a resulting trust, without the need for her to rely on the underlying illegality.

The possibility of a reverter to settlor occurring under a resulting trust in the event of a complete failure of beneficiaries should be avoided by the inclusion of an effective default clause in the settlement deed or will, since otherwise adverse capital taxes and income tax charges (in the case of a settlement) will result, even if the reverter is only a possibility. Inclusion of vested interests in the default clause or the inclusion of a charity or charities as the default beneficiaries will avoid these problems occurring.

Chapter 4

Subject Matter of the Trust

Nature of trust property

4.1   Depending upon the nature of the trust property, both initially and after subsequent additions have been made, the draftsman will need to consider what powers need to be included to permit the trustees to manage the particular trust property in question. Since the nature of the trust property may change during the lifetime of the settlement, the draftsman will usually include wide powers, both of investment and management, to permit the trustees to achieve the best overall return for the beneficiaries. As already mentioned, the Trustee Act 2000 contains certain default powers, but the draftsman may prefer to include specific powers in the settlement deed itself. Administrative powers are discussed more fully in CHAPTER 22: ADMINISTRATIVE PROVISIONS.

Whatever the nature of the trust property, the trustees will need to consider how best to manage it and they will need to choose appropriate investment managers to assist them with the proper management of the trust property. They will also need to adopt a sensible and proactive approach to reviewing their investment policy and the investments under their control and to measure the overall return achieved from the investments under their control, unless they wish to take the risk of a breach of trust action being pursued against them by the beneficiaries.

Both under the common law and the Trustee Act 2000, the trustees will need to consider whether the investments under their control should be varied and whether, in so far as is appropriate, the investments of the trust need to be diversified.

The draftsman will need to consider whether trust investment outside the United Kingdom is to be permitted and, if so, whether the trustees need to have power under the settlement to change the proper law of the settlement, being the law which will apply to the interpretation of the settlement and its provisions.

Certain types of trust property will necessitate special consideration by the draftsman.

Freehold and leasehold land

4.2   In the case of leasehold land settled at the outset, the terms of the lease will need to be considered by the settlor and the trustees will need to take any appropriate action required under the lease after the setting up of the settlement, for example concerning the service of any appropriate notices. In respect of later investment in leasehold land, the draftsman needs to consider whether this is to be permitted generally or whether the trustees are only to be permitted to invest in leasehold land where a certain specified minimum period of the lease is left to run.

Mortgaged freehold land which is initially settled will bring its own considerations, that is, who is to pay the ongoing mortgage payments and will the trustees have sufficient funds to pay such payments, both capital and interest? The trustees will also need to consider the terms of any mortgage when deciding whether or not to accept the role of trustee or the particular trust property into the trust fund.

Section 6(3) of the Trusts of Land and Appointment of Trustees Act 1996 and section 8(1), (2) of the Trustee Act 2000 permit trustees to acquire freehold or leasehold land in the UK as an investment, for occupation by a beneficiary, or for any other reason. The term 'freehold or leasehold land' has a specific definition (Trustee Act 2000, s 8(2)) because of the fact that trustees cannot acquire any undivided share in land in England and Wales under their statutory powers, since an undivided share exists only in equity and cannot subsist as a legal estate. Where it is thought that trustees might need to invest in an undivided share of land, an express power to that effect should be included. This is most often necessary where trustees are to hold a share of a property occupied by a beneficiary who is a co-owner.

Section 12(1) of the Trusts of Land and Appointment of Trustees Act 1996 makes provision for a right of occupation for a beneficiary 'who is beneficially entitled to an interest in possession' in land subject to a trust of land at any time if at that time either the purposes of the trust include making the land available for his occupation (or for the occupation of a class of which he is a member or of beneficiaries in general); or the land is held by the trustees so as to be so available. This is subject to the right not being available if the land is either unavailable or unsuitable for occupation by him.

The statutory right of occupation is not confined in its application to residential property held on trust, but can be relevant to any kind of land in England and Wales held on trust which is capable of being occupied by a beneficiary, such as a farm or business premises. However, the statutory right is only available in respect of a beneficiary who is beneficially entitled to an interest in possession in the land and no right is conferred on a beneficiary if the land is either unavailable or unsuitable for his occupation. When it is intended that the trust property might include land (whether freehold or leasehold), careful thought should be given as to whether the land is likely to be available or suitable for the occupation of one or more beneficiaries and whether any of the beneficiaries will have an interest in possession in the land.

Chattels

4.3 A settled gift of chattels (for example, for life) should be actively discouraged. Not only is it inconvenient but it raises problems of maintenance, fair wear and tear, loss, destruction, insurance, safe-keeping and taking inventories. The case of a settled gift of chattels usually arises in the case of a home-made will where a testator fails to appreciate the difficulties which might arise. Sometimes a settled gift of chattels arises where a testator creates a life interest of the whole of his estate. There is much to be said for chattels being excluded from the life interest and being made the subject of an absolute gift in such circumstances. The trustees' position may become invidious if the chattels are lost and it will usually not be practicable for trustees to take actual possession of chattels which are comprised in the trust fund. Certain powers for trustees in respect of chattels comprised in the trust fund will usually be included in the settlement deed by the draftsman but it is best to avoid a trust of chattels if at all possible.

Agricultural and business property

4.4 Where such property is settled and this qualifies for relief for inheritance tax purposes, the draftsman, for example in the case of a trust established by a will, especially a nil rate band discretionary legacy trust, will need to consider whether or not the property which qualifies for relief is intended to be settled.

If shares in a private limited company are settled as the initial trust property, the settlor and his professional advisers will need to consider the terms of the memorandum and articles of association of the company concerned to ensure that they permit the transfer of shares to the trustees and whether any specific provisions need to be observed in order to ensure that the shares are validly settled. If the company is in liquidation the consent of the liquidator to the transfer will need to be obtained.

In view of the increasing importance of taper relief for capital gains tax, especially for business property, the settlor will need to consider whether the settlement of the shares will enable the trustees to claim the higher rate of business taper relief and, where possible, to ensure that the higher rate of business taper relief is available to the trustees.

The settlement of private company shares and agricultural property will also often raise the issue of diversification and if the settlor does not wish for the trust property to be diversified, then this should be made expressly clear in the settlement deed itself.

Life assurance policies

4.5   Settlors will often wish to settle death benefits payable under life assurance and pension policies to ensure that they will not fall into their estates on death and thus be subject to inheritance tax.

The best solution for such benefits is for the settlor to settle the benefits under all such policies on trusts established by a single settlement, rather than settling the benefits due under each policy on separate trusts, for example using standard trust forms offered by life assurance companies. Such standard forms may not be adequate to permit sufficient flexibility or be appropriate to the particular circumstances of the settlor.

Before setting up such a settlement of policy death benefits, the prudent draftsman will send a copy of the draft settlement to the relevant life assurance companies to ensure that they will give effect to the terms of the trust when established. The draftsman will also need to address the state of health of the settlor at the time of establishing the trust since if, for example, the settlor is suffering from a terminal illness at that time and then dies within a relatively short time thereafter, say, two years or possibly longer, then an inheritance tax charge may arise under section 3 of the Inheritance Tax Act 1984 following the creation of the settlement and premature death.

Part II: Fiscal Classification of Trusts

Chapter 5

Types of Trust

Practical and fiscal definitions of trusts

5.1   Various definitions of the concept of a 'trust' were considered in CHAPTER 1: WHAT ARE TRUSTS but that is not the end of the matter. There are many different types of trust which vary according to the way in which they operate and the way in which they are treated by the tax system.

Most private trusts fall into two main categories: those where the trustees are obliged under the terms of their trust to give the income arising or the benefit of the trust property (dividends, interest, rents, free use of property, among other benefits) to a specific beneficiary or a class of beneficiaries (life interest or interest in possession trusts) and those where they are not so obliged, but have a discretion to allocate the income or other benefits to any one or more of a class of beneficiaries or to accumulate the income and add it to the capital for a period (discretionary trusts).

In turn there are different kinds of discretionary trust, each of which permits the trustees to allocate the capital and/or income to any one or more of a class of beneficiaries or objects which may either be stated at the outset or, possibly, nominated at a later date. The beneficiaries or objects of such a trust will not have any fixed interest under the trust but any entitlement will be strictly subject to the exercise by the trustees of their discretionary powers under the trust. Pending the exercise by the trustees of their powers, such beneficiaries or objects therefore have a potential interest (or, put in its pure form, a 'hope' of benefiting) only under the trust.

The settlor will choose one type of trust over another according to what it is that he hopes to achieve at a practical level. However, one of the most important driving factors in both the decision to create a trust and in the choice of trust is the avoidance of taxation, in particular, inheritance tax. The inheritance tax treatment of interest in possession and discretionary trusts is quite different and the settlor will be guided in his choice of trust according to advice which he receives about the fiscal treatment of the trust which he hopes to create.

In addition to the above trust types, modern trust draftsmen sometimes draft trusts in such a way as to give trustees all of the powers usually seen in a discretionary trust with wide discretion to appoint income or capital to any one or more of a class of beneficiaries, but subject to and in default of any exercise by them of their powers, the trustees are directed to pay the income or apply the other benefits arising in respect of the trust property to a specified individual, object or a class of individuals or objects, for example, for life or for a specified period.

This type of trust is sometimes called a hybrid settlement and offers complete flexibility to trustees to change the form of the trust at any time in their discretion and to override the interest in possession which would otherwise subsist. Such a trust is sometimes used where the person who is given the interest in possession is impecunious and may become bankrupt or where a divorce is a possibility, in order to permit the trustees to exercise their discretion to remove the interest of such beneficiary and either to redirect the benefits to another beneficiary or to permit the accumulation of such income.

Such an exercise by the trustees of their powers may then defeat the interest of the trustee in bankruptcy or the spouse, direct or indirect, in the income entitlement. When the bankruptcy or divorce is no longer in issue then, depending upon the terms of the trust, the interest of the original income beneficiary may be restored or even enhanced to an interest in capital, if desired.

These various trusts and the tax treatment of them are examined in the remainder of this PART. It is first appropriate to discuss the tax treatment of trusts in more general terms.

Trusts defined for fiscal purposes

5.2   The three principal tax regimes of income, capital gains and inheritance tax are not consistent in their treatment of trusts whether on their creation, during their lifetime or at their termination.

Since a desire to avoid inheritance tax is generally the most powerful fiscal motive for the creation of a trust, it is sensible to look at the inheritance tax treatment of trusts first.

Inheritance tax

5.3   The governing legislation for inheritance tax is the Inheritance Tax Act 1984. It is a development of capital transfer tax which replaced estate duty with effect from 26 March 1974. Inheritance tax is a tax on transfers of value which may be chargeable, potentially exempt, exempt or subject to relief. The inheritance tax treatment of property subject to trusts is not trivial and provides the structure of this Part.

The Inheritance Tax Act 1984 does not attempt to define 'a trust' but instead relies upon the concept of 'a settlement' which is any disposition or dispositions of property, whether effected by instrument by parol or by operation of law, or partly in one way and partly in another, whereby the property is for the time being –

(a)   held in trust for persons in succession or for any person subject to a contingency, or

(b)   held by trustees on trust to accumulate the whole or part of any income of the property or with power to make payments out of that income at the discretion of the trustees or some other person, with or without power to accumulate surplus income, or

(c)   charged or burdened (otherwise than for full consideration in money or money's worth paid for his own use or benefit to the person making the disposition) with the payment of any annuity or other periodical payment payable for a life or any other limited or terminable period,

or would be so held or charged or burdened if the disposition or dispositions were regulated by the law of any part of the United Kingdom; or whereby, under the law of any other country, the administration of the property is for the time being governed by provisions equivalent in effect to those which would apply if the property were so held, charged or burdened. (Inheritance Tax Act 1984, s 43(2)).

The section continues in the following way: A lease of property which is for life or lives, or for a period ascertainable only by reference to a death, or which is terminable on, or at a date ascertainable only by reference to, a death, shall be treated as a settlement, and the property as settled property, unless the lease was granted for full consideration in money or money's worth; and where a lease not granted as a lease at a rack rent is at any time to become a lease at an increased rent it shall be treated as terminable at that time. (Inheritance Tax Act 1984, s 43(3)).

Inheritance tax draws a distinction between the two practically distinct categories of settlement identified above, settlements in which there is an interest in possession and settlements in which there is no interest in possession. The latter category includes fully discretionary trusts, accumulation and maintenance trusts, protective trusts and trusts for the disabled. The tax treatment of trusts in which there is an interest in possession is discussed in CHAPTER 6: TRUSTS WITH AN INTEREST IN POSSESSION and the treatment of trusts in which there is no interest in possession in CHAPTER 7: DISCRETIONARY TRUSTS and subsequent chapters. The same distinction is not drawn by capital gains tax and income tax.

For inheritance tax purposes 'settlor', in relation to a settlement, includes any person by whom the settlement was made directly or indirectly. In particular (but without prejudice to the generality of that definition) it includes any person who has provided funds directly or indirectly for the purpose of or in connection with the settlement or who has made with any other person a reciprocal arrangement for that other person to make the settlement: Inheritance Tax Act 1984, s 44(1).

The 1984 Act supposes that the identity of the trustees is obvious but also provides that a 'trustee', in relation to a settlement in relation to which there would be no trustees apart from this section, means any person in whom the settled property or its management is for the time being vested: Inheritance Tax Act 1984, s 45.

Capital gains tax

5.4   The governing legislation for capital gains tax is the Taxation of Chargeable Gains Act 1992 which is a piece of consolidating legislation. By way of definition it does something similar to the Inheritance Tax Act 1984 in that it does not define 'trust' but relies on an unwritten understanding of what a trust is. Instead, capital gains tax starts with the concept of settled property providing that, unless the context otherwise requires, 'settled property' means any property held in trust other than property held by nominees or bare trustees: Taxation of Chargeable Gains Act 1992, ss 60 and 68.

Where inheritance tax is a tax on transfers of value, capital gains tax is a tax on chargeable gains and the key concept for capital gains tax purposes is between property treated as that of trustees and property treated as belonging to the beneficiaries. Thus, for the purposes of capital gains tax the trustees of the settlement are treated as being a single and continuing body of persons (distinct from the persons who may from time to time be the trustees). The effect of this is that on the appointment of a new trustee in place of a retiring trustee there is no capital gains tax charge because the body of trustees has remained the same.

If, on the other hand, a beneficiary becomes absolutely entitled to the settled property as against the trustees or it is appointed to new trustees to hold on new trusts there is what is called a deemed disposal and there may be a capital gains tax charge.

Property held by nominees or bare trustees is not included in the definition of settled property because assets held by nominees or bare trustees are treated for capital gains tax purposes as the assets of the beneficiary or beneficiaries for whom those assets are held and not as the assets of the trustees: Taxation of Chargeable Gains Act 1992, s 60.

Apart from the distinct treatment of nominees or bare trustees, capital gains tax does not draw the same distinction as inheritance tax between settlements in which there is an interest in possession and settlements in which there is no interest in possession.

Income tax

5.5   The governing legislation for income tax is the Income and Corporation Taxes Act 1988. This also uses the description 'settlement' which it defines as including 'any disposition, trust, covenant, agreement, arrangement or transfer of assets' (Income and Corporation Taxes Act, s 660G(1)).

The Income and Corporation Taxes Act 1988 defines 'settlor' in relation to a settlement as any person by whom the settlement was made but goes on to provide that a person shall be deemed to have made a settlement if he has made or entered into the settlement directly or indirectly, and, in particular (but without prejudice to the generality of that definition) if he has provided or undertaken to provide funds directly or indirectly for the purpose of the settlement, or has made with any other person a reciprocal arrangement for that other person to make or enter into the settlement: Income and Corporation Taxes Act 1988, s 660G(1) and (2).

Stamp duty

5.6   Confusion often surrounds the issue of stamp duty and settlements. That confusion may be alleviated with the introduction of stamp duty land tax.

Under the stamp duty regime the creation of a settlement by the conveyance or transfer of property operating as a voluntary disposition inter vivos for no consideration for money or money's worth nor any consideration referred to in section 57 of the Stamp Act 1891 (conveyance in consideration of a debt etc) was generally regarded as exempt from stamp duty (provided that it bears a certificate to that effect) and was not required to be stamped: Stamp Duty (Exempt Instruments) Regulations 1987 (SI 1987 No 516). The appropriate category was category L. Wills are not subject to stamp duty.

If the category L exemption was not available the settlement deed would need to be stamped with a £5 Inland Revenue stamp as a declaration of trust. Confusion often arose since an assumption is made by some that because the setting up of a settlement essentially constitutes a gift, the inclusion of a category L certificate is appropriate. Category L, however, does not apply to declarations of trust for which a fixed duty of £5 was retained in 1987. If a certificate was included, however, the Inland Revenue Stamp Office would generally not stamp the deed. If a deed was not duly stamped within 30 days, a stamp duty penalty would be payable.

The position was further confused, however, in respect of instruments transferring the trust property into the names of the trustees. The established position appears to be as follows:

(a)   where a settlor made a settlement, the deed establishing it should be stamped with a £5 Inland Revenue stamp as a declaration of trust;

(b)   where the settlor subsequently executed an instrument transferring the trust property into the names of the trustees to hold it upon the trusts set out in the settlement, a certificate under category L should be included since the instrument constitutes a voluntary conveyance for no consideration;

(c)   where the settlor simultaneously executed both the settlement and the instrument effecting the transfer, the transfer should contain a category L certificate and the settlement deed should be stamped with a £5 Inland Revenue stamp;

(d)   a category L certificate is not appropriate if the transfer was made for actual consideration, for example, in consideration of a debt;

(e)   the category L certificate, where appropriate, had to be signed either by the settlor or his solicitors;

(f)   the category L certificate, where appropriate, had either to be included as a clause in the relevant instrument or endorsed upon it, or be physically attached to it; and

(g)   if the category L certificate, where appropriate, was omitted accidentally, it could be made at any later time. No penalty would attach in respect of the later addition of the certificate.

Stamp duty land tax

5.7   Under the stamp duty land tax regime introduced by the Finance Act 2003 with effect from 1 December 2003, all land transactions are chargeable to stamp duty land tax unless they are specifically exempted by the legislation or they are for no chargeable consideration. If a transaction is exempt there is no need to file a land transaction return but self-certification is required. What constitutes chargeable consideration is defined at section 50 of, and Schedule 4 to, the Finance Act 2003.

Gifts, testamentary dispositions, dispositions under the intestacy law, dispositions of property to beneficiaries under a trust in accordance with the terms of that trust, and most acquisitions by operation of law are not chargeable to stamp duty land tax. However, no land transaction, and no document evidencing or effecting such a transaction, can be registered at HM Land Registry unless either a Revenue certificate (in form SDLT5) is issued by the Inland Revenue evidencing the submission of a land transaction return and payment of stamp duty land tax if appropriate, or a self-certificate is completed by the purchaser certifying that no land transaction return is required for the transaction. The certificate must accompany the relevant application to enable the land transaction to be registered at the appropriate registry.

Under the provisions of Schedule 11 to the Finance Act 2003, a self-certificate will also be required for land transactions which are not 'notifiable transactions'. The self-certificate must be in the prescribed form, contain the prescribed information and include a signed declaration by the purchaser(s).

When the trustees of a settlement acquire land, the trustees will be regarded as the purchaser for stamp duty land tax. Therefore, all the normal rules regarding notification and payment relate to the responsible trustees. A gift into a settlement will be exempt from stamp duty land tax as it was exempt from stamp duty

Where a chargeable interest is acquired by virtue of the exercise of a power of appointment or the exercise of a discretion vested in trustees, then any consideration given for the person in whose favour the appointment was made or the discretion was exercised will be treated as chargeable consideration under paragraph 7 of Schedule 16 to the Finance Act 2003.

A settlement for stamp duty land tax is any trust arrangement other than a bare trust. Stamp duty land tax recognises interest in possession trusts, discretionary trusts and various hybrid trusts as settlements.

Fiscal consequences of failing to exclude the settlor or his spouse from benefit

5.8   This topic is particularly relevant in the case of discretionary trusts where it is most easily overlooked, but it should be considered in the case of all types of settlement. Many settlors hope to achieve a tax saving by creating trusts in which they intend to participate as beneficiaries. The draftsman and adviser cannot over-emphasise the fiscal (and practical) disadvantages of that approach, especially where the asset which the settlor hopes to settle is his home.

Inheritance tax

5.9   If the settlor is a beneficiary, even a discretionary beneficiary, there will be a reservation of benefit for inheritance tax purposes: Finance Act 1986, s 102 and Sch 20. That section provides that if there is a disposal of property by way of gift and either:

- possession and enjoyment of the property is not bona fide assumed by the donee at or before the beginning of the relevant period; or

- at any time in the relevant period the property is not enjoyed to the entire exclusion, or virtually the entire exclusion, of the donor and of any benefit to him by contract or otherwise,

the gift is treated as forming part of the donor's estate for inheritance tax purposes until the material date, being the earlier of the donor relinquishing the reservation or the death of the donor. Thus, where there is a reservation of benefit the discretionary trust does not have any inheritance tax advantage.

Special provisions now apply to inter-spouse transfers and to the position in respect of gifts of land and careful consideration should be given to the problems thrown up by the gifts with reservation provisions at the outset if the settlor and his spouse are not to be excluded for benefit altogether. Specialist advice should be taken where necessary.

Capital gains tax

5.10   Under section 77 of the Taxation of Chargeable Gains Act 1992, a capital gain is treated, not as the liability of the trustees, but as accruing to the settlor where any settled property, or any income which may arise under the settlement, is, or may become, applicable for the benefit of the settlor or his spouse in any circumstances whatsoever, or the settlor or spouse enjoys a benefit directly or indirectly from any settled property or any income arising from the settlement.

Income tax

5.11   Similarly, for income tax purposes, if the settlor or his spouse is an object of a discretionary power contained in the settlement, the income is treated as that of the settlor for all income tax purposes: Income and Corporation Taxes Act 1988, s 660A.

Reverter to settlor

5.12   If a declared trust is too uncertain or vague, fails to satisfy the requisite formalities, cannot be carried out, or in the event of a complete failure of the beneficiaries, or, for example, it becomes void as a result of infringing the rule against perpetuities and excessive accumulations, then since it appears from the trust instrument that the trustees were not intended to take beneficially, there will be a resulting trust in favour of the settlor.

If the trust property reverts to the settlor then there will be no inheritance tax payable on the reverter pursuant to section 54 of the Inheritance Tax Act 1984. The possibility of a reverter to settlor occurring under a resulting trust in the event of a complete failure of beneficiaries should, however, generally be avoided by the inclusion of an effective default clause in the settlement deed or will, since otherwise adverse capital taxes and income tax charges (in the case of a settlement) will result, even if the reverter is only a possibility. Inclusion of vested interests in the default clause or the inclusion of a charity or charities as the default beneficiaries will avoid these problems occurring.

Creating the trust and the potentially exempt transfer

5.13   Essentially, on the creation of a lifetime settlement, in the case of virtually all trusts, except discretionary trusts, provided that there is no reservation of benefit in the trust property in favour of the settlor pursuant to section 102 of, and Schedule 20 to, the Finance Act 1986, a potentially exempt transfer will have been made by the settlor under section 3A of the Inheritance Tax Act 1984. This is subject to the availability and application of any available reliefs for inheritance tax, so that provided that the settlor survives the date of the settlement for a period of at least seven years, the value of the property settled, on the loss to the settlor's estate valuation principle for inheritance tax, will be removed from the settlor's estate. This is of course subject to the application (if any) of the clawback provisions under sections 113A and 124A of the Inheritance Tax Act 1984 in the case of business property and agricultural property and to any taper relief which may be available under section 7(4) of the Inheritance Tax Act 1984.

The application of taper relief for inheritance tax purposes is one of the most commonly misunderstood provisions of the legislation by laymen. The relief operates to reduce the inheritance tax payable. It does *not* reduce the value transferred by a failed potentially exempt transfer. Thus the relief will only apply where the gift itself becomes the subject of an inheritance tax liability. Since the gift will, on a death within seven years, be treated as having occurred on the date when the potentially exempt transfer was made, taper relief will only be available if the nil rate band for inheritance tax purposes has been exceeded at that point on the tax payable on that excess. Taper relief will have no application if the nil rate band has not been exceeded at that date.

If death occurs within seven years of a potentially exempt transfer, any chargeable transfers made within fourteen years of the date of the last potentially exempt transfer will need to be taken into account to calculate the inheritance tax payable.

If the settlement created is a discretionary settlement, it will not, unless it qualifies as an accumulation and maintenance settlement or a disabled trust, be a potentially exempt transfer on its creation, and it will therefore be a chargeable transfer, provided that it avoids the application of the reservation of benefit provisions mentioned above, and the value transferred will be the value of the property settled (again on the loss to the settlor's estate principle for inheritance tax). Again any available exemptions or reliefs can be set against the value transferred, but if the net value exceeds the amount of the then current nil rate band, taking into account any other chargeable transfers made within the previous seven years, then there will be an immediate charge to inheritance tax at the lifetime rate (currently 20 per cent) on that net value with the potential for a further inheritance tax charge of 20 per cent if the settlor dies within seven years.

A reallocation of the nil rate band to take into account the sequence of chargeable and potentially exempt transfers may be necessary if death occurs within seven years.

It is generally considered to be sensible to make potentially exempt transfers before chargeable transfers if both are being considered because this will generally give a more favourable result in terms of the overall inheritance tax liability.

For capital gains tax purposes, holdover relief may be available under section 165 or section 260 of the Taxation of Chargeable Gains Act 1992 on the setting up of the trust. Subject to this, however, the application of capital gains tax, after deduction of any exemptions or reliefs available in respect of that tax, on the creation of a settlement needs to be carefully borne in mind by the practitioner establishing the trust to ensure that what might be an exemplary inheritance tax avoidance scheme does not give rise to an unwelcome capital gains tax charge.

Chapter 6

Trusts with an Interest in Possession

Nature of interest in possession settlements

6.1   This type of trust exists when a beneficiary, known as an 'income beneficiary', has a right to the income of the trust as it arises or, where the trust property does not produce income, would have that right if the property did produce income. The trustees must pass all of the income received, less any trustees' expenses and tax, to the beneficiary. A beneficiary who is entitled to the income of the trust for life is known as a 'life tenant'.

The income beneficiary often does not have any rights over the capital of this kind of trust. Normally the capital will pass to a different beneficiary or beneficiaries at a specific time in the future or following a specified future event.

Thus, a trust for A for life remainder to B for life remainder to C, gives A the right to income (but not capital) during his life and, after A's death gives B that right during his life but leaves the capital to C. A and then B have successive interests in possession.

In this chapter the income beneficiary or person entitled to an interest in possession in settled property is referred to as the life tenant but it is important to bear in mind that an interest in possession can subsist for a shorter period.

Why choose an interest in possession settlement?

6.2   Interest in possession trusts or life interest trusts used to be more common than they are today, particularly, for example, to provide for spouses in the case of will trusts. Lay clients are more likely to ask for a more flexible discretionary trust (which has a more exciting ring to it) than a life interest trust but the draftsman and adviser should always exercise independent thought before providing the lay client with a settlement. To an extent interest in possession trusts have become less attractive in recent years because stock market investments have produced lower income returns so that a larger capital fund is required in order to provide a reasonable level of income for the income beneficiary. However, if a house is to be the subject of a trust and it is intended that a beneficiary will occupy it, an interest in possession will normally arise anyway for inheritance tax purposes.

Interest in possession trusts have a place for some in ensuring an income benefit or the benefit of the trust property while protecting the trust capital and ensuring that the beneficiaries cannot sell or dissipate the trust property.

From the perspective of the life tenant the life interest trust offers the certainty of an entitlement to the income or the enjoyment of the trust property as it arises, rather than merely a potential interest in the income as with a discretionary trust. Interest in possession trusts are not generally to be recommended where the settlor wishes to make substantial provision for a young adult whose needs might change radically and rapidly but can be particularly important in the case of an elderly beneficiary (such as a surviving spouse) for whom certainty is important. They are also a useful means of providing a capital sum the income of which is to be used for the maintenance and education of a young child with the intention that the child should become entitled to the capital at some age in the future.

Interest in possession trusts are also useful where the sum to be settled greatly exceeds the available nil-rate band because their creation is a potentially exempt transfer.

Where there are many young children to cater for, the settlor should also consider a discretionary trust (see CHAPTER 7: DISCRETIONARY TRUSTS) or an accumulation and maintenance trust (see CHAPTER 8: ACCUMULATION AND MAINTENANCE TRUSTS). If the settlor would like to make provision for a single beneficiary of dubious financial acumen a protective trust should be considered (see CHAPTER 10: PROTECTIVE TRUSTS) and if the beneficiary is disabled the settlor might consider a disabled trust (see CHAPTER 11: TRUSTS FOR THE DISABLED).

Inheritance tax

6.3   The lifetime creation of an interest in possession trust is a potentially exempt transfer by the settlor: Inheritance Tax Act 1984, s 3A. No inheritance tax will be payable provided that there is no reservation of benefit, actual or potential, in favour of the settlor, and subject to the application of any available inheritance tax exemptions and reliefs, provided that the settlor survives the gift into settlement for at least seven years. The creation of an interest in possession trust on death has no specific inheritance tax consequences.

The fundamental point about the inheritance tax treatment of interest in possession trusts is that the life tenant is treated for the purposes of the Inheritance Tax Act 1984 as beneficially entitled to the property in which the interest subsists so, during the continuance of the interest in possession, the trust property is treated for inheritance tax purposes as if the capital belongs to the life tenant: Inheritance Tax Act 1984, s 49.

Thus, where, during the life of the life tenant his interest comes to an end, tax is charged as if the life tenant had made a transfer of value and the value transferred had been equal to the value of the property in which the interest in possession subsisted: Inheritance Tax Act 1984, s 52(1). However, no tax is charged if the property is excluded property or if the life tenant becomes, on the same occasion, beneficially entitled to the property or to another interest in possession in the property: Inheritance Tax Act 1984, s 52(2). That is in keeping with the principle that the settled property is treated for inheritance tax purposes as belonging to the life tenant.

Similarly, on the death of the life tenant the settled property is treated as part of his estate and taxed as such unless the settled property reverts to the settlor, the settlor's spouse or, if the settlor has died within two years, the settlor's widow or widower: Inheritance Tax Act 1984, s 54(1), (2). On the death of the life tenant, therefore, if the interest in possession still subsists, then there will be a potential for an inheritance tax charge to arise, with the value of the life tenant's own estate being aggregated with the capital value of the trust property, subject to the deduction, if available, of the nil rate band for inheritance tax and any available exemptions and reliefs.

Where the life tenant disposes of his interest the disposal is not a transfer of value, but is treated as the coming to an end of his interest and inheritance tax is charged accordingly under section 52 of the Inheritance Tax Act 1984 as above: Inheritance Tax Act 1984, s 51.

Capital gains tax

6.4   The capital gains tax legislation does not use the term 'interest in possession' but refers to a 'life interest'. The capital gains tax term 'life interest' and the inheritance tax term 'interest in possession' are not synonymous.

The lifetime creation of an interest in possession trust is a disposal by the settlor at market value and so gives rise to capital gains tax: Taxation of Chargeable Gains Act 1992, s 70. Reliefs may be available to militate against this charge, however. Holdover relief is generally not available although it may be available on creation and termination to the extent that qualifying business assets are involved: Taxation of Chargeable Gains Act 1992, s 165.

One big advantage of an interest in possession trust is that the disposal of a residential property occupied by the beneficiary should attract principal private residence relief under section 222 of the Taxation of Chargeable Gains Act 1992. The creation of an interest in possession trust on death does not give rise to any capital gains tax because of the tax-free uplift: Taxation of Chargeable Gains Act 1992, s 62. Provided that the interest in possession still subsists in favour of the original life tenant at his death there will also be a tax-free uplift on death.

While the interest in possession subsists, provided that it is not given by a settlor in favour of himself or his own spouse, subject to any exemptions and reliefs available, the trust tax rate will be payable on any chargeable gains, after deduction of any available losses. The trust tax rate applicable for capital gains tax is currently 34 per cent: Income and Corporation Taxes Act 1988, s 686(1); Taxation of Chargeable Gains Act 1992, s 4(1AA).

Income tax

6.5   The income will effectively belong to the life tenant (unless this is the settlor or his spouse) so the net effect is that the income will be taxed at the rates applicable to the life tenant's own income: Income and Corporation Taxes Act 1988, ss 686 and 687. If the life tenant is a higher rate taxpayer, therefore, the income tax rate payable on the income arising in an interest in possession settlement will be higher than the rate which is payable on the income accumulated within a discretionary settlement (that is, 40 per cent as compared with 34 per cent).

Drafting points

6.6   As already mentioned, the person entitled to the income arising from the trust property is often called and defined as the life tenant. In some trust deeds this person may be defined as the principal beneficiary.

When drafting the clause giving the interest in possession in income, the draftsman must ensure that the life tenant is given an immediate and absolute interest in the income as it arises, for example, 'the Trustees shall pay the income of the Trust Fund to A for life'. It should be noted at this point, however, that overriding powers of appointment, advancement and resettlement contained within an interest in possession settlement or in, for example, a hybrid settlement, are consistent with an interest in possession subsisting, since the life tenant does have an immediate and absolute interest in the income as it arises, unless and until the relevant powers are exercised.

The draftsman must, however, ensure that he avoids including provisions which are inconsistent with the existence of the interest in possession. Any power to accumulate income during the currency of the interest in possession will result in the settlement being taxed as a discretionary trust, since there will then be no immediate and absolute interest in the income as it arises. There is, however, nothing to prevent the inclusion of a power to accumulate income following the termination of the interest in possession.

Careful consideration needs to be given to what is to happen to the capital on the determination of the interest in possession or on the determination of both of the interests in possession, if both are included. Should the reversionary interest be vested or contingent? If it is vested then it is always open to the life tenant and the reversionary beneficiaries, if of full age, to wind up the trust under the rule in *Saunders v Vautier (1841) 4 Beav 115*. If it is contingent then this will not be possible. If vested, then no long-stop clause will be necessary, that is, in case the earlier trusts fail. If contingent, then a long-stop will need to be included to avoid a possibility of reverter to settlor and a consequent reservation of benefit by the settlor for inheritance tax and other taxation disadvantages.

There are three examples of interest in possession trusts in APPENDIX 1. At APPENDIX 1.1 is an interest in possession trust providing an interest in possession to the settlor for life, followed by an interest in possession for his or her spouse for life, followed by a gift to a class at 21. The settlor has a discretionary power to appoint among a class by deed during his life and by will or codicil at death. There is a power to advance capital to the settlor while alive but not to the settlor's spouse.

The precedent at APPENDIX 1.2 is an interest in possession trust providing an interest in possession to the settlor for life, followed by a gift to a class at 21. The settlor has a discretionary power to appoint among a class by deed during his life and by will or codicil at death. There is a power to advance capital to the settlor while alive and an overriding power to appoint income and/or capital amongst the beneficial class which is only exercisable with the consent of the settlor when alive. Charity also features as a beneficiary and there is an ultimate default gift in favour of charity but there is no fiscal reason for including that gift in this settlement.

APPENDIX 1.3 sets out a precedent for an interest in possession trust providing an interest in possession to the life tenant for life in much the same way as in the previous precedent but in this case the settlor is excluded from benefit.

The inclusion, as in the first two precedents, of a power of appointment in the settlor was common in older trust deeds. Thoroughly modern trust drafting tends to discourage the giving of powers to beneficiaries and to give the relevant powers to the trustees but where the life tenant is the beneficiary it makes sense to include such a power.

Minors as life tenants

6.7   In order to avoid the attribution of the income of a minor life tenant to his parent in a case where the parent is the settlor, and generally in all cases where a minor is the life tenant, whoever is the settlor, it is desirable to exclude the application of section 31 of the Trustee Act 1925 to the settlement expressly. Settlements of this sort are discussed more fully in CHAPTER 9: BARE TRUSTS.

Chapter 7

Discretionary Trusts

Nature of discretionary settlements

7.1   A discretionary trust is a trust the trustees of which have broad powers of the application of both income and capital amongst a class of beneficiaries. It permits the trustees to allocate the capital and/or income to any one or more of a class of beneficiaries or objects which may either be stated at the outset or, possibly, nominated at a later date. The beneficiaries or objects of such a trust will not have any fixed interest under the trust but any entitlement will be strictly subject to the exercise by the trustees of their discretionary powers under the trust. Pending the exercise by the trustees of their powers, such beneficiaries or objects therefore have a potential interest (or, put in its pure form, a 'hope' of benefiting) only under the trust.

A discretionary trust may have as its beneficiaries, for example, all of the settlor's children, grandchildren and remoter issue, their future spouses, widows and widowers, adopted children, stepchildren and charity.

Income arises from time to time and the trustees may accumulate it (subject to statutory restrictions) or make distributions of it to whichever members of the class they consider to be in need of it.

Trustees of discretionary trusts usually have wide powers of appointment over capital as well, which is to say that they are often given a power to pay capital to beneficiaries or to re-settle capital on new trusts for beneficiaries either permanently or for limited periods within the original trust period.

The beneficiaries of a discretionary trust do not control the trust and, subject to default trusts applicable at the end of the trust period, no one beneficiary has a right to either the trust income or capital so he cannot compel the trustees to apply either in a particular way. That does not mean that beneficiaries are entirely without protection but it is a measure of the discretion vested in the trustees that no one beneficiary has any greater interest in the fund than a mere hope or expectancy that the discretion might be exercised in his favour.

The idea of a 'discretionary trust' is popular amongst settlors but often misunderstood.

Why choose a discretionary settlement?

7.2   Put simply, the answer to this will generally be to retain the maximum flexibility to organise matters and for the trustees to decide the destination of the trust property as they consider to be appropriate in the light of the circumstances applicable at the time when they are considering exercising their powers.

A discretionary settlement is one where both capital and income may be paid or applied, at the discretion of the trustees, to any one or more of a class of beneficiaries as the trustees think fit. Settlors of such settlements confer great discretion and power on the trustees. Great care therefore needs to be taken by settlors when setting up such trusts to consider whom the trustees are to be and whether they really are appropriate persons to be given such wide discretions over the trust property. The fiscal consequences of setting up a discretionary trust will need to be borne in mind.

The fiscal advantages of discretionary trusts relate almost entirely to inheritance tax: there are income tax and capital gains tax disadvantages. The advantage arises because, unlike settled property subject to an interest in possession, property subject to a discretionary trust is not treated for inheritance tax purposes as if it were owned by one or more of the beneficiaries.

Where the settlor intends to settle a house with a view to one or more beneficiaries occupying it, a discretionary trust is usually not a sensible choice. The Revenue regard the exercise of a discretionary power to permit a beneficiary to occupy a property as creating an interest in possession: Inland Revenue Statement of Practice SP 10/79.

On the other hand, the flexibility and the tax advantages of creating discretionary trusts of business property are good reasons to select discretionary trusts. A disadvantage is that the inheritance tax treatment of discretionary trusts is quite complicated.

Inheritance tax

7.3   Currently, the principal inheritance tax advantage of a discretionary trust is that the death of any beneficiary will not result in an inheritance tax charge. This can be contrasted with the situation on the death of a beneficiary with an interest in possession in settled property.

In addition, the current regime for the application to discretionary trusts of inheritance tax is certainly not penal, especially bearing in mind the flexibility offered by such settlements. The inheritance tax provisions affecting discretionary trusts are set out in the Inheritance Tax Act 1984 Part III Chapter III (ss 58 to 85). This imposes a special tax regime on discretionary trusts, which is based upon charging 'relevant property' at each ten-year anniversary of its existence and at the time when it ceases to be relevant property on account of its leaving the settlement or otherwise where the value of the relevant property is diminished by a disposition ('exit charges').

A gift into a discretionary settlement is a chargeable transfer and inheritance tax is payable on the chargeable transfer on entry in the normal way so a gift into a discretionary trust is chargeable subject to the usual exemptions and reliefs. Thus, the creation of a discretionary trust is not a potentially exempt transfer.

Tax is levied every ten years after the commencement of the settlement (the ten-year charge) and when property ceases to be 'relevant property', for example where capital is appointed out of the settlement, and where the value of relevant property is diminished by a disposition made by the trustees of the settlement (the exit charge).

The ten-year charge arises on the tenth anniversary which is the tenth anniversary of the date on which the settlement commenced, being the date on which property first becomes comprised in it and not the date of the settlement. Where immediately before a ten-year anniversary all or any part of the property comprised in a settlement is relevant property, inheritance tax is charged on the value of the property or part at that time. Relevant property is defined as property in which no qualifying interest in possession subsists other than property to which certain exceptions (set out in section 58 of the Inheritance Tax Act 1984) apply. The rate at which tax is charged is currently three-tenths of the rate at which inheritance tax would be charged on a hypothetical lifetime transfer. Since the lifetime rates are currently half the death rates, the maximum ten-year charge on property which has been relevant property for a full ten years is currently 6 per cent. The rules and calculations are non-trivial and need to be carried out by the trustees with professional advice at the appropriate time.

The exit charge is levied where the property or part of the property comprised in a settlement ceases to be relevant property (whether because it ceases to be comprised in the settlement or otherwise) and, where that is not the case, where the trustees make a disposition as a result of which the value of the relevant property is less than it would be but for the disposition. The most common example of this is when the trustees appoint property to a beneficiary or if an interest in possession arises in a portion of the fund such as when a beneficiary is permitted to occupy trust property. The means by which the tax is calculated varies according to whether the exit charge occurs before the first ten-year anniversary or in between subsequent anniversaries.

In the former case, tax is charged at one-fortieth of the settlement rate for each complete successive quarter that has elapsed from the creation of the settlement to the date of the exit charge where the settlement rate is 30 per cent of the rate applicable to a hypothetical chargeable transfer at half of the full inheritance tax rates. There is thus a relatively low charge initially (and no charge at all within the first quarter) which gradually builds up over the course of a ten-year period.

In the latter case, the rate is one-fortieth of the rate charged at the previous ten-year anniversary for each completed quarter from the date of the first anniversary charge to the date of the exit charge.

As with the ten-year charge, the rules and calculations, especially in relation to added property, are non-trivial and should be carried out by the trustees with professional advice at the appropriate time. A more detailed discussion of the discretionary trust charging regime can be found in *Mellows: Taxation for Executors and Trustees* and *Foster's Inheritance Tax*.

Capital gains tax

7.4   The rate at which capital gains tax is charged on gains accruing to trustees of a discretionary trust is the same as the rate which for that year is applicable to trusts under section 686 of the Income and Corporation Taxes Act: Taxation of Chargeable Gains Act 1992, s 5(1). The current rate is 34 per cent.

The capital gains tax advantage on distributions made out of a discretionary trust is that holdover relief is available: Taxation of Chargeable Gains Act 1992, s 260; Inheritance Tax Act 1984, s 2(3). In the absence of any holdover, the usual rules (see CHAPTER 5: TYPES OF TRUST) will apply.

Income tax

7.5   There is an income tax advantage of discretionary trusts in that the trustees are able to distribute income to those beneficiaries who pay the least tax, but that 'advantage' is slight. The provisions for the taxation of the income of discretionary trusts are contained in sections 686 and 687 of the Income and Corporation Taxes Act 1988. Section 686 provides that the rate of income tax on discretionary trusts is determined as a single rate applicable to trusts which is currently 34 per cent.

A beneficiary who receives income under a discretionary trust and pays tax at a lower rate or who has unused personal reliefs available to him may be able to recover some part of the tax paid by the trustees in respect of such income: Income and Corporation Taxes Act 1988, s 687.

Income which is accumulated and subsequently treated as capital will be taxed at 34 per cent which will not then be recoverable if the accumulated income is paid to a beneficiary.

Drafting points

7.6   The discretionary trust is the most flexible form of settlement and because of this the drafting of such settlements is often easier and more standardised in its form, certainly more so than is the case with accumulation and maintenance settlements.

Often discretionary trusts are drafted with 80-year perpetuity periods and 21-year accumulation periods. Lay trustees and settlors sometimes think that this means that income must be accumulated for 21 years and that the trust cannot be brought to an end before the expiry of 80 years. This problem is exacerbated by the complex drafting of overriding powers of appointment which is often unavoidable.

Apart from drawing those points to the attention of the settlor, the draftsman should bear in mind the following:

(i) The class of beneficiaries may be fixed or the settlement may include a provision permitting the trustees to alter the class of beneficiaries either by adding or removing persons or objects from it. The precedent at APPENDIX 1.5 has a fixed class while the precedent at APPENDIX 1.6 is an example of a trust with a class which can be added to. Such powers are often limited by requiring the settlor's consent in writing to be obtained first, so that the class may not be altered after the settlor's death. Otherwise beneficiaries introduced into the class by the trustees, not known or contemplated by the settlor, may benefit from the trust property.

(ii) At the end of the accumulation period, the trustees will need to pay or apply the income to one or more of the persons in the class of beneficiaries, subject to the availability of the statutory accumulation power under section 31 of the Trustee Act 1925 (as may be amended in the settlement deed).

(iii) With regard to capital the trustees will have full discretion to apply the trust capital at any time within the trust period defined in the settlement to any one or more of the beneficiaries.

(iv) Great care needs to be taken to ensure that the power of appointment of new trustees and (if included) the power of removal of trustees are placed in the correct hands.

(v) In order to avoid a reverter of the trust capital to the settlor, or the possibility of such, which would result in a reservation of benefit for inheritance tax purposes, a long-stop or default clause will need to be included in the settlement in favour of a beneficiary or a class of beneficiaries living at the date of the settlement giving them a vested interest, subject to defeasance, or in favour of a charity or a number of charities.

(vi) Where, as in the precedent at APPENDIX 1.6, the settlor is to be excluded from the start, a clause excluding the settlor or his or her spouse from benefiting must be included. Both precedents in APPENDIX 1 include a power to add persons to the list of excluded persons in a form commonly used.

Chapter 8

Accumulation and Maintenance Trusts

Nature of accumulation and maintenance settlements

8.1   An accumulation and maintenance trust is a sub-class of discretionary trust but one to which special inheritance tax rules apply. The special requirements are described below: essentially, the accumulation and maintenance trust is the classic children's or grandchildren's trust which provides for maintenance of infants during their minorities but also gives them a capital interest in possession in a portion of the fund at a specified future age.

It should be noted that, depending upon its precise terms, by its nature an accumulation and maintenance settlement will often change during its life from being a type of discretionary settlement to a life interest settlement as and when, and to the extent that, each beneficiary attains an interest in income as of right. In order for the settlement to qualify as an accumulation and maintenance settlement, the entitlement to income will need to arise at an age not exceeding 25 years.

Although this change takes place during the life of the settlement, the settlement is not correctly described as a hybrid settlement in its true sense, since it is by its nature a 'changeling' and is never truly a discretionary trust or an interest in possession trust. It should also be appreciated that at any one time different taxation treatment may apply to different funds within the same accumulation and maintenance settlement, that is, one child may have attained an entitlement to income under the trust, having attained the relevant age, so that that fund has an interest in possession subsisting in it, while other funds under the same settlement may still be in the non-interest in possession regime, since no beneficiary has yet attained the relevant age whereby a beneficiary becomes entitled to income as of right.

Why choose an accumulation and maintenance settlement?

8.2   The principal reason (perhaps the only reason) to choose an accumulation and maintenance settlement is because of certain taxation advantages that accrue. Accumulation and maintenance trusts, when properly drafted as trusts which satisfy the conditions set out in section 71 of the Inheritance Tax Act

1984, have significant tax advantages, combining the flexibility of discretionary trusts with a more favourable tax regime.

Because accumulation and maintenance trusts are, in reality, a type of discretionary trust for younger beneficiaries, they are the ideal vehicle for investments settled for the maintenance and education of children and grandchildren.

Like discretionary trusts, the fiscal advantages of accumulation and maintenance trusts relate almost entirely to inheritance tax: there may be income tax and capital gains tax disadvantages. The advantage arises because, so long as an accumulation and maintenance trust satisfies the strict provisions of section 71 of the Inheritance Tax Act 1984, they enjoy an inheritance tax holiday once created.

The favourable inheritance tax treatment of accumulation and maintenance trusts was introduced by a Labour government and so they are perceived as being less susceptible to political interference than fully discretionary trusts.

Inheritance tax

8.3   As with interest in possession settlements, a lifetime gift to an accumulation and maintenance settlement is a potentially exempt transfer: Inheritance Tax Act 1984, s 3A(1)(c). No inheritance tax will be payable if the settlor survives the gift into settlement by seven years and there is no reservation of benefit.

Unlike an interest in possession settlement, however, there is no deemed entitlement to the underlying capital while no interest in possession subsists, so that there will be no inheritance tax charge on the death of any beneficiary who has not attained an interest in possession under the settlement. Additionally, unlike fully discretionary settlements, no ten-year charges or exit charges will attract.

The conditions which must be satisfied if the trust is to qualify as an accumulation and maintenance trust are set out in section 71 of the Inheritance Tax Act 1984. They are that:

(1)   one or more beneficiaries will, on or before attaining a specified age not exceeding 25, become entitled to, or to an interest in possession in, the settled property; and

(2)   in the meantime no interest in possession subsists in the settled property and the income is to be accumulated so far as not applied for the maintenance, education or benefit of a beneficiary; and

(3)   either:

     (a)   not more than twenty-five years have elapsed since the commencement of the settlement or, if it was later, since the time (or latest time) when the conditions stated in (1) and (2) above became satisfied with respect to the property; or

(b)　all the persons who are or have been beneficiaries are or were either:

　(i)　grandchildren of a common grandparent, or

　(ii)　children, widows or widowers of such grandchildren who were themselves beneficiaries but died before the time when, had they survived, they would have become entitled as mentioned above.

During the lifetime of the settlement, so long as the property continues to be held on accumulation and maintenance trusts to which section 71 of the Inheritance Tax Act 1984 applies, the trust property is not relevant property for the purposes of Part III Chapter III of the Inheritance Tax Act 1984, so the ten-year anniversary charge normally applicable to discretionary trusts does not apply and there is no proportionate periodic charge when capital distributions are made to a beneficiary under the specified age or when the beneficiary becomes entitled to the trust property or to an interest in possession in it or dies: Inheritance Tax Act 1984, s 58(1) and s 71(4).

In section 71(1) 'persons' includes unborn persons provided there is or has been a living beneficiary and, for the purposes of the section, a person's children are be taken to include his illegitimate children, his adopted children and his stepchildren.

Capital gains tax

8.4　The creation of an accumulation and maintenance settlement is a disposal by the settlor for capital gains tax purposes. In the absence of any appropriate exemption or relief, capital gains tax will be payable. Subject to the availability of holdover relief under section 165 of the Taxation of Chargeable Gains Act 1992, however, there will be no holdover relief available on the setting up of the settlement.

Holdover relief under section 260 of the Taxation of Chargeable Gains Act 1992 will be available on the termination of an interest in possession settlement if the beneficiaries become entitled to capital at the same time as income under the terms of the settlement. This may often be lost, however, due to the provisions of section 31 of the Trustee Act 1925 which are very wide in their application and should be carefully considered at the outset by the draftsman of an accumulation and maintenance settlement.

The perceived advantage of holdover relief for capital gains tax in respect of entitlements arising under accumulation and maintenance settlements is often illusory because of the provisions of section 31 of the Trustee Act 1925 and the loss of taper relief when the beneficiary becomes entitled to a share of the trust property, so that the beneficiary starts with the need to build up a taper period of his own from nil.

Income tax

8.5   For income tax purposes, if a parent establishes a settlement for his own children he will need to appreciate that during the minority of his children any income will be taxed as his, unless during such minority the provisions of section 31 of the Trustee Act 1925 are excluded. In that case only income actually paid out to a minor child will be treated as the income of the parent: Income and Corporation Taxes Act 1988, s 660B. This provision does not, of course, apply to settlements established by grandparents for their grandchildren.

Subject to the above, any income arising from the property in the settlement will be taxed at the trust tax rate or the dividend trust tax rate, depending upon the nature of the trust property, while no interest in possession subsists in that property, and thereafter in accordance with the income tax regime applicable to interest in possession settlements.

Drafting points

8.6   Drafting accumulation and maintenance settlements is not a task for the faint-hearted. The rules laid down by section 71 of the Inheritance Tax Act 1984 (set out above) need to be satisfied in order for the settlement to qualify as an accumulation and maintenance settlement.

In order for the settlement to qualify as an accumulation and maintenance settlement there must be at least one living beneficiary who satisfies the test set out in section 71 of the Inheritance Tax Act 1984 at the date when the settlement is established. Provided that this condition is satisfied no difficulty will be encountered if all other, or many of the other, beneficiaries are unborn at the date of the settlement, provided that the overriding test which needs to be satisfied for the settlement to qualify as an accumulation and maintenance settlement, and the rule against perpetuities and excessive accumulations, are satisfied.

By their nature the drafting of accumulation and maintenance settlements is complex and the need to comply with the statutory requirements means that the drafting needs to be considered carefully. Often a discretionary trust or an interest in possession trust will be a more appropriate vehicle, being simpler to administer and offering greater flexibility.

If the settlement is an accumulation and maintenance settlement then the body of the deed will make this clear and a clause will usually be included to indicate that the powers given to the trustees in the settlement will not permit them to breach the terms of section 71 of the Inheritance Tax Act 1984.

The precedent used for an accumulation and maintenance settlement at APPENDIX 1.4 will create interests in possession in favour of the relevant principal beneficiary in respect of that share upon attaining the age of 25 years. While the beneficiary is under that age the income may be paid or applied for the maintenance, education or benefit of any principal beneficiary aged under 25 years, or may be accumulated, provided that not more than 21 years have elapsed since the creation of the settlement. If more than 21 years have elapsed then the income must be paid out for the maintenance, education or benefit of one or more of the principal beneficiaries who are then under 25 years.

By its nature an accumulation and maintenance settlement will include provisions that while no interest in possession subsists in the settlement, the income or any part of it may be applied for the maintenance, education or benefit of the relevant beneficiary, or it may be accumulated. For drafting purposes it is much simpler in cases where there is a class of beneficiaries to divide the trust fund into shares, one for each of the principal beneficiaries, but in order to ensure maximum flexibility the trustees should be permitted to apply the income arising from each share to any of the principal beneficiaries, while no interest in possession subsists in it.

Similarly, if the income of a share is accumulated while no interest in possession subsists, it is more sensible to provide that the accumulations will be added to the whole of the trust fund rather than to the particular share concerned. This will ease the administration of the trust, which would otherwise be unnecessarily complex with the various funds becoming of different sizes over time.

Where the class of principal beneficiaries includes persons unborn, then accumulation under the statutory power set out in section 31 of the Trustee Act 1925 will need to be included as a default provision, that is, to apply after the end of the defined accumulation period specified in the settlement. The precedent set out at APPENDIX 1.4 extends the statutory power.

It is a requirement that one or more persons 'will' become entitled to an interest in possession in the settled property. While this is not inconsistent with the statutory power of advancement, an overriding power of appointment in favour of a broad beneficial class of the sort seen in ordinary discretionary trusts will prevent the trusts from satisfying the strict requirements of section 71: *Lord Inglewood v IRC [1983] STC 133.*

Chapter 9

Bare Trusts

Nature of bare trusts

9.1   A bare trust is a trust by which property is held by one person upon trust for another absolutely. There is a simple separation of the legal and equitable interests but usually there is no more to it than that and so, in many cases, the terms 'bare trustee' and 'nominee' are interchangeable. There is a bare trust where land is held for an adult absolutely entitled to it.

A custodian trustee appointed under the Public Trustee Act 1906 is not a bare trustee, the distinction being that the custodian trustee is not bound to give effect to the wishes or directions of the beneficiaries although the distinction is described as a fine one but a real one: *IRC v Silverts Ltd [1951] 1 All ER 703*.

Why choose a bare trust?

9.2   More often than not a bare trust arises by default on, say, the termination of all successive interests under a settlement at which point the trustees hold property to distribute it to those absolutely beneficially entitled in default. That is not really an example of a bare trust being chosen – it is merely a vehicle which arises by default.

Bare trusts are commercially useful and are deliberately created either expressly or by implication where a professional such as a solicitor gives an undertaking to his client in relation to property held by him. *Target Holdings Limited v Redferns (a firm) [1995] 3 All ER 785* is a well-known example. Sometimes, perhaps in the course of a tax planning scheme, a settlor transfers property into the names of trustees or nominees to hold on trust for himself. The well-known case of *Gray v IRC [1960] AC 1* includes an example of a bare trust in these circumstances.

Where a parent accepts a legacy on behalf of a child the effect is as if a bare trust has arisen, the terms of which are dictated by section 31 of the Trustee Act 1925 (which is reproduced in APPENDIX 2). Strictly, trustees for a minor or other person under a disability should not be classified as bare trustees because they have duties to perform independent of any direction given by the beneficiary but for fiscal purposes they are bare trustees, which can be advantageous.

Inheritance tax

9.3   A bare trust, whether for an adult or a minor, is not treated as a settlement for inheritance tax purposes. It will be remembered from CHAPTER 5: TYPES OF TRUST that the Inheritance Tax Act 1984 does not rely upon a definition of 'trust' but instead relies upon the concept of 'a settlement'. A bare trust does not satisfy the concept of a settlement for inheritance tax purposes and a person for whom property is held on bare trust is simply treated as being beneficially entitled to the property without the need to consider the rules relating to settled property.

Capital gains tax

9.4   The Taxation of Chargeable Gains Act 1992 does not refer to a bare trust but to the case of an asset held by a person as trustee for another person absolutely entitled as against the trustee. This describes the case in which that 'beneficiary' has the exclusive right, subject only to satisfying any outstanding charge, lien or other right of the trustees to resort to the asset for payment of duty, taxes, costs or other outgoings, to direct how that asset shall be dealt with.

For capital gains tax purposes a bare trust is not regarded as a trust at all. Section 60 of the Taxation of Chargeable Gains Act 1992 provides that where property is held by a person as nominee for another person or on a bare trust the Act applies as if the property were vested in, and the acts of the nominee or bare trustee in relation to the property were the acts of, the person or persons for whom he is the nominee or bare trustee.

A bare trust for these purposes includes a trust by which property is held by a trustee for a person who would be absolutely entitled as against the trustee, but for being an infant or other person under disability, or for two or more persons who are or would be jointly so entitled.

The effect of treating the beneficiary of a bare trust as the owner of the property is that a full capital gains tax allowance (rather than the trustees' half allowance) will be available.

Income tax

9.5   A bare trust is a trust for income tax purposes. It will be remembered from CHAPTER 5: TYPES OF TRUST that section 660G of the Income and Corporation Taxes Act 1988 defines a 'settlement' as including any disposition, trust, covenant, agreement, arrangement or transfer of assets. A bare trust is plainly within the contemplation of this definition.

Hence, for example, where a settlor settles property on trust to pay the income to his unmarried minor children there is a bare trust but for income tax purposes the property is not treated as that of the children. The income is instead treated as that of the settlor by section 660B of the Income and Corporation Taxes Act 1988. If, on the other hand, the income is accumulated, there is no special rule which applies merely because the settlement is for the benefit of the settlor's children but it will be taxed at the trustee rate of 34 per cent. Where income is accumulated and subsequently paid to the child, section 660B will apply.

Where, on the other hand, the relationship between settlor and beneficiary is not one of parent and child, income which is not accumulated but cannot be paid to the child (because the child is a minor) will be taxed at the child's lower rate and the child's personal allowance will be available. In order to achieve this, section 31 of the Trustee Act 1925 should be excluded.

Drafting points

9.6   If a trust is genuinely a bare trust the trustees will have no duties other than to do what they are told by the beneficiary or beneficiaries. The inclusion of dispositive powers and discretions will necessarily involve the creation of some trust other than a bare trust but administrative powers and a power of advancement, which must necessarily be limited to a power to advance to the beneficiary of the bare trust, will not prevent a bare trust from arising.

Where the beneficiary is the settlor's child there may be little point in excluding section 31 of the Trustee Act 1925 because, if the section is excluded, the income will be taxed as that of the settlor. However, if the relationship between the settlor and the beneficiary is not one of parent and child, section 660B of the Income and Corporation Taxes Act 1988 does not result in the income being taxed as that of the settlor if section 31 is excluded.

The precedent at APPENDIX 1.7 is intended as a bare trust declared by a parent as settlor for his or her child and so an amended section 31 of the Trustee Act 1925 is included. In other cases it should be excluded. It should be noticed that, unlike the other precedents, this is a simple declaration of trust by which the settlor declares himself trustee.

Chapter 10

Protective Trusts

Nature of protective trusts

10.1   Protective trusts combine an interest in possession determinable on the happening of an event of forfeiture with a discretionary trust which arises upon the forfeiture. Protective trusts usually arise by simple incorporation of the provisions of section 33 of the Trustee Act 1925 which will occur whenever the settlement refers to property being held on 'protective trusts'. Express protective trusts which are at variance with the statutory protective trusts are sometimes encountered but these are a less common species.

Protective trusts are trusts designed to prevent funds from, amongst other things, falling into the hands of a trustee in bankruptcy in the event of an incautious beneficiary becoming insolvent or committing or suffering other acts of forfeiture in respect of the trust property. This is achieved by section 33(1) of the Trustee Act 1925 (set out in APPENDIX 2) which provides that where any income is directed to be held on protective trusts for the benefit of any person ('the principal beneficiary') for the period of his life or for any less period, then, during that period ('the trust period') the income shall, without prejudice to any prior interest, be held in the first instance:

> '(i)   upon trust for the principal beneficiary during the trust period or until he . . . does or attempts to do or suffers any act or thing, or until any event happens, other than an advance under any statutory or express power, whereby, if the said income were payable during the trust period to the principal beneficiary absolutely during that period, he would be deprived of the right to receive the same or any part thereof, in any of which cases, as well as on the termination of the trust period, whichever first happens, this trust of the said income shall fail or determine'.

Thus, where trustees hold property upon protective trusts for a beneficiary for life, there is initially an interest in possession in the property but if the beneficiary suffers, does, or attempts to do, any act which would deprive him of the right to receive the whole of the income of the fund (an act of forfeiture), his life interest in the property is forfeited and automatically comes to an end. The acts of forfeiture which deprive the beneficiary of his interest in possession include selling, assigning and mortgaging the life interest under the trust, and the bankruptcy of the principal beneficiary, each of which deprives the principal beneficiary of the right to receive the income.

Section 33(1) goes on to provide that if an act of forfeiture occurs during the trust period the following discretionary trust arises in place of the interest in possession:

'(ii) . . . during the residue of [the trust] period, the . . . income shall be held upon trust for the application thereof for the maintenance or support, or otherwise for the benefit, of all or any one or more exclusively of the other or others of the following persons (that is to say)—

(a) the principal beneficiary and his or her wife or husband, if any, and his or her children or more remote issue, if any; or

(b) if there is no wife or husband or issue of the principal beneficiary in existence, the principal beneficiary and the persons who would, if he were actually dead, be entitled to the trust property or the income thereof . . .;

as the trustees in their absolute discretion, without being liable to account for the exercise of such discretion, think fit'.

The effect of all of that is to prevent a trustee in bankruptcy or some other creditor of the principal beneficiary to whom he might wish to charge his interest in possession from becoming entitled to the trust income in the stead of the principal beneficiary.

That does not enable a settlor to settle his own property on protective trusts for himself before being declared bankrupt because section 33(3) expressly provides that it does not have the effect of validating any trust which would, if contained in the instrument creating the trust, be liable to be set aside, as such a trust would.

Why choose a protective trust?

10.2   Protective trusts serve a variety of uses and are often included in wills. They are primarily used by settlors who wish to make income available for a child who is prone to rash and incautious investments, who is, or may be likely to become insolvent, has an immature attitude to money or is easily led. The classic immature beneficiary is one whose past behaviour evidences a propensity to fritter away capital on get rich quick schemes, drink, drugs, fast cars and loose women or untrustworthy men and who, if given an unprotected interest in possession, is likely to sell or mortgage that interest in order to raise disposable capital.

Inheritance tax

10.3   For inheritance tax purposes protective trusts are interest in possession trusts while the principal beneficiary is entitled to receive the whole of the income from the fund. If there were no special provision, there would be a charge to inheritance tax when, upon forfeiture, the discretionary trust arises because the interest in possession would then terminate.

Section 88 of the Inheritance Tax Act 1984 applies to property which is held on trusts to the like effect as those specified in section 33(1) of the Trustee Act 1925. The section provides that for inheritance tax purposes the failure or determination, before the end of the trust period, of the interest in possession element of the protective trusts shall be disregarded and the principal beneficiary shall be treated as beneficially entitled to an interest in possession in any property which is held on the discretionary trusts of section 33(1)(ii).

The Revenue's view of this, as expressed in Statement of Practice E7, is that trusts 'to the like effect' are trusts which are not materially different in their tax consequences. A minor variation or the introduction of additional administrative duties or powers will not, according to the Revenue, affect the application of section 88 but the Revenue's view is otherwise quite strict, as discussed below.

As a consequence of the section 88 relief, if a capital distribution is made to the principal beneficiary, whether before or after a forfeiture, there will be no inheritance tax liability but if the principal beneficiary dies, whether before or after a forfeiture, there will be a notional transfer of value of the whole of the property in which the principal beneficiary's interest subsisted. Similarly, where the principal beneficiary's interest comes to an end because of a permitted capital distribution to a remainderman by way of advancement of capital or otherwise, there will be a termination of the interest in possession with the consequences described in CHAPTER 6: TRUSTS WITH AN INTEREST IN POSSESSION.

Capital gains tax

10.4   There are no capital gains tax provisions which correspond with those for inheritance tax. If there is an act of forfeiture during the lifetime of the principal beneficiary, that will not give rise to a deemed disposal of the settled property for capital gains tax purposes. However, if the trust continues at the principal beneficiary's death there will not be an uplift in the value of the assets at his death. Instead, if the property ceases to be settled on the principal beneficiary's death, there will be a deemed disposal and re-acquisition at that time but no exemption in respect of any gains which are realised.

Income tax

10.5   Similarly, there are no income tax provisions which correspond with those for inheritance tax. The rules applicable to interests in possession and then discretionary trusts will apply.

Drafting points

10.6   Where a settlor uses the term 'protective trusts' in the settlement, the reference is taken to be a reference to protective trusts under section 33 of the Trustee Act 1925. Thus, where in a settlement income is directed to be held upon protective trusts for any person for life or any less period then, subject to any prior interests, it is to be held during that period upon the statutory discretionary trusts of section 33 which are set out above. If the settlor wishes to vary the terms of the statutory trusts, the settlement can specify in full and precise terms the circumstances in which the discretionary trust will arise and, if properly drafted, the effect of section 69 of the Trustee Act 1925 (see APPENDIX 2) is that the settlor's directions will override the statutory provisions.

The precedent at APPENDIX 1.9 incorporates the statutory protective trusts which is the form most commonly used. If drafting express protective trusts the draftsman should remember to incorporate the three basic elements of protective trusts:

(a)   an initial interest in possession determinable on the occurrence of certain specified events, such as bankruptcy;

(b)   a provision cutting down or forfeiting the interest in possession in the event of certain specified events occurring;

(c)   a discretionary trust that automatically replaces the interest in possession upon the determination of that interest.

It should also be remembered that express protective trusts might not be accepted by the Revenue as being within section 88 of the Inheritance Tax Act 1984. For example, rightly or wrongly, the Revenue does not regard the extension of the list of potential beneficiaries to brothers and sisters as a minor variation: Statement of Practice E7. 'Similar words' have been held to mean similarity in substance, not in form or detail or wording: *Re Wallace's Settlements [1968] 2 All ER 209.*

Chapter 11

Trusts for the Disabled

Nature of disabled trusts

11.1   A disabled trust is a trust for a person who is incapable of administering his property or managing his affairs, which is extended for inheritance and capital gains tax purposes to include a person in receipt of attendance allowance or disability living allowance.

These trusts can be drafted as interest in possession trusts but they are usually drafted as discretionary trusts in order to militate against the loss of state or local authority benefits.

Such trusts have been accorded special inheritance tax treatment under section 89 of the Inheritance Tax Act 1984. Where the conditions of the section are satisfied, the disabled person is treated for inheritance tax purposes as being beneficially entitled to an interest in possession, so that the ten-year charge and exit charges for inheritance tax do not apply but the settlement is taxed as an interest in possession settlement for inheritance tax purposes on the death of the disabled person.

Why choose a disabled trust?

11.2   Provision can be made for a disabled person by way of an interest in possession trust but if the disabled person is in receipt of means-tested benefits, such as income support or the provision of residential care by the local authority, an interest in possession trust will normally be taken into account in assessing those benefits or the local authority's contribution to the cost of residential care.

If the disabled person is a beneficiary of a discretionary trust (of which he is not the settlor) which attracts the special inheritance tax treatment applicable to disabled trusts, the settled property in a disabled trust will not be taken into account save to the extent that it is actually applied for his benefit. The situation may be the same where the disabled person is the settlor of an award such as an award of compensation for personal injury but in other cases in which the disabled person is the settlor the property will usually still be taken into account.

Inheritance tax

11.3   Section 89 of the Inheritance Tax Act 1984 makes special provision for disabled trusts created after 9 March 1981. The inheritance tax treatment of disabled trusts created before 10 March 1981 is different and is beyond the scope of this book.

For inheritance tax purposes, a person is disabled if he is:

- incapable, by reason of mental disorder within the meaning of the Mental Health Act 1983, of administering his property or managing his affairs: Inheritance Tax Act 1984, s 89(4)(a);

- in receipt of an attendance allowance under section 64 of the Social Security Contributions and Benefits Act 1992 or section 64 of the Social Security Contributions and Benefits (Northern Ireland) Act 1992: Inheritance Tax Act 1984, s 89(4)(b); or

- in receipt of a disability living allowance under section 71 of the Social Security Contributions and Benefits Act 1992 or the Social Security Contributions and Benefits (Northern Ireland) Act 1992 by virtue of entitlement to the care component at the highest or middle rate: Inheritance Tax Act 1984, s 89(4)(c).

This definition includes both patients of the Court of Protection and persons whose affairs are being managed under an enduring power of attorney which has been registered with the Court of Protection. Attendance allowance is available for those over 65 while disability living allowance is available below that age. These are social security benefits available to persons with severe physical or mental disability who require frequent, prolonged or repeated attention or supervision during the day or night and who are not in state funded accommodation. For inheritance tax purposes the disabled person must be receiving the relevant allowance, mere entitlement is not enough.

Section 89 of the Inheritance Tax Act 1984 applies where property is transferred to a settlement after 9 March 1981 and held on trusts:

(a)   under which, during the life of a disabled person, no interest in possession in the settled property subsists; and

(b)   which secure that not less than half of the settled property which is applied during his life is applied for his benefit.

Where those conditions are satisfied and the disabled person qualifies as such at the time when the property is transferred into the settlement, the disabled person is treated as beneficially entitled to an interest in possession in the settled property: Inheritance Tax Act 1984, s 89(2).

As a consequence of the section 89 relief, if a capital distribution is made to the disabled person there will be no inheritance tax liability but if the disabled person dies there will be a notional transfer of value of the whole of the property.

Similarly, where the disabled beneficiary's interest comes to an end because of a permitted capital distribution to another person by way of advancement of capital or otherwise, there will be a termination of the interest in possession with the consequences described in CHAPTER 6: TRUSTS WITH AN INTEREST IN POSSESSION.

Capital gains tax

11.4   Where settled property is held on trusts which secure that, during the lifetime of a person who by reason of mental disorder is incapable of administering his property or managing his affairs, or a person in receipt of an attendance allowance or of a disability living allowance by virtue of entitlement to the care component at the highest or middle rate, and

(a)   not less than half of the property which is applied is applied for the benefit of the disabled person; and

(b)   the disabled person is entitled to not less than half of the income arising from the property or no such income may be applied for any other person,

the trustees are able to claim the full annual exemption amount as an individual and not the reduced rate usually applicable to trustees: Taxation of Chargeable Gains Act 1992, Sch 1 para 1(1).

Unlike section 89 of the Inheritance Tax Act 1984, for which the disabled person need only qualify when property is transferred into the settlement, the disabled person must qualify for every year in which the full capital gains tax exemption is claimed.

Income tax

11.5   There are no income tax provisions which correspond with those for inheritance tax. The trust will either be an interest in possession trust or a discretionary trust with the income tax consequences described in CHAPTERS 6 and 7.

Drafting points

11.6   The settlement deed itself will need to satisfy the conditions of section 89 of the Inheritance Tax Act 1984 expressly. The section provides that a disabled person for these purposes means either a person who is mentally disabled (that is, incapable of administering his property or managing his affairs by reason of mental disorder under the Mental Health Act 1983) or physically

disabled (that is, in receipt of attendance allowance or disability living allowance under the Social Security Contributions and Benefits Act 1992) and that
fact should be recited.

To attract the full capital gains tax exemption, the disabled person must have an
interest in possession in at least half of the fund. That breaches the inheritance
tax requirements. If income is accumulated, then relief under section 89 of the
Inheritance Tax Act 1984 and also capital gains tax relief can be claimed but
after the accumulation period one will have to be lost. The capital gains tax
relief is the less valuable and that should be sacrificed. However, unless the trust
fund is substantial it will be preferable in many cases to use an ordinary
discretionary trust rather than comply with the provisions of the Taxation of
Chargeable Gains Act 1992 because the trustees will be able to avoid capital
gains tax by using their ordinary annual exemption, and an exemption of twice
that amount will not be of particular advantage.

There is a precedent for a disabled trust at APPENDIX 1.8.

Chapter 12

Employee Trusts

Nature of employee trusts

12.1   Employee trusts deserve to be mentioned because of their favoured tax treatment, particularly the inheritance tax treatment. They are trusts by which property is held on discretionary trusts for a class of beneficiaries defined by reference to employment.

The Inland Revenue Trusts and Estates Manual recognises that the general employee benefit trust is known by a variety of names such as employee benefit trust, employee trust, business trust, employee share trust or scheme, employee share ownership plan or trust, employee profit sharing scheme or trust, pre-retirement employee benefit scheme or trust, incentive plan trust, discretionary bonus trust, remuneration trust and staff benevolent fund. Sometimes the word 'equity' or 'stock' is used instead of 'share' but they all amount to the same thing.

The organisation of employee trusts is largely tax driven. In addition to the general employee benefit trust, the Revenue recognise retirement benefits schemes and employee share ownership schemes (amongst others) as quite different classes of employee trust. The scope of employee benefit trusts, in particular the fiscal treatment, is an extremely complex topic, detailed discussion of which is largely beyond the scope of this book.

Why choose an employee trust?

12.2   Although the use of employee trusts is principally driven by their favoured tax treatment, they are also useful for more generally benevolent purposes. They are able to provide some level of comfort by way of discretionary payments to those employees who participate amongst the discretionary beneficial class and so help to foster good relations between employees and employers and can provide something of an incentive to the employee beneficiaries.

Employee trusts also have commercial benefits for the company in that they can provide a certain amount of funding and enable shares to be held *en bloc* in a manner which is most unlikely to assist a hostile takeover.

The rationale behind the creation of employee trusts is such that most are created by companies.

Inheritance tax

12.3   The inheritance tax treatment of employee trusts is contained in section 86 of the Inheritance Tax Act 1984. That section applies where settled property is held on trusts which, either indefinitely or until the end of a period (whether defined by a date or in some other way), do not permit any of the settled property to be applied otherwise than for the benefit of:

(a)   persons of a class defined by reference to employment in a particular trade or profession, or employment by, or office with, a body carrying on a trade, profession or undertaking, or

(b)   persons of a class defined by reference to marriage or relationship to, or dependence on, persons of a class defined as mentioned in paragraph (a) above.

Trusts which also permit the settled property to be applied for charitable purposes will still satisfy this definition.

Where the class is defined by reference to employment by or office with a particular body, the section applies to the settled property only if:

(a)   the class comprises all or most of the persons employed by or holding office with the body concerned, or

(b)   the trusts on which the settled property is held are those of a profit sharing scheme approved in accordance with Schedule 9 to the Income and Corporation Taxes Act 1988.

Where a trust satisfies those requirements, the property subject to the trust is to be treated as comprised in one settlement, whether or not it would otherwise be so treated apart from section 86, and an interest in possession in any part of the property is disregarded for the purposes of the Inheritance Tax Act 1984 (except section 55) if that part is less than 5 per cent of the whole.

Furthermore, section 58(1)(b) of the Inheritance Tax Act 1984 provides that settled property which satisfies the requirements of section 86 is not relevant property within the discretionary trust tax regime so, for example, there will be no ten-year anniversary charge on the property. Section 86(5) provides:

'Where any property to which this section applies ceases to be comprised in a settlement and, either immediately or not more than one month later, the whole of it becomes comprised in another settlement, then, if this section again applies to it when it becomes comprised in the second settlement, it shall be treated for all the purposes of this Act as if it had remained comprised in the first settlement.'

In addition to the above provisions, section 28 of the Inheritance Tax Act 1984 provides that a transfer of value made by an individual who is beneficially entitled to shares in a company is an exempt transfer to the extent that the value transferred is attributable to shares in or securities of the company which become comprised in a settlement if:

(a)   the trusts of the settlement are of the description specified in section 86(1), and

(b)   the persons for whose benefit the trusts permit the settled property to be applied include all or most of the persons employed by or holding office with the company.

However, in section 28(2) there are further requirements which must be satisfied if the exemption is to apply. These are that:

(a)   the trustees hold more than one half of the ordinary shares in the company, and have powers of voting on all questions affecting the company as a whole which if exercised would yield a majority of the votes capable of being exercised on them; and

(b)   there are no provisions in any agreement or instrument affecting the company's constitution or management or its shares or securities whereby the condition in paragraph (a) above can cease to be satisfied without the consent of the trustees.

To add to the complication, section 28(4) provides that the exemption does not apply if the trusts permit any of the settled property to be applied at any time for the benefit of a person who is a participator in the company; or any close company that has made a disposition whereby property became comprised in the same settlement; any other person who has been a participator in the company or close company during the previous ten years; or any person who is connected with any of those persons. There are conditions so that the participators in a company do not include any participator who is not beneficially entitled to, or to rights entitling him to acquire, 5 per cent or more of, or of any class of, the shares comprised in, its issued share capital, and on a winding-up of the company would not be entitled to 5 per cent or more of its assets.

Capital gains tax

12.4   Set out in section 239 of the Taxation of Chargeable Gains Act 1992 are special capital gains tax provisions relating to gifts to employee benefit trusts. Thus, where a close company disposes of an asset to trustees within section 13 of the Inheritance Tax Act 1984 or an individual disposes of an asset to trustees within section 28 of that Act, the market value rule in section 17 of the Taxation of Chargeable Gains Act 1992 is disapplied.

This can have knock-on effects where distributions are made to employee beneficiaries but Extra-Statutory Concession D35 may provide the trustees with some measure of relief where the beneficiary is liable for income tax on the full value of the shares in question.

Income tax

12.5   Employee benefit trusts are essentially discretionary trusts: the trustees have discretion to apply all or part of any income in favour of one or more of the beneficiaries. In view of the trustees' discretion (and possible power of accumulation), income is chargeable at the rate applicable to trusts under section 686 of the Income and Corporation Taxes Act 1988.

Where discretionary income payments are not chargeable under Schedule E on the recipient beneficiary, section 687 of the Income and Corporation Taxes Act 1988 will apply. The trustees will be chargeable under section 687(2)(b) in respect of payments to beneficiaries that are within section 687 after deducting the set off under section 687(3).

Employees who receive payments from an employee benefit trust are usually chargeable to income tax under Schedule E. If the payment is an emolument assessable to tax on the employees, there is a charge on the trustees as trust income and on the employees as an emolument. The employees cannot have credit for the tax paid by the trustees. This is in contrast to the tax rules that normally apply to trust distributions. The result is that tax is effectively charged twice. The trustees may be entitled to concessionary repayment under Extra-Statutory Concession A68 which applies only to employee trusts which are defined as 'discretionary trusts created by funds provided by employers for the benefit of their employees'. The concession partially relieves a double charge arising.

Drafting points

12.6   There is a straightforward precedent for an employee benefit trust at APPENDIX 1.10. This is a precedent for contributions by an individual settlor. Trusts created by employers are more common but beyond the scope of this book.

In settling employee trusts, care should be taken to have regard to the provisions of sections 28 and 86 of the Inheritance Tax Act 1984 and, where dispositions are made by close companies for the benefit of employees, section 13 of the Act should be borne in mind. Since employee benefit trusts are a form of discretionary trust, care should also be taken in defining the beneficial class and in providing adequate dispositive powers.

Where the settlor is an individual, an ordinary clause excluding the settlor and his spouse for the time being from benefit should be included.

Chapter 13

Charitable Trusts

Nature of charitable trusts

13.1   Charitable trusts are the only type of purpose trusts which, if valid, are enforceable, even though there may not be an identifiable beneficiary. Additionally, a valid and enforceable charitable trust is a public, rather than a private, trust. Enforcement and regulation concerning charitable trusts is made by the Attorney-General or the Charity Commissioners.

In order to qualify as a valid charitable trust, the trust must be able to demonstrate an element of public benefit, that is, that all members of the public or a significant section of the relevant community have the same opportunity of benefiting, unless the charity is established for the relief of poverty. Additionally the charity must be established as exclusively charitable according to law, unless the non-charitable purposes are purely incidental to the main charitable purposes.

The original test of what is charitable was set out in the preamble to the Charitable Uses Act (43 Eliz 1, C 4) which included within the definition:

> 'the relief of aged, impotent, and poor people; the maintenance of sick and maimed soldiers and mariners, schools of learning, free schools and scholars of universities; the repair of bridges, havens, causeways, churches, sea banks and highways; the education and preferment of orphans; the relief, stock or maintenance of houses of correction; marriages of poor maid . . .'

. . . and so on.

The preamble was repealed by the Charities Act 1960 and no new definition was introduced. The question of what is or is not charitable is now determined by case law and, more recently, reported decisions of the Charity Commissioners. In *Commissioners for Special Purposes of Income Tax v Pemsel [1891] AC 531* Lord MacNaghten summarised what are still recognised as the four classes of charitable purposes:

(a)   the relief of poverty;

(b)   the advancement of education;

(c)   the advancement of religion; and

(d)   other purposes for the benefit of the community.

The application of the fourth head is sometimes difficult to construe and particular difficulty has arisen in relation to trusts for sport and recreation. The position was clarified to some extent by the Recreational Charities Act 1958 which provides that in the case of a trust or institution for the public benefit it shall be and be deemed always to have been charitable to provide, or assist in the provision of, facilities for recreation or other leisure-time occupation, if the facilities are provided in the interests of social welfare. Facilities are provided in the interests of social welfare if they are provided with the object of improving the conditions of life for the persons for whom they are primarily intended and either those persons have need for such facilities by reason of their youth, age, infirmity or disablement, poverty or social and economic circumstances or the facilities are to be available to the members or female members of the public at large.

Reform

13.2   Four hundred years after the commencement of the Charitable Uses Act the Cabinet Office Strategy Unit was asked to consider how to improve the legal and regulatory framework relating to charities. The Cabinet Office Strategy Unit Report, *Private Action, Public Benefit – A Review of Charities and the Wider Not-For-Profit Sector*, was published in September 2002.

The Strategy Unit has proposed a new definition of charity under which there will be ten recognised heads of charity. The proposed definition is:

A charity should be defined as an organisation which provides public benefit and which has one or more of the following purposes:

(1)   The prevention and relief of poverty.

(2)   The advancement of education.

(3)   The advancement of religion.

(4)   The advancement of health. Including the prevention and relief of sickness, disease or of human suffering.

(5)   Social and community advancement. Including the care, support and protection of the aged, people with a disability, children and young people.

(6)   The advancement of culture, arts and heritage.

(7)   The advancement of amateur sport.

(8)   The promotion of human rights, conflict resolution and reconciliation.

(9)   The advancement of environmental protection and improvement.

(10) Other purposes for the benefit of the community.

In addition (or possibly in contradiction) the Strategy Unit has emphasised that the Government considers that public benefit should continue to be one of the essential requirements of charitable status with the result that there would not be a presumption that certain categories are for public benefit. Thus, in addition to being within one of the ten proposed heads of charity, all charities will have to demonstrate public benefit. One consequence of this might be that the proposed ten separate heads of charity become redundant in the face of a single public benefit test.

Some commentators see this as essentially a complex disguise under cover of which it will be possible to launch a political assault on the system of private education which exists in this country without openly taking on particular institutions. That may be a rather cynical view: the Strategy Unit's report goes further than to propose a redefinition of charity and much of it is devoted to an overhaul of the regulatory system applicable to charities. Nonetheless, there can be little doubt that, if carried into effect, the Strategy Unit's proposals would adversely affect independent schools: see paragraph 4.26 of the report.

There is no guarantee that all institutions which are presently regarded as charitable will continue to be treated as such. The report, which was prepared without the rigour usually employed by the Law Commission and apparently without any detailed canvassing of experienced legal opinion, has completely failed to address the question of what is to happen to the capital and income of charitable trusts which cease to be charitable under the new regime.

It is possible that, because the proposals do not originate from the Law Commission, if they are not immediately implemented they will disappear without trace when their political parents move on.

Why choose a charitable trust?

13.3   If being asked to set up a charity, it is important for the draftsman to consider whether the charity should be constituted as a charitable trust, as an unincorporated association or as an incorporated charitable company.

The Charity Commission suggests that it may be appropriate to establish an unincorporated association where the organisation is to be relatively small in terms of assets or is to be a local branch of a national charity which has a standard constitution for branches. It is also appropriate where the organisation is to have a membership, and the charity trustees are to be elected by members (whether or not they hold office for a fixed period of time); where the views of local residents, local councils, and other bodies need to be represented through membership, or as users of the facilities; and the objects of the organisation are to be carried out wholly or partly by, or through, the members (that is, where the members undertake office or voluntary work on behalf of the organisation).

A charitable company, on the other hand, is more likely to be appropriate where the organisation is to be quite large; will have employees; will deliver charitable services under contractual agreements; will regularly enter into commercial contracts; and will be a substantial owner of freehold or leasehold land or other property.

The charitable trust usually falls between these two. Looking again at the Charity Commission's recommendations, appropriate circumstances in which to create a charitable trust include the following: the organisation of the trust, administration of which should be relatively simple, is to be run by a fairly small group of people but by trustees and not members so that it will not rely on a membership for any part of its administration or for the appointment of new trustees which will be left in the hands of the existing trustees. There need be no time limit on how long the charity trustees remain in office although the Charity Commission prefers to see regular reviews of the trustees. It is also suggested that a charitable trust will be appropriate where land and buildings are to be held on trust for permanent use for the purposes of the charity and there is to be a restriction on spending capital or the organisation is to be a grant-making body only.

If a trust is appropriate, the advantages of a charitable trust as compared with a private trust include the following:

(a)   Considerable tax advantages result from charitable status being recognised. Income can be received by charities gross and a tax reclaim can be made in respect of any tax deducted from income received net. Charities do not need to pay capital gains tax on gains made on disposals and for inheritance tax purposes any gifts made by individuals to charities are exempt.

(b)   Charities are able to hold property in perpetuity and to hold the same as permanent endowment.

(c)   Gifts from one charity to another charity which might take effect outside the perpetuity period are not void, as would be the case in respect of a gift over from one person to another person under a private trust.

(d)   If the charitable trust is valid and enforceable, the purposes for which it exists will not be allowed to fail for uncertainty of objects, so long as general charitable intention in the creation of the settlement can be shown. In such cases a *cy près* scheme may be made to enable the original intention to be put into effect 'as nearly as possible'.

Some of the tax advantages are discussed in the following paragraphs.

Inheritance tax

13.4   There is a general exemption for transfers on the creation of a charitable trust (Inheritance Tax Act 1984, s 23). The exemption is available if the property transferred becomes owned by a charity, or is held on trust for charitable purposes only. This exemption only applies to charities established within the United Kingdom (Inheritance Tax Act 1984, s 272) and is subject to the conditions specified in section 23(2)–(5) of the Inheritance Tax Act 1984. A detailed discussion of those conditions and their tax planning implications is beyond the scope of this book.

There is, however, no monetary limit on the exemption, whether the charitable trust is created by a lifetime transfer or on death. Likewise, in general there is no exit charge where property subject to discretionary trusts is distributed to a charity (Inheritance Tax Act 1984, s 76).

Capital gains tax

13.5   Where, on the creation of a charitable trust, assets are disposed of to the charity by way of gift, or by way of sale at a value which does not exceed the cost to the disponor, the disponor is treated as making the disposal for a consideration which gives rise neither to a gain nor a loss (Taxation of Chargeable Gains Act 1992, s 257(1) and (2)).

Similarly, where a charity becomes absolutely entitled to settled property, the trustees are deemed to dispose of the settled property for a consideration which gives rise neither to a gain nor a loss, and to re-acquire the property at that value as bare trustees for the charity – and the same approach is adopted where property becomes held on trust for the charity following the lifetime termination of a life interest (Taxation of Chargeable Gains Act 1992, s 257(3)).

These special rules apply only if the charity becomes entitled without any person receiving consideration. It makes little sense to sell assets and pass the proceeds of sale to the charity if a capital gain would arise when they could be given in specie. Conversely, the rules do not permit a donor to take advantage of a loss for capital gains tax purposes. In that instance it makes more sense to sell the assets first. Many charities offer advice on the most tax-efficient means of giving to them.

A gain which accrues to a charity, and is applied for charitable purposes, is not a chargeable gain but when property which has been held on charitable trusts ceases to be so held, it is deemed to be disposed of and re-acquired at its market value at the time when it ceases to be held on charitable trusts and the gain is a chargeable gain to the extent that it represents the consideration for the disposal (Taxation of Chargeable Gains Act 1992, s 256(1)).

Income tax

13.6   All sums received by way of interest, annuities, annual payments, and income from land such as rents and premiums on leases, are exempt from income tax provided that they are applied for charitable purposes and the recipient is a body of persons or a trust established for charitable purposes only (Income and Corporation Taxes Act 1988, s 505)). Where one charity makes an outright payment to another charity, the charity making the payment applies its income to charitable purposes, even if the recipient charity merely accumulates it.

Much of the investment income of a charity may have been received subject to deduction of tax, and in this case a repayment claim can be made.

The profits of a trade carried on by a charity are subject to abstruse tax rules. These will be exempt from income tax only if applied solely to its purposes and either:

(i)   the purpose, or one of the primary purposes, of the charity is to carry on that business; or

(ii) the work in connection with that trade is mainly carried on by beneficiaries of the charity.

Extra-statutory concession ESC C4 also assists in that it exempts income from events organised for charitable purposes where the primary purpose is the raising of money. There is a further de minimis trading exemption for charitable companies of £5,000 or, if the turnover is greater than £5,000, 25 per cent of the charity's gross income subject to a maximum exemption of £50,000.

As a rule, however, it is best if the charity itself does not trade but permits trade to be carried on by wholly-owned trading subsidiaries of the charity operating according to normal commercial principles with all profits covenanted to the parent charity.

Drafting points

13.7   A precedent for a charitable trust in the model form approved by the Charity Commissioners is included at APPENDIX 1.11. The Charity Commission also produces model forms of a memorandum and articles of association and a constitution which are also available, free of charge, on their website (www.charitycommission.gov.uk) or by calling their Contact Centre on 0870 333 0123. A list of other organisations for which a standard governing document has been agreed can also be found on the website.

The Charity Law Association also produces suitable model governing documents for which a charge is made. Copies can be ordered from the administrator, on Charitylaw@aol.com. Other enquiries relating to these governing documents should be directed to the secretary Ros Harwood at Rollits, Rowntree Wharf, Navigation Road, York YO1 9WE. Tel: 01904 625790; Fax: 01904 625807.

Adopting a model charitable trust which has already been approved by the Charity Commission is not absolutely necessary but it speeds up the process of registration because the administrative provisions have already been agreed so that only the objects need to be considered. Where an agreed standard governing document is used, the objects will also be understood by the Charity Commission. However, there is no guarantee that the use of a model form will be accepted as charitable since its objects must be charitable for it to be accepted.

As is apparent from the model form at APPENDIX 1.11, charity trustees are not limited in number and are able to take decisions by majority vote but there are specific statutory controls on who can and cannot be a charity trustee. The model form includes provisions for six trustees. Special provisions also relate to the ownership of charity land and those which are referred to in the precedent are set out in APPENDIX 2.

Great care must be taken in identifying and specifying the objects of a charity (clause 3 of the model form). These must be drafted in such a way as to provide with clarity what the beneficial objects of the charity are intended to be with an eye to the recognised heads of charity and with a view to public benefit.

Following the execution of a charitable trust it should be sent for registration. The Charity Commission has produced an Application to Register a Charity pack which includes an application form (APP 1) and a declaration form (DEC 1) both of which must be completed. In addition, the Charity Commission must be provided with two certified copies of the dated trust deed showing the names of the first charity trustees and the witnesses to their signatures; evidence of adjudication by a local Stamp Office or a valid exemption certificate; and certified copies of any supplemental deeds or deeds of variation showing subsequent amendments, duly signed and witnessed, showing evidence of stamping if necessary. Further information can be obtained from the Charity Commission website and, in particular, from Note CC22 'Choosing and Preparing a Governing Document'.

Chapter 14

Trusts Arising on Death

Trusts arising on intestacy

14.1   The succession to real and personal estate on intestacy is governed by the table of distribution in section 46 of the Administration of Estates Act 1925 which is set out in APPENDIX 2. Thus, where a person dies intestate leaving a spouse and no issue and no parent, or brother or sister of the whole blood, or issue of a brother or sister of the whole blood, then the surviving spouse takes the whole of the residuary estate absolutely under the first paragraph in the table set out in section 46(1)(i) of the Administration of Estates Act 1925.

Where, however, a person dies intestate leaving a spouse and issue, the second paragraph in the table in section 46(1)(i) of the Administration of Estates Act 1925 provides that the surviving spouse takes the personal chattels absolutely; a fixed net sum (currently £125,000) and, subject to that, the residuary estate is held as to one-half upon trust for the surviving spouse during his or her life; and, subject to that, on the statutory trusts for the issue of the person dying intestate; and as to the other half, on the statutory trusts for the issue. The fixed net sum of £125,000 was set in 1993 and an increase in the figure is long overdue.

The statutory trusts are set out in section 47 of the Administration of Estates Act 1925 which is also reproduced in APPENDIX 2. It is sometimes necessary for the draftsman to incorporate the statutory trusts into a settlement. For example, where the surviving spouse exercises the right to have his or her life interest redeemed under section 47A of the Administration of Estates Act 1925 (see APPENDIX 2) and that life interest is then capitalised in accordance with the provisions of the Intestate Succession (Interest and Capitalisation) Order 1977, it will be prudent to draft a settlement in respect of the remainder. Such a settlement should recite the death, the exercise of the right under section 47A and might then expressly identify the beneficiaries and set out the statutory trusts as recorded in section 47.

Will trusts

14.2   A will trust is simply a trust created by will. By their very nature will trusts do not come into effect until the death of the testator (the maker of the will in question). They can be effected either in respect of specified property or in respect of the residue of the testator's estate. A will is an ambulatory document: provided that he has the required testamentary capacity the testator can change the terms of his will, and therefore the terms of any trusts within it, at any time during his lifetime.

The language employed when drafting will trusts is usually slightly different from that used when drafting lifetime settlements, but this difference is of little significance. What is of rather more significance is that will trusts are often much less carefully drafted than lifetime settlements. There are a variety of reasons for this. Many wills are homemade and the unskilled draftsman is unlikely to anticipate all of the difficulties thrown up by his attempt at drafting. Professionally drawn wills are also prone to sloppier drafting than lifetime settlements. To a small degree this is because the quality of will-draftsmen varies – there is no requirement as to the qualification of will draftsmen as there is in relation to lifetime settlements under section 22 of the Solicitors Act 1974. However, the most significant factor lies in the price. Wills are generally drafted cheaply and quickly and so there is little incentive for the draftsman to put time and effort into the drafting. That is no excuse. Exactly the same care and skill need to be applied to the drafting of will trusts as to the drafting of lifetime settlements.

In order to establish a trust validly the will in question must be validly made. No will of a person under the age of eighteen years is valid (Wills Act 1837, s 7) and any valid will must be executed in accordance with section 15 of the Wills Act 1837. These and other important provisions of the Wills Act 1837 which draftsmen ought to bear in mind are reproduced in APPENDIX 2. The draftsman should take note of the provisions as to revocation by marriage (Wills Act 1837, s 18), destruction (s 20), alteration (s 21) and revival (s 22). The effect of dissolution or annulment of marriage is also important (s 18A) and it is important to remember that gifts to attesting witnesses will be void (Wills Act 1837, s 15; Wills Act 1968, s 1). There are also specific provisions relating to the meaning of the words 'die without issue' and the death of children or other issue (Wills Act 1837, ss 29 and 33).

This chapter deals with certain types of will trusts, but a thorough analysis of wills and will drafting is beyond the scope of this book. A more thorough account can be found in *Parker's Modern Wills Precedents* (4th Edition, 2003) or *Williams on Wills* (8th Edition, 2002). The trusts mentioned below are the most common forms of will trusts encountered in practice.

Interest in possession trusts

14.3   When drafting a will containing an interest in possession trust, it will often be sensible for the draftsman to include sufficient flexibility for the trustees to override or extend the interest in possession, for example, by permitting them to appoint capital to the life tenant, or by the trustees having discretionary powers over the capital.

Sometimes it will be appropriate to include successive interests in possession. This can be especially useful, for example, where the successive life tenants are spouses, since on the death of the first of them to die, spouse exemption for inheritance tax will attract on the capital value of the fund.

In order to establish that an interest in possession subsists, the life tenant must be given the right to the trust income as it arises. There must not be any power to accumulate the income while the life interest subsists, otherwise this will vitiate the interest in possession. There is, of course, no objection to the inclusion of a power for the trustees to accumulate income after the termination or ceasing of the interest in possession, for example, if there is a discretionary trust of capital to follow the life interest.

Since annuity rates have fallen in recent years, the incorporation of interest in possession trusts in wills has become less popular. Interest in possession trusts are, however, still often used in wills to give rights of occupation of land. The disadvantage of an interest in possession trust for inheritance tax purposes for a life tenant, however, is that while the interest in possession subsists then for inheritance tax purposes the life tenant is deemed to be entitled to the underlying capital value of the fund. The aggregation of the capital value of the trust fund in which the interest in possession subsists immediately before death, or within seven years of death, with the deceased's free estate is often perceived as a substantial and real disadvantage to the life tenant, particularly where there are different beneficiaries entitled to the capital value of the trust fund on his death, as compared with those entitled to his free estate, for example, in a second marriage situation.

In older wills establishing trusts, it was common to see a provision giving the life tenant the power to appoint a life interest to his widow, or occasionally to appoint the capital to his widow or others, usually by his will or codicil. This option gave the life tenant power to redirect the income or capital effectively at his discretion. The problem was that often the power to appoint was not evident or apparent to the draftsman of the life tenant's will, or was otherwise overlooked. The exercise of such a power required some positive action on the part of the life tenant and required the life tenant to be aware of and actually to take some action to exercise the power.

Accumulation and maintenance trusts

14.4   Wills will often incorporate accumulation and maintenance trusts in their simplest form, for example, a gift to such of the testator's children as survive him and attain the age of 21 years. Some commentators have suggested that the incorporation of an age requirement in such gifts represents poor drafting. The reason for this is that there will exist the potential for a capital gains tax charge to arise in such an arrangement if the income vests at a different age from capital. Unless excluded, section 31 of the Trustee Act 1925 will usually mean that an interest in possession subsists from the age of 18 and if the capital vests at a later age under the terms of the gift, there is a potential for a capital gains tax charge with no holdover available, since there will be no simultaneous entitlement to income and capital. This is discussed in more detail in CHAPTER 8: ACCUMULATION AND MAINTENANCE TRUSTS.

The better solution is therefore thought to be to include a simultaneous entitlement to both income and capital, for example, 'to such of my children as shall be living at my death and if more than one in equal shares absolutely'. One potential disadvantage of this type of gift is that if any child survives the deceased but then dies, the gift will pass under the deceased child's intestacy. This may or may not be what the testator requires and the testator's particular requirements should be considered in each case.

Discretionary trusts

14.5 In addition to their use for the inheritance tax nil-rate band, discussed below, discretionary trusts can be used to ensure that maximum flexibility is retained in the hands of the trustees over the residuary estate.

Any use of a discretionary trust over residue should obviously be accompanied by a letter of wishes for the comfort of both the testator and the trustees.

A precedent for a discretionary trust of the residue of a testator's estate is included at APPENDIX 1.17. When giving trustees discretionary powers over the residue of the testator's estate, careful consideration needs to be given by the draftsman and the testator as to who the trustees are to be, whether they will be able to function effectively as a body and whether the executors are the appropriate persons to fulfil this role or whether separate trustees of the particular trust should be appointed.

Nil-rate band discretionary legacy trusts

14.6 When taking will instructions the draftsman will need to establish the nature and extent of the testator's estate, that is, the property which the testator can dispose of by will. If inheritance tax is likely to be payable on the death of the survivor of spouses from whom the draftsman is taking instructions, then the incorporation of a nil-rate band discretionary trust legacy should be considered.

Such a trust in the will of each of two spouses should be drafted so that it will only operate on the death of the first spouse to die and usually only if the surviving spouse survives for the chosen survivorship period (usually 30 days) which applies in respect of the residuary provision in favour of the surviving spouse. The reason for this is that there will be no need for the trust to operate on the death of the surviving spouse since the survivor will have no spouse to provide for and so no spouse exemption will be available in respect of residue. His (or, more usually, her) estate will attract its own nil-rate band, unless already used, for example, against lifetime gifts which become chargeable as a result of the death, subject to any aggregation applicable in respect of settled property, for example, because the testator was entitled to an interest in possession in it immediately before his death.

When a nil-rate band discretionary trust is used the operative trust will provide for maximum flexibility for the surviving spouse to reorganise his or her affairs or to benefit from the trust fund at a later date if this is considered to be necessary. The trust can be wound up at any time following the first death but should not be distributed until after the expiry of three months (see CHAPTER 7: DISCRETIONARY TRUSTS). If the surviving spouse does not need to have access to the fund it might be distributed in favour of the children or be administered and run as a continuing trust under the terms of which the surviving spouse is one of the potential beneficiaries, in respect of either or both of income and/or capital, together with, for example, the children and remoter issue of the testator.

In cases where nil-rate band discretionary trusts are used, it is usually desirable for the wills to provide that on the death of the first of two spouses to die, the personal chattels of the first spouse to die will pass to the surviving spouse absolutely, and that subject to the amount passing into the nil-rate band discretionary legacy trust, the residue of the estate will pass to the surviving spouse, either absolutely, or for life under an interest in possession trust. The result of this will be that there will be no inheritance tax payable on the first death and maximum flexibility will have been retained in the hands of the trustees of the will in respect of the nil-rate band discretionary trust fund, and possibly in respect of the residue, if, for example, an interest in possession is included and the trustees have discretionary powers of appointment over the residuary fund.

An interest in possession in the residue in favour of the surviving spouse will only generally be appropriate, however, where the survivor is very old and will not need access to capital, or the estate is substantial and is likely to provide a worthwhile amount of income or other benefits for the surviving spouse. Otherwise an absolute interest in the residue will generally be appropriate.

The effective use of the nil-rate band in these circumstances will achieve a saving of inheritance tax, as compared with the scenario where the surviving spouse takes an absolute interest or an interest in possession in the whole estate, of 40 per cent, at current rates, of the nil-rate band current at the date of death of the first spouse to die on the basis that the combined value of the estate of both spouses exceeds the nil-rate band. The use of this type of planning is therefore extremely important in these circumstances.

Shares in the matrimonial home

14.7   Settling a share of the matrimonial home as an asset of a discretionary trust is becoming increasingly popular. A variety of schemes have grown up in recent years which incorporate a share of the matrimonial home as an asset of a nil-rate band discretionary trust. However popular schemes which make use of the matrimonial home as an asset of a discretionary trust may be, they ought to be used only in the last resort. If there are sufficient income-yielding assets to make up a nil-rate band discretionary trust, the trust should be constituted out of those assets in the first instance.

Unfortunately, not many people are able to make up the discretionary trust without making use of the matrimonial home and schemes have been devised, therefore, which vest assets equal to the nil-rate band in such a trust but, directly or indirectly, make them available to the surviving spouse if required. In the case of testators who are less well off the inclusion of the matrimonial home within the nil-rate band is attractive because, if a non-income producing asset is hived off, it leaves more income-producing assets available to the survivor. This is sometimes unacceptable because the survivor wishes to retain absolute control of the house while living in it and that is something which needs to be considered.

Where the testator wishes to constitute a nil-rate band discretionary trust using the matrimonial home or a share in the matrimonial home, it is important that the settlement does not create an interest in possession. Practitioners must always bear in mind the dangers of creating an interest in possession in what, on the face of it, appears to be a discretionary trust. For a discretionary or contingent interest trust to succeed in mitigating inheritance tax, it is crucial that the survivor does not have an interest in possession. There are two highly artificial but popular schemes, the debt scheme and the charge scheme which, at present, are accepted by the Revenue as not creating an interest in possession.

Detailed discussion of these schemes is beyond the scope of this book and readers are referred to *Parker's Modern Wills Precedents* (4th Edition, 2003), *Williams on Wills* (8th Edition, 2002) and Robert Venables QC's specialised treatment of the subject in 'Inheritance Tax Planning for the Family Home', *The Personal Tax Planning Review*, Vol 9, Issue 2, 2003.

Definition of nil-rate band passing into the trust and other drafting points

14.8   Careful thought needs to be given to how the nil-rate band passing into the trust is defined. There are several points to note here:

(a)   The decision as to what property passes into the trust does not need to be taken by the draftsman. The trusts should be drafted in such a way as to permit the executors of the will to decide what property is appropriated into the trust to satisfy the gift.

(b)   Since the amount or value of the nil-rate band for inheritance tax is likely to change between the date of the will and the date of death, the will should be drafted in such a way that the nil-rate band amount passing into the trust is defined by reference to the maximum amount which is permitted to be passed into the trust at the date of death, after taking into account any chargeable potentially exempt transfers or chargeable transfers made within seven years of the date of death, the value of any aggregable settled property, and the value of any other gifts given by the will or any codicil to it, other than residuary gifts. At the time of writing, the nil-rate band is £255,000.

(c)   The use of a nil-rate band discretionary trust will only be relevant in the case of the survival, for the chosen survivorship period, of a surviving spouse. If there is no surviving spouse who survives for the chosen survivorship period then there will be no fiscal need for the trust to come into being at all.

(d)   In view of the inherent uncertainty as to the value of the nil-rate band applicable at the date of death, that is, it could be significantly higher (or, but this is most unlikely, lower) than that applicable at the date of the will, the surviving spouse should always be included as a potential beneficiary of the trust.

(e)   A decision needs to be taken by the testator and the draftsman as to whether any business or agricultural property qualifying for inheritance tax business property relief or agricultural property relief at his death is intended to pass into the trust. Depending upon the decision reached, the definition of the amount intended to pass into the nil-rate band discretionary trust will need to be drawn appropriately.

(f)   Careful consideration obviously needs to be given as to which other persons are to be included in the class of beneficiaries. Subject to questions of certainty, the class can be drafted as narrowly or as widely as the testator desires.

(g)   Since, by its nature, the trust is a discretionary trust the choice of trustees is crucial. The testator will need to decide who will be able and willing to fulfil this important function. He needs to ensure that the trustees appointed will be able to act as a body and will know enough about his family and property to act in accordance with the wishes of the testator. A letter of wishes written by the testator to guide the trustees may obviously assist in this.

An example of a nil-rate band discretionary legacy clause appears at APPENDIX 1.16.

Alternatives to nil-rate band discretionary trusts for married testators

14.9   Some testators who are averse to accepting provisions that they consider to be complicated and difficult to understand may wish to have their wills drafted in such a way as to leave the provisions in them extremely simple, for example, leaving the whole estate either absolutely or on an interest in possession trust in favour of the surviving spouse. The idea is that the surviving spouse can then, if he or she wishes to do so, vary the will following the first death by executing a deed of variation of the will or a deed of disclaimer to utilise the nil-rate band, or to disclaim his or her interest to utilise the nil-rate band. Both of these courses of action are dependent upon their being available at the relevant time (that is, that there is no change in the law in the meantime) and rely upon the surviving spouse to take the appropriate action at the relevant time.

Unless the testator has strong feelings on the matter, however, it is generally preferable to incorporate nil-rate band discretionary trusts in these circumstances to ensure that matters are better ordered. The survivor may, for example, not wish to engage in fairly complex and involved restructuring at a sensitive and difficult time following the death of his or her spouse.

Unmarried persons

14.10   Where a testator is not married there is no fiscal need for a nil-rate band discretionary trust unless the testator wishes to make an exempt gift of residue, for example, to charity.

Other provisions contained in nil-rate band discretionary legacy clauses

14.11   In order to minimise administration costs where an existing settlement is in place prior to death, where there is at least one beneficiary common to both the lifetime settlement and the nil-rate band discretionary legacy trust, a power for the nil-rate band discretionary legacy trustees to transfer the trust fund into the lifetime settlement might be included.

A power to lend with or without security, and with or without charging interest, might also be included in the nil-rate band discretionary legacy trust, particularly if the trust assets are likely to include land or a share in land.

In order to protect the interests of the surviving spouse with regard to the discretionary fund, a provision could be included providing that no appointment should be made by the trustees out of the trust fund without the written consent of the surviving spouse, while the surviving spouse is alive and is mentally capable of giving consent.

Secret trusts

14.12   Sometimes a testator wishes to incorporate a secret trust in his will. The inclusion of such a trust places great reliance upon the trustee receiving the gift to carry out the testator's wishes which, by the nature of the trust being secret, will not be evident or apparent to the outside world. Usually a discretionary trust, accompanied by a letter of wishes, will be a more appropriate vehicle.

There are two kinds of secret trust. A fully secret trust arises where neither the trust nor its terms are apparent from the gift itself, for example, an absolute gift to a beneficiary.

A half-secret trust arises where the trust is apparent from the terms of the gift, for example, in the will, but the terms of the trust itself are not specifically spelt out. In both cases there must be intention, communication and acquiescence (see *Blackwell v Blackwell [1929] AC 318*).

In the recent case of *Kasperbauer v Griffith [2000] WTLR 333*, Gibson LJ confirmed these requirements saying:

> '. . . what is needed is (i) an intention by the testator to create a trust, satisfying the traditional requirement of three certainties (that is to say certain language in an imperative form, certain subject matter and certain objects or beneficiaries); (ii) the communication of the trust to the legatee; and (iii) the acceptance of the trust by the legatee, which acceptance can take the form of silent acquiescence'.

These principles were reconfirmed by the Court of Appeal in *Margulies v Margulies [2000] 2 ITELR 641* where the claim that a secret trust could be inferred from a series of letters was struck out.

In England and Wales there is a significant difference between fully secret and half-secret trusts. In the case of the former the terms of the trust can be communicated either before or after the date of the testamentary document; in the case of the latter, in order to be valid, the terms of the trust must be communicated either before the testamentary document is executed or at the same time.

If a fully secret trust fails the property given will belong to the donee; in the case of a half-secret trust the property will pass into the residue, unless there is a gift over in default in respect of that property, or in accordance with an intestacy, if the subject matter of the gift is residuary estate.

A precedent for a secret trust, particularly useful for personal chattels, is included at APPENDIX 1.18. In essence this is an absolute gift to the trustees, but will enable a testator to incorporate flexibility in his will concerning such items and will permit the amendment of such wishes rather than requiring frequent changes of the will itself, whether by codicil or otherwise.

Care should be taken to ensure that any accompanying memorandum is not incorporated by reference if anything other than an absolute gift to the trustees is included, since usually, by its nature, the testator will not wish for his personal memorandum to become a public document.

Trusts giving rights of occupation

14.13   The grant of a right of occupation by will almost invariably creates an interest in possession for inheritance tax purposes: if the will directs that the trustees are not to seek to enforce a sale or to demand rent from the survivor then the position appears to be that the survivor will be treated as entitled to an interest in possession in the deceased's half share of the matrimonial home which will therefore be taxable as part of the survivor's estate on his or her death. See *IRC v Lloyd's Private Banking [1998] STC 559.*

The use of clauses granting such rights can, however, be useful, for example to ensure that a surviving spouse or partner has protection by way of being able to continue to reside in the family home, and, if desired, to move into an alternative property, whilst ensuring that the capital value of the home will pass in accordance with the testator's wishes when the surviving spouse or partner dies or no longer wishes to live there.

Two precedents giving rights of occupation are included in APPENDIX 1. The first (at APPENDIX 1.20) creates a life interest so that the beneficiary will be entitled to the income generated on any investment of the proceeds of sale. The second (at APPENDIX 1.21) grants a right of occupation only but does include a provision enabling the trustees and beneficiary to change properties (which can be omitted, if desired). No termination of the right on remarriage is included. Such provisions are often desired by testators but tend to give rise to claims under the Inheritance (Provision for Family and Dependants) Act 1975.

The responsibility for payment of outgoings on the property and the need to consider who is to be responsible for repairs during the subsistence of the right to occupy should be made clear by the draftsman in such clauses, as should the terms on which the rights are granted and the circumstances in which they will be terminated. Trustees' powers in relation to the occupation of land by a beneficiary are discussed more fully in CHAPTER 22: ADMINISTRATIVE PROVISIONS.

Separate trustees of such a trust may be appointed or the testator may be happy for the executors to be the trustees.

Another important consideration to be borne in mind when including such a clause in a will is whether a settled gift or an absolute gift of chattels, including the household furniture, needs to be included. Where a settled gift of chattels is included, a provision for an inventory to be made and agreed by the trustees and the occupying beneficiary within a short specified time after the death of the testator needs to be incorporated. Careful consideration also needs to be given in such circumstances as to the replacement of chattels when they wear out, are broken or are lost.

Trusts created by deeds of variation

14.14   The disposition of the deceased's estate can be varied by a deed of variation or by disclaimer. For inheritance tax and capital gains tax purposes a variation or disclaimer, if made within two years of the death, can take effect as if the dispositions effected by it were made by the deceased provided the requirements of the legislation are satisfied. See section 142 of the Inheritance Tax Act 1984 and section 62 of the Taxation of Chargeable Gains Act 1992.

For inheritance and capital gains tax purposes it is not possible to make more than one variation in respect of the same property in the same estate, so it is always sensible to try to include all variations in one document if at all possible. Similarly, the tax provisions do not apply to a variation or disclaimer made for any consideration in money or money's worth, other than consideration consisting of the making in respect of another of the deceased's dispositions of a variation or disclaimer to which section 142(1) of the Inheritance Tax Act 1984 applies. Difficult questions can arise in connection with this provision and the practitioner should seek specialist advice where necessary. Variations carried out within two years of death for no consideration in money or money's worth other than the making of a variation of another disposition will be exempt from charge under stamp duty land tax by virtue of paragraph 4 of Schedule 3 to the Finance Act 2003.

A deed of variation can relate to property passing under the deceased's will, his intestacy or by survivorship. If the statutory requirements are complied with, the property to which the variation relates will pass to the beneficiary receiving it under the variation as if he had been entitled under the will or intestacy. In the case of a variation affecting property passing by survivorship, the deceased's severable half share in the property will be treated as part of his estate and not passing to the surviving joint owner.

Variations are usually effected by deed, with the personal representatives, the original beneficiary and the substituted beneficiary as parties, with the necessary statement under section 142 of the Inheritance Tax Act 1984 and section 62 of the Taxation of Chargeable Gains Act 1992 included as a clause in the deed. An example of a simple deed of variation in included at APPENDIX 1.23. However, the drafting of deeds of variation is quite a specialised topic and should be carefully considered both in the context of the tax implications and under the general law. It is all too easy to rush through the drafting and execution of the deed in order to meet an artificial tax deadline without considering the real consequences of what has been done. Many practitioners have very little experience of deeds of variation and there is no shame in engaging the services of specialist counsel when necessary.

Distributions made in accordance with the testator's wishes

14.15   A gift over by a specific legatee in accordance with the testator's wishes within two years of the testator's death will be treated by section 143 of the Inheritance Tax Act 1984 as having been made by the testator's will.

Any distribution of chattels within two years of the testator's date of death by trustees in accordance with the provisions of a secret trust (see above, and APPENDIX 1.18) will be treated as gifts made by the testator.

Trusts of this nature are often called precatory trusts but, except for secret trusts, they are not trusts at all but merely an expression of a wish. Probably it is better to keep out of the will declarations like this and to rely on the ostensible beneficiary fulfilling the moral obligations imposed on him by an extra-testamentary document.

Powers of appointment in discretionary trusts within two years of death

14.16   Section 144 of the Inheritance Tax Act 1984 permits dispositions made by trustees out of a discretionary trust more than three months but less than two years after the testator's death to be read back into the will. This enables wills to be drafted with considerable flexibility giving an opportunity for the trustees to take stock before making a decision about the manner in which the estate should be distributed.

The trustees are able to appoint the capital among the beneficiaries so as to produce the best practical result in the circumstances which have emerged at the time of death or shortly afterwards. The trustees are better placed to do this than the testator was because they know the value of the estate, the current inheritance tax rates and the foreseeable requirements of the widow and other beneficiaries. The short-term discretionary trust requires the trustees to exercise their discretion and bring the trust to an end within two years of the death so that the appointments of capital which they make will be treated as dispositions under the will for inheritance tax purposes.

This has disadvantages. It limits the trustees' scope and, for capital gains tax purposes, the recipient acquires the property appointed at its market value at the date of appointment and not at the date of death. There might also be a cash flow problem during the administration of an estate in which tax must be paid at an early stage.

It is, however, a popular means of incorporating significant flexibility into will drafting. If a short-term discretionary trust is used the executors will be able to form a view as to the various moral claims and needs of members of the beneficial class after the testator's death without having their hands tied by provisions incorporated into a will made many years before the death and in quite different circumstances.

Chapter 15

Trusts with an Overseas Element

Domicile, residence and ordinary residence

15.1   There is an important distinction between domicile and residence. Many people are resident in one country but domiciled in another. This has important inheritance tax implications and confusion between the two leads many to create offshore settlements which are of little or no fiscal benefit to them or the intended beneficiaries. In April 2003 the Revenue produced a background paper: *Reviewing the residence and domicile rules as they affect the taxation of individuals*. The Revenue has been concerned about the use of offshore settlements for some time.

Domicile

15.2   Domicile is important for inheritance tax purposes.

The short point about domicile is that a person can only have one domicile at any one time and the default position is that a person's domicile is his domicile of origin: ie the domicile of his father at his birth. A person under the age of 16 will have a domicile of dependency: their domicile will follow that of the person on whom they are legally dependent. After attaining the age of 16 years a person can acquire a domicile of choice elsewhere by laying down permanent roots in another state with the intention of making that state his permanent home. However, a domicile of choice is difficult to set up and easy to lose and, as a rule, a person who lives abroad because his work demands it will have the most severe difficulty in establishing a domicile of choice in that state, particularly if he intends to return home when his work comes to an end. That is the common law position. Statute has also intervened in the form of section 267 of the Inheritance Tax Act 1984 to introduce the concept of deemed domicile but there is no equivalent deemed non-domicile.

Residence

15.3   Residence is determined in accordance with statutory rules and is particularly important in the context of capital gains tax and income tax.

A settlor will be treated as UK resident for tax purposes if he spends 183 days or more in the UK in any tax year or more than 90 days on average over a period of up to four years; or if he moves to the UK to live permanently for at least three years; or if he usually lives in the UK but goes abroad for short periods.

Ordinary residence

15.4   Ordinary residence in the UK means being resident in the UK year after year. A person will be ordinarily resident if he usually lives in the UK or comes to the UK regularly and his visits average 91 days or more in each fiscal year.

Use of overseas settlements by a UK domiciled settlor

15.5   No inheritance tax savings can be made through the creation of overseas trusts by a settlor domiciled in the UK. There may be capital gains tax advantages if the settlor is resident abroad and remains abroad but these generally evaporate once the settlor returns to the UK if the settlor retains an interest or if distributions are made to beneficiaries who are domiciled and resident in the UK. On the whole, a UK domiciled settlor creating a settlement in favour of UK domiciled and UK resident beneficiaries gains no advantage by creating an overseas settlement but suffers increased administrative costs instead.

Inheritance tax

15.6   If the settlor is domiciled in the UK at the time the settlement is made, there are no inheritance tax savings to be made through the creation of an overseas trust.

Section 48(3)(a) of the Inheritance Tax Act 1984 provides that where property comprised in a settlement is situated outside the United Kingdom the property (but not a reversionary interest in the property) is excluded property unless the settlor was domiciled in the United Kingdom at the time the settlement was made.

Capital gains tax

15.7   A trust is non-resident for capital gains tax purposes where the general administration of the trust is ordinarily carried on outside the UK and the trustees or a majority of them for the time being are not resident or not ordinarily resident in the UK: Taxation of Chargeable Gains Act 1992, s 69(1). Further, a person carrying on a business which consists of or includes the management of trusts, and acting as trustee of a trust in the course of that business, is treated in relation to that trust as not resident in the UK if the whole of the settled property consists of or derives from property provided by a person who was not then domiciled, resident or ordinarily resident in the UK.

Section 86 of the Taxation of Chargeable Gains Act 1992 provides that where the settlor of a settlement is domiciled in the UK and is either resident in the UK during any part of the year or ordinarily resident in the UK during the year and at any time during the year the settlor has an interest in the settlement then, if the settlement is a 'qualifying settlement' of which the trustees are not resident or ordinarily resident in the UK during any part of the year, or they are resident in the UK during any part of the year or ordinarily resident in the UK during the year, but at any time of such residence or ordinary residence they fall to be regarded for the purposes of any double taxation relief arrangements as resident in a territory outside the UK, then chargeable gains are treated as accruing to the settlor, and those gains are treated as forming the highest part of the amount on which he is chargeable to capital gains tax for the year. Qualifying settlements are defined in Schedule 5 to the Act.

That is a punitive and complex provision but, if the various conditions are satisfied, it has the effect of making the settlor chargeable for non-resident trustees' gains if those gains would have attracted a capital gains tax charge had the trustees been resident in the UK.

Section 87 of the Taxation of Chargeable Gains Act 1992 includes similarly complex provisions which have the effect of rendering UK resident beneficiaries in receipt of capital payments liable for capital gains tax in respect of non-resident settlements.

These provisions are not trivial. Justice cannot be done to them in a book of this nature but they must be considered with great care by both the draftsman and the settlor's tax advisers.

Income tax

15.8   Non-resident trustees are only subject to UK income tax on UK income. The position is different if a settlor domiciled in the UK retains an interest because he may then be liable: see Income and Corporation Taxes Act 1988, s 739.

A UK resident beneficiary entitled to the income generated by a foreign trust will be taxed whether it is paid to him or not, as will a beneficiary who, though not entitled to the income as of right, is in receipt of it because of an exercise of the trustees' discretion. Capital payments may be taxable under section 740 of the Income and Corporation Taxes Act 1988.

Part III: Drafting Trusts

Chapter 16

Drafting Style

16.1   A distinction should be drawn between drafting in a traditional style by structuring the trust deed and using language in a manner which would be recognisable to a draftsman of the mid-twentieth century or earlier and drafting substantive trusts in a traditional way. There is nothing at all wrong with drafting a trust deed in a manner which makes it look and sound traditional but trusts which are traditional in substance are now unfashionable and largely unacceptable to the modern settlor.

The difference is that, traditionally, trust draftsmen were accustomed to drafting trusts in restrictive and definite ways which often left trustees with what are now regarded as inadequate trust powers and insufficient discretion. In particular, a rigid trust may not allow trustees to take advantage of changing circumstances to maximise opportunities and to promote the interests of the beneficiaries in the most appropriate and sensible manner and, above all, to adapt to human and fiscal circumstances which may have been entirely unforeseen by the settlor and his draftsman when establishing the trust. The form of the statutory powers of maintenance and advancement set out in sections 31 and 32 of the Trustee Act 1925 reflect the form of express powers of that nature commonly used in the nineteenth century but they are now generally regarded as overly restrictive and the vast majority of modern settlements extend both powers using a simple and widely understood formula. This is dealt with more fully in CHAPTER 22: ADMINISTRATIVE PROVISIONS.

The vogue in recent years has been to draft trusts in an entirely flexible (sometimes too flexible) manner which permit, for example, the class of beneficiaries to be extended or restricted, the addition or restriction of trust powers and the ability for settlors or others to retain control over the appointment and removal of trustees and other matters with options for the settlor or others to pass on such powers.

Modern trust drafting would, no doubt, have been anathema to the draftsmen of old, but the reasons for the retention of a large degree of flexibility are evident and the balance generally now seems to be irrevocably tipped in favour of the incorporation of flexibility when drafting settlements.

This chapter is principally concerned, however, with the style rather than the substance of trust drafting.

Traditional style

16.2   The criticism often levelled at older trust deeds and wills is that the drafting style adopted is now considered to be over-complex and wordy. The older-style format will usually include no punctuation, no clause headings and extremely long and complex sentences. The advantage of the style is that the phrases used were often the result of generations of fine tuning and included tried and tested formulae with well understood meanings. Unfortunately, when coupled with substantive trusts which have little flexibility in terms of permitting discretion to trustees in the way in which the trust is administered, it often appeared that the draftsmen of such settlements intended the trustees to be locked into a strait-jacket of the draftsmen's making. That might have been true and in some cases was probably justified but nonetheless it is no longer an attractive format.

A further disadvantage of the more traditional style (which is not the fault of the draftsman but of the reader) is that the use of English has altered since the traditional stock phrases developed. Many people, including some lawyers, have difficulty with the apparently archaic language of more traditional settlements.

Modern style

16.3   Modern trust drafting will usually comprise short sentences and include punctuation. This is obviously easier for the settlor or testator to read and understand and, provided that the draftsman's intentions and the meaning of the words used are clear, then such drafting in a modern format will often be preferable. This is especially so where lay trustees are to be appointed.

The modern format will often include clause headings which makes deeds easier to read and to follow. A clause heading should not, however, control what a clause actually does and so in almost all cases in which headings are included there is an additional clause providing that the clause headings are not an aid to the interpretation of the deed.

The disadvantage of the modern drafting style is that if the draftsman does not take care, his clear use of modern English may lead to ambiguity in the result. Although the use of modern English in a modern style might appear to be an attractive option, it can often prove to be a harder task than simply using traditionally accepted precedents. The Trustee Act 2000 itself is a prime example of modern drafting style, but as with all novel statutes, litigation may be necessary to determine the extent and precise effect of some of its provisions.

Traditional or modern?

16.4   On the whole, practitioners prefer to draft in a modern style but most do so without entirely surrendering their use of quite traditional and well understood means of expressing the essential concepts of the trust.

Whichever style is adopted the draftsman will not be judged on the literary content of his work but on the precision, accuracy and effectiveness with which the meaning is communicated. The discipline of using tried and tested set forms is an enormous benefit to clients and draftsmen alike and the use of plain language can help a clear thinker to express himself precisely and a muddled thinker to focus his mind. Certainly, the muddled thinker should not attempt to excuse himself by hiding behind dated drafting practices and language. Such practices including sheltering behind tortuous or unnecessary technical words and phrases which often serve only to conceal a lack of thought.

In a well drafted settlement a complicated provision should be expressed simply, clearly and concisely in a manner which can be understood by laymen and lawyers alike. However, the draftsman should remember that the lay client (the settlor) is mainly, if not exclusively, interested in the effect rather than the fine technical detail of the vehicle and the route used to get there. The draftsman, on the other hand, must take care to ensure that what he produces will achieve the settlor's aims: sloppy, vague, ambiguous and ill thought out attempts to impose plain language in place of meaningful and precise technical phrases do much more harm than good.

The use of precedents and standard clauses can save much time, but in each case the draftsman needs to consider whether the precedent deed or clause precisely reflects the needs and intentions of the settlor. The draftsman should, in all cases, exercise clear-headed, independent judgment in selecting and tailoring precedents and should not try to force an ill-fitting precedent on to a settlor.

There is much to be said for making clear the intentions and aims of the settlor or testator when establishing the trust. Modern drafting will often deal with this by including appropriate recitals establishing why the trust has been established and what the settlor's or testator's intentions were when establishing the trust, or at least these matters will be set out in a letter of wishes, where appropriate. However, the pattern of modern life is uncertain and the modern trust draftsman will wish to incorporate sufficient flexibility in the trust to ensure that the trustees can properly see that the interests and needs of the beneficiaries can be looked after and be provided for, whatever the circumstances presenting themselves at the appropriate time.

The inclusion of accurate punctuation is generally desirable unless the draftsman is adopting clear and short phrasing. Clarity is obviously the watchword here in terms of the particular will or settlement being clear as to its meaning in given circumstances. Since, in most cases, the trust may run for a considerable number of years, it is important that the trustees and beneficiaries and future administrators of the terms of the trust understand what was intended since all relevant persons alive when the settlement was made may be dead or unable to remember relevant details at the time when the relevant provision needs to be interpreted.

The use of clause headings is generally desirable, certainly in the case of settlements where clauses can often be long and complex. In the case of wills, the use of clause headings is a matter for the draftsman, but will often be unnecessary since the clauses in wills are generally shorter and are presented in a more easily followed and standardised format.

Many older trust deeds and wills do not include adequate administrative provisions. Although to an extent many of the problems frequently encountered in this respect have been resolved by the provisions of the Trusts of Land and Appointment of Trustees Act 1996 and the Trustee Act 2000, the draftsman will need to consider whether the provisions in those Acts are sufficient, or whether they are deficient in certain respects and need to be clarified and extended.

Incorporation by reference is sometimes seen in older forms of trust documents, particularly in wills – for example statutory will forms 1925 – and definitions contained in statutes – for example, those in the Administration of Estates Act 1925 – were (and still are) commonly used. The use of such tools avoids trust deeds and wills becoming cluttered with unnecessary verbiage, which is obviously a worthy aim. The Society of Trust and Estate Practitioners recommends the incorporation by reference of STEP standard provisions. This is discussed further in CHAPTER 22: ADMINISTRATIVE PROVISIONS.

Flexibility

16.5   As previously mentioned, older trust deeds and wills often incorporate little or no flexibility for trustees or for those advising the trustees in the administration of trusts to act in any way which is divergent or different from the intentions of the settlor or testator (or, often, the draftsman). While this is admirable in some respects (in terms of the intentions of the settlor or testator), it can cause considerable difficulties if, for example, an unexpected divorce, bankruptcy or an inconvenient or unexpected order of deaths among the beneficiaries occurs.

Since modern life is often so much less certain and the world of investment, for example, is so much more complex and unpredictable, modern trust instruments will usually include numerous administrative provisions. These generally include the power to add to or alter the administrative powers, and possibly overriding trust powers for the trustees, including, for example, powers for the trustees, with the written consent of the settlor first having been obtained, to add to or alter the class of beneficiaries in the case of a discretionary trust. Generally speaking, where the trustees have overriding discretionary powers of any sort, such powers will be limited by the draftsman so that, while the settlor is alive, they will only be able to be exercised by the trustees after they have obtained the written consent of the settlor.

Since the very essence of the settlor having set up the trust is that he has avoided the beneficiaries becoming absolutely entitled to the trust property given by him to the trustees, and the trust will often have the capability to run for a considerable period, the inclusion of flexibility for the trustees when running the trust is only sensible. Not only might the beneficiaries' circumstances or the settlor's wishes concerning who is to benefit under the terms of the trust alter during the currency of the trust, but tax legislation also becomes ever more complex and is changed on a regular basis by Parliament.

The inclusion of powers for trustees to override the initial trusts or effectively to rewrite them is a sensible way for the modern trust deed to be drafted. The inclusion of such powers does not mean that the trustees will, or must, exercise them, but it simply means that they have the powers to do so which can be exercised, if necessary.

The inclusion of a power to resettle trust property within the same trust can also be an important and useful tool for trustees and can be used by them in appropriate circumstances to ensure that matters can be reorganised usually without any tax charges arising. Both of these aspects are discussed further in CHAPTER 24: BRINGING TRUSTS TO AN END.

Provided that the correct body of trustees is chosen at the outset and adequate protection is inserted concerning the appointment and removal of trustees (if desired), then the trust fund and the beneficiaries will be adequately protected.

The settlor may start off with trustees whom he knows well and trusts and who know his particular circumstances intimately and are aware of his wishes in most respects, but that may not always be the case in respect of the trustees appointed in the future.

Flexibility is often highly desirable in the modern world, but the draftsman will need to incorporate appropriate checks and balances in the trust instrument to ensure, so far as is possible, that the trustees are accountable and are controllable.

In the trust instrument, therefore, the settlor will need to reserve powers to enable him to exercise some control as to who the trustees are and to correct the position, for example by using an appropriate power to dismiss trustees, if things start to go wrong or if the settlor loses confidence in the trustees. Similarly, if trustees cannot agree on several issues or see things in a different light continually, the exercise by the settlor of such a power may break what appears to be an otherwise intractable log-jam, with the settlor then having the power to appoint an alternative trustee.

A transmissible power for the settlor to appoint and dismiss trustees by deed or by will is often incorporated in modern trust instruments, but detailed care and thought needs to be given by the settlor with regard to the exercise of this power, which can obviously be fundamentally significant to the whole administration and working of the trust itself. Sometimes the powers to appoint and dismiss trustees are given to persons other than the settlor in the trust instrument at the outset, but the irrevocable surrender by the settlor of these powers to others at the outset is not for the faint-hearted. There is potential for a settlor being left impotent at a later date as someone else exercises potentially disastrous and complete control over trust property which once belonged to the settlor.

Trust drafting, however, which permits the settlor to retain excessive and overpowering control over the exercise of trust functions and where the trustees have virtually no power to act without first obtaining the written, or other, agreement of the settlor should be avoided. It might, for example, lead to a charge that the trust is essentially a sham. Similarly, trusts drafted in such a way that the trustees are able to act by a majority vote as a matter of course or whereby the trustees have power to add persons into the class of beneficiaries can lead to abuse and bizarre and unfortunate results. Where a majority vote is included the questions arise: where does that leave the dissentient trustees and what does that do to their liability *inter se*?

The unfortunate side effects of extremely flexible trust drafting will often be wholly outside the contemplation or scope of conception of the settlor. Flexibility is desirable, subject to limits, the application of the settlor's particular wishes or circumstances and the application of common sense. Thus while there appears to be no good reason why the trustees, being at least two in number but acting unanimously, or a trust corporation, should not have the power while the settlor is alive, mentally capable and consents in writing, to add persons to the class of beneficiaries (but not any of the trustees for the time being or their spouses) or to remove persons from the class of beneficiaries, powers for the trustees to add persons to the class of beneficiaries, if two of the trustees think fit, whether the settlor is alive or not and whether he consents or not, would be regarded by many as excessive.

In terms of trusts being used to permit flexibility in different circumstances, many modern trusts, if not drafted as discretionary trusts at the outset, often give trustees overriding powers or powers to appoint capital, subject to certain safeguards being incorporated. Even interest in possession trusts frequently nowadays contain powers of revocation of the interest in possession, giving the trustees the discretion to change direction in terms of who benefits at any time.

Although letters of wishes can address this issue to a certain extent, it needs to be remembered that they are by their nature just that, that is, letters of wishes, not binding on the trustees and not creating any trust or obligation upon them.

Clarity

16.6   The essence of trust drafting is to achieve clarity and to avoid ambiguity. It does not really matter whether the draftsman favours or adopts a traditional drafting style or a modern drafting style, provided that the overriding intention is clear, both in terms of the settlor's initial intentions when establishing the trust and in terms of what the settlor is permitting the trustees to do, or not to do, in the future. Most advocates of modern format trust drafting will claim, often with justification, that modern format trust drafting is much clearer, at least in terms of understanding, than traditional format trust drafting. Certainly, a trust drafted in a modern style should be much more readily understood by both lawyers and laymen. If not, something has gone badly awry.

Clarity is obviously better achieved if unnecessary and over-wordy phrasing and terminology are avoided. Clarity is also an important aim to be achieved in order to ensure that the trust itself is valid. This is discussed in more detail in CHAPTER 3: VALIDITY OF THE TRUST.

Who should draft a trust?

16.7   Proliferation of precedents on floppy disk, CD and online has made a large number of stock phrases and clauses available for general public use. That is not necessarily a 'good thing'. While anybody can draft a trust, most will only do it badly producing trusts which are invalid, unintelligible, ambiguous and sometimes completely pointless.

Section 22 of the Solicitors Act 1974 requires any person who draws or prepares an instrument relating to real or personal estate *for a fee* to be a solicitor or barrister. This restriction operates where the property settled is situate in England and Wales. A similar restriction operates for the drafting of trust deeds in respect of trust property situate in Scotland under section 32 of the Solicitors (Scotland) Act 1980. A person who acts in breach of these restrictions commits a criminal offence.

While these offences clearly restrict who may draft settlement deeds, they do not relate to wills, codicils or stock transfers. However, transfers of land in accordance with the terms of a settlement would be caught. The criminalisation of these acts clearly has other ramifications, such as the negation of any professional indemnity cover for non-qualified persons undertaking these activities and the fact that solicitors employed by others, for example, a trust corporation, an independent financial adviser or a firm of accountants, undertaking such work would render the trust corporation or other body liable to a criminal conviction and penalty under these provisions. The drafting of other trust documentation, for example, a deed of appointment of property out of a settlement or a deed of appointment or retirement of trustees, would also be caught by these provisions.

Even when working from a precedent a trust or settlement should be drafted by or under the supervision of a draftsman of sufficient experience to be able to tailor the precedent to the needs of the particular settlor. A good draftsman will identify ambiguities and uncertainties and, if asked, will be able to explain what each clause of his settlement does and why it has been included.

Most modern trusts are driven by fiscal considerations. The draftsman should have a good working knowledge of the inheritance, capital gains and income tax treatment of different kinds of settlements as summarised in PART II. Where the settlor's needs demand specialist advice that should be provided by an appropriate person but there is little point in separating the drafting from the fiscal advice since the draftsman needs to have a good grasp of the tax treatment of what he is producing.

Where there may be an overseas element it is important that the settlor seeks and receives appropriate specialist advice on the drafting and establishment of the trust and that the settlor or testator properly identifies and understands what his circumstances and wishes are and what the framework of the law allows him to do, and, just as important, what it does not. Some discussion of the overseas approach appears in CHAPTER 15: TRUSTS WITH AN OVERSEAS ELEMENT.

In case of doubt the draftsman should not be afraid to seek the assistance of others with more experience than him and in the more difficult cases or where the draftsman does not have experienced support he should not be afraid to seek the assistance of Chancery counsel. The Chancery Bar Association publishes a directory of members which can be obtained from its administrator, Mary Block, at 21 Goodwyns Vale, London N10 2HA. It is far better to seek help in advance than to suffer the embarrassment and expense of watching one's work travel to Lincoln's Inn to be picked apart in the Chancery Division for all to see.

If counsel is instructed then it is usually desirable to instruct counsel to draft the settlement deed and to advise on any unusual drafting issues rather than for the instructing party to attempt to draft a deed for counsel to comment upon. Counsel will usually have a preferred format for the trust instrument and it is usually a waste of time and money to try to draft documents which may or may not coincide with counsel's viewpoint on particular issues. However, except in the most complex cases, instructing counsel will not generally be necessary in the drafting of the trust instrument and, provided that a suitably qualified solicitor is chosen and the relevant instructions are clearly given and understood, an entirely appropriate deed will be drawn.

Use of letters of wishes

16.8   Where trustees have wide discretionary powers, for example in discretionary trusts or where trustees have overriding discretionary powers, it is incumbent upon the draftsman to suggest to the settlor that he makes a memorandum of wishes setting out how he wishes the trustees to exercise such powers in particular circumstances. The memorandum of wishes can be inserted in the trust document itself, but it is usually drafted as a separate document.

There is a strengthening body of opinion that suggests that the reasons why a trust is being made should be inserted in the recitals to the trust deed. The reason for this is that certain elements of the Trusts of Land and Appointment of Trustees Act 1996 and the Trustee Act 2000 are more easily interpreted in certain given circumstances if a clear statement of the reasons why the trust has been established is evident from the settlement deed itself. These recitals need only be short, if they are included at all, and it is generally considered to be better practice to include detailed or lengthy wishes in a separate memorandum.

If the statement of wishes is included in the settlement deed then the beneficiaries will plainly have the right to see it. If it is separate then it will be confidential between the trustees and the settlor if this is the clear understanding upon which the document was made by the settlor (and preferably if it expressly states this on its face): *Re Londonderry's Settlement [1964] 3 All ER 855; Schmidt v Rosewood Trust Ltd [2003] 3 All ER 76*. Otherwise it may be considered to be part of the trust documents and may have to be disclosed to the beneficiaries: *Hartigan Nominees Pty Ltd v Rydge (1992) 29 NSWLR 405* and *Re Rabaiotti's Settlements [2000] WTLR 953*. Since most settlors will prefer that their particular wishes should be confidential, it is better practice to state this expressly in the relevant memorandum of wishes. It is, of course, always open to a settlor to update and add to or alter his memorandum at any time if it is a separate document.

The intention of the memorandum is not to bind the trustees, but to provide guidance to the trustees as to how the settlor might expect or hope them to exercise their powers and discretions in certain circumstances. The settlor will need to give detailed consideration to the contents of the memorandum to ensure that it is not ambiguous and is of real use to the trustees, and does not simply create problems for them in attempting to interpret it.

Clearly the memorandum of wishes must be drafted in such a way that it does not fetter or attempt to control the way in which trustees exercise their discretions, otherwise the beneficiaries might argue that they are committing a breach of trust by not exercising their own independent discretion. The memorandum must make it clear on its face that it is a statement of wishes and does not, and is not intended to, create any binding trust or obligation upon the trustees. Words like the trustees 'shall' or 'must' should be avoided if the document is not to be read as an adjunct to, or extension of, the trust deed itself.

Subject to the above comments, letters of wishes can be of great use to trustees, possibly many years after the settlement has been created and after several changes of trustees have occurred, to guide the trustees with regard to the settlor's intentions and wishes at the outset of the trust. Wherever possible, reasons for the settlor expressing his wishes in the way that he does in the memorandum of wishes should be specified by him.

Name of settlement

16.9   Many settlements are given a name. The draftsman of a lifetime settlement will usually include a clause in the settlement deed giving the settlement a name which can be chosen by the settlor. This will not usually be appropriate in the case of a trust established by a will, but it may be, for example, in the case of a will establishing several different trusts. This is not compulsory and should not be used as an aid to interpretation but is useful as a means of identifying the particular settlement being established at a later date, especially if the settlor has established more than one settlement.

Chapter 17

Content of Trust Deed

Basic structure of trust deeds

17.1 A modern trust deed has six formal parts. The first three of these are usually compressed into a set of formal definitions comprising the words describing the deed as a settlement, the date and the names of the parties. Where appropriate these are followed by recitals which concisely summarise the facts evidenced by the deed. The bulk of the deed is made up of the operative or witnessing part technically known as the testatum and the whole is rounded off by the testimonium. Many modern deeds include schedules which are incorporated into the deed by references within the recitals or testatum. Schedules should always be set out below the testimonium but above the signatures of the parties and witnesses.

Following the commencement of the Law of Property (Miscellaneous Provisions) Act 1989 on 31 July 1990, an instrument may not be a deed unless it makes clear on its face that the parties intend it to be a deed and it is validly executed as a deed by those parties.

Description, date and parties

17.2 There is a concise and traditional means of setting out the words of description, the date and the names and addresses of the parties which, if used properly, spares the draftsman the need to introduce lengthy definitions of the parties in the operative parts of the deed. The format used in the precedents in APPENDIX 1 is as follows:

> THIS DECLARATION OF TRUST is made the [*date in the month*] day of [*month*] Two Thousand and [*Four*] BY [*NAME OF SETTLOR*] of [*Address of Settlor*] (hereinafter referred to as 'the Settlor') of the First Part and [*NAME OF FIRST TRUSTEE*] of [*Address of First Trustee*] and [*NAME OF SECOND TRUSTEE*] of [*Address of Second Trustee*] (hereinafter together referred to as the Original Trustees')

Some draftsmen prefer 'SETTLEMENT' or 'DEED OF TRUST' to 'DECLARATION OF TRUST' but the effect is the same. Many eschew the words 'hereinafter referred to as' relying only on ('the Settlor') or ('the Trustees').

Deeds with definitions in that form still make sense and look more modern but they are somehow less elegant than the form set out above. Some draftsmen only put 'Settlor' and 'Trustees' in quotation marks so that the definition appears as (the 'Settlor') but they invariably go on to refer to 'the Settlor' throughout the remainder of the deed, a practice which the author finds difficult to comprehend.

If the settlor is also one of the trustees it is not necessary to repeat the settlor's name *and* address. It suffices to use the formula 'the said [*NAME OF SETT-LOR*]'. The same rule applies where any person appears as more than one party to the deed.

Recitals

17.3   In most settlements the recitals come immediately after the statement of the parties to the trust deed. Deeds subsequent to a settlement and (rarely) declarations of trust themselves occasionally contain two separate recitals, the first of which recites the identity, dates and parties of previous instruments. This additional recital is introduced by 'SUPPLEMENTAL TO:' followed by a list identifying the instruments which have led to the deed. The type of previous instrument referred to, the names of the parties to them, and the dates on which they were executed should all be given. Thus, a deed might be made:

SUPPLEMENTAL TO:

(A)   The Will dated [*date*] (hereinafter referred to as 'the Will') of [*name of Testator*] late of [*Address*] who died the [*date of death*] (hereinafter referred to as 'the Testator') probate of which was granted out of the Principal Probate Registry to [*names of Executors*] (hereinafter referred to as 'the Executors') on [*date of probate*]

(B)   A Deed of Family Arrangement ('the Deed of Family Arrangement') dated [*date*] and made between [*name of first party*] (hereinafter referred to as 'the Settlor') (1) [*name of second party*] (2) and the Executors (3)

(C)   A Settlement ('the Settlement') made on [*date*] between the Settlor (1) and [*names of trustees*] (hereinafter referred to as 'the Original Trustees') (2)

Few settlements include provisions in those terms and many of those which recite preceding deeds do so by setting them out in a schedule referred to in one of the recitals.

Recitals in general have in recent years become rather short in modern trust drafting although there are circumstances in which even the minimalist modern draftsman must explain the factual background to the creation of the trust. An example of when this might be necessary is that of the widow of an intestate who has elected to redeem her life interest in the residuary estate and has required the personal representatives to appropriate the matrimonial home towards satisfaction of her interest in the intestacy leaving a sum to be invested on behalf of the intestate's children. Some explanation as to how the trust in favour of the children has arisen in that case would normally be appropriate.

Following the enactment of the Trusts of Land and Appointment of Trustees Act 1996 and the Trustee Act 2000, a trend may develop of expanding recitals to enter into rather more detail as to why the trust is being established. This is particularly important where land is to be purchased for the occupation of a beneficiary. See CHAPTER 22: ADMINISTRATIVE PROVISIONS.

Recitals are traditionally introduced with the word 'WHEREAS:' followed by one or more statements of fact. Where there is just one statement the whole recital should comprise one paragraph but if the recitals are longer the paragraphs should be numbered. As a matter of common sense and clarity the numbering of recitals and of the paragraphs in the testatum ought to be distinct. Where recitals appear in the precedents in APPENDIX 1 they are numbered in parentheses whereas the paragraphs of the testatum are numbered without.

Unless a settlor specifically reserves for himself or another person the right to revoke a trust deed, then it will be irrevocable. If such a power is reserved it is wise to recite the fact so that the reader's attention is drawn to it early on. There is no need to recite that a deed is irrevocable but it is often done as a matter of good practice.

Testatum or operative part

17.4   The testatum is the business end of the deed. This is the part which describes what property the trustees hold, for whom they hold it, the terms on which they hold it and the powers which they have while doing so. The testatum is usually divided into definitions, administration trusts, beneficial trusts, overriding powers, additional powers (such as powers of addition or exclusion) and administrative powers.

The testatum is traditionally introduced with the words 'NOW THIS DEED WITNESSETH as follows:' but some prefer 'NOW THIS DEED WITNESSES:' and the ultra-modern draftsman settles for 'OPERATIVE PART' as a heading before moving into the trusts themselves.

Definitions

17.5   Definitions are used to make the trust deed easier to read and to identify the key players or *dramatis personae* in relation to the settlement, for example, 'the Settlor', 'the Trustees', and 'the Beneficiaries'. Self-evidently the use of definitions will avoid restating the full names of the persons concerned each time their names appear in the trust deed, or the full descriptions of the terms defined. They will avoid the text of the document becoming over-long and will enable the text to be broken up into reasonable and manageable clauses.

All definitions do not need to appear in one clause. Some fundamental definitions, such as the Settlor and the Trustees or the Original Trustees, are often set out when the parties are described at the head of the deed as in the form set out above. Apart from those two it is often more convenient, and the settlement is easier to read, if the majority of the definitions appear in one clause so that the reader is able to refer back to a single reference point, rather than having to search through several different clauses to find where the particular definition appears. Where a number of terms are defined in the early parts of the deed, as is sometimes necessary if there are many recitals, many draftsmen include amongst the definitions a gathering provision such as 'the terms "the Settlor", "the Original Trustees", "the Principal Beneficiary", "the Settlor's Children" and "Lady Margaret" shall have the meanings hereinbefore assigned to them'.

When defining 'the Trustees', a common technique is to define 'the Original Trustees' by reference to their names and addresses, being the trustees initially appointed under the trust deed, and then to define 'the Trustees' as the Original Trustees or other the trustee or trustees for the time being of the settlement. This is a useful technique and gives a clear example of how definitions can be used to make the draftsman's intentions clear.

Defined terms are best shown with the particular term defined having a capital letter, for example, 'the Trustees', and 'the Beneficiaries'. This makes it clear to the reader that the particular term has a specific definition and enables use to be made of the same words in the settlement where the defined use is not intended. Emboldening defined terms (putting them in bold type) and italicising them should be avoided partly because, as a matter of style, they often affront the reader's eye but also because even quite advanced word processing software can sometimes eradicate subtle codification of the text.

Capitalising the whole defined term should also be avoided both as a matter of style and because capitalisation in a deed is traditionally reserved for proper nouns and the introductory words of some clauses so that its appearance elsewhere can be confusing.

Whatever style is adopted, it is important that each definition used clearly explains what is intended by the draftsman. Consistency in drafting is very important and where the draftsman adopts a particular style for definitions or for other matters in the text of his draft, this should be adopted throughout. If not, the reader might become confused as to the sense intended by the draftsman and this may lead to problems of interpretation.

The draftsman should bear in mind the statutory provisions which confirm that in every document, for example, the singular includes the plural and vice versa and the masculine the feminine and vice versa. If the draftsman bears in mind these fundamental rules then the drafting will be made easier both to the eye of the reader and generally for interpretation purposes. The use by the draftsman of clause headings will also break up the text and will be helpful for the reference of the reader. Clearly they will not override the text of the clause, but will be indicative of what is the subject-matter of each clause.

Administration trusts

17.6   The administration trusts are those which simply provide that the trustees are holding the trust property on trust. Before the commencement of the Trusts of Land and Appointment of Trustees Act 1996, there was usually a provision for a trust for sale and conversion. That is no longer necessary or important because the Settled Land Act 1925 will no longer apply to land comprised in a trust where no trust for sale is specified. If land is held on trust it will be a 'trust of land' within the Trusts of Land and Appointment of Trustees Act 1996 and there is little if anything to be gained by employing a trust for sale.

Settlors and lay trustees alike are often confused by the inclusion of a trust for sale and so it makes sense not to use a trust for sale where possible.

Beneficial trusts

17.7   The beneficial trusts are those which describe for whom the trustees hold the trust property and the terms on which they hold it. In the case of a bare trust this can be as simple as a direction that the trustee holds the property on trust for one beneficiary absolutely. At the other extreme the beneficial trusts can appear quite complicated. Take the case, for example, of an accumulation and maintenance trust for a class of children with provisions taking effect in the event of a child dying before attaining a vested interest leaving or not leaving children or leaving children who also fail to attain a vested interest with cross accruers and ultimate default gifts. The description of those beneficial trusts is not trivial so the draftsman should not expect to use only a few words to give effect to them.

Some powers may be so intimately linked to the beneficial trusts that they ought to be included at this stage. In a discretionary settlement, if powers are to be reserved to add discretionary objects to and to remove discretionary objects from the class of beneficiaries, then they are usually included here. Similarly, in an accumulation and maintenance trust, powers to vary the shares of beneficiaries should be included as part of the beneficial trusts.

In drafting the beneficial trusts it is important to remember to include clauses dealing with both the trust income and the capital. A power of accumulation of income, if it is included in the particular trust, is often set out at this stage as is a default clause to avoid a reverter of the trust capital to the settlor.

Overriding powers

17.8   The settlor will initially have ensured that the settlement has been drafted to reflect his wishes. Sometimes the settlor intends only that the trustees should manage a portfolio for the benefit of his beneficiaries with as much flexibility as possible, but more often than not the settlor will have strong views as to how his wishes should be put into effect. Those wishes may change, however, over time or the circumstances of the beneficiaries may change, for example as a result of divorce, bankruptcy or a death.

The inclusion of flexible overriding powers will enable the trustees, often with the consent of the settlor, to redirect or resettle the trust fund or to reshape the beneficial interests under the settlement. The inclusion of a consent provision in favour of the settlor will prevent the settlor's original intentions from being circumvented or ignored, at least while the settlor is alive.

An overriding power may give the trustees the power to revoke the original trusts and to appoint the capital or income to another beneficiary or other beneficiaries, to appoint the trust fund to any one or more of the class of beneficiaries at their discretion, that is, to create absolute entitlements, to resettle the capital or income on different trusts within the same settlement or to transfer the trust fund to the trustees of another settlement.

The form of the overriding power will need to specify how, in what circumstances and in whose favour it can be exercised. Usually the power will have to be exercised by deed and will be able to be exercised revocably or irrevocably, to ensure maximum flexibility. The terms of the power should be worded with sufficient width to enable the trustees to create whatever trusts they determine to be appropriate at the particular time when the power is exercised, subject to appropriate restrictions and safeguards.

In view of the different possible uses of the overriding powers, it is often best to include separate powers dealing with the power of absolute appointment, the power to resettle within the same settlement and the power to transfer the trust fund to another settlement in separate clauses of the trust deed (see below). These powers are discussed further in CHAPTER 22: ADMINISTRATIVE PROVISIONS and CHAPTER 24: BRINGING TRUSTS TO AN END.

Additional and extended powers

17.9   One of the most useful forms of overriding power is the power of advancement. The most common form is that contained in section 32 of the Trustee Act 1925. The statutory power permits trustees to transfer trust property to a person absolutely or to apply it for his 'advancement or benefit'. As explained in CHAPTER 22: ADMINISTRATIVE PROVISIONS, the statutory power is often extended by the draftsman to permit advancement in more flexible circumstances than contemplated by the statute.

The clause providing for an extended power of advancement should appear within the body of the deed and is often placed with other extending clauses such as clauses extending the statutory power of maintenance and express powers to resettle within the existing settlement or to transfer property to another settlement, if these have not been mentioned earlier.

Other matters which might appear in this part of the deed include: powers of appointment and removal of trustees (see CHAPTER 19: CHOICE OF TRUSTEES); powers permitting the exclusion of the settlor and the settlor's spouse from benefiting from the trust in any way (see CHAPTER 20: TRUSTEES' DUTIES AND POWERS); powers of addition to or exclusion from the beneficial class; a charging clause for professional trustees (see CHAPTER 19: CHOICE OF TRUS- TEES); a clause permitting the trustees to amend their administrative powers; a clause specifying the governing law of the trust; and a clause giving the settlement a name, or title, by which it can be identified.

Administrative powers

17.10   In modern settlements the administrative powers themselves are usu- ally set out in a separate schedule to the trust deed but, whatever form they take, administrative powers should be incorporated into the deed by a clause within the testatum. It is usual to provide that administrative powers are in addition to the trustees' ordinary powers. Administrative powers are discussed more fully in CHAPTER 22: ADMINISTRATIVE PROVISIONS.

Testimonium

17.11   Where the parties to the deed are individuals the testimonium clause traditionally appears in the following form:

> IN WITNESS whereof the Parties hereto have executed these presents as their deed the day and year first above written.

Some draftsmen do not enter the date at the head of a deed but at its foot, in which case it should appear in the testimonium clause thus:

> IN WITNESS whereof the Parties hereto have executed these presents as their deed the [*date in the month*] day of [*month*] Two Thousand and [*Four*].

Schedules

17.12   Schedules incorporated into the deed by words in the recitals or the testatum should appear between the testimonium and the signatures. Some draftsmen include a marker referring back to the clause incorporating the schedule thus:

SCHEDULE

(excluded persons, clause 4(3))

That, like a clause heading, is a matter of choice. The following often appear in schedules: administrative powers, additional administrative powers, a description of the trust property, a list of preceding instruments, a list of beneficiaries, a list of excluded persons and provisions relating to the appointment and removal of trustees.

Signature

17.13   Where the parties to a deed are individuals, the deed should be signed by each party and each signature should be witnessed. A person who is a party to a deed in more than one capacity (for example, as settlor and trustee) need only sign once since it would be absurd to allow such a person to claim to have executed the deed as trustee but not as settlor.

For reasons of space, the precedents in APPENDIX 1 do not include lengthy provision for all the parties' and witnesses' signatures. Where the precedents refer to 'SIGNED ETC.', the following should be set out:

SIGNED and DELIVERED   )

as a deed by the said [*NAME*   )

OF PARTY] in the presence of:)

Space should be left in between the name of each party for a witness to sign, print his or her name and give his or her address. It is often helpful to include the following formula under the name of each party in faint ink as a reminder of what the witness should add.

W	Signature ....
I	Name ....
T	Address ....
N	....
E	....
S	....
S	....

Chapter 18

Constituting Trusts

Post-trust creation steps

18.1   After the execution of the settlement deed in respect of a lifetime settlement a number of steps will need to be taken.

Transfer of trust property to the trustees

18.2   Depending upon the type of trust property, the draftsman will need to ensure that the settlement is properly established by preparing an appropriate instrument to transfer the trust property to the trustees. Shares are transferred to the trustees by the delivery of an executed stock transfer form and share certificates. The transfer is then completed by registration of the trustees as owners of the shares. Land is transferred by a conveyance (if unregistered) or transfer (if registered). A cheque or bank transfer suffices for a settlement of cash while chattels may be delivered or made the subject of a deed of gift. In the case of a life assurance policy, notice should be given to the life assurance company.

If the trust property is incapable of assignment, the declaration of trust will still be effective unless there is some statutory or contractual prohibition on declarations of trust of the property. The transfer of the trust property should always be made as soon as possible after the creation of the settlement.

Taxation issues

18.3   A form 41G (Trusts) will need to be completed and sent to the relevant Inland Revenue trusts district to advise it of the setting up of the settlement for income tax purposes. Following submission of the form, the relevant Inland Revenue trusts district will open a file for the settlement and will allocate a unique ten digit taxpayer reference number for the trustees. Inland Revenue trusts districts no longer need to see the settlement deed and will simply rely upon the information contained in the form 41G (Trusts) to establish the basis of taxation of the trustees.

If the settlement constitutes a chargeable transfer for inheritance tax purposes, that is, it constitutes a transfer into a discretionary settlement, an account in form IHT 100 will need to be submitted to the Inland Revenue Capital Taxes Office, unless the gift into the discretionary settlement is valued at £10,000 or less.

Depending upon the type of settlement set up and the nature of the trust property settled, a holdover election for capital gains tax purposes may need to be made by the settlor within six years of the end of the tax year in which the gift is made.

As already discussed in CHAPTER 5: TYPES OF TRUST, the settlement deed might attract stamp duty land tax and require certification.

Also depending upon the type of settlement created and who is to bear any inheritance tax payable, for example if the settlor dies within seven years, the settlor may wish to make life assurance arrangements to cover the possibility of him dying within seven years and to ensure that the proceeds of any such policy pass outside his estate to the persons who will be liable to bear the inheritance tax, by use of a trust. The primary responsibility for payment of inheritance tax due in respect of a potentially exempt transfer which becomes chargeable is that of the donee, that is, the trustees, but others may face liability for the tax if it is not paid within twelve months. In the case of a chargeable transfer, that is, a gift into a discretionary settlement, the primary liability will be that of the settlor, but he will usually arrange matters such that the donee will be liable for the tax since otherwise grossing up will apply for inheritance tax.

In the case of a discretionary settlement, or an accumulation and maintenance settlement, the trustees will need to be aware of the occasions when taxation charges may arise, that is, ten-year charges and exit charges for inheritance tax in the case of discretionary settlements and capital gains tax charges arising in certain circumstances in the case of accumulation and maintenance settlements, during the currency of such settlements.

In the case of interest in possession settlements, an inheritance tax charge may arise on the occasion of the death of a life tenant. The trustees should be aware of this.

In the case of both a will and the creation of a lifetime settlement, a decision will need to be made as to where the original document or deed is to be held and a note of this should be kept by the settlor.

A will will need to be reviewed periodically by a testator and the draftsman may be able to assist with this by arranging for a forward diary reminder system to be established, say every three to five years.

The testator will also need to be aware of relevant changes of circumstances, however, when changes to his will may become necessary, since these may occur more frequently than three to five years, for example the death or bankruptcy of any beneficiary and the birth of grandchildren.

Memorandum of wishes

18.4   Although this will usually be prepared by the draftsman or settlor at the same time as the settlement deed is prepared, it will usually need to be updated over time, if appropriate, as circumstances change. If a memorandum of wishes is not prepared simultaneously with the settlement deed, it will need to be completed as soon as possible after the settlement has been set up to ensure that the trustees are aware of the settlor's wishes in certain, given circumstances, particularly where any element of discretion is given to the trustees under the settlement deed or will. The memorandum of wishes should be stored with the settlement deed or will since it might otherwise be lost. Letters or memoranda of wishes are discussed further in CHAPTER 16: DRAFTING STYLE.

Chapter 19

Choice of Trustees

Who to appoint?

19.1   The choice of who the trustees are to be will be one which often will exercise the testator or settlor since he will have to choose persons who are both suitable and able to carry out the role and who will be able to function effectively and properly as a body. This is particularly so where there is any element of dispositive discretion to be given to the trustees, which will usually be the case in a modern well-drafted trust.

In addition, a testator will regularly need to update and reconsider his decision as to whom he has appointed and whether their appointment is still relevant and apposite to his circumstances. A settlor will need to consider whether the relevant powers to remove or appoint trustees are included within the trust instrument at the outset and, subsequently, whether they ought to be exercised.

The role of the trustees is to hold the trust property for the benefit of the beneficiaries of the trust, and to exercise for the benefit of the beneficiaries the powers and discretions given to them by the trust instrument and by the law. The capacity to exercise these powers and discretions and the duties of trusteeship, and the manner in which the settlor intends that such powers are to be exercised will have a great influence on the particular trustees chosen by the settlor. The identity and choice of the trustees is often crucial to the way in which the trust will be carried out.

The trustees will be responsible for ensuring that effect is given to the testator's or settlor's wishes in terms of the beneficial provisions of the trust and for other matters, such as the investment of the property subject to the trust. The trustees will obviously need to be able to act in a sensible, prudent and businesslike manner as a body and be able to understand the needs and interests of the beneficiaries.

Anyone (other than a minor, a person of unsound mind or, in certain cases, a bankrupt) can act as a trustee, but the law imposes certain restrictions which may affect the appointment of trustees when the trust is established or where trustees of existing trusts are appointed. For the latter, section 36 of the Trustee Act 1925 will be relevant. Trustees are normally chosen from the following: the settlor (or the settlor's spouse), beneficiaries, individuals such as friends, professional individuals and trust corporations.

Number of trustees

19.2   Usually, in the case of a non-charitable trust, unless a trust corporation is appointed, the number of trustees will be between two and four. In the case of a charitable trust there is no limit on the number of trustees who can be appointed. In the case of a non-charitable trust, section 34(2) of the Trustee Act 1925 provides that there shall be no more than four trustees of a settlement of land and section 36(6) provides that upon an appointment of additional trustees, the number of trustees may not be increased to more than four. These sections are set out in APPENDIX 2.

Section 27 of the Law of Property Act 1925 provides that a minimum of two trustees or a trust corporation is required to give a valid receipt for the proceeds of sale of land. As a result, the settlement deed will usually provide that certain powers, particularly dispositive powers under the trust deed, will only be validly exercised by the trustees if there are at least two trustees or a trust corporation to exercise the powers.

If a trustee is also a beneficiary the trust deed may sometimes indicate that in any exercise of a trust power in his own favour, the power will only be validly exercised if there are trustees, other than the beneficiary, or a trust corporation who exercise the power. Alternatively the trust deed may contain a specific provision that a beneficiary-trustee may exercise or join in powers, including dispositive powers, notwithstanding that he may derive a personal or indirect benefit from the exercise of the power.

Section 37(1)(c) of the Trustee Act 1925 provides that it is not obligatory to appoint more than one trustee where only one trustee was initially appointed, or to fill up the original number of trustees where more than two trustees were originally appointed. The subsection further provides, however, that, except where only one trustee was originally appointed, and a sole trustee when appointed will be able to give valid receipts for all capital money (that is, where the settlement deed does not require two trustees to do this and the trust fund contains personalty only), a trustee will not be discharged from a trust, for example on his retirement, unless there will be either a trust corporation or at least two individuals to act as trustees to perform the trust. Thus, if the settlor appoints two trustees initially it will not be possible for one of them to retire without another being appointed.

Settlor as a trustee

19.3   There are no fiscal disadvantages to the settlor (or his spouse) being a trustee provided neither is to benefit from the trust. If so, the gifts with reservation rules may apply: see CHAPTER 5: TYPES OF TRUST. Even a benefit as simple as charging for work done as trustee could have this consequence. Otherwise, unless the settlor does not wish to have the bother of exercising trust functions, there are no disadvantages to him being a trustee. Usually a settlor will wish to be a trustee in order to retain some control of the trust assets. A settlor should not ordinarily be a sole trustee.

An alternative to the settlor being a trustee, where he wishes to retain some degree of control over the trust property, is to provide in the trust instrument that certain powers are not to be exercisable by the trustees without the written consent of the settlor having first been obtained.

Beneficiary as a trustee

19.4   Similarly, there is no general fiscal or other bar to a beneficiary being a trustee. It may, in certain circumstances, be a positive benefit to include one or more of the beneficiaries as trustees to ensure that the administration of the trust proceeds smoothly and to ensure that the investments comprised in the trust fund are closely and properly managed and reviewed. Indeed, who could have a closer or keener interest in this than someone who stands to benefit from the trust?

Unless all of the beneficiaries are trustees, and this may not, of course, be practicable or desirable, then the appointment of one of many actual or potential beneficiaries as a trustee may cause distrust or suspicion among those not appointed and lead to real or imagined conflicts of interest in the beneficiary appointed. This can be overcome to an extent by the trust deed providing that a trustee, who is also a beneficiary, may not participate in the appointment of property out of the settlement in his favour. However, this may not be sufficient to dispel the suspicions of the other beneficiaries since the beneficiary-trustee may have taken part in the decision-making process, even though he was not a formal party to the deed by which the appointment was made.

Great care must be taken in appointing a beneficiary trustee as this is often quite a delicate matter. The settlor might not be aware of differences of opinion or disagreements between different beneficiaries which might render his appointment fatally divisive.

Confusion often arises in the mind of the settlor that a trustee cannot also be a beneficiary, in view of the general trust principle that 'a trustee cannot profit from his own trust'. This principle does not apply to a situation where a trustee, who is also a beneficiary under the trust, benefits as a beneficiary. The rule simply prohibits a trustee from benefiting in his capacity as a trustee, unless specifically authorised by the trust instrument or the beneficiaries. The confusion is simply an example of the failure of many laymen to appreciate that individuals can simultaneously act in different legal capacities. It is usually satisfied by careful explanation.

When considering whether to appoint a beneficiary as a trustee, the settlor will need to balance the possible conflict of interest and distrust which may arise, with the benefit of having someone who has a direct and personal interest in ensuring that the trustees act responsibly and in the best interests of the beneficiaries. The settlor will wish to ensure, before appointing a beneficiary as a trustee, that he is going to be able to balance the interests of all of the beneficiaries and to act in a proper and businesslike manner in carrying out the terms of the trust given to him.

Other individuals as trustees

19.5   Professional trustees charge for their services (see below) and so the settlor is often tempted to ask others such as friends and relatives to accept an appointment as trustees. It is particularly common for testators to ask their friends and relatives to act as their executors and so, in the ordinary course of things, as their trustees.

While this is often superficially a good idea the draftsman should encourage the exercise of caution. There are a number of reasons for this. Laymen rarely comprehend either the extent of their powers as trustees or the onerous nature of the duties which they undertake when agreeing to their appointment. As an exercise in saving professional fees the appointment of lay trustees often fails because the trustees, who have no understanding of what they can and cannot do, incur professional charges acquiring the most elementary legal knowledge. Where lay trustees do not seek professional help and advice they can make quite basic errors. On the whole these go unnoticed but there are sometimes catastrophic fiscal consequences and occasionally these lead to expensive and bitter trust litigation.

Nonetheless, the appointment of a trusted friend or impartial relative as a trustee to act alongside professional trustees has much to recommend it. During his lifetime the settlor might still have a degree of legitimate influence over the trustees' exercise of their dispositive powers because of his ongoing relationship with the lay trustee and he has the reassurance that after his death the trust will not be left in the hands of professionals with no relationship with the beneficiaries.

Professional trustees

19.6   Often the best result in terms of achieving a balance in the appointment of a body of trustees who will best be able to manage the administration of the trust in a businesslike manner will be for the settlor to appoint trustees, some of whom will have a detailed knowledge of his family (or whoever are the beneficiaries) and his and their circumstances and a professional trustee who will be able to guide and remind the trustees as to their powers and duties under the trust and their responsibilities to all of the beneficiaries. The lay trustees appointed may be beneficiaries or trusted relatives or friends, in whom the settlor has the requisite confidence.

As explained above, a body of exclusively lay trustees may lead to breaches of trust occurring if they do not have sufficient knowledge or understanding of their responsibilities as trustees, or do not take advice in relevant circumstances. A body of exclusively professional trustees may lead to concerns arising among the beneficiaries that they are too remote or are charging professional fees which the beneficiaries consider to be too high, leading to concerns that the professional trustees have a vested interest in continuing to run the trust for an over-long period of time.

Individuals

19.7   Individual professionals are often appointed as trustees of settlements. The settlor's family solicitor is a popular choice but it is sometimes more sensible for the settlor to appoint his accountant or a combination of solicitor and accountant. Individual professional trustees will usually wish for an appropriate charging clause and exoneration clause to be included in the trust deed.

Corporate trustees and trust corporations

19.8   If the settlor decides to appoint a professional trustee, an individual professional trustee will usually be preferred, since although a trust corporation or corporate trustee will never die and will provide a continuum, the high charges levied and the perception of remoteness and inflexibility in the minds of the beneficiaries will often be more acute and real in the case of a trust corporation or corporate trustee. Corporate professional trustees will insist on an appropriate charging clause and exoneration clause being included in the trust deed.

Corporate trustees usually charge scale fees for which an express power is required and care should be taken to ensure that the scale charges are not limited to those charged by the corporate trustee initially appointed since, if no other trust corporation is able to charge scale fees, it may be difficult to transfer the trust business elsewhere. Some larger professional firms have set up their own trust corporations.

A company, other than a trust corporation, may be appointed to be a trustee provided that its memorandum and articles of association permit it to act as such, but, in order to act as a sole trustee, the company will still need to comply with the restrictions mentioned above in respect of companies qualifying as trust corporations, unless the company is entitled to be treated as a trust corporation under section 35 of the Charities Act 1993, set out in APPENDIX 2.

Charging clauses

19.9   It was formerly the case that, generally, a solicitor or other professional person could not charge for acting as executor or trustee unless the settlement authorised him to charge for his services. Now, under section 29(2) of the Trustee Act 2000, in the absence of an express remuneration clause, a trustee or personal representative acting in a professional capacity and who is not a sole trustee is entitled to receive reasonable remuneration for any services he provides (including services capable of being provided by a lay trustee) if each other trustee has agreed in writing that he may be remunerated: section 28(1), (2) and (5)–(6) of the Trustee Act 2000. Similarly, in the absence of an express remuneration clause, a trust corporation is entitled to receive reasonable remuneration for any services provided to or on behalf of the trust including services which are capable of being provided by someone who is not a trust corporation: sections 29(1), 28(1), (2) and (6) of the Trustee Act 2000. Section 29 does not apply to charitable trusts, or to trusts where a charging clause is included in the deed, even if such clause is ineffective or faulty.

Notwithstanding these provisions, where professional trustees or a trust corporation are appointed they ought to insist on express provision enabling the trustees to charge fees because, in the case of a professional trustee, it will still be necessary for the trustee to obtain the consent of his co-trustees and, in the case of a trust corporation, the statutory reasonable remuneration might not extend to the scale fees often charged by such institutions. Where the trustees are likely to require professional advice the settlor should not have any qualms about this but the plain truth is that a professional trustee will not agree to act without an appropriate charging provision so that even if lay trustees are appointed in the first instance it may be difficult to appoint a professional trustee in the future without express provision.

Lay trustees will only be entitled to be reimbursed for out-of-pocket expenses, as confirmed by section 31 of the Trustee Act 2000, set out in APPENDIX 2.

Professional trustees and exemption clauses

19.10   As with charging provisions, professional trustees will seek appropriate protection in order to limit their personal liability, unless loss is suffered to the trust fund through the dishonesty or fraud of the professional trustee.

Since the common law and now the Trustee Act 2000 both require higher standards of care from professional trustees, in certain respects, as regards the exercise of their duties and powers, it is probably not surprising that professional trustees will often seek to limit or restrict their liability. These attempts to limit liability are sometimes resented by beneficiaries and the higher courts might yet look carefully at such attempts to limit or restrict liability in terms of the particular wording used in the trust deed, since if professional trustees are charging for their services and are holding themselves out as having special knowledge or skill, it may be considered that they should take responsibility where they are at fault, for example through their negligence.

It is sometimes thought that section 61 of the Trustee Act 1925 (see APPENDIX 2) offers some relief since this section empowers the court to relieve a trustee, either wholly or partially, from personal liability for any breach of trust if he has acted honestly and reasonably and ought fairly to be excused for the breach of trust and for omitting to obtain the directions of the court in the matter in which he committed such a breach. Section 61 is, in practice, a defence of last resort and the court will generally be slow to offer protection under the section to professional trustees in view of the higher standards of care expected of them.

In *Armitage v Nurse [1997] 2 All ER 705*, the exemption clause in question read:

'No Trustee shall be liable for any loss or damage which may happen to [the Trust Fund] or any part thereof or the income thereof at any time or from any cause whatsoever unless such loss or damage shall be caused by his own actual fraud.'

The Court of Appeal held that 'actual fraud' meant dishonesty; that the clause was not void for public policy reasons; and that the trustee would not be liable, therefore, unless there was dishonesty which caused loss to the trust fund. Even if the trustee acted in breach of trust, provided that he did so in the overall best interests of the beneficiaries and was not dishonest, then the clause would operate to protect him.

Millett LJ, however, stated that in his opinion more was to be expected of a professional trustee and that where a professional trustee had acted in a grossly negligent manner then an exemption clause would not exculpate him. He said:

'At the same time it must be acknowledged that the view is widely held that these clauses have gone too far, and that trustees who charge for their services and who, as professional men, would not dream of excluding liability for ordinary professional negligence, should not be able to rely on a trustee exemption clause excluding liability for gross negligence.'

More usually such clauses refer to exemption from liability unless 'actual fraud or dishonesty' or 'wilful fraud or dishonesty' can be made out. Such a clause was in question in the case of *Walker v Stones [2000] 4 All ER 412; [2001] 2 WLR 623*. The court there indicated that in the case of a professional trustee such a clause would not afford exemption to the trustee where no reasonable professional trustee, judged on an objective basis, could have acted in such a way and claimed that what he had done was for the overall best interests of the beneficiaries. This therefore appears to add a 'gloss' on the *Armitage v Nurse* principle and to confirm that a higher standard is to be expected of professional trustees. This attitude is confirmed in other, but similar, respects in section 1 of the Trustee Act 2000 (set out in APPENDIX 2).

It appears to be settled law now, however, that liability can be excluded except in the cases of 'knowing dishonesty' or unreasonable and reckless disregard for the interests of the beneficiaries.

The case of *Bogg v Raper [1998] The Times 22 April, [1998] CLY 4592* confirms that similar principles apply in respect of trustee exemption clauses in wills.

Trustees will not wish to be held liable in cases where they make an honest mistake nor will they want to have to fall back on the relieving provision of section 61 of the Trustee Act 1925. Lay trustees should also feel comforted by the inclusion of an appropriate trustee exemption clause in a trust deed or will. The message appears to be, however, that where trustees are professionals, charging fees and holding themselves out as having special skills, then they will be expected to achieve a higher standard in respect of their actions. Unless a tightly worded and clear exemption clause is included at the outset, usually indicating that liability will only lie where actual wilful fraud or negligence is shown, then the court will hold them to account, not least because they will hold professional indemnity insurance to cover for negligence, at least.

The Law Commission has issued a consultation paper on trustee exemption clauses. One possible outcome of the consultation process is that professional trustees might no longer be able to rely on exemption clauses of such breadth. Discussions are still at a relatively early stage.

Power of appointment of trustees

19.11   The initial trustees of a settlement are usually appointed in the trust instrument and their appointment is confirmed by their acceptance of the appointment. This is usually achieved by them executing the trust deed.

Section 36 of the Trustee Act 1925 requires any subsequent appointment to be made in writing. This will usually be done by deed, particularly since section 40 of the Trustee Act 1925 only applies to vest trust property in new or continuing trustees, for example following the retirement of a trustee, where the new trustee is appointed by deed. These sections are set out in APPENDIX 2.

The appointment of trustees subsequent to the initial appointment of trustees in the trust deed can be effected in four main ways:

(a)   by statutory power of appointment;

(b)   by exercise of an express power of appointment, for example pursuant to a power in the trust instrument;

(c)   by the court; and

(d)   by the beneficiaries of the trust.

Statutory power of appointment

19.12   Section 36 of the Trustee Act 1925 provides that the power of appointing new trustees vests in the person nominated to do so in the trust instrument and, in default of this, in the trustees for the time being of the trust, and, in the event of the death of the last surviving trustee, the personal representatives of such trustee.

Most modern trust deeds will contain either a modification of the statutory power or an express power of appointment of trustees, usually in favour of the settlor during his lifetime, but, if not, then the statutory power will apply and may be used to appoint new or additional trustees or to replace existing trustees, for example on the retirement of a trustee. Sometimes the trust deed provides that the statutory power of appointment applies and is exercisable by the trustees for the time being or by the settlor or someone else and the deed may go on to provide that the settlor may by deed or deeds pass on the power to appoint new or additional trustees, or indicate that on the settlor's death the power to appoint new or additional trustees will be vested in the trustees for the time being of the trust.

Under section 36(1) of the Trustee Act 1925, power is given for the appointment of one or more new trustees in place of a trustee who has died, remains outside the United Kingdom for twelve months or more, decides to retire, refuses to act, is unfit to act or is a minor (that is, is under the age of 18 years). A trust deed may also include a power, usually exercisable by the settlor, to remove a trustee and will specify a procedure to be followed to achieve this. If such a power of removal is contained in the trust deed and is exercised, then section 36(2) of the Trustee Act 1925 extends the statutory power to appoint one or more new trustees. These powers permit any person exercising the power of appointment, for example the settlor if he holds the power under the terms of the trust deed, to appoint himself.

In addition to the above powers, section 36(6) of the Trustee Act 1925 extends the statutory power to permit the appointment of an additional trustee, that is, where there is no retirement or removal, provided that there are not already more than three trustees. This power cannot be used by the person holding the power of appointment under the terms of the trust deed (if applicable) to appoint himself.

A deed of appointment of new trustees, where there is a simultaneous retirement and there is no person under the trust deed holding the power of appointment, will usually state that the new appointment is being made by both the continuing trustees and the retiring trustee or trustees, but strictly the appointment only needs to be made by the continuing trustees under the terms of section 36 of the Trustee Act 1925.

Section 8 of the Trustee Delegation Act 1999 inserted four new subsections into section 36(6) of the Trustee Act 1925 which provide that in certain circumstances an attorney under an enduring power of attorney registered at the Court of Protection may exercise the statutory power of appointment conferred on the trustees.

Express power of appointment

19.13   If an express power of appointment is included in the trust deed, then the trustees will need to take great care in order to ensure that the precise terms of the express power are followed so that the power is validly exercised and the new trustees are duly and properly appointed.

Appointment by the court

19.14   Section 41 of the Trustee Act 1925 provides that whenever it is expedient to do so the court may appoint one or more new trustees where it is inexpedient, difficult or impracticable for this to be achieved without the assistance of the court. The court may exercise this power to appoint a trustee either in substitution for, or in addition to, any existing trustee or trustees, and in cases where there is no existing trustee. Such an application may therefore become necessary where all of the trustees have died and the personal representatives of the last survivor of them cannot be established or found. Section 41 of the Trustee Act 1925 (see APPENDIX 2) makes it clear that the power given to the court will be exercisable, for example, to appoint a new trustee in place of a trustee who is incapable by reason of mental disorder within the meaning of the Mental Health Act 1983 of acting as a trustee, is bankrupt or is a corporation which is in liquidation or has been dissolved. These examples are specifically stated to be non-exhaustive.

Appointment by the beneficiaries of the trust

19.15   Powers are given by section 19 of the Trusts of Land and Appointment of Trustees Act 1996 (see APPENDIX 2), in certain circumstances, to beneficiaries to appoint and to remove trustees. Section 20 of the 1996 Act contains similar provisions where a trustee is incapable of exercising his functions as a trustee by reason of mental disorder. The power given by section 19 of the 1996 Act is exercisable where the statutory power of appointing new trustees is held by the trustees for the time being of the trust (that is, there is no other person given the statutory power of appointment of new trustees under the trust deed) and where all of the beneficiaries are of full age and capacity and between them are absolutely entitled to the trust property (that is, under the principle in *Saunders v Vautier (1841) 4 Beav 115*, the beneficiaries could bring the trust to an end).

The section 19 power will usually be specifically excluded by the trust drafts-man, since the settlor will not generally want the beneficiaries to decide who are to be the trustees of the trust because this could lead to abuse undermining the very purpose of the trust.

Power of removal of trustees

19.16   The power to remove a trustee is now more often seen in modern trust deeds. The power is usually exercisable by the settlor, but it is sometimes provided in the trust deed that the settlor may pass on the power to another person by a revocable or irrevocable deed. It is generally considered that such a power contained in a will will not be valid.

Clearly the settlor will usually have given considerable thought to the persons being appointed as trustees at the outset, and he will hope that as a result he will not need to remove any of the trustees, but the power will give him some added security if things go wrong, or if the trustees, for one reason or another, are not able to act together as a body.

The position of the trustees, however, needs to be considered by the draftsman. The exercise of such a power may leave the dismissed trustee in an unsatisfactory position and may lead to wider family or other disruption or disagreement; and the inclusion of such a power may lead to the new trustee not wishing to take on the role of a trustee, since it might affect his ability to act independently as a trustee.

A power to dismiss a trustee is a fiduciary power and the holder of the power will need to exercise the power in the interests of the beneficiaries and not to satisfy a vendetta or to resolve a personal grievance.

Perhaps in view of lack of proximity in terms of exercising control or influence over the trustees, the inclusion of such a power of dismissal of trustees is more usually included in offshore rather than UK-resident trusts.

Occasionally the power to dismiss trustees can be included or passed on by the settlor (if there is a power given by the settlement to do so) to a beneficiary, for example the life tenant. The inclusion of such a power or the passing on of such a power by a settlor to a beneficiary is now unusual, since the overall balance between the trustees and the beneficiaries would be upset by its exercise and the holding by a beneficiary of such a power would probably over-endow the beneficiary, particularly where the beneficiary also has the power to appoint new trustees under the terms of the trust, and, for example, the trust deed contains discretionary powers over capital.

Removal of trustees by the court

19.17   Section 41 of the Trustee Act 1925 enables the court to appoint replacement trustees but can also be used to remove trustees. It has been held, for example, that a trustee can be removed where his whereabouts are unknown: *Re Harrison's Trusts (1852) 22 LJ Ch 69*. The statutory power is in the widest possible terms and is of general application: *Re Henderson, Henderson v Henderson [1940] Ch 764, [1940] 3 All ER 295.*

On an application under section 41 of the Trustee Act 1925 a trustee can be removed or an appointment made against his will if the court is satisfied that it is expedient to make such an appointment. In addition, the High Court has inherent jurisdiction to remove a trustee from office even without replacing him if sufficient trustees remain. A trustee may be removed whenever the welfare of the beneficiaries requires it, even if guilty of no misconduct: *Re Wrightson [1908] 1 Ch 789*; *Letterstedt v Broers (1884) 9 App Cas 371*.

Retirement of trustees

19.18   Unless an express power of retirement is included in the trust deed, which is relatively unusual, section 39 of the Trustee Act 1925 will apply. That section provides that a trustee may retire, with the consent of his co-trustees or the person who has the power to appoint new trustees, provided that following his retirement as a trustee there will be at least two persons or a trust corporation remaining in that role.

On retirement a trustee, particularly a professional trustee, may seek an indemnity from the remaining trustees (including any new trustees being concurrently appointed). However, such indemnities are usually little more than 'comfort blankets'. If a breach of trust has been committed by a retiring trustee then he will be personally liable whether or not an indemnity is given and the retiring trustee cannot be liable for breaches of trust of others which occur after he has ceased to be a trustee. Any retiring trustee will in any event have a lien over the trust fund for any fiscal or other liabilities which arose, and were properly incurred, while he was a trustee.

Trustees giving an indemnity will need to ensure that the indemnity is only given in respect of liabilities properly incurred and that the indemnity is limited to the value of the trust fund in the hands of the trustees.

Chapter 20

Trustees' Duties and Powers

Introduction

20.1   Initially the draftsman will need to distinguish what he intends to be duties (obligations upon the trustees to do or not to do certain things) and powers (permissions to trustees to act or not to act in a certain way). Appropriate language needs to be adopted in the trust deed or will to make it clear whether the provisions included are intended to be duties or powers. What are being considered in this chapter are not administrative provisions, for example, powers of investment, insurance, to deal with land, etc and the powers of maintenance and advancement, which are covered in CHAPTER 22: ADMINIS-TRATIVE PROVISIONS, but more general overriding duties and powers, especially those powers permitting the trustees to dispose of property comprised in the trust fund to the beneficiaries. More specific administrative duties are considered in CHAPTER 21: ADMINISTRATIVE DUTIES.

To achieve clarity in the minds of the settlor or testator, the beneficiaries and the trustees, being both those initially appointed and subsequent trustees, and in order to avoid later problems and conflicts concerning the interpretation of what was or was not intended, the draftsman's clearest technique will be to phrase duties using the word 'shall' and powers using the word 'may'.

Duties

20.2   In addition to duties imposed by the will or trust deed, trustees have other duties imposed either by common law or by statute, for example, by the Trustee Act 2000.

Some of the common law duties of trustees, discussed more fully in CHAPTER 21: ADMINISTRATIVE DUTIES, are as follows:

(a)   Duties to inform beneficiaries of their rights and to pay to the correct persons. This includes advising beneficiaries of fixed entitlements either to income or capital, whether vested or contingent, and probably advising discretionary beneficiaries of their potential interests (although it is difficult to envisage what remedy a potential beneficiary under a discretionary trust would have if a trustee failed to inform him of his potential interest). This is really the corollary of beneficiaries having rights of obtaining certain information from trustees and the ability of beneficiaries to hold trustees to account. If beneficiaries do not know of their actual, contingent or potential interests, then obviously they will not be able to exercise these rights. It seems that beneficiaries under wills and other testamentary dispositions do not have similar rights against executors since wills and other testamentary documents become public documents after probate is granted.

(b)   Duty to act with reasonable care and skill. For a lay trustee this duty requires a trustee to act, judged on an objective standard, as an ordinary prudent man of business would have acted in similar circumstances, but a higher standard will be required of professional trustees.

(c)   Duty to obey the directions of the settlement. Breach of this duty is likely to result in a breach of trust and to lead, as in the case of the other duties mentioned here, to personal liability for the trustees. The duty will not apply if the terms of the settlement are illegal, unenforceable or void for uncertainty.

(d)   Duty to keep and produce accounts and other trust documents. For clarification of what is and what is not a trust document for these purposes reference should be made to the cases of *Re Londonderry's Settlement [1964] 3 All ER 855* and *Re Rabaiotti's Settlements [2000] WTLR 953*. The duties relating to accounts require trustees to keep clear and accurate accounts and to produce them and any back-up information used in preparing the accounts, to beneficiaries and their advisers. The cost of supplying trust documents and accounts to beneficiaries must be met by the beneficiaries requiring these.

(e)   Duty to deal fairly. This duty requires trustees to act fairly between beneficiaries and not to take any advantage whatsoever in their capacity as trustees over the beneficiaries.

(f)   Duty not to profit from trust property and not to cause loss to the trust property as a result of any conflict of interest between the trustees' personal interests and their duties as trustees. This is often called 'the self-dealing rule' and results from the trustees' overriding duty to act in the utmost good faith. Subject to some exceptions, any disposition involving self-dealing by a trustee of trust property will be voidable, however fair.

(g)   Duty to act jointly where there is more than one trustee. In the case of charitable trusts, trustees can act by a majority, but in private trusts unanimity among all of the trustees is generally required unless the court otherwise directs. The counter-side of this is that unless all of the trustees for the time being agree to the course of action proposed then it will need to be abandoned. Essentially this is the equivalent of a right of veto for each of the trustees. This duty generally requires trustees to retain investments in the names of all of them, unless the settlement or will otherwise provides (but see CHAPTER 22: ADMINISTRATIVE PROVISIONS and the provisions of the Trustee Act 2000).

It must be emphasised that the above list is not exhaustive of the common law duties of trustees.

Powers

20.3   What are being considered here are beneficial powers under the terms of the settlement deed, and not administrative powers, which are covered in CHAPTER 22: ADMINISTRATIVE PROVISIONS.

In general terms, the beneficial powers will be exercisable by the trustees under the terms of the settlement deed or will. There may, however, be requirements in the settlement deed or will for a minimum number of trustees, usually two or a trust corporation, to exercise certain powers validly (see CHAPTER 19: CHOICE OF TRUSTEES) or a requirement for the consent of an individual, for example, the settlor or a protector, if used, to be obtained before the power can be exercised validly. The reasons for the insertion of a requirement for a minimum number of trustees or a provision requiring consent can be various but one important consideration is to offer protection to the beneficiaries and to avoid a 'rogue' sole trustee wreaking havoc with the trust property. Under the general law, a sole trustee will generally be able to exercise most powers required of a trustee, but this may not be acceptable to the settlor. The requirement for consent to be obtained or for a minimum number of trustees will only be part of a web of protection woven by the draftsman, however. Other strands of the web will include consideration of who is to exercise the powers of appointment and, if included, the power to dismiss trustees.

Since beneficial powers in settlement deeds or wills will offer wide discretion to trustees, particularly in the case of discretionary trusts and discretionary powers, a settlor or testator will often make a memorandum of wishes intended to guide the trustees as to how the settlor envisages the trustees exercising such powers. By their very nature, memoranda of wishes are not binding on the trustees. These are discussed in CHAPTER 16: DRAFTING STYLE.

Section 11 of the Trusts of Land and Appointment of Trustees Act 1996 (see APPENDIX 2), in the case of trusts comprising land, requires trustees to consult with beneficiaries of full age who are beneficially entitled to an interest in possession in the land and to give effect to the wishes of those beneficiaries (or, in the event of a dispute, to the majority of them according to the value of their combined interests) so far as is consistent with the general interests of the trust.

This duty sits rather uncomfortably on the shoulders of most trustees and most draftsmen will exclude it as a matter of course. Settlors will have given careful thought as to whom they wish to appoint as trustees and will not wish the position of the trustees to be compromised or undermined by the beneficiaries and, although clearly the terms of section 11 will need to be discussed with the settlor by the draftsman in cases where it is applicable, most settlors will wish for it to be excluded. The 1996 Act specifically permits the exclusion of section 11.

Although the settlor may not wish to fetter trustees with, for example, the provisions of sections 11 and 19 of the Trusts of Land and Appointment of Trustees Act 1996 (the latter conferring powers on beneficiaries in certain circumstances to remove trustees – see CHAPTER 19: CHOICE OF TRUSTEES), he will usually wish to insert some checks and balances in respect of the exercise by the trustees of some of their dispositive powers. Clearly the settlor, when considering the draft deed prepared by the draftsman, will need to consider which powers should be subject to control and who is to exercise whatever form of control is chosen to be appropriate. In reality, the draftsman will have already inserted some standard checks and balances in the draft deed prepared, and it will be for the settlor to consider whether those which have been inserted are appropriate and sufficient. The powers over which the settlor might wish to see some control being exercised will include, for example, discretionary dispositive powers, powers of resettlement and powers of advancement of capital.

The settlement deed will usually provide that such powers are only validly exercisable by two trustees or a trust corporation and only with the written consent of the settlor having first been obtained. The settlor will then need to consider whether he wishes any similar control to be exercised after he has died by means of a requirement for the written consent of another person to be obtained. If so, the draftsman may use the device of a protector, which is considered later in this chapter.

In older settlement deeds, particularly in interest in possession trusts, settlors sometimes conferred on the life tenant either the power to confer an interest in possession to follow his own by deed, or even the power to appoint capital by deed, with such appointment to operate on his death. Such powers in favour of life tenants or other beneficiaries are now infrequently used. The main reason for this is that most commentators suggest that settlors usually prefer for the trustees, who will have an overall perspective of the interests of all of the beneficiaries, to exercise such powers (on the basis of a minimum number of trustees being required to exercise such powers), rather than a single beneficiary having such control.

For those settlors who wish to exercise a larger measure of control, the best solution is for the settlor himself to be appointed as a trustee initially, and then for the administration of the settlement to move forward from there.

Fraud on a power of appointment

20.4   Unless the settlement deed permits it, a beneficial power of appointment will be void if exercised in favour of a holder of the power, for example, the trustee under the terms of the settlement. This is not usually a problem in modern settlements, since a special power permitting such appointments will usually be included as a matter of course. Dispositive powers of appointment are, however, fiduciary powers and must be exercised in ways which the trustees, and any consent holders, consider to be in the best interests of the beneficiaries. It follows that the trustees, and any consent holders, will need to consider the needs and interests of all of the beneficiaries in conjunction with any memorandum of wishes of the settlor.

A purported exercise of a power of appointment will be void where it is exercised to benefit a person who is not the object of the power, for example, where trustees exercise a power knowing that the beneficiary to whom the property is appointed has agreed or intends to give the property appointed to another person who is not within the class of objects permitted to benefit from the exercise by the trustees of their discretions under the power. Such an exercise by the trustees is said to constitute 'a fraud on the power'.

This doctrine was recently considered in the case of *Netherton v Netherton [2000] WTLR 1171* (where the court decided that the exercise of the power in question was valid).

When exercising a power of appointment the trustees will need to consider the precise terms of the power and to ensure that they take into account all relevant facts and that the exercise of the power achieves the result intended, if the exercise of the power is to be effective. Extremely difficult questions can arise in the context of an appointment which may be a fraud on the power or in excess of the trustees' power.

The rule in Hastings-Bass

20.5   The rule in *Hastings-Bass* may be stated in the following terms: the exercise of a power on the part of trustees may be vitiated if, though they have considered the matter without impropriety, they have failed to take into account considerations which they should have taken into account or have taken into account considerations which they should not have taken into account. However, and this is really no more than common sense, the court cannot interfere unless it is clear that had the trustees had a proper understanding of the effect of their act they would not have acted as they did.

The rule in *Hastings-Bass* is a principle labelled as such by Warner J in *Mettoy Pension Trustees v Evans [1990] 1 WLR 1587*. The principle was summarised by Buckley LJ in *Re Hastings-Bass deceased [1975] Ch 25* at *41F* in the following way:

> '. . . in our judgment, where by the terms of a trust . . . a trustee is given a discretion as to some matter under which he acts in good faith, the court should not interfere with his action notwithstanding that it does not have the full effect which he intended, unless: (1) what he achieved is unauthorised by the power conferred upon him; or (2) it is clear that he would not have acted as he did: (a) had he not taken into account considerations

which he should not have taken into account; or (b) had he not failed to take into account considerations which he ought to have taken into account.'

In *Mettoy Pension Trustees v Evans* Warner J applied the rule to the case before him saying (at *1624B-C*) that:

'I do not think the application of the principle is confined . . . to cases where an exercise by trustees of a discretion vested in them is partially ineffective because of some rule of law or because of some limit on their discretion which they overlooked. If, as I believe, the reason for the application of the principle is the failure by the trustees to take into account considerations that they ought to have taken into account, it cannot matter whether that failure is due to their having overlooked (or to their legal advisers having overlooked) some relevant rule of law or limit on their discretion, or is due to some other cause.'

The rule in *Hastings-Bass* has been applied recently in *Abacus Trust Company (Isle of Man) Ltd v NSPCC [2001] WTLR 953* in which case the court held that the appointment in question was invalid. Commenting (at *963C*) on the statement of the rule cited above, Patten J said that 'the factors which, if overlooked, may vitiate the exercise of the power are not limited to the legal effect or consequences of the exercise of the power in question'.

In all cases in which trustees are exercising powers they should consider and understand the scope and extent of those powers.

Trustee Act 2000

20.6   This important Act, which came into force on 1 February 2001, has introduced a number of fundamental changes to the powers and duties of trustees, including the introduction of a new statutory duty of care. In addition, the major changes introduced by the Act are to repeal the main provisions of the Trustee Investments Act 1961, and to replace them with a much more flexible and acceptable framework for investment by trustees (but with the liberalisation in terms of powers comes the creation and reinforcement of duties); the power for trustees collectively to delegate; the power for trustees to use nominees and custodians; the power to insure trust property; and powers concerning the remuneration of professional trustees. These powers are discussed more fully in CHAPTER 22: ADMINISTRATIVE PROVISIONS and CHAPTER 19: CHOICE OF TRUSTEES. The Act is set out in APPENDIX 2.

One important point to note is that, although the Law Commission indicated that many of the provisions of the Act were intended to consolidate and codify in statutory form certain existing common law duties of trustees, the reality is that the powers given by the Act are generally applicable in addition to (and not in place of) existing common law duties and are in addition to (and not in place of) powers expressly given by new or existing trusts. The provisions of the Act generally apply both to existing trusts and trusts established after 1 February 2001.

The Act is written in a modern English format. The disadvantage of this is that the precise meaning of the language used is unlikely to become clear, unless and until some of the relevant provisions have been litigated. For example, section 4(3)(b) indicates that the standard investment criteria, in relation to a trust, include the need for diversification of investments of the trust 'in so far as is appropriate to the circumstances of the trust'; when considering whether to take investment advice either on initial investment or when reviewing the investments of the trust, section 5 indicates that a trustee *must* obtain and consider *proper* advice, unless (s 5(3)) '... he reasonably considers that in all the circumstances it is unnecessary or inappropriate to do so'; and section 5(4) advises trustees that proper advice in this context is the advice of a person '... who is reasonably believed by the trustees to be qualified to give it by his ability ...' in certain respects. Quite what the extent of these duties is will only become clear after they have been litigated by trustees and beneficiaries. Even then their intended meaning might be difficult to discern. Section 8 is drafted in a rather intriguing way. It provides that a trustee may acquire freehold or leasehold land in the United Kingdom:

'(a)   as an investment,

(b)   for occupation by a beneficiary, or

(c)   for any other reason'.

Quite what was the point of including (a) and (b) in view of the wording of (c) is unclear.

Statutory duty of care

20.7   The new duty of care is set out in section 1 of the Trustee Act 2000 and applies to a trustee whenever exercising the power of investment conferred by the Act or any other power of investment however conferred, for example, one given by the trust deed, and when carrying out a duty to which a trustee is subject under the following:

(a)   section 4 (relating to the review of investments and when having regard to the standard investment criteria);

(b)   section 5 (relating to taking advice);

(c)   section 8 (acquisition of land);

(d)   section 11 (the power of delegation);

(e)   section 16 (the power of appointing and using nominees);

(f)   section 19 of the Trustee Act 1925, as amended by section 34 of the Trustee Act 2000 or under the trust deed (the power of insurance).

This list is not exhaustive and it should be noted that the duty applies whenever the new statutory powers are exercised or when equivalent powers under the trust deed are exercised. Paragraph 7 of Schedule 1 to the Trustee Act 2000 states that the statutory duty of care does not apply if or in so far as it appears from the trust instrument that it is not meant to apply. It remains to be seen, however, what attitude will be taken by the court if the statutory duty of care is routinely excluded, as is likely.

In the circumstances where the statutory duty of care applies, a trustee must exercise such care and skill as is reasonable in the circumstances having regard in particular:

(i)   to any special knowledge or experience that the trustee has or holds himself out as having; and

(ii)   if he acts as a trustee in the course of a business or profession, to any special knowledge or experience that it is reasonable to expect of a person acting in the course of that kind of business or profession.

It is clear, therefore, that a greater standard will be expected of professional trustees (and probably even greater from specialist professional trustees), than of lay trustees. It should be noted that (i) above imposes a subjective test while (ii) above imposes an objective test.

Two important points should be noted, however, in connection with the statutory duty of care. First, it does not replace the common law duty of care, already mentioned, that trustees 'are bound only to use such due diligence and care in the management of the estate as businessmen of ordinary prudence and vigilance would use in the management of their own affairs' (*Brice v Stokes (1805) 11 Ves 319*), so that it imposes an additional duty, where it applies. As noted earlier, however, a higher standard will be required of paid, professional trustees. Secondly, where it applies, the statutory duty of care does not apply to omissions, although the common law duty will.

The other main provisions of the Trustee Act 2000 are considered in more detail in CHAPTER 22: ADMINISTRATIVE PROVISIONS.

Trustee Delegation Act 1999

20.8   The issue of collective delegation by trustees is discussed in detail in CHAPTER 22: ADMINISTRATIVE PROVISIONS, but the Trustee Delegation Act 1999 (set out in APPENDIX 2), which came into effect on 1 March 2000, permits delegation by individual trustees in certain respects. Since delegation by individual trustees relates to the trustee delegating his responsibility to take trust decisions, it is more properly considered in this chapter.

Individual delegation by trustees is permitted only in the following circumstances:

- if it is specifically authorised by the trust deed;

- if all of the beneficiaries are of full age and capacity, are between them absolutely entitled to the trust property and specifically authorise it; or

- where statute permits it.

Before 1 March 2000, the usual way for trustees to delegate their functions was by an enduring power of attorney. Section 3(3) of the Enduring Powers of Attorney Act 1985 provided that when any individual validly granted an enduring power of attorney, the delegation of his powers as a trustee happened automatically unless specifically restricted or excluded in the deed itself. This rather rendered redundant the other means of individual delegation of powers by trustees, namely under section 25 of the Trustee Act 1925 (as amended by sections 9 and 11 of the Powers of Attorney Act 1971).

Section 25 of the Trustee Act 1925 contained restrictions that the delegation under that section could not be for more than twelve months at a time and that before the power of attorney under section 25 came into effect, or within seven days thereafter, a written notice specifying certain required matters needed to be given to or served on all co-trustees and any person having the power to appoint new trustees. These requirements did not apply to individual trustee delegation under an enduring power of attorney.

Section 4 of the Trustee Delegation Act 1999 repealed section 3(3) of the Enduring Powers of Attorney Act 1985 in respect of enduring powers created after 1 March 2000. Instead, a new statutory power of delegation is given by sections 1–3 of the Trustee Delegation Act 1999 permitting the donee of a power of attorney to carry out trustee functions of the donor in relation to land, the proceeds of sale of land or income from land if the donor has any beneficial interest in the land, the proceeds or the income.

In relation to land, the proceeds of sale of land or the income arising from land, therefore, a donor can delegate his powers in respect thereof either by an enduring power of attorney or by a general power of attorney, without being subject to the requirements of section 25 of the Trustee Act 1925. In relation to the co-ownership of land, the delegation may be to the only other co-owner, but in respect of the receipt of capital monies these must be paid to at least two different persons. These provisions may be restricted or excluded in the trust deed or in the power of attorney.

The Trustee Delegation Act 1999 provides that the donor will be liable for the acts or defaults of his attorney and that a purchaser from the attorney may rely on a statement made at the time of the sale or within three months of the sale by the attorney confirming that the donor has a beneficial interest in the relevant property.

In respect of trust property other than land, section 6 of the Trustee Delegation Act 1999 has the effect of permitting an enduring power of attorney to be used to delegate the trustee functions but states that the requirements of section 25 of the Trustee Act 1925 will apply.

An attorney under a registered enduring power of attorney created after 1 March 2000 is given a limited power under the Trustee Delegation Act 1999 of appointing new trustees.

Sections 5 and 6 of the Trustee Delegation Act 1999 amend the provisions of section 25 of the Trustee Act 1925 and provide for a new statutory form of power of attorney for use by trustees.

The amended provisions of section 25 of the Trustee Act 1925 provide that:

(a)   a trustee can either delegate all of his trust functions under one or more trusts of which he is a trustee or any one or more of such functions;

(b)   as before, the period of delegation may not endure for more than twelve months;

(c)   the donor can appoint a trust corporation to be his attorney;

(d)   a sole co-trustee can be the only attorney appointed, but, as mentioned, the previously applicable requirement for at least two separate trustees to receive capital monies is preserved;

(e)   the requirement for a written notice to be given by the donor to all other trustees and the person holding the power of appointment (if any) before, or within seven days of, the creation of the power of attorney specifying certain required matters is preserved. If written notice is not given, however, then acts carried out by the attorney will not be invalidated; and

(f)   the donor is personally liable for the acts or defaults of the attorney.

Influence of the settlor

20.9   While a settlor may wish to be a trustee or provide in his trust deed that certain powers may not be exercised without his written consent first having been obtained, care must be taken to ensure that his control and influence do not become overbearing on the trustees to the detriment of the beneficiaries. Similarly, when drafting the trust deed, the draftsman will need to ensure that the trustees are permitted to act independently in certain respects, otherwise an argument may be pursued that the trust is merely a 'sham', or device, of the settlor, and that the trust and the trustees are merely 'creatures' of the settlor, or an 'alter ego' of the settlor.

When exercising trust powers, especially in the case of discretionary trusts and powers, the trustees must make it clear that it is they who are exercising their own powers and are properly exercising their trust functions. Trustees' meetings should take place on a regular basis and accurate minutes of those meetings should be kept. This is discussed in CHAPTER 23: TRUST ADMINISTRATION.

Although the settlor, or another person, may have a veto in the form of giving or withholding his consent under the terms of the trust deed, this by itself will not be sufficient to make the trust a sham. However, if, for example, all of the powers of the trustees, both dispositive and administrative, require the prior written consent of the settlor to be given, or if the trustees simply act on the instructions of the settlor without further due consideration, or if the settlor, when not a trustee, insists on being present at all trustees' meetings and insists on his agenda being followed, then inevitably suggestions will be made that the trust is a sham or that the trustees are not acting independently.

Two cases illustrate the problem. In the Jersey case of *Rahman v Chase Bank (CI) Trust Co Ltd (1991) JLR 103*, the court decided that in view of the conduct of the settlor and the trustees which showed that it was never intended that the property should be held for anyone other than the settlor, despite the existence of the trust deed, then the trust veil (or, rather more accurately, 'smokescreen') would be pierced and the property would be treated as having belonged to the settlor throughout.

In *Turner v Turner [1984] Ch 100*, the trustees' pattern of behaviour was that they automatically followed the instructions of the settlor when exercising their powers. Even though the appointments made by the trustees were within their powers as set out in the trust deed, and would have been properly exercised if they had used their own independent judgment, the court set them aside because they had not in fact exercised their own independent judgment at all and had merely acted at the whim of the settlor.

Protectors

20.10   Protectors are often appointed by settlors of offshore trusts, to add an element of protection and to attempt to control trustees who may otherwise seem, and often are (geographically at least) remote. The problem which gave rise to the litigation in *Schmidt v Rosewood Trust Ltd [2003] 3 All ER 76* is instructive in this regard. In United Kingdom trusts, protectors may have a role in certain cases, but generally the appointment of a protector is unusual in a United Kingdom trust since a similar result can be achieved, at least during the life of the settlor, by requirements in the trust deed for the trustees to obtain the settlor's written consent in advance of the exercise by them of certain powers under the trust. The use of a protector can, however, extend the requirement by the trustees to obtain the written consent of another person before exercising certain powers, beyond the lifetime of the settlor.

Where a protector is appointed, the trust deed usually provides that it is necessary for the protector's prior written consent to be obtained before certain beneficial powers of the trustees under the trust deed are exercised and for the protector to be given the power of appointment and, if included, the power of dismissal of trustees, and possibly the power to authorise the trustees to self-deal in certain circumstances.

The protector can be the settlor initially, or a trustee and the settlor, or another person. A protector can be given the power by deed to appoint a successor as protector, or the trust deed can simply specify the order and names of future protectors. The trustees can be given the power to appoint a future protector, or the role of the protector can lapse on the death of the first protector, with the powers exercisable previously by, or requiring the consent of, the protector then becoming powers exercisable by the trustees in their discretion.

Sometimes trust deeds establishing discretionary trusts provide that the settlor, or possibly the trustees, with the prior written consent of the protector, can add persons to the class of beneficiaries. Such powers are to be avoided, since they confer too much power and flexibility on the trustees, or the protector. These powers should be limited to be exercisable by the trustees during the lifetime of the settlor and only with the settlor's prior written consent having been obtained. Otherwise persons not known, or even contemplated, by the settlor could receive the whole or part of the trust property, the possibility of which will rarely be acceptable to the settlor.

Any powers given to a protector are likely to be fiduciary in nature, rather than personal powers. If a protector is appointed, the settlement deed will need to be drafted carefully to ensure that the protector is not deemed to be a trustee for taxation purposes and to consider precisely what powers the protector should have. The latter will usually be analogous, but not identical, to the powers usually reserved to the settlor.

Exclusion of certain powers

20.11   As already mentioned, when drafting the settlement deed the draftsman will need to consider whether certain statutory, or common law, powers and duties need to be excluded. Examples of such matters which might be excluded are the new statutory duty of care under section 1 of the Trustee Act 2000, sections 11 and 19 of the Trusts of Land and Appointment of Trustees Act 1996, and the trustees' duties of care under the common law, in so far as they can be limited.

The settlor may wish for certain statutory powers conferred on trustees to be modified, extended or restricted, even if he does not wish for them to be excluded altogether, for example, the statutory power of advancement under section 32 of the Trustee Act 1925. This power is considered in more detail in CHAPTER 22: ADMINISTRATIVE PROVISIONS.

Chapter 21

Administrative Duties

Trustees' administrative duties

21.1   When administering a trust, trustees will need to fulfil certain administrative duties. The role of a trustee has certainly become far more onerous in recent times, partly as a result of the introduction of new statutory duties, some of which cannot be excluded, and partly as a result of recent case law, which has extended and clarified the duties of trustees to beneficiaries. The position of trustee is not a comfortable one for the nervous, inexperienced or unconscientious.

Lay trustees often make two quite basic errors. First, they do not always appreciate that where trustees fall into error they will incur personal liability. Secondly, they often fail to grasp that they may be liable for the acts and defaults of their fellow trustees. Many lay trustees believe that the primary responsibility for the management of the trust and of the exercise of trustees' powers and discretions lies with the trustee first named in the trust deed. They ought to be disabused of that notion by their legal advisers at the earliest opportunity.

The duties set out in this chapter are unwritten duties. They are not set out in the trust deed because they do not need to be expressly included in order to take effect. Indeed, an attempt to exclude them may result in the trust being held a sham. Although the draftsman should not set out these duties in the trust deed he should be familiar with them and ought to draw the attention of the settlor and, where appropriate, the trustees to their existence and effect.

Duty to carry out the terms of the trust

21.2   This heading expresses two duties. First, the trustees must be aware of and familiarise themselves with the terms of their trust and, secondly, they must comply with those terms. The trustees will need to refer regularly to the settlement deed or will and the powers given to them, both by the settlement deed or will and the law. This means that they must discover the extent of the trust property, the contents of all deeds, notices and other documents and papers relating to the property: *Hallows v Lloyd (1888) 39 Ch D 686*. They should also ascertain the identity of the beneficiaries and the extent of their powers. If they do not do so, the trustees cannot fulfil their other duties to the beneficiaries at all.

If trustees do not carry out the terms of their trust, for example, by distributing the trust property to the wrong persons or by exceeding or acting outside the powers given to them, then they will be liable to be sued by the beneficiaries for breach of trust. This will have dramatic and far-reaching consequences for the trustees who will face personal liability for all loss flowing from the breach. The usual rules relating to remoteness of damage and causation do not apply to breach of trust actions: *Target Holdings Ltd v Redferns [1996] AC 421.*

Trustees must pay income and capital to those who are beneficially entitled without demand: *Hawkesley v May [1956] 1 QB 304, [1955] 3 All ER 353.* If they are under a duty to distribute amongst a discretionary class, trustees should do so: *Re Locker's Settlement Trusts [1978] 1 All ER 216.* Distribution to the wrong person is a breach of trust.

In cases where the trustees can show that they have acted honestly and reasonably and ought fairly to be excused for the breach of trust and for failing to obtain the sanction of the court to the proposed action before committing the breach of trust, the trustees can apply for relief from the court under section 61 of the Trustee Act 1925. The court will sometimes grant trustees relief in cases of misdistribution of the trust property by trustees to the wrong persons after taking legal advice.

Generally the settlor in the settlement deed or the testator in his will will seek to limit the liability of the trustees so as to render trustees liable only where they have acted dishonestly or fraudulently. These restriction of liability clauses will generally be effective. See CHAPTER 19: CHOICE OF TRUSTEES concerning attempts by professional trustees to limit their liability under such clauses.

In the event of uncertainty, the proper way for trustees to proceed is for them to seek the directions of the court before taking the action in question. Many trustees prefer to avoid this course if possible because they fear that the beneficiaries will object to them incurring legal costs in resolving what, to the beneficiaries, seem trivial or insubstantial points. However, in taking risks to save the trust expense the trustees may be exposing themselves to unnecessary personal liability to the very beneficiaries whose funds they are trying to preserve.

Duty to get in, hold and preserve the trust property

21.3   This duty requires the trustees to ensure that all of the trust property settled is collected in by them and that appropriate steps are taken to collect in the trust property, if not held by them at the outset. They must then keep the trust property under their control and separate from their own property and any other trust property held by them as trustees of other trusts and ensure that the trust documents and the documents relating to the trust property are kept in the custody of at least one of the trustees. The trust property should be vested in the names of the trustees, that is, all of them jointly if more than one, and prudent trustees ought to list their trust property, especially in the case of chattels, and to keep the list up to date.

Subject to certain limited statutory exceptions, prior to the Trustee Act 2000 trustees were not permitted to transfer to or place trust property in the names of nominees and were not permitted to appoint a custodian to look after the trust documents unless their trust instrument expressly permitted it. These restrictions caused problems for trustees in practice, particularly in view of the general trend to dematerialise Stock Exchange-based investments into uncertificated form, following the introduction of the CREST settlement system.

Again, in modern trust deeds and wills adequate powers are usually included by draftsmen to permit this, but in older trust deeds such powers were often not included and trustees were left with the dilemma of either committing a breach of trust (and being responsible for the consequences of such) or retaining the trust property under their control and possibly being penalised in terms of being able to proceed swiftly and efficiently with the administration of the trust.

With effect from 1 February 2001, trustees have been given express powers to appoint a person to act as a nominee or custodian in relation to any trust property and, in the case of a nominee, to take such steps as are necessary to ensure that the trust property is vested in the persons so appointed, provided that such appointment is made in writing or is evidenced in writing (Trustee Act 2000, ss 16 and 17). These powers are discussed more fully in CHAPTER 22: ADMINISTRATIVE PROVISIONS.

Duty to keep accounts

21.4   A fundamental duty of trustees is 'to keep clear and accurate accounts of the trust property' or, as some put it, 'to be ready with their accounts': *Pearse v Green (1819) 1 Jack & W 135*. In order to establish their entitlements and to ensure that the trust is being administered properly, the beneficiaries are entitled to see the trust accounts and to question the trustees on issues arising from the accounts.

The cost of drawing up accounts is a proper trust expense chargeable to the trust. If a beneficiary wishes to inspect the trust accounts the cost of making copies available to him is not a trust expense and must be borne by the beneficiary.

Although audited accounts will not generally be required to be prepared by trustees of non-charitable trusts (charitable trusts have their own specific requirements depending on the value of the trust income and capital), trustees do have the power under section 22(4) of the Trustee Act 1925 (see APPENDIX 2) to have accounts audited by an independent accountant, if they wish to do so, at the expense of the trust fund.

The duty to keep accounts is related to the duty to disclose information.

Duty to disclose information

21.5   Although not an absolute right, beneficiaries will generally be entitled to see all documents relating to the trust (trust documents) and to have copies of them at their own expense. Confusion often arises in the minds of trustees both as to who is entitled to information and as to what information they are entitled to see.

Trustees often claim that that they have no duty to disclose information to discretionary beneficiaries because they do not have any identifiable interest under the trust but have only a hope of benefiting. In so doing, trustees are confusing the kind of information which they can disclose with the persons entitled to see it. It is now clear that both beneficiaries with fixed interests and discretionary beneficiaries whose interests arise under a discretionary settlement are entitled to see the trust documents. The point was confirmed in *Re Rabaiotti's Settlements [2000] WTLR 953* where it was held that, unless exceptional circumstances exist, all beneficiaries will have the right to see all trust documents. In *Schmidt v Rosewood Trust Ltd [2003] 3 All ER 76* the Privy Council held that the trustees' duty to disclose information is not dependent on the nature of the beneficiaries' interests but arises as a result of the court's inherent jurisdiction to supervise the administration of trusts.

Determining what are and what are not trust documents is not so straightforward because there is no comprehensive definition as to what constitutes a trust document. The decisions referred to above and *Re Londonderry's Settlement [1965] Ch 918, [1964] 3 All ER 855* give some guidance as to what will and what will not be regarded as a trust document for these purposes. It is generally accepted, however, that the following are trust documents:

(a)   Trust accounts. This will generally mean, as a minimum, annual trust accounts.

(b)   Trust deeds. This will generally include the settlement deed and any subsequent deeds and the deeds or documents of title relating to the trust property.

(c)   Legal advice, including opinions of counsel, given to trustees and the instructions upon which that advice was based. This is true of all advice obtained at the expense of the trust but does not apply to advice obtained by the trustee for his own protection or to the evidence on a *Beddoe* application.

(d)   Other documents generated by or for the trustees which set out the trustees' understanding of their duties or of the factual background upon which their decisions are made. This does not, however, include records of their deliberations, reasons or the material on which those reasons are based. This is because trustees are not bound to disclose their reasons. If they were, they might face a continuous barrage of litigation from disappointed beneficiaries.

There is some doubt whether letters or memoranda of wishes should be treated as trust documents within the last category or whether they fall within the exceptions to it. Trustees sometimes wish to disclose the contents of a letter of wishes but it is often expressed to be a document confidential to the settlor and the trustees which is not disclosable to the beneficiaries. It appears that the court may have an overriding jurisdiction to order disclosure in appropriate cases: *Re Rabaiotti's Settlements*. There are cases in which the trustees' over-reliance on a letter of wishes is the principal issue in a claim brought against them by the beneficiaries. In such cases the court is likely to order disclosure in the ordinary course of litigation.

Duty to act fairly and impartially between the beneficiaries

21.6   A fundamental duty of trustees is not to act partially when considering the interests of the beneficiaries and to treat beneficiaries in the same class equally when exercising their administrative and dispositive powers. Not only should trustees treat beneficiaries in the same class equally but they should act fairly and impartially between all beneficiaries. In doing so, the trustees must act reasonably and not act capriciously.

It does seem, however, that a trustee may pay the share of one beneficiary who has attained a vested interest before paying others whose interests have not vested if sufficient property is retained to satisfy those shares. Many modern trust deeds expressly permit trustees to do this.

Duty to act unanimously

21.7   Except in the case of charitable trusts (where trustees may act by a majority), unless the trust instrument permits it trustees must exercise their powers unanimously. Many settlors and lay trustees do not appreciate that a majority cannot bind the minority and the point should be drawn to their attention. A distinction should be made between powers and duties of trustees. When discharging duties in relation to the trust property, one trustee may be able to bind all of the trustees since the trustees as a body, in such circumstances, are under a duty which must be carried out, irrespective of whether they all agree or not. Powers, on the other hand, should be exercised unanimously.

Duty of trustees not to profit from their trust

21.8   A fundamental principle of trust law is that a trustee must not profit from his trust. This is both a duty not to profit from trust property and a duty not to cause loss to the trust property as a result of any conflict of interest between the trustees' personal interests and their duties as trustees. This is often called 'the self-dealing rule' and results from the trustees' overriding duty to act in the utmost good faith.

Any disposition involving self-dealing by a trustee of trust property will be voidable, however fair, except in so far as:

(i) an express or necessarily implied power exists in the settlement;

(ii) leave is obtained of the court;

(iii) a contractual arrangement in respect of the self-dealing existed before the trustee was appointed;

(iv) it is carried out under section 68 of the Settled Land Act 1925;

(v) all of the beneficiaries agreed to the transaction (this will require all of the beneficiaries to be over 18 and of full mental capacity); or

(vi) very exceptional circumstances exist.

When drafting the powers and provisions of the trust instrument, the draftsman will generally incorporate a provision overriding this general duty, which will then exclude the application of the duty. Confusion can sometimes arise as to whether the duty applies where no exclusion of the duty is incorporated in the trust instrument and a trustee is appointed by the trust instrument who is also a beneficiary or potential beneficiary under the trust instrument. It is generally thought that it does not, but for the avoidance of doubt it is better to include an appropriate clause excluding the application of the duty in these circumstances.

A clause permitting a trustee to purchase trust property will often also be included in the trust instrument to prevent the rule applying, since purchases by nominees of trustees; indirect purchases through third parties; purchases by companies in which trustees hold substantial shareholdings; and the convenient retirement of trustees to enable them to purchase trust property will all fall foul of the rule if it has not been excluded.

Where a problem arises under this rule in connection with the trustees exercising their powers, it should not be forgotten that even if the trust instrument does not exclude the application of the rule, if the beneficiaries are all of full age and are between them absolutely entitled to the trust property they may authorise the trustees to undertake the appropriate action notwithstanding that a profit may result, and similarly the court can sanction such an action if an application is made to it in advance of the action being taken.

Remuneration of professional trustees used to cause problems under this rule, where an appropriate provision authorising the remuneration of trustees was not contained in the trust instrument, but the Trustee Act 2000 now largely remedies these problems. There are, however, good reasons for extending the statutory power as discussed in CHAPTER 19: CHOICE OF TRUSTEES.

Duty to exercise reasonable care and skill

21.9   At common law the duty of trustees is to act by taking such steps in managing the affairs of the trust as a businessman of ordinary prudence and vigilance would use in managing affairs of his own: *Bartlett v Barclays Bank Trust Co Ltd [1980] Ch 515, [1980] 1 All ER 139*. Paid trustees and professional trustees, particularly paid professional trustees, were expected to meet a higher standard of care, taking into account the particular skill and care to be reasonably expected of a trustee possessing the relevant skills and qualifications concerned.

Section 1 of the Trustee Act 2000 now creates a new statutory duty of care, as previously discussed in CHAPTER 20: TRUSTEES' DUTIES AND POWERS. The statutory duty of care can be excluded, restricted or modified by the trust instrument. Although the statutory duty of care will apply to acts of trustees it will not apply to omissions. The statutory duty of care, unless excluded, restricted or modified in the trust instrument, will co-exist with the previous common law duty of care.

The statutory duty of care imposes a higher standard for professional trustees, and probably also for paid trustees.

As mentioned in CHAPTER 19: CHOICE OF TRUSTEES, trustees, and particularly professional trustees, will usually seek to limit their liability in the trust instrument. In some cases it may be appropriate for the trustees to consider making an application for directions from the court under section 61 of the Trustee Act 1925 (see APPENDIX 2), although in respect of such applications it is generally considered that the court will be more reluctant to excuse professional and paid trustees, and in cases of doubt the court is likely to construe the relevant provision against a professional trustee.

Duty to act personally and not to delegate powers

21.10   Although there is a general duty imposed upon trustees to act personally and not to delegate the exercise of their powers, the position has been fundamentally changed in recent years, by the Trustee Delegation Act 1999 in respect of individual delegation (dealt with in detail in CHAPTER 20: TRUSTEES' DUTIES AND POWERS), and by sections 11 to 15 of the Trustee Act 2000 in respect of collective delegation by a body of trustees.

Modern trust deeds and wills will usually include a specific power permitting trustees to delegate collectively, but in trust deeds and wills operative before the commencement of the Trustee Act 2000, section 23 of the Trustee Act 1925 gave trustees a limited power to employ agents to do certain administrative acts, but it did not allow the delegation of trust discretions (for example, decisions about the sales and purchases of particular trust property).

Section 11 of the Trustee Act 2000 now gives trustees of non-charitable trusts powers to employ an agent or otherwise authorise any person to carry out any of their 'delegable functions' as their agent, which functions are defined as any of the trustees' functions other than:

(a)   any function relating to whether, or in what way, any assets of the trust should be distributed;

(b)   any power to decide whether any fees or payments due to be made out of the trust funds should be made out of income or capital;

(c)   any power to appoint a person to be a trustee of the trust; or

(d)   any power conferred by statute, or by the trust instrument, permitting the trustees to delegate any of their functions or to appoint a person to act as nominee or custodian.

These non-delegable functions are essentially the dispositive functions of trustees fundamental to the character of trusteeship. The Trustee Act 2000 does not, for example, enable trustees to delegate responsibility for determining which member or members of a beneficial class are to receive distributions out of the income or capital of the fund. The common law rule still applies to that situation – the rule at common law being that a trustee is personally responsible for the exercise of his judgement and the performance of his duty and it is no excuse to delegate that responsibility to another, even to a co-trustee. This rule still applies to the non-delegable functions in respect of which the trustees remain personally responsible.

In the case of charitable trusts, the trustees can delegate to agents the following 'delegable functions':

 (i)   any function consisting of carrying out a decision that the trustees have already taken;

 (ii)   any function relating to the investment of the trust property;

(iii)   any function relating to fund-raising for the trust, otherwise than by means of profits of a trade which is an integral part of carrying out the purpose of the charitable trust; or

(iv)   any other function prescribed by an order made by the Secretary of State.

Chapter 22

Administrative Provisions

Introduction

22.1   If trustees purport to exercise powers which are not given to them by the trust instrument, by statute or by the common law, then the consequences for them will be serious since a breach of trust action may well be pursued against them. Trustees will therefore need to examine their powers carefully from time to time to ensure that they are adequate and the draftsman at the outset will need to consider what powers the trustees might reasonably require during the currency of the trust.

The draftsman should ensure that the trustees are given sufficient powers to enable them to observe and perform the duties imposed upon them by the trust instrument and by the law and achieve the aims of the settlor or testator.

In cases where inadequate powers are given and the trustees do not have power under the trust instrument to vary their administrative powers, any trustee or beneficiary may apply to the court under section 57 of the Trustee Act 1925 for an order that the relevant power or powers should be given by the court to the trustees to enable them to proceed with the relevant transaction or disposition and, if it is in the opinion of the court 'expedient to do so', it may confer the relevant power or powers on the trustees. In reaching its decision the court will consider the interests of all of the income beneficiaries collectively on the one hand, and the interests of all of the capital beneficiaries collectively on the other.

If a variation of the terms of the trusts is considered necessary, trustees might also make an application under the Variation of Trusts Act 1958, discussed more fully in CHAPTER 24: BRINGING TRUSTS TO AN END.

Both applications are expensive and best avoided by giving careful thought to the form and contents of the settlement or will at the outset.

Incorporating powers by reference

22.2   Older settlement deeds often include what, to the modern practitioner, appear to be inadequate powers. In the case of settlements which have been in existence for a long time this can often make the lot of the trustees in trying to achieve the efficient administration of the trust for the benefit of all of the beneficiaries much more difficult. A modern draftsman would regard such restrictive drafting as quite unacceptable and a well-drafted will or settlement drawn by a skilled professional should clearly give adequate and full powers to the trustees to enable them properly to carry out their role.

As mentioned in CHAPTER 17: CONTENT OF TRUST DEED, many modern draftsmen choose to set out administrative powers in a schedule to the trust deed and then incorporate them into the trusts by use of a single clause. This is a relatively new phenomenon: older settlements tend to set out all express powers in the course of the testatum. An even more modern innovation is to incorporate by reference powers which do not appear anywhere in the deed. Many simpler modern trust deeds and wills will often incorporate the Society of Trust and Estate Practitioners (STEP) standard administrative provisions by using one simple referential clause (see 22.4 below).

The difficulty with incorporation of powers by reference is twofold. First, incorporated powers are too often used to shorten the thought process involved in choosing powers and other provisions. It is all too easy for the busy draftsman to incorporate unnecessary and perhaps inconsistent provisions in a mechanical way without having due regard to the consequences. The author recommends that if a practitioner is to incorporate the STEP standard provisions or any other standard provisions, no express provisions should be incorporated without exercising great care. Secondly, the incorporation of powers not reproduced in the settlement can lead to uncertainty (real or imagined) as to what powers are in fact available. Lay trustees in particular prefer to see their powers clearly set out than to have to look elsewhere to discover what they can and cannot do.

The difficulty caused by the incorporation by reference of relevant provisions is sometimes avoided in modern trust drafting by draftsmen who try to set out in full the intended trust provisions in plain English. This is, of course, quite acceptable provided that the words used clearly reflect the draftsman's intention.

Statutory powers

22.3 There have for a long time been statutory powers intended to introduce certainty into trust drafting and to save the draftsman time. These have not always been satisfactory. For example, prior to the commencement of the Trustee Act 2000 the provision relating to insurance contained in section 19 of the Trustee Act 1925 was widely regarded as inadequate so that, despite the possibility of relying on the statutory power, most draftsmen set out their own express power of insurance.

The enactment of the provisions of the Trusts of Land and Appointment of Trustees Act 1996 and the Trustee Act 2000 is likely to result in most modern trust deeds being generally shorter. As already mentioned, however, the drafts-man needs to consider whether these provisions are adequate for the purposes intended or anticipated by the settlor, or whether they need to be extended or amended in certain respects. That can lead to complication and some draftsmen will wish to continue with their own express powers.

The statutory provisions referred to in this chapter are all set out in full in APPENDIX 2.

STEP standard provisions

22.4   The incorporation in a settlement deed of these standard provisions can reduce the length of the settlement deed considerably. They are generally appropriate for simple, straightforward settlements. The powers, which have been drafted for such use on behalf of STEP, are available free of charge from the STEP website at www.step.org. As already mentioned, whilst administra-tive powers are generally set out in a schedule to the settlement deed, the STEP standard provisions can be incorporated without setting them out in a schedule.

The provisions have the following advantages:

- they can be incorporated in both wills and lifetime settlements, and

- their inclusion will avoid the possibility of relevant powers being omitted in error, and

- they will save the draftsman a considerable amount of time.

There are disadvantages in using the STEP standard provisions. Not all practi-tioners are familiar with their terms and it is all too easy to incorporate terms which might conflict with those expressly set out in the settlement. This is true, of course, both in respect of the STEP provisions and a reliance on statute and the general law.

A possible problem with incorporating such standard provisions is that the settlor or testator and the trustees or executors will need to refer to a separate document setting out the powers given. Where, alternatively, a schedule setting out all administrative powers is included in the settlement deed, the particular powers given will be evident to all.

Although the STEP standard provisions have advantages, most draftsmen continue to use their own provisions which, in all but the simplest cases, are fully set out in a schedule to the settlement deed. Nonetheless, the usefulness and ease of incorporation of standard provisions should not be forgotten or overlooked by the draftsman, where appropriate.

Wide powers and flexibility

22.5   In order to ensure that the trustees can carry out their duties as trustees properly and fulfil their paramount duty to act in the best interests of the beneficiaries, they will need to be given sufficiently wide administrative powers in the settlement deed, taken in conjunction with those given under the general law, to ensure that they can properly manage and deal with the trust property.

Trustees will need to have sufficient administrative powers to enable them to administer the trust flexibly, given that the circumstances and nature of the trust property confronting them at the outset of the trust may change several times during the currency of the trust.

There has been a raft of legislative changes in recent years which has had the effect of improving and extending the statutory powers given to trustees. The Trusts of Land and Appointment of Trustees Act 1996, the Trustee Delegation Act 1999 and the Trustee Act 2000 have all helped the contemporary draftsman in certain ways in this area.

The administrative powers given by statute will apply in addition to those given by the settlement deed or will, unless expressly excluded in the settlement deed or will.

However, draftsmen will usually still include wide administrative powers in the settlement deed or will, since some of the powers given by the recent legislation are not as wide as most draftsmen and trustees may wish to see.

Trustee Act 2000

22.6   The reform of the law relating to trustees' powers and duties made by the Trustee Act 2000 was the most comprehensive and basic reform of the law in this area since 1925. Generally, the powers and duties set out in the Trustee Act 2000 will apply to trusts whenever established, but, as with the Trustee Act 1925, most of them apply only in so far as they are not overridden or excluded by the settlement deed or will.

The Trustee Act 2000 introduced new, and consolidated existing, trust powers in relation to trustees' investment powers; collective delegation by trustees; the use of nominees and custodians; insurance; and remuneration of professional trustees. The Act also introduced a new statutory duty of care that will apply unless excluded. The duty of care is discussed more fully in CHAPTER 20: TRUSTEES' DUTIES AND POWERS.

The significance of these changes should not be understated, particularly for older trust deeds containing no, limited or inadequate powers, but the Act does not provide a panacea for all problems faced by trustees in these areas. Rather than relying exclusively on the statutory powers, many draftsmen will continue to use their own extended trust powers which are often wider and, at least in the draftsmen's view, clearer and more exact in defining precisely the scope of such powers. Whether this early view changes over time remains to be seen.

Investment

22.7   The first change introduced by the Trustee Act 2000 related to powers of investment. In many cases, expressly extending powers of investment and management will not now be necessary because of the wide statutory powers introduced by the Trustee Act 2000. The Act repealed important provisions of the Trustee Investments Act 1961 and portions of the Trustee Act 1925 and confers on trustees and personal representatives newer and wider powers of investment, powers to delegate investment and investment-holding powers, and powers to charge, while imposing an excludable statutory duty of care.

The general power of investment

22.8   In order to ensure that they comply with their duty to act in the best interests of the beneficiaries, the trustees will be under a duty to invest or to maintain the investment of the trust property appropriately.

The Trustee Act 2000 has replaced the Trustee Investments Act 1961 as the source of trustees' power of investment. One consequence of the 2000 Act is that it makes all kinds of investment (apart from equitable interests in land) authorised investments. The power conferred on trustees and personal representatives by the Trustee Act 2000 is referred to as 'the general power of investment': s 3.

Trustees now have a power to make any kind of investment, including loans secured on land but otherwise excluding land (power to invest in which is dealt with separately), that they could make if they were absolutely entitled to the assets of the trust: Trustee Act 2000, s 3(1)–(3).

The new statutory power of investment is in addition to any other powers conferred on the trustees, but subject to any restriction or exclusion imposed by the trust instrument: Trustee Act 2000, s 6(1).

The general power of investment is subject to two express duties: the duty to have regard to standard investment criteria (s 4) and the duty to take advice (s 5).

Duty to have regard to standard investment criteria

22.9   In exercising the general power of investment (or indeed any investment power) trustees or personal representatives must have regard to 'the standard investment criteria'. These criteria are: the suitability to the trust of investments of the same kind as any particular investment proposed to be made or retained and of that particular investment as an investment of that kind (s 4(3)(a)) and the need for diversification of investments of the trust, in so far as is appropriate to the circumstances of the trust (s 4(3)(b)). If diversification is not to be expected of the trustees, the prudent draftsman will specify this in the trust instrument.

The trustees must also, from time to time, review the investments of the trust and consider whether, having regard to the standard investment criteria, they should be varied. No indication is given as to how often trustees must review the investment, but in the case of a large trust fund or one invested on the stock market at times of particular volatility or depression, frequent reviews might be required. Section 4 of the Trustee Act 2000 makes it clear that the requirement of having regard to the standard investment criteria applies to all powers of investment.

Section 6 provides that the general power of investment in section 3 is capable of being excluded or restricted, but does not permit any such exclusion or restriction in respect of the standard investment criteria of section 4.

Duty to take advice

22.10   Before exercising their statutory investment power (or indeed any investment power) and when reviewing their investments, trustees must obtain and consider proper advice about the way in which, having regard to the standard investment criteria, their powers to invest or vary investments should be exercised: Trustee Act 2000, s 5. They do not need to obtain such advice if they reasonably conclude that in all the circumstances it is unnecessary or inappropriate to do so. Proper advice is the advice of a person who is reasonably believed by the trustees to be qualified to give it by his ability and practical experience of financial and other matters relating to the proposed investment: s 5(4). The nature of the trust fund and the size of the proposed investment, and of the trust fund as a whole, are likely to be taken into account in deciding whether the trustees have acted reasonably in this regard.

The duty applies to all types of investment and to the exercise of any power of investment, not just the statutory power: s 5(1). As with the duty to have regard to the standard investment criteria, the duty to take advice cannot be excluded.

Delegation to investment managers and nominees

22.11   The conventional power of investment, however wide as to type of investment, confers the power to select investments and decide when to sell them on the trustees only, and is not a power which the trustees can delegate without express power. Sections 11 to 26 of the Trustee Act 2000 now confer on trustees and personal representatives a power to delegate their investment functions to investment managers and to vest trust assets in nominees. The question which the draftsman must face is whether he should rely on the statutory powers or whether express provision should still be made. In most cases the statutory powers will probably be sufficient but express powers should still be considered.

The statutory power to delegate

22.12   The statutory power to delegate enables trustees to authorise an agent to exercise any of their delegable functions. Delegable functions are all functions other than those specified in section 11 of the Trustee Act 2000. The non-delegable functions specified include the exercise of dispositive powers relating to asset distribution such as powers of appointment; the power to decide whether fees or other payments should be made out of capital or income; the power to appoint new trustees; and powers of delegation and appointment of nominees. These are quite obvious reservations: there are some functions which are fundamental to the character of trusteeship and simply cannot be delegated. Agents to whom functions have been delegated are under the same duty in relation to the exercise of those functions as were the trustees themselves: Trustee Act 2000, s 13.

Agents

22.13   In exercise of the power of delegation trustees may authorise one or more of their number to exercise functions as their agent (Trustee Act 2000, s 12(1)) but may not authorise two or more persons to exercise the same function severally. Only a joint exercise of a delegable function is permitted: s 12(2). A beneficiary is not a person who may be appointed to exercise the functions of trustees as their agent even if that beneficiary is also a trustee: s 12(3).

Trustees may authorise an agent to receive remuneration. The trustees may remunerate agents out of the trust fund for services if the terms of engagement include agreement for remuneration and the amount of the remuneration does not exceed what is reasonable in the circumstances: Trustee Act 2000, s 32. Unless it is reasonably necessary, an agent may not be authorised to appoint a substitute, restrict his liability to the trustees or beneficiaries, or act in circumstances giving rise to a conflict of interest: Trustee Act 2000, s 14.

Asset management

22.14   In respect of their functions relating to the investment of assets, the acquisition of property and the management of property subject to the trust (the asset management functions) trustees may not authorise a person to act as their agent except by an agreement in or evidenced in writing: Trustee Act 2000, s 15(1), (5). They may not do so unless they have prepared a statement in or evidenced in writing as to how the asset management functions should be exercised (a policy statement) and their agreement includes a term to the effect that the agent will comply with the policy statement: s 15(2), (4). A standard investment policy statement is included in APPENDIX 1 at A1.29.

Nominees and custodians

22.15   Trustees may appoint a person to act as their nominee in relation to the assets of the trust and may take such steps as are necessary to secure that the assets are vested in the nominee: Trustee Act 2000, s 16(1). The appointment of a nominee must be in or evidenced in writing: s 16(2).

Trustees may also appoint a person to undertake safe custody of the assets of the trust or of any documents or records concerning the assets (a custodian): Trustee Act 2000, s 17(1), (2). The appointment of a custodian must also be in or evidenced in writing: s 17(3). If the trustees invest in bearer securities they must appoint a person to act as custodian of the securities unless the trust instrument permits them to invest in bearer securities without appointing a custodian: s 18(1), (2). Trustees may authorise a nominee or custodian to receive remuneration: s 20(1). The trustees may remunerate nominees and custodians out of the trust fund for services if the terms of engagement include agreement for remuneration and the amount of the remuneration does not exceed what is reasonable in the circumstances: s 32. Unless it is reasonably necessary, a nominee or custodian may not be authorised to appoint a substitute, restrict his liability to the trustees or beneficiaries, or act in circumstances giving rise to a conflict of interest: s 20(2), (3).

A person may not be appointed as a nominee or custodian unless the person carries on a business which consists of or includes acting as a nominee or custodian, is a body corporate controlled by trustees or is a body corporate recognised under section 9 of the Administration of Justice Act 1985: Trustee Act 2000, s 19(1), (2). Trustees may appoint one of their number if that one is a trust corporation, or two or more of their number if they are to act jointly: Trustee Act 2000, s 19(5). The trustees may also appoint the same person to be nominee and custodian and their agent: s 19(6), (7).

Review of and liability for agents and nominees

22.16   Where trustees have authorised a person to exercise functions as their agent or appointed a person to act as their nominee or custodian then, while that person continues to act for the trust, the trustees must keep under review the arrangements by which the agent, nominee or custodian acts and how those arrangements are being put into effect and, if appropriate, consider whether to exercise any power of intervention: Trustee Act 2000, ss 21, 22(1). If the trustees consider that they need to exercise a power of intervention they must do so.

Similarly, where an agent has been authorised to exercise asset management functions the trustees are under a duty to consider whether there is any need to revise or replace the policy statement and must replace it if there is a need to do so: Trustee Act 2000, s 22(2). Trustees are also under a duty to assess whether the policy statement is being complied with. Trustees are not liable for the acts or defaults of agents, nominees or custodians unless they have failed to comply with their duty of care (s 23), and a failure by trustees to act within the limits of their powers in authorising a person to act as their agent or in appointing a nominee or custodian does not invalidate the authorisation or appointment (s 24).

The powers to authorise a person to exercise functions as an agent or to appoint a person to act as a nominee or custodian are in addition to powers conferred on trustees otherwise than by the Trustee Act 2000 but subject to any restriction or exclusion imposed by the trust instrument: s 26. The draftsman will want to consider whether these powers should be extended, excluded or restricted.

Power to insure

22.17   At common law the position is that although trustees have a power to insure (paying the premiums for this out of capital), there is no duty to do so.

Prior to the commencement of the Trustee Act 2000, the position was regulated, unless specifically covered in the trust instrument, by the Trusts of Land and Appointment of Trustees Act 1996 in relation to land (by which trustees had all the powers of an absolute owner to insure the land) and by section 19(1) of the Trustee Act 1925 in relation to personalty (by which trustees were authorised to insure against fire up to an amount not exceeding three-quarters of the value of the trust property and to pay the premiums out of income).

Section 34 of the Trustee Act 2000 substituted a new section 19 of the Trustee Act 1925. A trustee may insure any property subject to the trust against risks of loss or damage due to any event, and pay the premium out of any income or capital funds of the trust. The power is subject to a contrary direction on the part of beneficiaries of full age and capacity who are absolutely entitled to the property of the trust or each of whom is of full age and capacity and who (taken together) are absolutely entitled to the property subject to the trust. The statutory power is now adequate and in almost all cases no express power of insurance will be necessary.

Appropriation

22.18   The power of appropriation allows a trustee or personal representative to satisfy an entitlement of a beneficiary, wholly or partly, by the transfer of specific assets.

A statutory power is given to personal representatives by section 41 of the Administration of Estates Act 1925, but this power cannot be used without the consent of those beneficiaries who are absolutely entitled to the trust property or, in respect of settled interests of the trustees, of the person entitled to an interest in possession in the trust property.

The requirement for consents is generally dispensed with by draftsmen who routinely incorporate an extended statutory power in this way. The power is a fiduciary power, such that the trustees must exercise the power taking into account the interests of all of the beneficiaries, unless the trust deed excludes or amends this. Most modern trust deeds and wills will include a provision indicating that the trustees can exercise fiduciary powers in their own favour in cases where trustees are also beneficiaries.

The fact that the power is a fiduciary power was clearly shown in the case of *Kane v Radley-Kane [1998] 3 All ER 753* where a sole administrator under an intestacy purported to exercise the statutory power in her own favour to partially satisfy her statutory legacy arising on an intestacy. The court held that an exercise by a personal representative or trustee of the statutory power in his own favour can only be achieved legitimately in the following cases:

(a)   under an express or necessarily implied power in the settlement or will;

(b)   by leave of the court;

(c)   under a contract or option made before the fiduciary relationship arose;

(d)   under section 68 of the Settled Land Act 1925;

(e)   where the beneficiaries have agreed to the transaction; and

(f)   where very exceptional circumstances exist.

The court also held that an appropriation by an executor or administrator to himself in respect of a pecuniary or statutory legacy could only be made where the assets appropriated were cash or equivalent to cash, for example, government stock, or possibly quoted shares, but not other assets. Such an appropriation in respect of a share of residue of an estate by an executor to himself would be permitted in certain cases in respect of either cash or other assets.

Provisions relating to specific types of property

22.19   When considering what administrative powers should be included in the trust instrument, the draftsman will need to have regard both to the type of property being settled and to any other property which may become comprised in the trust fund at any future time. For this reason, the widest variety of trust powers possible will usually be included in the trust instrument.

Appropriate provisions dealing with and widening the trustees' powers will routinely be included in respect of the following:

•   the ownership and management of land;

•   private company shares;

•   chattels;

•   insurance and assurance policies;

•   the appropriation of trust property without obtaining consents;

•   delegation;

- trading;

- the appointment of servants or agents;

- the power to charge in the case of professional trustees;

- the variation of administrative provisions;

- the power to act even though personally interested;

- the power to accept receipts on behalf of infants or charities; and

- investment.

Provisions relating to land in the trustees' ownership deserve special attention.

Provisions relating to land

22.20 Apart from the appointment of trustees, the Trusts of Land and Appointment of Trustees Act 1996 had four consequences:

- it affected powers of management of land (s 6) which were then further affected by the Trustee Act 2000;

- it introduced powers to delegate the powers of management of land to beneficiaries (ss 9–9A);

- it introduced consultation with beneficiaries (ss 10–11); and

- it expressly dealt with rights of occupation of trust land (ss 12–13).

Powers of management of land

22.21 Trustees' powers of management of land are derived from the Trusts of Land and Appointment of Trustees Act 1996 and the Trustee Act 2000 which heavily amended the 1996 Act in this regard. Trustees of land have in relation to the land subject to the trust all the powers of an absolute owner: Trusts of Land and Appointment of Trustees Act 1996, s 6(1). The powers of management of land may be extended or restricted by the trust: Trusts of Land and Appointment of Trustees Act 1996, s 9. The duty of care applies to trustees of land when exercising their powers of management of land but that, too, can be excluded if desired.

Trustees may acquire freehold or leasehold land in the UK as an investment, for occupation by a beneficiary, or for any other reason: Trusts of Land and Appointment of Trustees Act 1996, s 6(3); Trustee Act 2000, s 8(1), (2). 'Land' is defined in the Interpretation Act 1978: it includes buildings and other structures, land covered with water, and any estate, interest, easement, servitude or right in or over land.

The term 'freehold or leasehold land' is specifically defined to mean, in relation to England, Wales and Northern Ireland, a legal estate (including, in relation to Northern Ireland, land held under a fee farm grant), and, in relation to Scotland, the estate or interest of the proprietor of the dominium utile, or in the case of land not held on feudal tenure, the estate or interest of the owner, or a tenancy: Trustee Act 2000, s 8(2). Trustees cannot therefore acquire any undivided share in land in England and Wales under the statutory power, since an undivided share exists only in equity and cannot subsist as a legal estate.

Where it is thought that trustees might need to invest in an undivided share of land, an express power to that effect should be included by the draftsman. This is most often necessary where trustees are to hold a share of a property occupied by a beneficiary who is a co-owner.

Trustees acquiring land as an investment are under duties to have regard to the standard investment criteria and to obtain and consider proper advice, and also the statutory duty of care, if it has not been limited or excluded by the trust instrument. If, however, they are acquiring land for a non-investment purpose, such as for occupation by a beneficiary, trustees will only be subject to the statutory duty of care. The powers may be restricted or excluded or made subject to consents: Trusts of Land and Appointment of Trustees Act 1996, s 8. As part of the general power of investment, trustees may invest in loans secured on land.

Delegation to beneficiaries

22.22 Trustees of land acting together jointly as trustees are given power to delegate by power of attorney to any beneficiary or beneficiaries of full age and beneficially entitled to an interest in possession in land any of their functions which relate to the land, for any period or indefinitely: Trusts of Land and Appointment of Trustees Act 1996, s 9(1). Beneficiaries to whom functions have been delegated are, in relation to the exercise of those functions, subject to the same duties and liabilities as trustees.

The duty of care applies to trustees in deciding whether to delegate any of their functions to beneficiaries. If the delegation is not irrevocable, the trustees remain under a continuing duty to keep the delegation under review and, if the circumstances make it appropriate to do so, must consider whether there is a need to exercise any power of intervention that they have and, if they consider that there is a need to exercise such a power, they must do so: Trusts of Land and Appointment of Trustees Act 1996, s 9A.

Consultation with beneficiaries

22.23 In the exercise of any function relating to land subject to the trust, trustees of land are under a duty 'so far as practicable' to consult the beneficiaries of full age and beneficially entitled to an interest in possession in the land,

and so far as consistent with the general interest of the trust to give effect to the wishes of those beneficiaries, or (in the event of a dispute) the majority by value: s 11 Trusts of Land and Appointment of Trustees Act 1996.

The duty to consult the beneficiaries adds appreciably to the burdens and difficulties of the trustees and, in general, it is routinely excluded with a simple clause declaring that the section is not to apply. In relation to a gift into a settlement where it is intended that any land shall be sold and the proceeds divided, it is particularly advisable to exclude the duty to consult. Sometimes there are special reasons for not excluding the duty to consult, such as in the case of a co-ownership trust of a house in which the co-owners are going to live, or in the case of a trust to provide a residence for a beneficiary, or any other land where it is intended that a beneficiary will occupy it. In such circumstances it will usually be desirable to provide the occupying beneficiary with the assurance of knowing that trustees must consult him (or, as is usually the case, her).

The right of occupation

22.24 Section 12 of the Trusts of Land and Appointment of Trustees Act 1996 makes provision for a right of occupation for a beneficiary 'who is beneficially entitled to an interest in possession' in land subject to a trust of land at any time if at that time either the purposes of the trust include making the land available for his occupation (or for the occupation of a class of which he is a member or of beneficiaries in general); or the land is held by the trustees so as to be so available.

The statutory right of occupation is not confined in its application to residential property held on trust, but can be relevant to any kind of land in England and Wales held on trust which is capable of being occupied by a beneficiary, such as a farm or business premises. However, the statutory right is available only in respect of a beneficiary who is beneficially entitled to an interest in possession in the land. Interest in possession is not defined for these purposes but probably connotes a lesser interest than that contemplated by the use of the same words in the Inheritance Tax Act 1984. No right of occupation is conferred on a beneficiary if the land is either unavailable or unsuitable for his occupation.

Trustees may impose reasonable conditions on a beneficiary in relation to his occupation of land including payment of outgoings and assuming any other obligation in relation to the land or any activity conducted there: Trusts of Land and Appointment of Trustees Act 1996, s 13(3), (5). Where two or more beneficiaries are entitled to occupy land, trustees may exclude or restrict the entitlement to occupy of one or more but not all of them, but may not do so unreasonably or to an unreasonable extent.

If a beneficiary is excluded, trustees can require compensatory provision to be made for anyone excluded by a beneficiary in occupation. For example, the trustees might impose a condition on the occupying beneficiary which requires him to pay a 'rent' to an excluded beneficiary or beneficiaries, or a condition that he forgoes benefit from another part of the trust fund so that a compensating additional benefit from that other part is received by the excluded beneficiary or beneficiaries: Trusts of Land and Appointment of Trustees Act 1996, s 13(6).

The powers of exclusion or restriction must be exercised having regard to the intentions of the person who created the trust, the purposes for which the land is held and the circumstances and wishes of the beneficiaries who are entitled to occupy the land: Trusts of Land and Appointment of Trustees Act 1996, s 13(4). A settlor or testator can include an express declaration of his intentions in the trust instrument or will, and can provide that a property is to be retained *in specie* for the purpose of providing a particular beneficiary with a home. In doing so, the settlor testator will strongly influence what is subsequently done with the land because the powers of exclusion or restriction cannot be exercised so as to prevent a person who is in occupation of land from continuing to occupy the land, or in a manner likely to result in his ceasing to occupy the land, unless he consents or the court has given approval: Trusts of Land and Appointment of Trustees Act 1996, s 13(7). Should the matter come to court, the testator's intentions and the purposes for which the land is held will be taken into account: Trusts of Land and Appointment of Trustees Act 1996, s 13(8).

Many draftsmen include a broad and unrestricted power to permit beneficiaries to enjoy trust property such as land (and sometimes chattels) in kind. In this the draftsman has an opportunity to include terms which will affect the subsequent management of the trust property in an important way. Where land is to be held by the trustees and it might be occupied by a beneficiary the draftsman should consider whether a statement as to the settlor's intentions or the purposes of the settlement should be included in the recitals.

Lending and borrowing

22.25   In addition to permitting beneficiaries to enjoy trust property in kind, many draftsmen include express powers to make loans (including unsecured loans) of property and to borrow. These are often useful powers where maximum flexibility is desired. However, the draftsman should take care to ensure that the powers are sufficiently restrictive that they cannot be abused by unscrupulous trustees and that their incorporation and misuse does not lead to a charge that the settlement is a sham. It is also important to ensure that, if there is a class of excluded persons who cannot benefit from the trusts for fiscal reasons, it is not possible to lend to or borrow from them.

Provisions relating to minority and contingent interests

Receipts

22.26   Draftsmen usually include an infant receipt clause in wills and settlements under which minors are included as beneficiaries or potential beneficiaries. This gives the trustees the power to accept the receipt of the parent or guardian of the minor in question as a sufficient receipt for monies or property paid over or transferred to or for such minors during their minorities. Such powers will usually also permit the minor himself to give a valid receipt for monies or property transferred to him, or on his behalf in certain circumstances, often from the age of sixteen years.

Under section 3 of the Children Act 1989 trustees may, in any event, pay funds belonging to a child to the person who has parental responsibility for the child and the receipt of that person will be a good receipt under the general law. It is prudent, however, for the draftsman to include a specific provision permitting trustees to accept the receipt of a person with parental responsibility for the minor.

Powers of advancement

22.27   The most common type of power of advancement is that contained in section 32 of the Trustee Act 1925, which enables trustees to advance trust capital to any beneficiary prospectively entitled to capital for his 'advancement or benefit'. Those words are not now commonly understood.

In *Pilkington v IRC [1964] AC 612* at *635*, Lord Radcliffe explained that 'advancement or benefit' meant 'the use of the money which will improve the material situation of the beneficiary'. The statutory power applies whether the beneficiary is entitled absolutely or contingently on attaining any specified age, or on the occurrence of any other event, and whether the beneficiary's interest is in possession, remainder, or reversion, and even if it can be defeated by the exercise of a power of appointment or revocation. Unless a life tenant has a prospective interest in capital, the statutory power cannot be exercised in his favour.

It should be noted that if a beneficiary who has received an advancement under the statutory power becomes entitled to a share in the trust fund the advancement must be brought into account as part of the share. Additionally, no advancement may be made under the statutory power so as to prejudice the interests of a person entitled to a prior life or other interest, whether vested or contingent, unless that person is alive, is adult and gives written consent. The section does not, however, require the consent of a person who is one of a number of a discretionary class of beneficiaries.

The power of advancement contained in section 32 of the Trustee Act 1925 can be extended by the trust instrument and often is. There are four common extensions employed by trust draftsmen:

(a)   The power permits trustees to transfer trust property to a person absolutely or to apply it for his 'advancement or benefit'. The words 'advancement or benefit' are often extended by the draftsman to permit advancement under section 32 for the 'advancement, education or benefit' of the relevant beneficiary.

(b) Section 32 restricts advancement to beneficiaries who, under the settlement, have an actual or potential interest in the trust capital, that is, advancement of capital to a life tenant is not permitted under the section. A common and useful extension is for the trustees to be given express power to advance capital to a life tenant.

(c) Not more than half of the beneficiary's vested or presumptive share may be advanced under the statutory power. This limit is generally removed as a matter of course by draftsmen of modern trust deeds and wills.

(d) The section 32 power can be exercised only with the consent of any beneficiary with a prior interest, for example, any life tenant whose interest it is proposed should be overridden. Leaving this restriction in place can severely restrict the trustees' exercise of their power of advancement and it is often removed.

No deed is necessary where the section 32 power is being exercised – provided that the conditions for its valid exercise are fulfilled, it can be exercised simply by a resolution of the trustees.

Where a wide overriding power of advancement is included in a settlement it is unnecessary to consider the statutory power in addition, but trust draftsmen often overlook this and include both the standard extensions to the section 32 power and a wide overriding power.

Clearly, in addition to absolute advancements, section 32 also offers the scope for resettlement by advancement provided that the terms of section 32 (as may be extended by the settlement) are properly observed. This is dealt with in CHAPTER 24: BRINGING TRUSTS TO AN END.

Power of maintenance and accumulation

22.28 Section 31 of the Trustee Act 1925 contains an express power of maintenance. The section provides that where any property is held by trustees on trust for any person for any interest, whether vested or contingent, during the infancy of the beneficiary the trustee may pay to his parent or guardian, or otherwise for his maintenance, education or benefit, the whole or such part of the income of the property as may in all the circumstances be reasonable. The section requires income to be paid to any beneficiary who has attained the age of 18, notwithstanding that he has no vested interest in the income under the settlement or will, until he attains a vested interest, or dies, or the failure of his interest.

Income which is not paid or applied for the beneficiary shall be accumulated for the beneficiary, although the accumulations may be applied for maintenance as if they were current income.

Section 31 can be excluded in the will or settlement deed.

Draftsmen of modern trust instruments frequently extend the provisions of the section to state that they shall apply in such circumstances as the trustees in their discretion 'think fit' instead of '. . . as may, in all the circumstances, be reasonable . . .' and to state that the proviso to section 31(1) will be omitted. This proviso states that in deciding whether the whole or any part of the income is to be paid, or applied, for the minor, the trustees will have regard to the age of the minor, what other income is applicable for the same purposes, and that where trustees have notice that the income of more than one fund is applicable then, so far as is practicable, unless the entire income of the funds is paid or applied, a proportion only of the income of each fund shall be so paid or applied.

Power to vary administrative provisions

22.29   Although such power is unlikely to be used, it is often included to permit trustees to add to or vary the administrative powers in case, for example, fiscal or other legal provisions change, making additional or different powers desirable. Again, the inclusion of such a power simply adds to the flexibility available to the trustees.

Similarly, modern trust deeds will usually include a power for trustees to release or restrict their powers. Again, such a power is probably unlikely to be exercised, but will offer flexibility if, in any future circumstances, the trustees need to alter the powers given to them, for example, in the case of changes in the law.

Remuneration of trustees

22.30   Under the common law, the basic trust principle that a trustee cannot profit from his trust generally precluded a trustee from being remunerated for acting unless the trust deed or will specifically included a power for trustees to be remunerated.

Sections 28–33 of the Trustee Act 2000 have made fundamental changes to the law in relation to trustees' remuneration for professional trustees and trust corporations, as a result of which it might be thought that express powers relating to remuneration are no longer necessary. However, as explained in CHAPTER 19: CHOICE OF TRUSTEES, express powers to charge are still desirable.

Part IV: Managing Trusts

Chapter 23

Trust Administration

Compliance with duties and exercise of powers

23.1   The common law duties of trustees are discussed in CHAPTER 21: ADMINISTRATIVE DUTIES.

In order to comply with their duties the trustees must meet, discuss the trust and the investments of the trust fund, and form decisions as to how to proceed with the exercise of their powers in compliance with their duties. The frequency and length of meetings will depend upon the nature of the trust itself, the value and composition of the trust fund and, perhaps, the skill and knowledge of the trustees.

It should be remembered that trustees are under a common law duty of care and, if it is not excluded, a statutory duty of care arising under the Trustee Act 2000. Where the statutory duty of care applies, a trustee must exercise such care and skill as is reasonable in the circumstances. A greater standard will be expected of a trustee who has or holds himself out as having any special knowledge or experience or who acts as a trustee in the course of a business or profession, as a result of which he ought reasonably to be expected to have special knowledge or experience.

Trustees should, of course, keep an eye on the investment of the trust fund and, where they have delegated the day-to-day management of the trust investments they should ensure that the performance of those investments is, within reason, regularly reviewed.

They must do so in order to comply with their duty to keep and produce accounts and to comply with their duties in relation to the Revenue.

Trustees should also keep track of their investments in order to comply with their duty to deal fairly between the beneficiaries. Not only does this duty require that trustees do not take any advantage in their capacity as trustees over the beneficiaries, but it also requires that they balance the competing interests of income and capital beneficiaries. Trustees should not invest in income producing assets to the detriment of the beneficiaries interested in capital, and vice versa. To do this effectively they must review the investments under their control to ensure that the competing interests are being balanced.

Finally, when exercising powers, the trustees (other than charity trustees) are under a duty to act jointly. Unless the trust deed authorises them to act severally, trustees cannot act by majority decision so that if they are unable to reach unanimous agreement to a particular course of action they cannot take it.

Revocable and irrevocable exercises of powers

23.2   On the whole, exercises of administrative powers take effect without any question arising as to their revocation. If trustees authorise investment in a particular fund and the investment does not perform as well as expected they simply change their minds and authorise investment in a different fund instead.

Exercises of dispositive powers such as powers of advancement and appointment are not so easy to reverse. When dispositive powers are exercised, trustees will appoint property out of the settlement or on to new and separate trusts or appoint or advance property to or for the benefit of a beneficiary absolutely. On the whole these powers are exercised irrevocably but, when the trust deed permits and there is good cause to do so, trustees may exercise their powers revocably with a view to unravelling an appointment at a later date.

Where a trust deed authorises trustees to exercise a power revocably it should also provide that the power cannot be revoked after the end of the perpetuity period applicable to the trust and the deed by which the power is exercised should at least recite the fact that the power is not exercised irrevocably.

Exercising powers of advancement

23.3   The most common power of advancement seen in settlements is the statutory power set out in section 32 of the Trustee Act 1925; see CHAPTER 22: ADMINISTRATIVE PROVISIONS. By that power, trustees may advance trust capital to any beneficiary prospectively entitled to capital for his 'advancement or benefit'. The power of advancement can be effected by resolution of the trustees (an example can be found at APPENDIX 1.25) but it is sometimes effected by deed. If the power is used to settle property but without creating a new settlement for capital gains tax purposes (see CHAPTER 24: BRINGING TRUSTS TO AN END) a deed should normally be used.

As with the exercise of any other dispositive power, the trustees ought to act in good faith with the principal purpose of benefiting the object of the power and not a stranger to it. Often the beneficiary or his guardian makes a request for an advancement before the trustees consider whether or not to exercise their power and, where there are prior interests to be taken into account, the trustees will have to obtain the consent of those beneficiaries with prior interests before making an advancement. A common amendment to the statutory power removes the need to obtain consents.

Exercising powers of appointment

23.4   Appointments should be exercised by deed and care should be taken to ensure that the appointment is a valid exercise of the power contained in the trust deed within the parameters of the power. Trustees should ensure that they have exercised their own discretion to utilise the power in good faith.

They should also satisfy themselves that what they intend to do is within the ambit of the power as to the time of exercise, the extent of the exercise and as to the beneficial objects. A failure to do this may result in the appointment being declared void or voidable.

An example of a simple deed of appointment can be found at APPENDIX 1.24.

Chapter 24

Bringing Trusts to an End

Practical means

24.1   Modern discretionary trusts often have a trust period chosen with an eye on the long perpetuity period which is a rather daunting 80 years and it is often necessary to bring trusts to an end or partially to an end before the end of such a trust period. Lay trustees often fail to appreciate that a discretionary trust, in particular, does not have to run its course and can usually be brought to an end well before the end of the trust period. Often they do not realise that the trust period is the long-stop by which they must exercise their powers if they are to exercise them at all, without appreciating that they can exercise them at any time.

Most modern trusts incorporate broad powers of appointment and advancement which are available to be used as a means of bringing the trusts to an end long before the trust period prescribed by the settlor has ended. The means of bringing trusts to an early end are not limited to powers of appointment and advancement. Sometimes the beneficiaries are able to terminate trusts under the rule in *Saunders v Vautier* and, if there is no other means available, trusts can sometimes be ended by way of variation.

Appointment

24.2   In many trusts, particularly in discretionary trusts, the trustees are given a power of appointment so broad that they are able to appoint any or all of the trust capital to one or more of the beneficiaries absolutely. If a power in the wider form is exercised to its full extent the trusts can be brought to an end for all practical purposes with immediate effect, regardless of the trust period or beneficial interests which take effect in default.

Most modern discretionary trusts are drafted with powers of appointment which enable this to be done but which also permit the trustees to resettle beneficial interests within the existing trusts. At APPENDIX 1.24 is an example of a deed of appointment under a nil-rate band discretionary trust which can easily be adapted for use in a lifetime settlement.

Advancement

24.3   Section 32 of the Trustee Act 1925 is described in detail in CHAPTER 22: ADMINISTRATIVE PROVISIONS. It sets out a statutory power of advancement which enables trustees to advance trust capital to any beneficiary prospectively entitled to capital for his 'advancement or benefit'.

The power of advancement contained in section 32 of the Trustee Act 1925 can be extended by the trust instrument and, in most modern trust instruments, often is. In particular, the statutory limitation that not more than one-half of the beneficiary's vested or presumptive share may be advanced under the statutory power is generally removed, as is the requirement that the section 32 power can only be exercised with the consent of any beneficiary with a prior interest whose interest it is proposed should be overridden.

Where property is held upon trust for a beneficiary subject to that beneficiary attaining the age of, say, 35 years, a power of advancement in the wider form could be used to advance the whole of that beneficiary's entitlement, thus bringing the trust to an end. The power of advancement can be effected by resolution of the trustees (see APPENDIX 1.25) so does not need to be exercised by deed although a deed is sometimes used.

At the direction of beneficiaries

24.4   Where the beneficiaries are all adults who are between themselves absolutely entitled to the trust property they are able, if they so wish, to direct the trustees to bring the trusts to an end under the rule in *Saunders v Vautier (1841) 4 Beav 115*. It is important to remember that the existence of minority and contingent interests prevents beneficiaries from bringing trusts to an end by this method.

Where the known beneficiaries are absolutely entitled they might also give a direction pursuant to section 19 of the Trusts of Land and Appointment of Trustees Act 1996 (see APPENDIX 2) with the result that intransigent trustees are replaced by others more willing to exercise their powers to wind up the trust.

Variation

24.5   Where the beneficiaries are not all adults who are between themselves absolutely entitled to the trust property, it is still sometimes possible to bring trusts to an end by way of application under section 1 of the Variation of Trusts Act 1958, which is reproduced in APPENDIX 2. The Act gives jurisdiction to the court to vary trusts or, rather, to approve a variation of trusts on behalf of persons or classes of persons who are unable to consent to the variation themselves.

The court cannot approve a variation under the Act on behalf of adults of full capacity who object to the proposed variation. The persons on whose behalf the court may approve a variation are:

(a)   any person who by reason of infancy or other incapacity is incapable of assenting;

(b)   any person (whether ascertained or not) who may become entitled, directly or indirectly, to an interest under the trusts as being at a future date or on the happening of a future event a person of any specified description or a member of any specified class of persons;

(c)   any person unborn; or

(d)   any person in respect of any discretionary interest of his under protective trusts where the interest of the principal beneficiary has not failed or determined.

In the case of the first three categories the court shall not approve an arrangement on behalf of any person unless the arrangement would be for the benefit of that person. There are a number of authorities on the various (often subtle) meanings of benefit, a discussion of which is beyond the scope of this book.

The increasing expense of litigation has resulted in a fall in the popularity of applications under the Variation of Trusts Act 1958 in recent years except in the case of applications under paragraph (d) (which may be approved by a Master in the Chancery Division) and in the case of very valuable settlements. Such applications are, for the most part, extremely complex and demanding of their proponents and should not be undertaken without the employment of specialist counsel.

Tax consequences

24.6   Tax often provides the driving force behind the continuation or determination of a settlement just as with the creation of a settlement. The tax consequences of termination of a trust are discussed in some detail in PART II but the inheritance and capital gains tax consequences can be summarised in the following way.

Inheritance tax

24.7   On the termination of an interest in possession trust by exercise of a power of advancement or appointment in favour of a beneficiary with an interest in possession in the whole of the settlement there will be no inheritance tax charge. This is consistent with the inheritance tax treatment of interest in possession trusts by which the beneficiary with an interest in possession is treated as beneficially interested in the underlying property. See CHAPTER 6: TRUSTS WITH AN INTEREST IN POSSESSION. Where, however, the interest in possession comes to an end and the beneficiary does not become absolutely entitled to the property or to another interest in possession in the property, he will be treated as making a transfer of value which may be a potentially exempt transfer.

On the termination of a discretionary trust there will be an exit charge because the trust property ceases to be relevant property. See CHAPTER 7: DISCRETION-ARY TRUSTS. The timing of the termination of a discretionary trust in relation to the ten-year anniversary can be an important consideration.

Capital gains tax

24.8   If, as is usually the intention on the termination of a settlement, the beneficiaries become absolutely entitled to the trust property as against the trustees, there will be a deemed disposal and reacquisition of the trust property at market value which will crystallise any gain in the hands of the trustees giving rise to a charge to capital gains tax: Taxation of Chargeable Gains Act 1992, s 71. To avoid this, much energy has been put into means of resettling trust property in a way which postpones the deemed disposal and reacquisition.

Resettling within existing settlement

24.9   For capital gains tax, the potential for a capital gains tax charge to arise under section 71 of the Taxation of Chargeable Gains Act 1992 will occur when property leaves a settlement, that is, the trustees will be deemed to dispose of the relevant trust property at its market value when a person becomes absolutely entitled to it as against the trustees. The Inland Revenue accept that a new settlement is only created if the exercise of the power results in property being removed from the settlement. This is confirmed by Inland Revenue Statement of Practice SP 7/84. This means that it is possible to resettle trust property in a way which avoids the section 71 charge: resettlement within the same settlement will not result in a capital gains tax charge arising, since no property will be leaving the settlement.

In *Roome v Edwards [1982] AC 279* Lord Wilberforce stressed that the question should be approached 'in a practical and common sense manner' and suggested that relevant indicia included separate and defined property, separate trusts and separate trustees, although he emphasised that such factors were helpful but not decisive and that the matter ultimately depended upon the particular facts of each case. Similarly, in *Swires v Renton [1991] STC 490* Hoffmann J pointed out that the question can only be answered on a case-by-case basis and is essentially determined on the basis of intention. In general a separate settlement would be created where particular assets were segregated, new trustees appointed, and fresh trusts created exhausting the beneficial interest in the assets and providing full administrative powers thus rendering further reference back to the original settlement unnecessary.

The question of whether the trust property is leaving the settlement or not is thus a question of fact, taking into account the circumstances of the particular appointment and the wording of the relevant deed or resolution. The prudent draftsman, when drafting a deed of appointment or a resolution in this respect, will expressly state whether or not the power is intended to have the effect of resettling the property within the same settlement or transferring property out of the settlement or into a new one, for example, 'freed and discharged from the trusts of the settlement'.

Usually this will be achieved by the exercise of an overriding power of appointment but, subject to the constraints of section 32 of the Trustee Act 1925 (as it may have been amended by the settlement deed), the statutory power of advancement can also be used to do this.

Transfer to another settlement

24.10   A final form of termination of a settlement is to make use of a power to transfer the trust property to another settlement, if such a power is included within the trusts. The exercise of such a power will usually have the tax consequences (particularly the capital gains tax consequences) highlighted above since the trustees of the new settlement will become absolutely entitled to the trust property as against the trustees of the old settlement.

When including a power of this nature, the settlor will need to consider precisely on what terms it is to be permitted to be exercised. Should the power only be exercisable where the beneficiaries of the transferor settlement are exactly the same as those of the transferee settlement or need there simply be one beneficiary common to both settlements? It is submitted that the latter is the more sensible solution, coupled with a provision stating that the power should be exercisable only during the lifetime of the settlor and then only with his written consent first having been obtained. It should be appreciated that the exercise of such a power could have the effect of inserting new beneficiaries (those of the transferee settlement) capable of benefiting from the trust property of the transferor settlement.

Administration costs may be saved by exercising such a power to avoid the cost of administering more than one settlement, but, as with so many aspects of the creation, management and termination of trusts, the potential taxation consequences will often be the primary concern and specialist advice should normally be taken.

Appendices

Contents

Appendix 1

Precedents

Contents

Precedent for life interest settlement with settlor life tenant with remainder to spouse for life and remainder for children

A1.1

THIS DECLARATION OF TRUST is made the [*date in the month*] day of [*month*] Two Thousand and [*Four*] BY

[*NAME OF SETTLOR*] of [*Address of Settlor*] (hereinafter referred to as 'the Settlor') of the First Part and

[*NAME OF FIRST TRUSTEE*] of [*Address of First Trustee*] and

[*NAME OF SECOND TRUSTEE*] of [*Address of Second Trustee*] (hereinafter together referred to as 'the Original Trustees') of the Second Part

WHEREAS the Settlor wishes to make this irrevocable Settlement for the benefit of the Settlor and the Settlor's family hereinafter mentioned and with a view to this Settlement has transferred to the Original Trustees the property specified in the First Schedule hereto to be held on the trusts hereof

NOW THIS DEED WITNESSETH as follows:

Definitions

1. IN this Settlement the following expressions shall have the following meanings:

   (a) 'the Settlor' and 'the Original Trustees' bear the meanings hereinbefore assigned to them;

   (b) 'the Trustees' means the Original Trustees or other the trustees or trustee for the time being of this Settlement;

   (c) 'the Trust Fund' means and includes:

      (i) the property described in the First Schedule hereto;

      (ii) all further assets added thereto whether by way of further settlement capital accretion or otherwise; and

      (iii) the assets from time to time representing the said assets and additions thereto

   (d) 'the Vesting Day' means the day on which shall expire the period of eighty years from the date of this deed or such earlier date as the Trustees by deed declare and the perpetuity period applicable to these trusts under the rule against perpetuities shall be the period of eighty years

   (e) 'the Beneficiaries' means:

      (i) the Settlor;

      (ii) the children and remoter issue of the Settlor whether now living or born hereafter before the Vesting Day;

171

(iii)   any spouse widow or widower of the Settlor or of any such child or remoter issue (including a widow or widower who has remarried)

Administration trust

2.   THE Trustees shall stand possessed of the Trust Fund upon trust at their discretion to retain the same in its existing form of investment or to sell the same or any part or parts thereof and to invest or apply the net moneys to arise from any such sale as aforesaid and any other capital moneys held subject to the provisions hereof in any of the investments or modes of application hereby authorised with power to vary any such investments or applications for any others hereby authorised

Beneficial trusts

3.   THE Trustees shall stand possessed of the Trust Fund upon trust:

(1)   DURING the life of the Settlor to pay the income to the Settlor PROVIDED that the Trustees shall have power at any time or times before the Vesting Day while the Settlor shall be living to pay transfer or apply the whole or any part or parts of the capital of the Trust Fund to or for the benefit of the Settlor in such manner as the Trustees shall in their absolute discretion think fit

(2)   SUBJECT to the life interest of the Settlor to pay the income to the spouse of the Settlor during [his]/[her] life

(3)   SUBJECT thereto to hold the capital and income of the Trust Fund in trust for all or such one or more exclusively of the others or other of the Beneficiaries for such interests at such ages or times in such shares and with and subject to such powers and discretions (including protective or discretionary trusts) exercisable over capital or income by any person or persons and in such manner generally as the Settlor shall before the Vesting Day by deed or deeds revocable or irrevocable or by will or codicil (without transgressing the rules against perpetuities) appoint

(4)   SUBJECT thereto to hold the capital and income of the Trust Fund for such of the children of the Settlor born before the Vesting Day as are living on the Vesting Day or earlier attain the age of twenty-one years if more than one in equal shares

Extended powers of maintenance and advancement

4.   In the trusts hereof:

(1)   Section 31 of the Trustee Act 1925 shall apply as if in paragraph (i) of subsection (1) the words 'as the trustees think fit' were substituted for the words 'as may in all the circumstances be reasonable' and there were no proviso to subsection (1).

(2)   Section 32 of the Trustee Act 1925 shall apply as if the words 'the whole of' were substituted for the words 'one half of' in proviso (a) to subsection (1).

Incorporation of administrative powers

5.   In addition and without prejudice to any powers conferred on them by law the Trustees shall have the further powers and provisions hereinafter set forth in the Second Schedule hereto PROVIDED that none of the powers shall be capable of being exercised in such a manner as to:

(1)   prevent any person who would otherwise have an interest in possession for the purposes of Part III of the Inheritance Tax Act 1984 in any part of the Trust Fund from having such an interest; or

(2)   prevent trusts which would otherwise be accumulation and maintenance trusts for the purposes of section 71 of the Inheritance Tax Act 1984 from qualifying as such

Exclusion of apportionment

6.   The statutory rules of apportionment shall not apply to this Settlement

Retirement and appointment of trustees

7.   (1)   The statutory power to appoint new and additional trustees shall be vested in the persons listed in the Third Schedule hereto in the order in which they appear PROVIDED always that the statutory power of appointing new trustees not be exercisable by reason only that a Trustee remains out of the United Kingdom for more than twelve months but shall be exercisable notwithstanding that one of the Trustees for the time being is a Trust Corporation.

(2)   A person or corporation in any part of the world may be appointed as a trustee hereof notwithstanding the lack of any connection with England and Wales and notwithstanding that none of the trustees hereof will on such appointment have any such connection.

(3)   Any trustee hereof may retire at any time provided he gives 30 days' written notice to the Settlor if the Settlor is living or after the Settlor's death to the person or persons who for the time being has or have the power to appoint new trustees.

(4)   A trustee retiring from the trusts hereof (whether with or without a new appointment) shall be discharged notwithstanding that there will not be either a trust corporation or at least two individuals to perform the trusts thereafter PROVIDED that a sole trustee may not retire so as to leave no person as a trustee hereof except with the approval of the Court.

(5) The persons listed in the Third Schedule hereto in the order in which they appear may at any time or times by deed remove any or all of the trustees hereof (but not without the appointment of a new trustee or trustees if the result of such removal would otherwise be to leave no trustee) and thereupon such trustee or trustees shall cease to be a trustee or trustees hereof except as to acts and deeds necessary for the proper vesting of the property subject to the trusts hereof in the continuing or new trustee or trustees hereof or otherwise as the circumstances may require.

Professional trustee charging

8. Any of the Trustees who is a professional, including a sole trustee, may charge fees for work done by him or his firm (whether or not the work is of a professional nature) on the same basis as if he were not one of the Trustees but employed to carry out the work on their behalf and a trust corporation may charge and be paid fees according to the scale fees which it charges from time to time

Protection, consultation and indemnities

9. (1) The Trustees shall exercise their powers of investment and carry out their duties as trustees without regard to the statutory duty of care and section 1 of the Trustee Act 2000 shall not apply to the trusts hereof.

(2) The Trustees shall be under no duty to review the acts of agents, nominees and custodians appointed by them and section 22 of the Trustee Act 2000 shall not apply to the trusts hereof.

(3) Section 11 of the Trusts of Land and Appointment of Trustees Act 1996 (consultation with beneficiaries) shall not apply to the trusts hereof.

(4) In the absence of proof of dishonesty or the wilful commission of an act known to be a breach of trust none of the Trustees shall be liable for any loss or bound to take proceedings against a co-trustee for any breach of trust.

(5) The Trustees shall be entitled to be indemnified out of the assets of the Trust Fund against all liabilities incurred in connection with the bona fide execution of their duties and powers.

(6) None of the Trustees shall be accountable for any remuneration or other benefit gained as an officer employee agent or adviser of any company body or firm in any way connected with the Trust Fund notwithstanding that his situation or office may have been obtained by reason of his position as one of the Trustees.

(7) The Trustees may enter into any transaction notwithstanding that one or more of their number may have some other interest therein whether in a personal or in a fiduciary capacity provided that at least one of their number has no such other interest.

Clause headings, name of settlement, proper law and irrevocability

10. (1) The clause headings are included only for ease of reference and are not to be used as an aid to the interpretation of this settlement.

(2)   This Settlement shall be known as '[*Insert name to be given to Settlement*]'.

(3)   The proper law of this Settlement is the law of England and Wales.

(4)   This Settlement is irrevocable.

IN WITNESS whereof the Parties hereto have executed these presents as their deed the day and year first above written

FIRST SCHEDULE

(The Trust Property, recital)

[*Specify the property subject to the trust*]

SECOND SCHEDULE

(Administrative Powers, clause 5)

[*Set out administrative powers if any powers in addition to the statutory powers are to be incorporated*]

THIRD SCHEDULE

(Persons with power to appoint new and additional trustees, clause 7)

[(a)   the Settlor during [his]/[her] life; and, after [his]/[her] death

(b)   such person (if any) as the Settlor shall by deed revocable or irrevocable appoint; and, in default of such appointment

(c)   [*name*] during [his]/[her] life]

SIGNED and DELIVERED as a deed by the said [*NAME OF PARTY*] in the presence of:–

W	Signature..
I	Name..
T	Address ....
N	....
E	....
S	....
S	....

Etc

Precedent for life interest settlement with settlor life tenant and remainder on discretionary trusts

A1.2

THIS DECLARATION OF TRUST is made the [*date in the month*] day of [*month*] Two Thousand and [*Four*] BY [*NAME OF SETTLOR*] of [*Address of Settlor*] (hereinafter referred to as 'the Settlor') of the First Part and

[*NAME OF FIRST TRUSTEE*] of [*Address of First Trustee*] and

[*NAME OF SECOND TRUSTEE*] of [*Address of Second Trustee*] (hereinafter together referred to as 'the Original Trustees') of the Second Part

WHEREAS the Settlor wishes to make this irrevocable Settlement for the benefit of the Settlor and the other beneficiaries hereinafter mentioned and with a view to this Settlement has transferred to the Original Trustees the property specified in the First Schedule hereto to be held on the trusts hereof

NOW THIS DEED WITNESSETH as follows:

1.   IN this Settlement the following expressions shall have the following meanings:

   (a)   'the Settlor' and 'the Original Trustees' bear the meanings hereinbefore assigned to them;

   (b)   'the Trustees' means the Original Trustees or other the trustees or trustee for the time being of this Settlement;

   (c)   'the Trust Fund' means and includes:

      (i)   the property described in the First Schedule hereto;

      (ii)   all further assets added thereto whether by way of further settlement capital accretion or otherwise; and

      (iii)   the assets from time to time representing the said assets and additions thereto

   (d)   'the Vesting Day' means the day on which shall expire the period of eighty years from the date of this deed or such earlier date as the Trustees by deed declare and the perpetuity period applicable to these trusts under the rule against perpetuities shall be the period of eighty years

   (e)   'the Beneficiaries' means:

      (i)   the Settlor;

      (ii)   the children and remoter issue of the Settlor whether now living or born hereafter before the Vesting Day;

      (iii)   any spouse widow or widower of the Settlor or of any such child or remoter issue (including a widow or widower who has remarried); and

(iv)   any charity, meaning an institution whether corporate or not (including any trust or undertaking) which is established for purposes which are exclusively charitable according to the law of England and Wales.

Administration trust

2.   THE Trustees shall stand possessed of the Trust Fund upon trust at their discretion to retain the same in its existing form of investment or to sell the same or any part or parts thereof and to invest or apply the net moneys to arise from any such sale as aforesaid and any other capital moneys held subject to the provisions hereof in any of the investments or modes of application hereby authorised with power to vary any such investments or applications for any others hereby authorised

Beneficial trusts

3.   SUBJECT TO and in default of the exercise of the powers set out in clause 4 hereof the Trustees shall stand possessed of the Trust Fund upon trust:

(1)   DURING the life of the Settlor to pay the income to the Settlor

(2)   SUBJECT thereto to hold the capital and income of the Trust Fund in trust for all or such one or more exclusively of the others or other of the Beneficiaries for such interests at such ages or times in such shares and with and subject to such powers and discretions (including protective or discretionary trusts) exercisable over capital or income by any person or persons and in such manner generally as the Settlor shall before the Vesting Day by deed or deeds revocable or irrevocable or by will or codicil (without transgressing the rules against perpetuities) appoint

(3)   SUBJECT thereto to hold the capital and income of the Trust Fund for such of the children of the Settlor born before the Vesting Day as are living on the Vesting Day or earlier attain the age of twenty-one years if more than one in equal shares

Overriding powers

4.   The Trustees shall stand possessed of the Trust Fund as to both capital and income upon trust for the benefit of all or such one or more exclusively of the others or other of the Beneficiaries for such interests in respect of capital or income or both at such ages or times in such shares and with and subject to such powers and discretions (including protective or discretionary trusts) and including powers of further delegation whether of a dispositive or an administrative nature and whether exercisable by the Trustees or any other person or persons and subject and without prejudice to any existing interests trusts or powers in such manner generally as the Trustees may at any time or times before the Vesting Day by deed or deeds revocable or irrevocable (without transgressing the rules against perpetuities) appoint PROVIDED that:

(a)   during the life of the Settlor and unless the Settlor shall by deed have released the Trustees from this condition the Trustees shall not exercise their powers hereunder without the written consent of the Settlor;

(b)   no exercise of their powers hereunder shall invalidate any prior payment transfer or application of capital or income;

(c)   no appointment in exercise of the said powers shall be made or revoked on or after the Vesting Day and in exercising the said powers the Trustees shall have due regard both to the rules against remoteness applicable hereto; and

(d)   none of the powers hereunder shall be exercised by a sole trustee other than a trust corporation.

Ultimate default provision in favour of charity

5.   SUBJECT as aforesaid the Trustees shall hold the Trust Fund and the income thereof Upon Trust for such charity or charities as the Trustees shall by deed or deeds before the Vesting Day appoint and in default of and subject to and until any such appointment Upon Trust for charitable purposes generally

Extended powers of maintenance and advancement

6.   In the trusts hereof:

(1)   Section 31 of the Trustee Act 1925 shall apply as if in paragraph (i) of subsection (1) the words 'as the trustees think fit' were substituted for the words 'as may in all the circumstances be reasonable' and there were no proviso to subsection (1).

(2)   Section 32 of the Trustee Act 1925 shall apply as if the words 'the whole of' were substituted for the words 'one half of' in proviso (a) to subsection (1).

Incorporation of administrative powers

7.   In addition and without prejudice to any powers conferred on them by law the Trustees shall have the further powers and provisions hereinafter set forth in the Second Schedule hereto PROVIDED that none of the powers shall be capable of being exercised in such a manner as to:

(1)   prevent any person who would otherwise have an interest in possession for the purposes of Part III of the Inheritance Tax Act 1984 in any part of the Trust Fund from having such an interest; or

(2)   prevent trusts which would otherwise be accumulation and maintenance trusts for the purposes of section 71 of the Inheritance Tax Act 1984 from qualifying as such

Exclusion of apportionment

8.   The statutory rules of apportionment shall not apply to this Settlement

Retirement and appointment of trustees

9.   (1)   The statutory power to appoint new and additional trustees shall be vested in the persons listed in the Third Schedule hereto in the order in which they appear PROVIDED always that the statutory power of appointing new trustees not be exercisable by reason only that a Trustee remains out of the United Kingdom for more than twelve months but shall be exercisable notwithstanding that one of the Trustees for the time being is a Trust Corporation.

(2)   A person or corporation in any part of the world may be appointed as a trustee hereof notwithstanding the lack of any connection with England and Wales and notwithstanding that none of the trustees hereof will on such appointment have any such connection.

(3)   Any trustee hereof may retire at any time provided he gives 30 days' written notice to the Settlor if the Settlor is living or after the Settlor's death to the person or persons who for the time being has or have the power to appoint new trustees.

(4)   A trustee retiring from the trusts hereof (whether with or without a new appointment) shall be discharged notwithstanding that there will not be either a trust corporation or at least two individuals to perform the trusts thereafter PROVIDED that a sole trustee may not retire so as to leave no person as a trustee hereof except with the approval of the Court.

(5)   The persons listed in the Third Schedule hereto in the order in which they appear may at any time or times by deed remove any or all of the trustees hereof (but not without the appointment of a new trustee or trustees if the result of such removal would otherwise be to leave no trustee) and thereupon such trustee or trustees shall cease to be a trustee or trustees hereof except as to acts and deeds necessary for the proper vesting of the property subject to the trusts hereof in the continuing or new trustee or trustees hereof or otherwise as the circumstances may require.

Professional trustee charging

10.   Any of the Trustees who is a professional, including a sole trustee, may charge fees for work done by him or his firm (whether or not the work is of a professional nature) on the same basis as if he were not one of the Trustees but employed to carry out the work on their behalf and a trust corporation may charge and be paid fees according to the scale fees which it charges from time to time

Protection, consultation and indemnities

11.   (1)   The Trustees shall exercise their powers of investment and carry out their duties as trustees without regard to the statutory duty of care and section 1 of the Trustee Act 2000 shall not apply to the trusts hereof.

      (2)   The Trustees shall be under no duty to review the acts of agents, nominees and custodians appointed by them and section 22 of the Trustee Act 2000 shall not apply to the trusts hereof.

      (3)   Section 11 of the Trusts of Land and Appointment of Trustees Act 1996 (consultation with beneficiaries) shall not apply to the trusts hereof.

      (4)   In the absence of proof of dishonesty or the wilful commission of an act known to be a breach of trust none of the Trustees shall be liable for any loss or bound to take proceedings against a co-trustee for any breach of trust.

      (5)   The Trustees shall be entitled to be indemnified out of the assets of the Trust Fund against all liabilities incurred in connection with the bona fide execution of their duties and powers.

      (6)   None of the Trustees shall be accountable for any remuneration or other benefit gained as an officer employee agent or adviser of any company body or firm in any way connected with the Trust Fund notwithstanding that his situation or office may have been obtained by reason of his position as one of the Trustees.

      (7)   The Trustees may enter into any transaction notwithstanding that one or more of their number may have some other interest therein whether in a personal or in a fiduciary capacity provided that at least one of their number has no such other interest.

Clause headings, name of settlement, proper law and irrevocability

12.   (1)   The clause headings are included only for ease of reference and are not to be used as an aid to the interpretation of this settlement.

      (2)   This Settlement shall be known as '[*Insert name to be given to Settlement*]'.

      (3)   The proper law of this Settlement is the law of England and Wales.

      (4)   This Settlement is irrevocable.

IN WITNESS whereof the Parties hereto have executed these presents as their deed the day and year first above written

FIRST SCHEDULE

(The Trust Property, recital)

[*Specify the property subject to the trust*]

SECOND SCHEDULE

(Administrative Powers, clause 7)

[Set out administrative powers if any powers in addition to the statutory powers are to be incorporated]

THIRD SCHEDULE

(Persons with power to appoint new and additional trustees, clause 9)

[(a)   the Settlor during [his]/[her] life; and, after [his]/[her] death

(b)   such person (if any) as the Settlor shall by deed revocable or irrevocable appoint; and, in default of such appointment

(c)   [*name*] during [his]/[her] life]

SIGNED and DELIVERED as a deed by the said [*NAME OF PARTY*] in the presence of:–

W   Signature...
I   Name...
T   Address ....
N   ....
E   ....
S   ....
S   ....

Etc

Precedent for life interest settlement with non-settlor life tenant

A1.3

THIS DECLARATION OF TRUST is made the [*date in the month*] day of [*month*] Two Thousand and [*Four*] BY

[*NAME OF SETTLOR*] of [*Address of Settlor*] (hereinafter referred to as "the Settlor") of the First Part and

[*NAME OF FIRST TRUSTEE*] of [*Address of First Trustee*] and

[*NAME OF SECOND TRUSTEE*] of [*Address of Second Trustee*] (hereinafter together referred to as "the Original Trustees") of the Second Part

WHEREAS the Settlor wishes to make this irrevocable Settlement for the benefit of the Life Tenant hereinafter named and the Life Tenant's family and of the Discretionary Beneficiaries hereinafter mentioned and with a view to this Settlement has transferred to the Original Trustees the property specified in the First Schedule hereto to be held on the trusts hereof

NOW THIS DEED WITNESSETH as follows:

1. IN this Settlement the following expressions shall have the following meanings:

    (a) 'the Settlor' and 'the Original Trustees' bear the meanings hereinbefore assigned to them;

    (b) 'the Trustees' means the Original Trustees or other the trustees or trustee for the time being of this Settlement;

    (c) 'the Trust Fund' means and includes:

         (i)   the property described in the First Schedule hereto;

         (ii) all further assets added thereto whether by way of further settlement capital accretion or otherwise; and

         (iii) the assets from time to time representing the said assets and additions thereto

    (d) 'the Vesting Day' means the day on which shall expire the period of eighty years from the date of this deed or such earlier date as the Trustees by deed declare and the perpetuity period applicable to these trusts under the rule against perpetuities shall be the period of eighty years

    (e) 'the Life Tenant' means [*NAME OF LIFE TENANT*];

    (f) 'the Excluded Persons' means and includes:

         (i)   the Settlor;

         (ii) any spouse for the time being of the Settlor.

    (g) 'the Discretionary Beneficiaries' means:

         (i)   the Life Tenant;

(ii) the children and remoter issue of the Life Tenant whether now living or born hereafter before the Vesting Day;

(iii) any spouse widow or widower of the Life Tenant or of any such child or remoter issue (including a widow or widower who has remarried); and

(iv) any charity, meaning an institution whether corporate or not (including any trust or undertaking) which is established for purposes which are exclusively charitable according to the law of England and Wales.

Administration trust

2. THE Trustees shall stand possessed of the Trust Fund upon trust at their discretion to retain the same in its existing form of investment or to sell the same or any part or parts thereof and to invest or apply the net moneys to arise from any such sale as aforesaid and any other capital moneys held subject to the provisions hereof in any of the investments or modes of application hereby authorised with power to vary any such investments or applications for any others hereby authorised

Beneficial trusts

3. SUBJECT TO and in default of the exercise of the powers set out in clause 4 hereof the Trustees shall stand possessed of the Trust Fund upon trust:

(1) DURING the life of the Life Tenant to pay the income to the Life Tenant

(2) SUBJECT thereto to hold the capital and income of the Trust Fund for such of the children of the Life Tenant born before the Vesting Day as are living on the Vesting Day or earlier attain the age of twenty-one years if more than one in equal shares

Overriding powers

4. The Trustees shall stand possessed of the Trust Fund as to both capital and income upon trust for the benefit of all or such one or more exclusively of the others or other of the Discretionary Beneficiaries for such interests in respect of capital or income or both at such ages or times in such shares and with and subject to such powers and discretions (including protective or discretionary trusts) and including powers of further delegation whether of a dispositive or an administrative nature and whether exercisable by the Trustees or any other person or persons and subject and without prejudice to any existing interests trusts or powers in such manner generally as the Trustees may at any time or times before the Vesting Day by deed or deeds revocable or irrevocable (without transgressing the rules against perpetuities) appoint PROVIDED that:

(a) during the life of the Life Tenant and unless the Life Tenant shall by deed have released the Trustees from this condition the Trustees shall not exercise their powers hereunder without the written consent of the Life Tenant;

(b) no exercise of their powers hereunder shall invalidate any prior payment transfer or application of capital or income;

(c) no appointment in exercise of the said powers shall be made or revoked on or after the Vesting Day and in exercising the said powers the Trustees shall have due regard both to the rules against remoteness applicable hereto;

(d) none of the powers hereunder shall be exercised by a sole trustee other than a trust corporation; and

(e) none of the powers hereunder shall be exercised for the benefit of an Excluded Person.

Ultimate default provision in favour of charity

5. SUBJECT as aforesaid the Trustees shall hold the Trust Fund and the income thereof Upon Trust for such charity or charities as the Trustees shall by deed or deeds before the Vesting Day appoint and in default of and subject to and until any such appointment Upon Trust for charitable purposes generally

Extended powers of maintenance and advancement

6. In the trusts hereof:

(1) Section 31 of the Trustee Act 1925 shall apply as if in paragraph (i) of subsection (1) the words 'as the trustees think fit' were substituted for the words 'as may in all the circumstances be reasonable' and there were no proviso to subsection (1).

(2) Section 32 of the Trustee Act 1925 shall apply as if the words 'the whole of' were substituted for the words 'one half of' in proviso (a) to subsection (1).

Incorporation of administrative powers

7. In addition and without prejudice to any powers conferred on them by law the Trustees shall have the further powers and provisions hereinafter set forth in the Second Schedule hereto PROVIDED that none of the powers shall be capable of being exercised in such a manner as to:

(1) prevent any person who would otherwise have an interest in possession for the purposes of Part III of the Inheritance Tax Act 1984 in any part of the Trust Fund from having such an interest; or

(2) prevent trusts which would otherwise be accumulation and maintenance trusts for the purposes of section 71 of the Inheritance Tax Act 1984 from qualifying as such

Exclusion of apportionment

8. The statutory rules of apportionment shall not apply to this Settlement

Retirement and appointment of trustees

9. (1) The statutory power to appoint new and additional trustees shall be vested in the persons listed in the Third Schedule hereto in the order in which they appear PROVIDED always that the statutory power of appointing new trustees not be exercisable by reason only that a Trustee remains out of the United Kingdom for more than twelve months but shall be exercisable notwithstanding that one of the Trustees for the time being is a Trust Corporation.

   (2) A person or corporation in any part of the world may be appointed as a trustee hereof notwithstanding the lack of any connection with England and Wales and notwithstanding that none of the trustees hereof will on such appointment have any such connection.

   (3) Any trustee hereof may retire at any time provided he gives 30 days' written notice to the Settlor if the Settlor is living or after the Settlor's death to the person or persons who for the time being has or have the power to appoint new trustees.

   (4) A trustee retiring from the trusts hereof (whether with or without a new appointment) shall be discharged notwithstanding that there will not be either a trust corporation or at least two individuals to perform the trusts thereafter PROVIDED that a sole trustee may not retire so as to leave no person as a trustee hereof except with the approval of the Court.

   (5) The persons listed in the Third Schedule hereto in the order in which they appear may at any time or times by deed remove any or all of the trustees hereof (but not without the appointment of a new trustee or trustees if the result of such removal would otherwise be to leave no trustee) and thereupon such trustee or trustees shall cease to be a trustee or trustees hereof except as to acts and deeds necessary for the proper vesting of the property subject to the trusts hereof in the continuing or new trustee or trustees hereof or otherwise as the circumstances may require.

Exclusion from benefit

10. NOTWITHSTANDING anything hereinelsewhere expressed or implied –

   (1) the Trust Fund and the income thereof shall be possessed and enjoyed to the entire exclusion of the Excluded Persons and of any benefit to any of them by contract or otherwise; and

   (2) no part of the capital or income of the Trust Fund shall be lent to or paid or applied for the benefit of any of the Excluded Persons and no power or discretion hereunder shall be capable of being exercised so as to confer any benefit on any of the Excluded Persons in any circumstances whatsoever.

Professional trustee charging

11. SUBJECT to clause 10 hereof any of the Trustees who is a professional, including a sole trustee, may charge fees for work done by him or his firm (whether or not the work is of a professional nature) on the same basis as if he were not one of the Trustees but employed to carry out the work on

their behalf and a trust corporation may charge and be paid fees according to the scale fees which it charges from time to time

Protection, consultation and indemnities

12. (1) The Trustees shall exercise their powers of investment and carry out their duties as trustees without regard to the statutory duty of care and section 1 of the Trustee Act 2000 shall not apply to the trusts hereof.

    (2) The Trustees shall be under no duty to review the acts of agents, nominees and custodians appointed by them and section 22 of the Trustee Act 2000 shall not apply to the trusts hereof.

    (3) Section 11 of the Trusts of Land and Appointment of Trustees Act 1996 (consultation with beneficiaries) shall not apply to the trusts hereof

    (4) In the absence of proof of dishonesty or the wilful commission of an act known to be a breach of trust none of the Trustees shall be liable for any loss or bound to take proceedings against a co-trustee for any breach of trust.

    (5) The Trustees shall be entitled to be indemnified out of the assets of the Trust Fund against all liabilities incurred in connection with the bona fide execution of their duties and powers.

    (6) None of the Trustees shall be accountable for any remuneration or other benefit gained as an officer employee agent or adviser of any company body or firm in any way connected with the Trust Fund notwithstanding that his situation or office may have been obtained by reason of his position as one of the Trustees

    (7) Subject to clause 10 hereof the Trustees may enter into any transaction notwithstanding that one or more of their number may have some other interest therein whether in a personal or in a fiduciary capacity provided that at least one of their number has no such other interest

Clause headings, name of settlement, proper law and irrevocability

13. (1) The clause headings are included only for ease of reference and are not to be used as an aid to the interpretation of this settlement.

    (2) This Settlement shall be known as '[*Insert name to be given to Settlement*]'.

    (3) The proper law of this Settlement is the law of England and Wales.

    (4) This Settlement is irrevocable.

IN WITNESS whereof the Parties hereto have executed these presents as their deed the day and year first above written

FIRST SCHEDULE

(The Trust Property, recital)

[*Specify the property subject to the trust*]

SECOND SCHEDULE

(Administrative Powers, clause 7)

[*Set out administrative powers if any powers in addition to the statutory powers are to be incorporated*]

THIRD SCHEDULE

(Persons with power to appoint new and additional trustees, clause 9)

[(a)   the Settlor during [his]/[her] life; and, after [his]/[her] death

(b)   such person (if any) as the Settlor shall by deed revocable or irrevocable appoint; and, in default of such appointment

(c)   [*name*] during [his]/[her] life]

SIGNED and DELIVERED as a deed by the said [*NAME OF PARTY*] in the presence of:–

```
W     Signature.........................................
I     Name..............................................
T     Address ..........................................
N           ....................................................
E           ....................................................
S           ....................................................
S           ....................................................
```

Etc

Precedent for accumulation and maintenance trust

A1.4

THIS DECLARATION OF TRUST is made the [*date in the month*] day of [*month*] Two Thousand and [*Four*] BY

[*NAME OF SETTLOR*] of [*Address of Settlor*] (hereinafter referred to as 'the Settlor') of the First Part and

[*NAME OF FIRST TRUSTEE*] of [*Address of First Trustee*] and

[*NAME OF SECOND TRUSTEE*] of [*Address of Second Trustee*] (hereinafter together referred to as 'the Original Trustees') of the Second Part

WHEREAS the Settlor wishes to make this irrevocable Settlement for the benefit of the various persons hereinafter mentioned and with a view to this Settlement has transferred to the Original Trustees the property specified in the First Schedule hereto to be held on the trusts hereof

NOW THIS DEED WITNESSETH as follows:

Definitions

1.   IN this Settlement the following expressions shall have the following meanings:

(a)   'the Settlor' and 'the Original Trustees' bear the meanings hereinbefore assigned to them;

(b)   'the Trustees' means the Original Trustees or other the trustees or trustee for the time being of this Settlement;

(c)   'the Trust Fund' means and includes:

(i)   the property described in the First Schedule hereto;

(ii)   all further assets added thereto whether by way of further settlement capital accretion or otherwise; and

(iii)   the assets from time to time representing the said assets and additions thereto

(d)   'the Vesting Day' means the day on which shall expire the period of eighty years from the date of this deed or such earlier date as the Trustees by deed declare and the perpetuity period applicable to these trusts under the rule against perpetuities shall be the period of eighty years

(e)   'the Accumulation Period' means the period of twenty one years immediately following the date of this Settlement

(f)   'the Principal Beneficiaries' means such of the grandchildren of the Settlor as are now living or are born hereafter before the Closing Day hereinafter defined including (without prejudice to the generality of the foregoing) the following children now living namely:–

(i)   [*name*] who was born on [*date*]; and

(ii)   [*name*] who was born on [*date*]

and 'Principal Beneficiary' means any one of the Principal Beneficiaries

(g) 'the Excluded Persons' means and includes:

(i) the Settlor;

(ii) any spouse for the time being of the Settlor; and

(iii) such person or persons or class or description of person (if any) as the Trustees shall from time to time have declared to be an Excluded Person or Excluded Persons in relation to the Trust Fund or any part thereof under the power conferred upon them by Clause 5 hereof (and in respect of whom in the case of a spouse of the Settlor such declaration – if revocable – remains unrevoked)

and 'Excluded Person' means any of the Excluded Persons

(h) 'the Specified Age' means:

(i) in relation to any person who shall have attained the age of four years or more at the date hereof the age of twenty five years;

(ii) in relation to any person who shall not have attained the age of four years at the date hereof but who shall be living at the date hereof the age of twenty one years; and

(iii) in relation to any other person the age of eighteen years.

(i) 'interest in possession' bears the same meaning as it bears in Part III of the Inheritance Tax Act 1984.

(j) 'accumulation and maintenance trusts' means trusts under which the conditions specified in sub-section (1) of Section 71 of the Inheritance Tax Act 1984 are for the time being satisfied in relation to the settled property subject thereto.

Administration trust

2. THE Trustees shall stand possessed of the Trust Fund upon trust at their discretion to retain the same in its existing form of investment or to sell the same or any part or parts thereof and to invest or apply the net moneys to arise from any such sale as aforesaid and any other capital moneys held subject to the provisions hereof in any of the investments or modes of application hereby authorised with power to vary any such investments or applications for any others hereby authorised

Primary beneficial trusts

3. The Trustees shall stand possessed of the Trust Fund upon trust for such of the Principal Beneficiaries as shall be living on the Vesting Day or shall earlier attain the Specified Age in such shares as the Trustees (being not fewer than two in number or being a corporation) shall by any deed or deeds revocable or irrevocable appoint in accordance with the provisions hereinafter contained and in default of and subject to any such appointment in equal shares PROVIDED ALWAYS that if any of the Principal Beneficiaries shall die before the Vesting Day without having attained the Specified Age leaving a child or children him or her surviving who shall be

living on the Vesting Day or shall earlier attain the Specified Age such child or children shall take if more than one equally between them the share of the Trust Fund which such deceased Principal Beneficiary would have taken (whether under an appointment or in default of appointment) if he or she had survived until the Vesting Day or had earlier attained the Specified Age PROVIDED FURTHER that:–

(a) no appointment under the foregoing power and no revocation of any such appointment shall alter (whether by increasing or diminishing the same) –

    (i) the share of any Principal Beneficiary who has at the date of such appointment or revocation attained the Specified Age; or

    (ii) any share in which a Principal Beneficiary who is under the Specified Age has at the said date an interest in possession; or

    (iii) the share (devolving on his or her child or children) of any Principal Beneficiary who has died on or before the said date under the Specified Age;

(b) no such appointment or revocation shall have the effect of reducing the value of the share of any living Principal Beneficiary (at the date of such appointment or revocation) to a value of less than £1000; and

(c) no such appointment shall be made or revoked on or after the Vesting Day

(2) THE foregoing trusts shall carry the intermediate income of the Trust Fund and Section 31 of the Trustee Act 1925 (as modified hereafter) shall apply thereto PROVIDED that in relation to the said trusts the said section shall take effect in all respects as if the age of majority were the Specified Age (and so that the expressions 'infancy' 'minority' and 'infant' and all references to the age of eighteen years in the said Section 31 shall be construed accordingly) To the intent and so that each of the Principal Beneficiaries (and any child of a deceased Principal Beneficiary who shall have died under the Specified Age before the Vesting Day) shall on attaining the Specified Age before the Vesting Day become entitled to an interest in possession in his or her share in accordance with the trusts hereinafter contained

(3) THE powers (relating to the payment or application of capital) conferred by Section 32 of the Trustee Act 1925 (as modified hereafter) shall apply to the presumptive share to which a Principal Beneficiary or a child of a deceased Principal Beneficiary is for the time being entitled under the foregoing trusts so as to be exercisable in respect of such presumptive share for the benefit of such person as if such person was contingently entitled to the capital of his or her share

Default trusts

4. SUBJECT as aforesaid the Trustees shall hold the Trust Fund and the income thereof Upon Trust for such of the Principal Beneficiaries as are living at the date hereof and if no longer living for their executors administrators and assigns in equal shares absolutely

Exclusion

5.   THE Trustees shall have power at any time and from time to time by any deed or deeds to declare that any person or persons or class or description of person shall thenceforth be an Excluded Person or Excluded Persons in relation to the whole or any part of the Trust Fund and the provisions of this Settlement shall thenceforth be construed and take effect accordingly in relation to the Trust Fund or such part thereof as aforesaid (subject to the exercise of any power of revocation authorised by paragraph (b) below).

   (a)   Without prejudice to the generality of the foregoing power the Trustees may in exercise thereof declare that all or any of the Settlor and the person or persons who shall then be or thereafter become the spouse of the Settlor shall thenceforth be Excluded Persons in relation to the Trust Fund or any part thereof.

   (b)   In relation to any spouse of the Settlor any declaration under the foregoing power shall continue to operate (and any such spouse shall continue to be an Excluded Person) notwithstanding the dissolution of the marriage or the death of the Settlor PROVIDED that any such declaration may (if the Trustees think fit) be made revocable by the Trustees (in so far only as it relates to any such spouse) at any time after the death of the Settlor but before the Vesting Day.

Extended powers of maintenance and advancement

6.   In the trusts hereof:

   (1)   Section 31 of the Trustee Act 1925 shall apply as if in paragraph (i) of subsection (1) the words 'as the trustees think fit' were substituted for the words 'as may in all the circumstances be reasonable' and there were no proviso to subsection (1).

   (2)   Section 32 of the Trustee Act 1925 shall apply as if the words 'the whole of' were substituted for the words 'one half of' in proviso (a) to subsection (1).

Incorporation of administrative powers

7.   In addition and without prejudice to any powers conferred on them by law the Trustees shall have the further powers and provisions hereinafter set forth in the Second Schedule hereto PROVIDED that none of the powers shall be capable of being exercised in such a manner as to:

   (1)   prevent any person who would otherwise have an interest in possession for the purposes of Part III of the Inheritance Tax Act 1984 in any part of the Trust Fund from having such an interest; or

   (2)   prevent trusts which would otherwise be accumulation and mainte-nance trusts for the purposes of section 71 of the Inheritance Tax Act 1984 from qualifying as such

Exclusion of apportionment

8.   The statutory rules of apportionment shall not apply to this Settlement

Retirement and appointment of trustees

9.   (1)   The statutory power to appoint new and additional trustees shall be

vested in the persons listed in the Third Schedule hereto in the order in which they appear PROVIDED always that the statutory power of appointing new trustees not be exercisable by reason only that a Trustee remains out of the United Kingdom for more than twelve months but shall be exercisable notwithstanding that one of the Trustees for the time being is a Trust Corporation.

(2)   A person or corporation in any part of the world may be appointed as a trustee hereof notwithstanding the lack of any connection with England and Wales and notwithstanding that none of the trustees hereof will on such appointment have any such connection.

(3)   Any trustee hereof may retire at any time provided he gives 30 days' written notice to the Settlor if the Settlor is living or after the Settlor's death to the person or persons who for the time being has or have the power to appoint new trustees.

(4)   A trustee retiring from the trusts hereof (whether with or without a new appointment) shall be discharged notwithstanding that there will not be either a trust corporation or at least two individuals to perform the trusts thereafter PROVIDED that a sole trustee may not retire so as to leave no person as a trustee hereof except with the approval of the Court.

(5)   The persons listed in the Third Schedule hereto in the order in which they appear may at any time or times by deed remove any or all of the trustees hereof (but not without the appointment of a new trustee or trustees if the result of such removal would otherwise be to leave no trustee) and thereupon such trustee or trustees shall cease to be a trustee or trustees hereof except as to acts and deeds necessary for the proper vesting of the property subject to the trusts hereof in the continuing or new trustee or trustees hereof or otherwise as the circumstances may require.

Exclusion from benefit

10.   NOTWITHSTANDING anything hereinelsewhere expressed or implied –

(1)   the Trust Fund and the income thereof shall be possessed and enjoyed to the entire exclusion of the Excluded Persons and of any benefit to any of them by contract or otherwise; and

(2)   no part of the capital or income of the Trust Fund shall be lent to or paid or applied for the benefit of any of the Excluded Persons and no power or discretion hereunder shall be capable of being exercised so as to confer any benefit on any of the Excluded Persons in any circumstances whatsoever

Professional trustee charging

11.   SUBJECT to clause 10 hereof any of the Trustees who is a professional, including a sole trustee, may charge fees for work done by him or his firm (whether or not the work is of a professional nature) on the same basis as if he were not one of the Trustees but employed to carry out the work on their behalf and a trust corporation may charge and be paid fees according to the scale fees which it charges from time to time

Protection, consultation and indemnities

12. (1) The Trustees shall exercise their powers of investment and carry out their duties as trustees without regard to the statutory duty of care and section 1 of the Trustee Act 2000 shall not apply to the trusts hereof.

(2) The Trustees shall be under no duty to review the acts of agents, nominees and custodians appointed by them and section 22 of the Trustee Act 2000 shall not apply to the trusts hereof.

(3) Section 11 of the Trusts of Land and Appointment of Trustees Act 1996 (consultation with beneficiaries) shall not apply to the trusts hereof.

(4) In the absence of proof of dishonesty or the wilful commission of an act known to be a breach of trust none of the Trustees shall be liable for any loss or bound to take proceedings against a co-trustee for any breach of trust.

(5) The Trustees shall be entitled to be indemnified out of the assets of the Trust Fund against all liabilities incurred in connection with the bona fide execution of their duties and powers.

(6) None of the Trustees shall be accountable for any remuneration or other benefit gained as an officer employee agent or adviser of any company body or firm in any way connected with the Trust Fund notwithstanding that his situation or office may have been obtained by reason of his position as one of the Trustees.

(7) Subject to clause 10 hereof the Trustees may enter into any transaction notwithstanding that one or more of their number may have some other interest therein whether in a personal or in a fiduciary capacity provided that at least one of their number has no such other interest.

Release of powers

13. THE Trustees shall have power by any deed or deeds to extinguish or to release or restrict in any manner and to any extent any of the powers and discretions hereby or by law conferred upon them (including this present power) PROVIDED that:

(a) during the life of the Settlor and unless the Settlor shall by deed have released the Trustees from this condition the Trustees shall not exercise their powers hereunder without the written consent of the Settlor;

(b) no exercise of their powers hereunder shall invalidate any prior payment transfer or application of capital or income;

(c) no exercise of their powers hereunder shall prejudice or affect the trusts in favour of charity contained in clause 4 hereof;

(d) no exercise of the said powers shall be made or revoked on or after the Vesting Day and in exercising the said powers the Trustees shall have due regard both to the rules against remoteness applicable hereto; and

(e)   none of the powers hereunder shall be exercised by a sole trustee other than a trust corporation.

Clause headings, name of settlement, proper law and irrevocability

14.   (1)   The clause headings are included only for ease of reference and are not to be used as an aid to the interpretation of this settlement.

(2)   This Settlement shall be known as '[*Insert name to be given to Settlement*]'

(3)   The proper law of this Settlement is the law of England and Wales

(4)   This Settlement is irrevocable.

IN WITNESS whereof the Parties hereto have executed these presents as their deed the day and year first above written

FIRST SCHEDULE

(The Trust Property, recital)

[*Specify the property subject to the trust*]

SECOND SCHEDULE

(Administrative Powers, clause 7)

[*Set out administrative powers if any powers in addition to the statutory powers are to be incorporated*]

THIRD SCHEDULE

(Persons with power to appoint new and additional trustees, clause 9)

[(a)   the Settlor during [his]/[her] life; and, after [his]/[her] death

(b)   such person (if any) as the Settlor shall by deed revocable or irrevocable appoint; and, in default of such appointment

(c)   [*name*] during [his]/[her] life]

SIGNED and DELIVERED as a deed by the said [*NAME OF PARTY*] in the presence of:–

W   Signature....................................
I   Name...
T   Address ....
N   ....
E   ....
S   ....
S   ....

Etc

Precedent for discretionary settlement with settlor included

A1.5

THIS DECLARATION OF TRUST is made the [*date in the month*] day of [*month*] Two Thousand and [*Four*] BY

[*NAME OF SETTLOR*] of [*Address of Settlor*] (hereinafter referred to as 'the Settlor') of the First Part and

[*NAME OF FIRST TRUSTEE*] of [*Address of First Trustee*] and

[*NAME OF SECOND TRUSTEE*] of [*Address of Second Trustee*] (hereinafter together referred to as 'the Original Trustees') of the Second Part

WHEREAS the Settlor wishes to make this irrevocable Settlement for the benefit of the Beneficiaries hereinafter mentioned and with a view to this Settlement has transferred to the Original Trustees the property specified in the First Schedule hereto to be held on the trusts hereof

NOW THIS DEED WITNESSETH as follows:

Definitions

1. IN this Settlement the following expressions shall have the following meanings:

 (a) 'the Settlor' and 'the Original Trustees' bear the meanings hereinbefore assigned to them;

 (b) 'the Trustees' means the Original Trustees or other the trustees or trustee for the time being of this Settlement;

 (c) 'the Trust Fund' means and includes:

  (i) the property described in the First Schedule hereto;

  (ii) all further assets added thereto whether by way of further settlement capital accretion or otherwise; and

  (iii) the assets from time to time representing the said assets and additions thereto

 (d) 'the Vesting Day' means the day on which shall expire the period of eighty years from the date of this deed or such earlier date as the Trustees by deed declare and the perpetuity period applicable to these trusts under the rule against perpetuities shall be the period of eighty years

 (e) 'the Accumulation Period' means the period of twenty one years immediately following the date of this Settlement

 (f) 'the Beneficiaries' means:

  (i) the Settlor;

  (ii) the children and remoter issue of the Settlor whether now living or born hereafter before the Vesting Day;

(iii) any spouse widow or widower of the Settlor or of any such child or remoter issue (including a widow or widower who has remarried); and

(iv) any charity, meaning an institution whether corporate or not (including any trust or undertaking) which is established for purposes which are exclusively charitable according to the law of England and Wales.

'Beneficiary' means any of the Beneficiaries.

(g) 'the Excluded Persons' means and includes such person or persons or class or description of person (if any) as the Trustees shall from time to time have declared to be an Excluded Person or Excluded Persons in relation to the Trust Fund or any part thereof under the power conferred upon them by Clause 6 hereof (and in respect of whom in the case of a spouse of the Settlor such declaration – if revocable – remains unrevoked) and 'Excluded Person' means any of the Excluded Persons

Administration trust

2. THE Trustees shall stand possessed of the Trust Fund upon trust at their discretion to retain the same in its existing form of investment or to sell the same or any part or parts thereof and to invest or apply the net moneys to arise from any such sale as aforesaid and any other capital moneys held subject to the provisions hereof in any of the investments or modes of application hereby authorised with power to vary any such investments or applications for any others hereby authorised

Overriding power of appointment

3. THE Trustees shall stand possessed of the Trust Fund upon trust for the benefit of all or such one or more exclusively of the others or other of the Beneficiaries for such interests in respect of capital or income or both at such ages or times in such shares and with and subject to such powers and discretions (including protective or discretionary trusts) exercisable over capital or income (including powers of further delegation) whether of a dispositive or an administrative nature and whether exercisable by the Trustees or any other person or persons in the same unrestricted manner (subject to the rules against remoteness) as if they were absolute beneficial owners of the property thereby appointed and subject and without prejudice to any existing interests trusts or powers in such manner generally as the Trustees may at any time or times before the Vesting Day by deed or deeds revocable or irrevocable (without transgressing the rules against perpetuities) appoint PROVIDED that:

(a) during the life of the Settlor and unless the Settlor shall by deed have released the Trustees from this condition the Trustees shall not exercise their powers hereunder without the written consent of the Settlor;

(b) no exercise of their powers hereunder shall invalidate any prior payment transfer or application of capital or income;

(c) no appointment in exercise of the said powers shall be made or revoked on or after the Vesting Day and in exercising the said powers the Trustees shall have due regard both to the rules against remoteness applicable hereto; and

(d)   none of the powers hereunder shall be exercised by a sole trustee other than a trust corporation.

Default trusts

4.   SUBJECT to and in default of the exercise of the powers contained in clause 3 hereof the Trustees shall stand possessed of the Trust Fund upon trust:

(1)   Until the Vesting Day to pay or apply the income of the Trust Fund to or for the benefit of all or such one or more exclusively of the others or other of the Beneficiaries if more than one in such shares and in such manner generally as the Trustees shall in their absolute discretion think fit PROVIDED that until the expiration of the Accumulation Period the Trustees shall have power to accumulate the whole or any part of such income by investing the same and the resulting income thereof in any manner hereby authorised so that any accumulations so made shall form an accretion to the capital from which such income arose for all purposes

(2)   NOTWITHSTANDING the foregoing trust of income the Trustees shall have power at any time or times before the Vesting Day to pay transfer or apply the whole or any part or parts of the capital of the Trust Fund to or for the benefit of all or such one or more of the Beneficiaries in such shares if more than one and in such manner generally as the Trustees shall in their absolute discretion think fit

(3)   SUBJECT to the trusts and powers aforesaid the Trustees shall hold the Trust Fund and the income thereof for such of the Beneficiaries other than charities as are living on the Vesting Day if more than one in equal shares absolutely

Ultimate default provision in favour of charity

5.   SUBJECT as aforesaid the Trustees shall hold the Trust Fund and the income thereof Upon Trust for such charity or charities as the Trustees shall by deed or deeds before the Vesting Day appoint and in default of and subject to and until any such appointment Upon Trust for charitable purposes generally

Exclusion

6.   THE Trustees shall have power at any time and from time to time by any deed or deeds to declare that any person or persons or class or description of person shall thenceforth be an Excluded Person or Excluded Persons in relation to the whole or any part of the Trust Fund and the provisions of this Settlement shall thenceforth be construed and take effect accordingly in relation to the Trust Fund or such part thereof as aforesaid (subject to the exercise of any power of revocation authorised by paragraph (b) below).

(a)   Without prejudice to the generality of the foregoing power the Trustees may in exercise thereof declare that all or any of the Settlor and the person or persons who shall then be or thereafter become the spouse of the Settlor shall thenceforth be Excluded Persons in relation to the Trust Fund or any part thereof.

(b)   In relation to any spouse of the Settlor any declaration under the foregoing power shall continue to operate (and any such spouse shall continue to be an Excluded Person) notwithstanding the dissolution of the marriage or the death of the Settlor PROVIDED that any such declaration may (if the Trustees think fit) be made revocable by the Trustees (in so far only as it relates to any such spouse) at any time after the death of the Settlor but before the Vesting Day.

Extended powers of maintenance and advancement

7.   In the trusts hereof:

(1)   Section 31 of the Trustee Act 1925 shall apply as if in paragraph (i) of subsection (1) the words 'as the trustees think fit' were substituted for the words 'as may in all the circumstances be reasonable' and there were no proviso to subsection (1).

(2)   Section 32 of the Trustee Act 1925 shall apply as if the words 'the whole of' were substituted for the words 'one half of' in proviso (a) to subsection (1).

Incorporation of administrative powers

8.   In addition and without prejudice to any powers conferred on them by law the Trustees shall have the further powers and provisions hereinafter set forth in the Second Schedule hereto PROVIDED that none of the powers shall be capable of being exercised in such a manner as to:

(1)   prevent any person who would otherwise have an interest in possession for the purposes of Part III of the Inheritance Tax Act 1984 in any part of the Trust Fund from having such an interest; or

(2)   prevent trusts which would otherwise be accumulation and mainte-nance trusts for the purposes of section 71 of the Inheritance Tax Act 1984 from qualifying as such

Exclusion of apportionment

9.   The statutory rules of apportionment shall not apply to this Settlement

Retirement and appointment of trustees

10.   (1)   The statutory power to appoint new and additional trustees shall be vested in the persons listed in the Third Schedule hereto in the order in which they appear PROVIDED always that the statutory power of appointing new trustees not be exercisable by reason only that a Trustee remains out of the United Kingdom for more than twelve months but shall be exercisable notwithstanding that one of the Trustees for the time being is a Trust Corporation.

(2)   A person or corporation in any part of the world may be appointed as a trustee hereof notwithstanding the lack of any connection with England and Wales and notwithstanding that none of the trustees hereof will on such appointment have any such connection.

(3)   Any trustee hereof may retire at any time provided he gives 30 days' written notice to the Settlor if the Settlor is living or after the Settlor's death to the person or persons who for the time being has or have the power to appoint new trustees.

(4)   A trustee retiring from the trusts hereof (whether with or without a new appointment) shall be discharged notwithstanding that there will not be either a trust corporation or at least two individuals to perform the trusts thereafter PROVIDED that a sole trustee may not retire so as to leave no person as a trustee hereof except with the approval of the Court.

(5)   The persons listed in the Third Schedule hereto in the order in which they appear may at any time or times by deed remove any or all of the trustees hereof (but not without the appointment of a new trustee or trustees if the result of such removal would otherwise be to leave no trustee) and thereupon such trustee or trustees shall cease to be a trustee or trustees hereof except as to acts and deeds necessary for the proper vesting of the property subject to the trusts hereof in the continuing or new trustee or trustees hereof or otherwise as the circumstances may require.

Exclusion from benefit

11.   NOTWITHSTANDING anything hereinelsewhere expressed or implied –

(1)   the Trust Fund and the income thereof shall be possessed and enjoyed to the entire exclusion of the Excluded Persons and of any benefit to any of them by contract or otherwise; and

(2)   no part of the capital or income of the Trust Fund shall be lent to or paid or applied for the benefit of any of the Excluded Persons and no power or discretion hereunder shall be capable of being exercised so as to confer any benefit on any of the Excluded Persons in any circumstances whatsoever

Professional trustee charging

12.   SUBJECT to clause 11 hereof any of the Trustees who is a professional, including a sole trustee, may charge fees for work done by him or his firm (whether or not the work is of a professional nature) on the same basis as if he were not one of the Trustees but employed to carry out the work on their behalf and a trust corporation may charge and be paid fees according to the scale fees which it charges from time to time

Protection, consultation and indemnities

13.   (1)   The Trustees shall exercise their powers of investment and carry out their duties as trustees without regard to the statutory duty of care and section 1 of the Trustee Act 2000 shall not apply to the trusts hereof.

(2)   The Trustees shall be under no duty to review the acts of agents, nominees and custodians appointed by them and section 22 of the Trustee Act 2000 shall not apply to the trusts hereof.

(3) Section 11 of the Trusts of Land and Appointment of Trustees Act 1996 (consultation with beneficiaries) shall not apply to the trusts hereof.

(4) In the absence of proof of dishonesty or the wilful commission of an act known to be a breach of trust none of the Trustees shall be liable for any loss or bound to take proceedings against a co-trustee for any breach of trust.

(5) The Trustees shall be entitled to be indemnified out of the assets of the Trust Fund against all liabilities incurred in connection with the bona fide execution of their duties and powers.

(6) None of the Trustees shall be accountable for any remuneration or other benefit gained as an officer employee agent or adviser of any company body or firm in any way connected with the Trust Fund notwithstanding that his situation or office may have been obtained by reason of his position as one of the Trustees.

(7) Subject to clause 11 hereof the Trustees may enter into any transaction notwithstanding that one or more of their number may have some other interest therein whether in a personal or in a fiduciary capacity provided that at least one of their number has no such other interest.

Release of powers

14. THE Trustees shall have power by any deed or deeds to extinguish or to release or restrict in any manner and to any extent any of the powers and discretions hereby or by law conferred upon them (including this present power) PROVIDED that:

(a) during the life of the Settlor and unless the Settlor shall by deed have released the Trustees from this condition the Trustees shall not exercise their powers hereunder without the written consent of the Settlor;

(b) no exercise of their powers hereunder shall invalidate any prior payment transfer or application of capital or income;

(c) no exercise of their powers hereunder shall prejudice or affect the trusts in favour of charity contained in clause 5 hereof;

(d) no exercise of the said powers shall be made or revoked on or after the Vesting Day and in exercising the said powers the Trustees shall have due regard both to the rules against remoteness applicable hereto; and

(e) none of the powers hereunder shall be exercised by a sole trustee other than a trust corporation.

Clause headings, name of settlement, proper law and irrevocability

15. (1) The clause headings are included only for ease of reference and are not to be used as an aid to the interpretation of this settlement.

(2) This Settlement shall be known as '[*Insert name to be given to Settlement*]'.

(3) The proper law of this Settlement is the law of England and Wales.

(4)   This Settlement is irrevocable.

IN WITNESS whereof the Parties hereto have executed these presents as their deed the day and year first above written

FIRST SCHEDULE

(The Trust Property, recital)

[*Specify the property subject to the trust*]

SECOND SCHEDULE

(Administrative Powers, clause 8)

[*Set out administrative powers if any powers in addition to the statutory powers are to be incorporated*]

THIRD SCHEDULE

(Persons with power to appoint new and additional trustees, clause 10)

[(a)   the Settlor during [his]/[her] life; and, after [his]/[her] death

(b)   such person (if any) as the Settlor shall by deed revocable or irrevocable appoint; and, in default of such appointment

(c)   [*name*] during [his]/[her] life]

SIGNED and DELIVERED as a deed by the said [*NAME OF PARTY*] in the presence of:–

```
W    Signature.........................................
I    Name..............................................
T    Address ..........................................
N         ...................................................
E         ...................................................
S         ...................................................
S         ...................................................
```

Etc

Precedent for discretionary settlement with settlor excluded

A1.6

THIS DECLARATION OF TRUST is made the [*date in the month*] day of [*month*] Two Thousand and [*Four*] BY

[*NAME OF SETTLOR*] of [*Address of Settlor*] (hereinafter referred to as "the Settlor") of the First Part and

[*NAME OF FIRST TRUSTEE*] of [*Address of First Trustee*] and

[*NAME OF SECOND TRUSTEE*] of [*Address of Second Trustee*] (hereinafter together referred to as "the Original Trustees") of the Second Part

WHEREAS the Settlor wishes to make this irrevocable Settlement for the benefit of the Discretionary Beneficiaries hereinafter mentioned and with a view to this Settlement has transferred to the Original Trustees the property specified in the First Schedule hereto to be held on the trusts hereof

NOW THIS DEED WITNESSETH as follows:

Definitions

1. IN this Settlement the following expressions shall have the following meanings:

    (a) 'the Settlor' and 'the Original Trustees' bear the meanings hereinbefore assigned to them;

    (b) 'the Trustees' means the Original Trustees or other the trustees or trustee for the time being of this Settlement;

    (c) 'the Trust Fund' means and includes:

        (i) the property described in the First Schedule hereto;

        (ii) all further assets added thereto whether by way of further settlement capital accretion or otherwise; and

        (iii) the assets from time to time representing the said assets and additions thereto

    (d) 'the Vesting Day' means the day on which shall expire the period of eighty years from the date of this deed or such earlier date as the Trustees by deed declare and the perpetuity period applicable to these trusts under the rule against perpetuities shall be the period of eighty years

    (e) 'the Accumulation Period' means the period of twenty one years immediately following the date of this Settlement

    (f) 'the Excluded Persons' means and includes:

        (i) the Settlor;

        (ii) any spouse for the time being of the Settlor; and

        (iii) such person or persons or class or description of person (if any) as the Trustees shall from time to time have declared to be an Excluded Person or Excluded Persons in relation to the

Trust Fund or any part thereof under the power conferred upon them by Clause 6 hereof (and in respect of whom in the case of a spouse of the Settlor such declaration – if revocable – remains unrevoked)

and 'Excluded Person' means any of the Excluded Persons

(g) 'the Discretionary Beneficiaries' means:

(i) the children and remoter issue of the Settlor whether now living or born hereafter before the Vesting Day;

(ii) any spouse widow or widower of the Settlor or of any such child or remoter issue (including a widow or widower who has remarried);

(iii) any charity, meaning an institution whether corporate or not (including any trust or undertaking) which is established for purposes which are exclusively charitable according to the law of England and Wales; and

(iv) any person or persons or class or description of person whom or which the Trustees shall by deed or deeds executed before the Vesting Day have directed to be added to the Discretionary Beneficiaries

and 'Discretionary Beneficiary' means any of the Discretionary Beneficiaries PROVIDED that the Trustees shall not add any person to the Discretionary Beneficiaries during the life of the Settlor without the written consent of the Settlor and PROVIDED further that no person who is an Excluded Person shall be included among the Discretionary Beneficiaries if and so long as he or she is or remains an Excluded Person

Administration trust

2. THE Trustees shall stand possessed of the Trust Fund upon trust at their discretion to retain the same in its existing form of investment or to sell the same or any part or parts thereof and to invest or apply the net moneys to arise from any such sale as aforesaid and any other capital moneys held subject to the provisions hereof in any of the investments or modes of application hereby authorised with power to vary any such investments or applications for any others hereby authorised

Overriding power of appointment

3. THE Trustees shall stand possessed of the Trust Fund upon trust for the benefit of all or such one or more exclusively of the others or other of the Discretionary Beneficiaries for such interests in respect of capital or income or both at such ages or times in such shares and with and subject to such powers and discretions (including protective or discretionary trusts) exercisable over capital or income (including powers of further delegation) whether of a dispositive or an administrative nature and whether exercisable by the Trustees or any other person or persons in the same unrestricted manner (subject to the rules against remoteness) as if they were absolute beneficial owners of the property thereby appointed and subject and without prejudice to any existing interests trusts or powers in such manner generally as the Trustees may at any time or times before the

Vesting Day by deed or deeds revocable or irrevocable (without transgressing the rules against perpetuities) appoint PROVIDED that:

(a) no exercise of their powers hereunder shall invalidate any prior payment transfer or application of capital or income;

(b) no appointment in exercise of the said powers shall be made or revoked on or after the Vesting Day and in exercising the said powers the Trustees shall have due regard both to the rules against remoteness applicable hereto; and

(c) none of the powers hereunder shall be exercised by a sole trustee other than a trust corporation.

Default trusts

4. SUBJECT to and in default of the exercise of the powers contained in clause 3 hereof the Trustees shall stand possessed of the Trust Fund upon trust:

(1) Until the Vesting Day to pay or apply the income of the Trust Fund to or for the benefit of all or such one or more exclusively of the others or other of the Discretionary Beneficiaries if more than one in such shares and in such manner generally as the Trustees shall in their absolute discretion think fit PROVIDED that until the expiration of the Accumulation Period the Trustees shall have power to accumulate the whole or any part of such income by investing the same and the resulting income thereof in any manner hereby authorised so that any accumulations so made shall form an accretion to the capital from which such income arose for all purposes

(2) NOTWITHSTANDING the foregoing trust of income the Trustees shall have power at any time or times before the Vesting Day to pay transfer or apply the whole or any part or parts of the capital of the Trust Fund to or for the benefit of all or such one or more of the Discretionary Beneficiaries in such shares if more than one and in such manner generally as the Trustees shall in their absolute discretion think fit

(3) SUBJECT to the trusts and powers aforesaid the Trustees shall hold the Trust Fund and the income thereof for such of the Discretionary Beneficiaries other than charities as are living on the Vesting Day if more than one in equal shares absolutely

Ultimate default provision in favour of charity

5. SUBJECT as aforesaid the Trustees shall hold the Trust Fund and the income thereof Upon Trust for such charity or charities as the Trustees shall by deed or deeds before the Vesting Day appoint and in default of and subject to and until any such appointment Upon Trust for charitable purposes generally

Exclusion

6. THE Trustees shall have power at any time and from time to time by any deed or deeds to declare that any person or persons or class or description of person shall thenceforth be an Excluded Person or Excluded Persons in relation to the whole or any part of the Trust Fund and the provisions of this Settlement shall thenceforth be construed and take effect accordingly

in relation to the Trust Fund or such part thereof as aforesaid (subject to the exercise of any power of revocation authorised by paragraph (b) below).

(a)   Without prejudice to the generality of the foregoing power the Trustees may in exercise thereof declare that all or any of the Settlor and the person or persons who shall then be or thereafter become the spouse of the Settlor shall thenceforth be Excluded Persons in relation to the Trust Fund or any part thereof.

(b)   In relation to any spouse of the Settlor any declaration under the foregoing power shall continue to operate (and any such spouse shall continue to be an Excluded Person) notwithstanding the dissolution of the marriage or the death of the Settlor PROVIDED that any such declaration may (if the Trustees think fit) be made revocable by the Trustees (in so far only as it relates to any such spouse) at any time after the death of the Settlor but before the Vesting Day.

Extended powers of maintenance and advancement

7.   In the trusts hereof:

(1)   Section 31 of the Trustee Act 1925 shall apply as if in paragraph (i) of subsection (1) the words 'as the trustees think fit' were substituted for the words 'as may in all the circumstances be reasonable' and there were no proviso to subsection (1).

(2)   Section 32 of the Trustee Act 1925 shall apply as if the words 'the whole of' were substituted for the words 'one half of' in proviso (a) to subsection (1).

Incorporation of administrative powers

8.   In addition and without prejudice to any powers conferred on them by law the Trustees shall have the further powers and provisions hereinafter set forth in the Second Schedule hereto PROVIDED that none of the powers shall be capable of being exercised in such a manner as to:

(1)   prevent any person who would otherwise have an interest in possession for the purposes of Part III of the Inheritance Tax Act 1984 in any part of the Trust Fund from having such an interest; or

(2)   prevent trusts which would otherwise be accumulation and mainte-nance trusts for the purposes of section 71 of the Inheritance Tax Act 1984 from qualifying as such

Exclusion of apportionment

9.   The statutory rules of apportionment shall not apply to this Settlement

Retirement and appointment of trustees

10.   (1)   The statutory power to appoint new and additional trustees shall be vested in the persons listed in the Third Schedule hereto in the order in which they appear PROVIDED always that the statutory power of appointing new trustees not be exercisable by reason only that a Trustee remains out of the United Kingdom for more than twelve

> months but shall be exercisable notwithstanding that one of the Trustees for the time being is a Trust Corporation.

    (2)   A person or corporation in any part of the world may be appointed as a trustee hereof notwithstanding the lack of any connection with England and Wales and notwithstanding that none of the trustees hereof will on such appointment have any such connection.

    (3)   Any trustee hereof may retire at any time provided he gives 30 days' written notice to the Settlor if the Settlor is living or after the Settlor's death to the person or persons who for the time being has or have the power to appoint new trustees.

    (4)   A trustee retiring from the trusts hereof (whether with or without a new appointment) shall be discharged notwithstanding that there will not be either a trust corporation or at least two individuals to perform the trusts thereafter PROVIDED that a sole trustee may not retire so as to leave no person as a trustee hereof except with the approval of the Court.

    (5)   The persons listed in the Third Schedule hereto in the order in which they appear may at any time or times by deed remove any or all of the trustees hereof (but not without the appointment of a new trustee or trustees if the result of such removal would otherwise be to leave no trustee) and thereupon such trustee or trustees shall cease to be a trustee or trustees hereof except as to acts and deeds necessary for the proper vesting of the property subject to the trusts hereof in the continuing or new trustee or trustees hereof or otherwise as the circumstances may require.

Exclusion from benefit

11.   NOTWITHSTANDING anything hereinelsewhere expressed or implied –

    (1)   the Trust Fund and the income thereof shall be possessed and enjoyed to the entire exclusion of the Excluded Persons and of any benefit to any of them by contract or otherwise; and

    (2)   no part of the capital or income of the Trust Fund shall be lent to or paid or applied for the benefit of any of the Excluded Persons and no power or discretion hereunder shall be capable of being exercised so as to confer any benefit on any of the Excluded Persons in any circumstances whatsoever

Professional trustee charging

12.   SUBJECT to clause 11 hereof any of the Trustees who is a professional, including a sole trustee, may charge fees for work done by him or his firm (whether or not the work is of a professional nature) on the same basis as if he were not one of the Trustees but employed to carry out the work on their behalf and a trust corporation may charge and be paid fees according to the scale fees which it charges from time to time

Protection, consultation and indemnities

13.   (1)   The Trustees shall exercise their powers of investment and carry out

their duties as trustees without regard to the statutory duty of care and section 1 of the Trustee Act 2000 shall not apply to the trusts hereof.

(2)   The Trustees shall be under no duty to review the acts of agents, nominees and custodians appointed by them and section 22 of the Trustee Act 2000 shall not apply to the trusts hereof.

(3)   Section 11 of the Trusts of Land and Appointment of Trustees Act 1996 (consultation with beneficiaries) shall not apply to the trusts hereof.

(4)   In the absence of proof of dishonesty or the wilful commission of an act known to be a breach of trust none of the Trustees shall be liable for any loss or bound to take proceedings against a co-trustee for any breach of trust.

(5)   The Trustees shall be entitled to be indemnified out of the assets of the Trust Fund against all liabilities incurred in connection with the bona fide execution of their duties and powers.

(6)   None of the Trustees shall be accountable for any remuneration or other benefit gained as an officer employee agent or adviser of any company body or firm in any way connected with the Trust Fund notwithstanding that his situation or office may have been obtained by reason of his position as one of the Trustees.

(7)   Subject to clause 11 hereof the Trustees may enter into any transaction notwithstanding that one or more of their number may have some other interest therein whether in a personal or in a fiduciary capacity provided that at least one of their number has no such other interest.

Release of powers

14.   THE Trustees shall have power by any deed or deeds to extinguish or to release or restrict in any manner and to any extent any of the powers and discretions hereby or by law conferred upon them (including this present power) PROVIDED that:

(a)   during the life of the Settlor and unless the Settlor shall by deed have released the Trustees from this condition the Trustees shall not exercise their powers hereunder without the written consent of the Settlor;

(b)   no exercise of their powers hereunder shall invalidate any prior payment transfer or application of capital or income;

(c)   no exercise of their powers hereunder shall prejudice or affect the trusts in favour of charity contained in clause 5 hereof;

(d)   no exercise of the said powers shall be made or revoked on or after the Vesting Day and in exercising the said powers the Trustees shall have due regard both to the rules against remoteness applicable hereto; and

(e)   none of the powers hereunder shall be exercised by a sole trustee other than a trust corporation.

Clause headings, name of settlement, proper law and irrevocability

15.   (1)   The clause headings are included only for ease of reference and are not to be used as an aid to the interpretation of this settlement.

(2)   This Settlement shall be known as '[*Insert name to be given to Settlement*]'.

(3)   The proper law of this Settlement is the law of England and Wales.

(4)   This Settlement is irrevocable.

IN WITNESS whereof the Parties hereto have executed these presents as their deed the day and year first above written

FIRST SCHEDULE

(The Trust Property, recital)

[*Specify the property subject to the trust*]

SECOND SCHEDULE

(Administrative Powers, clause 8)

[*Set out administrative powers if any powers in addition to the statutory powers are to be incorporated*]

THIRD SCHEDULE

(Persons with power to appoint new and additional trustees, clause 10)

[(a)   the Settlor during [his]/[her] life; and, after [his]/[her] death

(b)   such person (if any) as the Settlor shall by deed revocable or irrevocable appoint; and, in default of such appointment

(c)   [*name*] during [his]/[her] life]

SIGNED and DELIVERED as a deed by the said [*NAME OF PARTY*] in the presence of:–

```
W     Signature........................................
I     Name...........................................
T     Address ........................................
N        ...................................................
E        ...................................................
S        ...................................................
S        ...................................................
```

Etc

Precedent for bare trust for child of settlor

A1.7

THIS DECLARATION OF TRUST is made the [*date in the month*] day of [*month*] Two Thousand and [*Four*] BY [*NAME OF SETTLOR*] of [*Address of Settlor*] (hereinafter referred to as 'the Settlor')

WHEREAS the Settlor wishes to make this irrevocable Settlement for the benefit of [*NAME OF BENEFICIARY*] (a minor) and with a view to this Settlement has declared himself Trustee of the property specified in the First Schedule hereto to be held on the trusts hereof

NOW THIS DEED WITNESSETH as follows:

1. IN this Settlement the following expressions shall have the following meanings:

    (a) 'the Settlor' bears the meaning hereinbefore assigned to it;

    (b) 'the Trustees' means the Settlor or other the trustees or trustee for the time being of this Settlement;

    (c) 'the Trust Fund' means and includes:

        (i) the property described in the First Schedule hereto;

        (ii) all further assets added thereto whether by way of further settlement capital accretion or otherwise; and

        (iii) the assets from time to time representing the said assets and additions thereto

    (d) 'the Beneficiary' means [*NAME OF BENEFICIARY*] a [*son/daughter*] of the Settlor

2. THE Trustees shall stand possessed of the Trust Fund upon trust for the Beneficiary absolutely

3. (1) THE provisions of section 31 of the Trustee Act 1925 (relating to maintenance and accumulation) shall apply hereto as if the proviso to sub-section (1) thereof had been omitted therefrom

    (2) THE powers in section 32 of the Trustee Act 1925 (relating to the payment or application of capital) shall apply hereto as if the words "one-half of" were omitted from proviso (a) to sub-section (1) thereof

4. DURING the minority of the Beneficiary the Trustees shall have the further powers and provisions hereinafter set forth in the Second Schedule hereto in addition and without prejudice to any powers conferred on them by law

IN WITNESS whereof the Parties hereto have executed these presents as their deed the day and year first above written

FIRST SCHEDULE

(The Trust Property, recital)

[*Specify the property subject to the trust*]

SECOND SCHEDULE

(Administrative Powers, clause 4)

[*Set out administrative powers if any powers in addition to the statutory powers are to be incorporated*]

SIGNED and DELIVERED as a deed by the said [*NAME OF SETTLOR*] in the presence of:–

W	Signature..
I	Name..
T	Address ....
N	....
E	....
S	....
S	....

Etc

Precedent for a trust for the disabled

A1.8

THIS DECLARATION OF TRUST is made the [*date in the month*] day of [*month*] Two Thousand and [*Four*] BY

[*NAME OF SETTLOR*] of [*Address of Settlor*] (hereinafter referred to as 'the Settlor') of the First Part and

[*NAME OF FIRST TRUSTEE*] of [*Address of First Trustee*] and

[*NAME OF SECOND TRUSTEE*] of [*Address of Second Trustee*] (hereinafter together referred to as 'the Original Trustees') of the Second Part

WHEREAS:

(1) [*NAME OF PRINCIPAL BENEFICIARY*] (hereinafter referred to as 'the Principal Beneficiary') is [incapable, by reason of mental disorder within the meaning of the Mental Health Act 1983, of administering [his]/[her] property or managing his affairs]

(2) The Settlor wishes to make this irrevocable Settlement for the benefit of the Principal Beneficiary and with a view to this Settlement has transferred to the Original Trustees the property specified in the First Schedule hereto to be held on the trusts hereof

NOW THIS DEED WITNESSETH as follows:

1. IN this Settlement the following expressions shall have the following meanings:

   (a) 'the Settlor', 'the Original Trustees' and 'the Principal Beneficiary' bear the meanings hereinbefore assigned to them;

   (b) 'the Trustees' means the Original Trustees or other the trustees or trustee for the time being of this Settlement;

   (c) 'the Trust Fund' means and includes:

      (i) the property described in the First Schedule hereto;

      (ii) all further assets added thereto whether by way of further settlement capital accretion or otherwise; and

      (iii) the assets from time to time representing the said assets and additions thereto

   (d) 'the Vesting Day' means the day on which shall expire the period of eighty years from the date of this deed or such earlier date as the Trustees by deed declare and the perpetuity period applicable to these trusts under the rule against perpetuities shall be the period of eighty years

   (e) 'the Accumulation Period' means the period of twenty-one years immediately following the date of this Settlement

   (f) 'the Beneficiaries' means:

      (i) the Principal Beneficiary;

(ii)   the grandchildren and remoter issue of the parents of the Principal Beneficiary whether now living or born hereafter before the Vesting Day;

(iii)   any spouse widow or widower of the Principal Beneficiary or of any such grandchild or remoter issue of the parents of the Principal beneficiary including a widow or widower who has remarried);

(iv)   any charity, meaning an institution whether corporate or not (including any trust or undertaking) which is established for purposes which are exclusively charitable according to the law of England and Wales.

(g)   'the Excluded Persons' means and includes:

(i)   the Settlor;

(ii)   any spouse for the time being of the Settlor

and 'Excluded Person' means any of the Excluded Persons

Administration trust

2.   THE Trustees shall stand possessed of the Trust Fund upon trust at their discretion to retain the same in its existing form of investment or to sell the same or any part or parts thereof and to invest or apply the net moneys to arise from any such sale as aforesaid and any other capital moneys held subject to the provisions hereof in any of the investments or modes of application hereby authorised with power to vary any such investments or applications for any others hereby authorised

Beneficial trusts

3.   During the life of the Principal Beneficiary the Trustees shall hold the Trust Fund UPON TRUST:

(1)   TO HOLD the income of the Trust Fund on trust for such of the Beneficiaries if more than one in such shares and generally in such manner as the Trustees think fit PROVIDED that

(a)   not less than one half of any income applied during the lifetime of the Principal Beneficiary is applied for the benefit of the Principal Beneficiary;

(b)   during the Accumulation Period the Trustees shall have power to accumulate the whole or any part of such income by investing the same and the resulting income thereof in any manner hereby authorised so that any accumulations so made shall form an accretion to the capital from which such income arose for all purposes

(c)   the Trustees (being not fewer than two in number or a trust corporation) may at any time or times and from time to time during the life of the Principal Beneficiary apply the whole or any part or parts of the Trust Fund for or towards the maintenance support or benefit of the Principal Beneficiary in such manner as they think fit.

Power of appointment after death of principal beneficiary

4. FROM and after the death of the Principal Beneficiary the Trustees shall have power to appoint the whole or any part of the Trust Fund as to both capital and income upon trust for the benefit of all or such one or more exclusively of the others or other of the Beneficiaries for such interests in respect of capital or income or both at such ages or times in such shares and with and subject to such powers and discretions (including protective or discretionary trusts) and including powers of further delegation whether of a dispositive or an administrative nature and whether exercisable by the Trustees or any other person or persons and subject and without prejudice to any existing interests trusts or powers in such manner generally as the Trustees think fit PROVIDED that:

    (a)   no exercise of their powers hereunder shall invalidate any prior payment transfer or application of capital or income;

    (b)   no appointment in exercise of the said powers shall be made or revoked on or after the Vesting Day and in exercising the said powers the Trustees shall have due regard both to the rules against remoteness applicable hereto; and

    (c)   none of the powers hereunder shall be exercised by a sole trustee other than a trust corporation.

Default trusts

5. SUBJECT to the trusts and powers hereinbefore appearing the Trustees shall hold the Trust Fund and the income thereof for such of the Beneficiaries other than charities as are living on the Vesting Day if more than one in equal shares absolutely

Ultimate default provision in favour of charity

6. SUBJECT as aforesaid the Trustees shall hold the Trust Fund and the income thereof Upon Trust for such charity or charities as the Trustees shall by deed or deeds before the Vesting Day appoint and in default of and subject to and until any such appointment Upon Trust for charitable purposes generally

Extended powers of maintenance and advancement

7. In the trusts hereof:

    (1)   Section 31 of the Trustee Act 1925 shall apply as if in paragraph (i) of subsection (1) the words 'as the trustees think fit' were substituted for the words 'as may in all the circumstances be reasonable' and there were no proviso to subsection (1).

    (2)   Section 32 of the Trustee Act 1925 shall apply as if the words 'the whole of' were substituted for the words 'one half of' in proviso (a) to subsection (1).

Incorporation of administrative powers

8. In addition and without prejudice to any powers conferred on them by law the Trustees shall have the further powers and provisions hereinafter

set forth in the Second Schedule hereto PROVIDED that none of the powers shall be capable of being exercised in such a manner as to:

(1)   prevent any person who would otherwise have an interest in possession for the purposes of Part III of the Inheritance Tax Act 1984 in any part of the Trust Fund from having such an interest; or

(2)   prevent trusts which would otherwise be accumulation and maintenance trusts for the purposes of section 71 of the Inheritance Tax Act 1984 from qualifying as such

Exclusion of apportionment

9.   The statutory rules of apportionment shall not apply to this Settlement

Retirement and appointment of trustees

10.   (1)   The statutory power to appoint new and additional trustees shall be vested in the persons listed in the Third Schedule hereto in the order in which they appear PROVIDED always that the statutory power of appointing new trustees not be exercisable by reason only that a Trustee remains out of the United Kingdom for more than twelve months but shall be exercisable notwithstanding that one of the Trustees for the time being is a Trust Corporation.

(2)   A person or corporation in any part of the world may be appointed as a trustee hereof notwithstanding the lack of any connection with England and Wales and notwithstanding that none of the trustees hereof will on such appointment have any such connection.

(3)   Any trustee hereof may retire at any time provided he gives 30 days' written notice to the Settlor if the Settlor is living or after the Settlor's death to the person or persons who for the time being has or have the power to appoint new trustees.

(4)   A trustee retiring from the trusts hereof (whether with or without a new appointment) shall be discharged notwithstanding that there will not be either a trust corporation or at least two individuals to perform the trusts thereafter PROVIDED that a sole trustee may not retire so as to leave no person as a trustee hereof except with the approval of the Court.

(5)   The persons listed in the Third Schedule hereto in the order in which they appear may at any time or times by deed remove any or all of the trustees hereof (but not without the appointment of a new trustee or trustees if the result of such removal would otherwise be to leave no trustee) and thereupon such trustee or trustees shall cease to be a trustee or trustees hereof except as to acts and deeds necessary for the proper vesting of the property subject to the trusts hereof in the continuing or new trustee or trustees hereof or otherwise as the circumstances may require.

Exclusion from benefit

11.   NOTWITHSTANDING anything hereinelsewhere expressed or implied –

(1)   the Trust Fund and the income thereof shall be possessed and

enjoyed to the entire exclusion of the Excluded Persons and of any benefit to any of them by contract or otherwise; and

(2) no part of the capital or income of the Trust Fund shall be lent to or paid or applied for the benefit of any of the Excluded Persons and no power or discretion hereunder shall be capable of being exercised so as to confer any benefit on any of the Excluded Persons in any circumstances whatsoever

Professional trustee charging

12. SUBJECT to clause 10 hereof any of the Trustees who is a professional, including a sole trustee, may charge fees for work done by him or his firm (whether or not the work is of a professional nature) on the same basis as if he were not one of the Trustees but employed to carry out the work on their behalf and a trust corporation may charge and be paid fees according to the scale fees which it charges from time to time

Protection, consultation and indemnities

13. (1) The Trustees shall exercise their powers of investment and carry out their duties as trustees without regard to the statutory duty of care and section 1 of the Trustee Act 2000 shall not apply to the trusts hereof.

(2) The Trustees shall be under no duty to review the acts of agents, nominees and custodians appointed by them and section 22 of the Trustee Act 2000 shall not apply to the trusts hereof.

(3) Section 11 of the Trusts of Land and Appointment of Trustees Act 1996 (consultation with beneficiaries) shall not apply to the trusts hereof.

(4) In the absence of proof of dishonesty or the wilful commission of an act known to be a breach of trust none of the Trustees shall be liable for any loss or bound to take proceedings against a co-trustee for any breach of trust.

(5) The Trustees shall be entitled to be indemnified out of the assets of the Trust Fund against all liabilities incurred in connection with the bona fide execution of their duties and powers.

(6) None of the Trustees shall be accountable for any remuneration or other benefit gained as an officer employee agent or adviser of any company body or firm in any way connected with the Trust Fund notwithstanding that his situation or office may have been obtained by reason of his position as one of the Trustees.

(7) Subject to clause 10 hereof the Trustees may enter into any transaction notwithstanding that one or more of their number may have some other interest therein whether in a personal or in a fiduciary capacity provided that at least one of their number has no such other interest.

Clause headings, name of settlement, proper law and irrevocability

14. (1) The clause headings are included only for ease of reference and are not to be used as an aid to the interpretation of this settlement.

(2)   This Settlement shall be known as '[*Insert name to be given to Settlement*]'.

(3)   The proper law of this Settlement is the law of England and Wales.

(4)   This Settlement is irrevocable.

IN WITNESS whereof the Parties hereto have executed these presents as their deed the day and year first above written

FIRST SCHEDULE

(The Trust Property, recital)

[*Specify the property subject to the trust*]

SECOND SCHEDULE

(Administrative Powers, clause 8)

[*Set out administrative powers if any powers in addition to the statutory powers are to be incorporated*]

THIRD SCHEDULE

(Persons with power to appoint new and additional trustees, clause 10)

[(a)   the Settlor during [his]/[her] life; and, after [his]/[her] death

(b)   such person (if any) as the Settlor shall by deed revocable or irrevocable appoint; and, in default of such appointment

(c)   [*name*] during [his]/[her] life]

SIGNED and DELIVERED as a deed by the said [*NAME OF PARTY*] in the presence of:–

```
W     Signature...........................................
I     Name...............................................
T     Address ...........................................
N           ....................................................
E           ....................................................
S           ....................................................
S           ....................................................
```

Etc

Precedent for a protective trust

A1.9

THIS DECLARATION OF TRUST is made the [*date in the month*] day of [*month*] Two Thousand and [*Four*] BY

[*NAME OF SETTLOR*] of [*Address of Settlor*] (hereinafter referred to as 'the Settlor') of the First Part and

[*NAME OF FIRST TRUSTEE*] of [*Address of First Trustee*] and

[*NAME OF SECOND TRUSTEE*] of [*Address of Second Trustee*] (hereinafter together referred to as 'the Original Trustees') of the Second Part

WHEREAS the Settlor wishes to make this irrevocable Settlement for the benefit of [*NAME OF PRINCIPAL BENEFICIARY*] (hereinafter referred to as 'the Principal Beneficiary') and with a view to this Settlement has transferred to the Original Trustees the property specified in the First Schedule hereto to be held on the trusts hereof

NOW THIS DEED WITNESSETH as follows:

1.   IN this Settlement the following expressions shall have the following meanings:

    (a)   'the Settlor', 'the Original Trustees' and 'the Principal Beneficiary' bear the meanings hereinbefore assigned to them;

    (b)   'the Trustees' means the Original Trustees or other the trustees or trustee for the time being of this Settlement;

    (c)   'the Trust Fund' means and includes:

        (i)   the property described in the First Schedule hereto;

        (ii)   all further assets added thereto whether by way of further settlement capital accretion or otherwise; and

        (iii)   the assets from time to time representing the said assets and additions thereto

    (d)   the Vesting Day' means the day on which shall expire the period of eighty years from the date of this deed or such earlier date as the Trustees by deed declare and the perpetuity period applicable to these trusts under the rule against perpetuities shall be the period of eighty years

    (e)   'the Accumulation Period' means the period of twenty one years immediately following the date of this Settlement

    (f)   'the Beneficiaries' means:

        (i)   the Principal Beneficiary;

        (ii)   the children and remoter issue of the Principal Beneficiary whether now living or born hereafter before the Vesting Day;

        (iii)   any spouse widow or widower of the Principal Beneficiary or of any such child or remoter issue (including a widow or widower who has remarried); and

(g) 'Protective Trusts' bears the same meaning as it bears in section 33 of the Trustee Act 1925

(h) 'the Excluded Persons' means and includes:

(i) the Settlor;

(ii) any spouse for the time being of the Settlor

and 'Excluded Person' means any of the Excluded Persons

Administration trust

2. THE Trustees shall stand possessed of the Trust Fund upon trust at their discretion to retain the same in its existing form of investment or to sell the same or any part or parts thereof and to invest or apply the net moneys to arise from any such sale as aforesaid and any other capital moneys held subject to the provisions hereof in any of the investments or modes of application hereby authorised with power to vary any such investments or applications for any others hereby authorised

Beneficial trusts

3. THE Trustees shall stand possessed of the Trust Fund UPON TRUST:

(1) TO HOLD the income of the Trust Fund on Protective Trusts for the benefit of the Principal Beneficiary during [*his*]/[*her*] life PROVIDED that the Trustees shall have power at any time or times before the Vesting Day while the Principal Beneficiary shall be living and entitled to the income of the Trust Fund under this trust to pay transfer or apply the whole or any part or parts of the capital of the Trust Fund to or for the benefit of the Principal Beneficiary in such manner as the Trustees being two in number or a Trust Corporation shall in their absolute discretion think fit

(2) SUBJECT thereto to hold the capital and income of the Trust Fund one for such of the children of the Principal Beneficiary born before the Vesting Day as are living on the Vesting Day or earlier attain the age of twenty-one years if more than one in equal shares PROVIDED that if any one or more of the children or child of the Principal Beneficiary shall die without having attained a vested interest in the Trust Fund leaving children or a child him her or them surviving such children or child as shall be living at the death of the Principal Beneficiary shall take per stirpes and if more than one in equal shares the share in the Trust Fund that such deceased parent would have taken had he or she survived and attained a vested interest

Overriding powers and power to convert protective trusts

4. THE Trustees being two in number or a Trust Corporation shall have power exercisable by deed or deeds revocable or irrevocable executed at any time or times before the Vesting Day:

(1) WHILE the Principal Beneficiary shall be living and entitled to the income of the Trust Fund under this trust to declare that the income of the Trust Fund shall be paid to the Principal Beneficiary during [*his*]/[*her*] life freed from the Protective Trusts

(2) TO appoint the whole or any part of the Trust Fund as to both

capital and income upon trust for the benefit of all or such one or more exclusively of the others or other of the Beneficiaries for such interests in respect of capital or income or both at such ages or times in such shares and with and subject to such powers and discretions (including protective or discretionary trusts) and including powers of further delegation whether of a dispositive or an administrative nature and whether exercisable by the Trustees or any other person or persons and subject and without prejudice to any existing interests trusts or powers in such manner generally as the Trustees think fit PROVIDED that:

(a) during the life of the Principal Beneficiary and unless the Principal Beneficiary shall by deed have released the Trustees from this condition the Trustees shall not exercise their powers hereunder without the written consent of the Principal Beneficiary;

(b) no exercise of their powers hereunder shall invalidate any prior payment transfer or application of capital or income; and

(c) no appointment in exercise of the said powers shall be made or revoked on or after the Vesting Day and in exercising the said powers the Trustees shall have due regard both to the rules against remoteness applicable hereto

Extended powers of maintenance and advancement

5. In the trusts hereof:

(1) Section 31 of the Trustee Act 1925 shall apply as if in paragraph (i) of subsection (1) the words 'as the trustees think fit' were substituted for the words 'as may in all the circumstances be reasonable' and there were no proviso to subsection (1).

(2) Section 32 of the Trustee Act 1925 shall apply as if the words 'the whole of' were substituted for the words 'one half of' in proviso (a) to subsection (1).

Incorporation of administrative powers

6. In addition and without prejudice to any powers conferred on them by law the Trustees shall have the further powers and provisions hereinafter set forth in the Second Schedule hereto PROVIDED that none of the powers shall be capable of being exercised in such a manner as to:

(1) prevent any person who would otherwise have an interest in possession for the purposes of Part III of the Inheritance Tax Act 1984 in any part of the Trust Fund from having such an interest; or

(2) prevent trusts which would otherwise be accumulation and maintenance trusts for the purposes of section 71 of the Inheritance Tax Act 1984 from qualifying as such

Exclusion of apportionment

7. The statutory rules of apportionment shall not apply to this Settlement

Retirement and appointment of trustees

8. (1) The statutory power to appoint new and additional trustees shall be vested in the persons listed in the Third Schedule hereto in the order in which they appear PROVIDED always that the statutory power of appointing new trustees not be exercisable by reason only that a Trustee remains out of the United Kingdom for more than twelve months but shall be exercisable notwithstanding that one of the Trustees for the time being is a Trust Corporation.

(2) A person or corporation in any part of the world may be appointed as a trustee hereof notwithstanding the lack of any connection with England and Wales and notwithstanding that none of the trustees hereof will on such appointment have any such connection.

(3) Any trustee hereof may retire at any time provided he gives 30 days' written notice to the Settlor if the Settlor is living or after the Settlor's death to the person or persons who for the time being has or have the power to appoint new trustees.

(4) A trustee retiring from the trusts hereof (whether with or without a new appointment) shall be discharged notwithstanding that there will not be either a trust corporation or at least two individuals to perform the trusts thereafter PROVIDED that a sole trustee may not retire so as to leave no person as a trustee hereof except with the approval of the Court.

(5) The persons listed in the Third Schedule hereto in the order in which they appear may at any time or times by deed remove any or all of the trustees hereof (but not without the appointment of a new trustee or trustees if the result of such removal would otherwise be to leave no trustee) and thereupon such trustee or trustees shall cease to be a trustee or trustees hereof except as to acts and deeds necessary for the proper vesting of the property subject to the trusts hereof in the continuing or new trustee or trustees hereof or otherwise as the circumstances may require.

Exclusion from benefit

9.   NOTWITHSTANDING anything hereinelsewhere expressed or implied –

    (1)   the Trust Fund and the income thereof shall be possessed and enjoyed to the entire exclusion of the Excluded Persons and of any benefit to any of them by contract or otherwise; and

    (2)   no part of the capital or income of the Trust Fund shall be lent to or paid or applied for the benefit of any of the Excluded Persons and no power or discretion hereunder shall be capable of being exercised so as to confer any benefit on any of the Excluded Persons in any circumstances whatsoever

Professional trustee charging

10.   SUBJECT to clause 9 hereof any of the Trustees who is a professional, including a sole trustee, may charge fees for work done by him or his firm (whether or not the work is of a professional nature) on the same basis as if he were not one of the Trustees but employed to carry out the work on their behalf and a trust corporation may charge and be paid fees according to the scale fees which it charges from time to time

Protection, consultation and indemnities

11.   (1)   The Trustees shall exercise their powers of investment and carry out their duties as trustees without regard to the statutory duty of care and section 1 of the Trustee Act 2000 shall not apply to the trusts hereof.

    (2)   The Trustees shall be under no duty to review the acts of agents, nominees and custodians appointed by them and section 22 of the Trustee Act 2000 shall not apply to the trusts hereof.

    (3)   Section 11 of the Trusts of Land and Appointment of Trustees Act 1996 (consultation with beneficiaries) shall not apply to the trusts hereof.

    (4)   In the absence of proof of dishonesty or the wilful commission of an act known to be a breach of trust none of the Trustees shall be liable for any loss or bound to take proceedings against a co-trustee for any breach of trust.

    (5)   The Trustees shall be entitled to be indemnified out of the assets of the Trust Fund against all liabilities incurred in connection with the bona fide execution of their duties and powers.

(6)   None of the Trustees shall be accountable for any remuneration or other benefit gained as an officer employee agent or adviser of any company body or firm in any way connected with the Trust Fund notwithstanding that his situation or office may have been obtained by reason of his position as one of the Trustees.

(7)   Subject to clause 9 hereof the Trustees may enter into any transaction notwithstanding that one or more of their number may have some other interest therein whether in a personal or in a fiduciary capacity provided that at least one of their number has no such other interest.

(8)   None of the Trustees shall be liable or accountable for the payment of income to the Principal Beneficiary after the income interest of the Principal Beneficiary shall have failed or determined in accordance with section 33(1)(i) of the Trustee Act 1925 unless the Trustee or Trustees have actual knowledge of the same.

Clause headings, name of settlement, proper law and irrevocability

12.   (1)   The clause headings are included only for ease of reference and are not to be used as an aid to the interpretation of this settlement.

(2)   This Settlement shall be known as '[*Insert name to be given to Settlement*]'.

(3)   The proper law of this Settlement is the law of England and Wales.

(4)   This Settlement is irrevocable.

IN WITNESS whereof the Parties hereto have executed these presents as their deed the day and year first above written

FIRST SCHEDULE

(The Trust Property, recital)

[*Specify the property subject to the trust*]

SECOND SCHEDULE

(Administrative Powers, clause 6)

[*Set out administrative powers if any powers in addition to the statutory powers are to be incorporated*]

THIRD SCHEDULE

(Persons with power to appoint new and additional trustees, clause 8)

[(a)   the Settlor during [his]/[her] life; and, after [his]/[her] death

(b)   such person (if any) as the Settlor shall by deed revocable or irrevocable appoint; and, in default of such appointment

(c)   [*name*] during [his]/[her] life]

SIGNED and DELIVERED as a deed by the said [*NAME OF PARTY*] in the presence of:–

W	Signature...
I	Name...
T	Address ....
N	....
E	....
S	....
S	....

Etc

Precedent for an employee benefit trust

A1.10

THIS DECLARATION OF TRUST is made the [*date in the month*] day of [*month*] Two Thousand and [*Four*] BY

[*NAME OF SETTLOR*] of [*Address of Settlor*] (hereinafter referred to as 'the Settlor') of the First Part and

[*NAME OF FIRST TRUSTEE*] of [*Address of First Trustee*] and

[*NAME OF SECOND TRUSTEE*] of [*Address of Second Trustee*] (hereinafter together referred to as 'the Original Trustees') of the Second Part

WHEREAS the Settlor wishes to make this irrevocable Settlement for the benefit of the employees of [*NAME OF COMPANY*] (hereinafter also referred to as 'the Company') and with a view to this Settlement has transferred to the Original Trustees the property specified in the First Schedule hereto to be held on the trusts hereof

NOW THIS DEED WITNESSETH as follows:

Definitions

1.　IN this Settlement the following expressions shall have the following meanings:

　　(a)　'the Settlor', 'the Original Trustees' and 'the Company' bear the meanings hereinbefore assigned to them;

　　(b)　'the Trustees' means the Original Trustees or other the trustees or trustee for the time being of this Settlement;

　　(c)　'the Trust Fund' means and includes:

　　　　(i)　the property described in the First Schedule hereto;

　　　　(ii)　all further assets added thereto whether by way of further settlement capital accretion or otherwise; and

　　　　(iii)　the assets from time to time representing the said assets and additions thereto

　　(d)　Beneficiary' means and includes:

　　　　(i)　any person who is employed by or holds office with the Company or who has been employed by or held office with the Company;

　　　　(ii)　any person who is the spouse widow or widower or child or remoter issue of such person as is mentioned in (i) above;

　　　　(iii)　any person who, in the unfettered opinion of the Trustees is a dependant of any such person as is mentioned in (i) above; and

　　　　(iv)　any charity, meaning an institution whether corporate or not (including any trust or undertaking) which is established for purposes which are exclusively charitable according to the law of England and Wales.

(e) 'the Excluded Persons' means and includes:

    (i)   the Settlor;

    (ii)   any spouse for the time being of the Settlor; and

    (iii) such person or persons or class or description of person (if any) as the Trustees shall from time to time have declared to be an Excluded Person or Excluded Persons in relation to the Trust Fund or any part thereof under the power conferred upon them by Clause 6 hereof (and in respect of whom in the case of a spouse of the Settlor such declaration – if revocable – remains unrevoked)

and 'Excluded Person' means any of the Excluded Persons

(f) 'the Vesting Day' means the day on which shall expire the period of eighty years from the date of this deed or such earlier date as the Trustees by deed declare and the perpetuity period applicable to these trusts under the rule against perpetuities shall be the period of eighty years

(g) 'the Accumulation Period' means the period of twenty one years immediately following the date of this Settlement

Administration trust

2.   THE Trustees shall stand possessed of the Trust Fund upon trust at their discretion to retain the same in its existing form of investment or to sell the same or any part or parts thereof and to invest or apply the net moneys to arise from any such sale as aforesaid and any other capital moneys held subject to the provisions hereof in any of the investments or modes of application hereby authorised with power to vary any such investments or applications for any others hereby authorised

Principal beneficial trusts

3.   THE Trustees shall stand possessed of the Trust Fund upon trust for the benefit of all or such one or more exclusively of the others or other of the Beneficiaries for such interests in respect of capital or income or both at such ages or times in such shares and with and subject to such powers and discretions (including protective or discretionary trusts) exercisable over capital or Income (including powers of further delegation) whether of a dispositive or an administrative nature and whether exercisable by the Trustees or any other person or persons and subject and without prejudice to any existing interests trusts or powers in such manner generally as the Trustees may at any time or times before the Vesting Day by deed or deeds revocable or irrevocable (without transgressing the rules against perpetuities) appoint PROVIDED that:

(a) no exercise of their powers hereunder shall invalidate any prior payment transfer or application of capital or income;

(b) no appointment in exercise of the said powers shall be made or revoked on or after the Vesting Day and in exercising the said powers the Trustees shall have due regard both to the rules against remoteness applicable hereto; and

(c)   none of the powers hereunder shall be exercised by a sole trustee other than a trust corporation.

Default trusts

4.   SUBJECT to and in default of the exercise of the powers contained in clause 3 hereof the Trustees shall stand possessed of the Trust Fund upon trust:

(1)   Until the Vesting Day to pay or apply the income of the Trust Fund to or for the benefit of all or such one or more exclusively of the others or other of the Beneficiaries if more than one in such shares and in such manner generally as the Trustees shall in their absolute discretion think fit PROVIDED that until the expiration of the Accumulation Period the Trustees shall have power to accumulate the whole or any part of such income by investing the same and the resulting income thereof in any manner hereby authorised so that any accumulations so made shall form an accretion to the capital from which such income arose for all purposes

(2)   NOTWITHSTANDING the foregoing trust of income the Trustees shall have power at any time or times before the Vesting Day to pay transfer or apply the whole or any part or parts of the capital of the Trust Fund to or for the benefit of all or such one or more of the Beneficiaries in such shares if more than one and in such manner generally as the Trustees shall in their absolute discretion think fit

(3)   SUBJECT to the trusts and powers aforesaid the Trustees shall hold the Trust Fund and the income thereof for such of the Beneficiaries other than charities as are living on the Vesting Day if more than one in equal shares absolutely

Ultimate default provision in favour of charity

5.   SUBJECT as aforesaid the Trustees shall hold the Trust Fund and the income thereof Upon Trust for such charity or charities as the Trustees shall by deed or deeds before the Vesting Day appoint and in default of and subject to and until any such appointment Upon Trust for charitable purposes generally

Exclusion

6.   THE Trustees shall have power at any time and from time to time by any deed or deeds to declare that any person or persons or class or description of person shall thenceforth be an Excluded Person or Excluded Persons in relation to the whole or any part of the Trust Fund and the provisions of this Settlement shall thenceforth be construed and take effect accordingly in relation to the Trust Fund or such part thereof as aforesaid (subject to the exercise of any power of revocation authorised by paragraph (b) below).

(a)   Without prejudice to the generality of the foregoing power the Trustees may in exercise thereof declare that all or any of the Settlor and the person or persons who shall then be or thereafter become the spouse of the Settlor shall thenceforth be Excluded Persons in relation to the Trust Fund or any part thereof.

(b)   In relation to any spouse of the Settlor any declaration under the foregoing power shall continue to operate (and any such spouse shall continue to be an Excluded Person) notwithstanding the dissolution of the marriage or the death of the Settlor PROVIDED that any such declaration may (if the Trustees think fit) be made revocable by the Trustees (in so far only as it relates to any such spouse) at any time after the death of the Settlor but before the Vesting Day.

Extended powers of maintenance and advancement

7.   In the trusts hereof:

(1)   Section 31 of the Trustee Act 1925 shall apply as if in paragraph (i) of subsection (1) the words 'as the trustees think fit' were substituted for the words 'as may in all the circumstances be reasonable' and there were no proviso to subsection (1).

(2)   Section 32 of the Trustee Act 1925 shall apply as if the words 'the whole of' were substituted for the words 'one half of' in proviso (a) to subsection (1).

Incorporation of administrative powers

8.   In addition and without prejudice to any powers conferred on them by law the Trustees shall have the further powers and provisions hereinafter set forth in the Second Schedule hereto PROVIDED that none of the powers shall be capable of being exercised in such a manner as to:

(1)   prevent any person who would otherwise have an interest in possession for the purposes of Part III of the Inheritance Tax Act 1984 in any part of the Trust Fund from having such an interest; or

(2)   prevent trusts which would otherwise be accumulation and mainte-nance trusts for the purposes of section 71 of the Inheritance Tax Act 1984 from qualifying as such

Exclusion of apportionment

9.   The statutory rules of apportionment shall not apply to this Settlement

Retirement and appointment of trustees

10. (1)   The statutory power to appoint new and additional trustees shall be vested in the persons listed in the Third Schedule hereto in the order in which they appear PROVIDED always that the statutory power of appointing new trustees not be exercisable by reason only that a Trustee remains out of the United Kingdom for more than twelve months but shall be exercisable notwithstanding that one of the Trustees for the time being is a Trust Corporation.

(2)   A person or corporation in any part of the world may be appointed as a trustee hereof notwithstanding the lack of any connection with England and Wales and notwithstanding that none of the trustees hereof will on such appointment have any such connection.

(3)   Any trustee hereof may retire at any time provided he gives 30 days' written notice to the Settlor if the Settlor is living or after the Settlor's death to the person or persons who for the time being has or have the power to appoint new trustees.

(4)   A trustee retiring from the trusts hereof (whether with or without a new appointment) shall be discharged notwithstanding that there will not be either a trust corporation or at least two individuals to perform the trusts thereafter PROVIDED that a sole trustee may not retire so as to leave no person as a trustee hereof except with the approval of the Court.

(5)   The persons listed in the Third Schedule hereto in the order in which they appear may at any time or times by deed remove any or all of the trustees hereof (but not without the appointment of a new trustee or trustees if the result of such removal would otherwise be to leave no trustee) and thereupon such trustee or trustees shall cease to be a trustee or trustees hereof except as to acts and deeds necessary for the proper vesting of the property subject to the trusts hereof in the continuing or new trustee or trustees hereof or otherwise as the circumstances may require.

Exclusion from benefit

11.   NOTWITHSTANDING anything hereinelsewhere expressed or implied –

(1)   the Trust Fund and the income thereof shall be possessed and enjoyed to the entire exclusion of the Excluded Persons and of any benefit to any of them by contract or otherwise; and

(2)   no part of the capital or income of the Trust Fund shall be lent to or paid or applied for the benefit of any of the Excluded Persons and no power or discretion hereunder shall be capable of being exercised so as to confer any benefit on any of the Excluded Persons in any circumstances whatsoever.

Application of section 86 of the Inheritance Tax Act 1986

12.   No power or discretion contained in this deed shall be exercisable by the Trustees in any manner which might prevent the trusts hereof from complying with the requirements of section 86 of the Inheritance Tax Act 1984 or of any amendment or re-enactment of that section from time to time in force.

Professional trustee charging

13.   SUBJECT to clause 11 hereof any of the Trustees who is a professional, including a sole trustee, may charge fees for work done by him or his firm (whether or not the work is of a professional nature) on the same basis as if he were not one of the Trustees but employed to carry out the work on their behalf and a trust corporation may charge and be paid fees according to the scale fees which it charges from time to time

Protection, consultation and indemnities

14.   (1)   The Trustees shall exercise their powers of investment and carry out their duties as trustees without regard to the statutory duty of care and section 1 of the Trustee Act 2000 shall not apply to the trusts hereof.

(2)   The Trustees shall be under no duty to review the acts of agents, nominees and custodians appointed by them and section 22 of the Trustee Act 2000 shall not apply to the trusts hereof.

(3)   Section 11 of the Trusts of Land and Appointment of Trustees Act 1996 (consultation with beneficiaries) shall not apply to the trusts hereof.

(4)   In the absence of proof of dishonesty or the wilful commission of an act known to be a breach of trust none of the Trustees shall be liable for any loss or bound to take proceedings against a co-trustee for any breach of trust.

(5)   The Trustees shall be entitled to be indemnified out of the assets of the Trust Fund against all liabilities incurred in connection with the bona fide execution of their duties and powers.

(6)   None of the Trustees shall be accountable for any remuneration or other benefit gained as an officer employee agent or adviser of any company body or firm in any way connected with the Trust Fund notwithstanding that his situation or office may have been obtained by reason of his position as one of the Trustees.

(7)   Subject to clause 11 hereof the Trustees may enter into any transaction notwithstanding that one or more of their number may have some other interest therein whether in a personal or in a fiduciary capacity provided that at least one of their number has no such other interest.

Release of powers

15.   THE Trustees shall have power by any deed or deeds to extinguish or to release or restrict in any manner and to any extent any of the powers and discretions hereby or by law conferred upon them (including this present power) PROVIDED that:

(a)   during the life of the Settlor and unless the Settlor shall by deed have released the Trustees from this condition the Trustees shall not exercise their powers hereunder without the written consent of the Settlor;

(b)   no exercise of their powers hereunder shall invalidate any prior payment transfer or application of capital or income;

(c) no exercise of their powers hereunder shall prejudice or affect the trusts in favour of charity contained in clause 5 hereof;

(d) no exercise of the said powers shall be made or revoked on or after the Vesting Day and in exercising the said powers the Trustees shall have due regard both to the rules against remoteness applicable hereto; and

(e) none of the powers hereunder shall be exercised by a sole trustee other than a trust corporation.

Clause headings, name of settlement, proper law and irrevocability

16. (1) The clause headings are included only for ease of reference and are not to be used as an aid to the interpretation of this settlement.

(2) This Settlement shall be known as '[*Insert name to be given to Settlement*]'.

(3) The proper law of this Settlement is the law of England and Wales.

(4) This Settlement is irrevocable.

IN WITNESS whereof the Parties hereto have executed these presents as their deed the day and year first above written

FIRST SCHEDULE

(The Trust Property, recital)

[*Specify the property subject to the trust*]

SECOND SCHEDULE

(Administrative Powers, clause 8)

[*Set out administrative powers if any powers in addition to the statutory powers are to be incorporated*]

THIRD SCHEDULE

(Persons with power to appoint new and additional trustees, clause 10)

[(a) the Settlor during [his]/[her] life; and, after [his]/[her] death

(b) such person (if any) as the Settlor shall by deed revocable or irrevocable appoint; and, in default of such appointment

(c) [*name*] during [his]/[her] life]

SIGNED and DELIVERED as a deed by the said [*NAME OF PARTY*] in the presence of:–

W   Signature...
I   Name...
T   Address ....
N   ....
E   ....
S   ....
S   ....

Etc

Precedent for a charitable trust

This precedent is in the model form approved by the Charity Commission, and is reproduced with the permission of the Charity Commission.

A1.11

THIS DECLARATION OF TRUST is made the [date in the month] day of [month] Two Thousand and [Four] BY

[*Name of First Trustee*] of [*Address of First Trustee*]

[*Name of Second Trustee*] of [*Address of Second Trustee*]

[*Name of Third Trustee*] of [Address of Third Trustee]

[*Name of Fourth Trustee*] of [*Address of Fourth Trustee*]

[*Name of Fifth Trustee*] of [*Address of Fifth Trustee*] and

[*Name of Sixth Trustee*] of [*Address of Sixth Trustee*] ('the Original Trustees')

The Original trustees hold the sum of £.......on the trusts declared in this deed and they expect that more money or assets will be acquired by them on the same trusts.

NOW THIS DEED WITNESSES AS FOLLOWS:

1. Administration

The charitable trust created by this deed ('the charity') shall be administered by the trustees. (In this deed, the expression 'the trustees' refers to the individuals who are the trustees of the charity at any given time. It includes the first trustees and their successors. The word 'trustee' is used to refer to any one of the trustees.)

2. Name

The charity shall be called ....but the trustees may change the charity's name from time to time. Before doing so they must obtain the written approval of the Charity Commissioners for England and Wales ('the Commission') for the new name.

3. Application of income

The trustees must apply the income of the charity in furthering the following objects ('the objects') . . . [set out objects here]

4. Application of capital

At their discretion, the trustees may spend all or part of the capital of the charity in furthering the objects.

5. Powers

In addition to any other powers they have, the trustees may exercise any of the following powers in order to further the objects (but not for any other purpose):

 (i) to raise funds. In exercising this power, the trustees must not undertake any substantial permanent trading activity and must comply with any relevant statutory regulations;

 (ii) to buy, take on lease or in exchange, hire or otherwise acquire property and to maintain and equip it for use;

(iii) to sell, lease or otherwise dispose of all or any part of the property belonging to the charity. In exercising this power, the trustees must comply as appropriate with sections 36 and 37 of the Charities Act 1993;

(iv) to borrow money and to charge the whole or any part of the property belonging to the charity as security for repayment of the money borrowed. The trustees must comply as appropriate with sections 38 and 39 of the Charities Act 1993 if they wish to mortgage land owned by the charity;

 (v) to co-operate with other charities, voluntary bodies and statutory authorities and to exchange information and advice with them;

(vi) to establish or support any charitable trusts, associations or institutions formed for any of the charitable purposes included in the objects;

(vii) to create such advisory committees as the trustees think fit;

(viii) to employ and remunerate such staff as are necessary for carrying out the work of the charity;

(ix) to do any other lawful thing that is necessary or desirable for the achievement of the objects.

6. Statutory powers

Nothing in this deed restricts or excludes the exercise by the trustees of the powers given by the Trustee Act 2000 as regards investment, the acquisition or disposal of land and the employment of agents, nominees and custodians.

7. Delegation

 (i) In addition to their statutory powers, the trustees may delegate any of their powers or functions to a committee of two or more trustees. A committee must act in accordance with any directions given by the trustees. It must report its decisions and activities fully and promptly to the trustees. It must not incur expenditure on behalf of the charity except in accordance with a budget previously agreed by the trustees.

 (ii) The trustees must exercise their powers jointly at properly convened meetings except where they have:

   (a) Delegated the exercise of the powers (either under this provision or under any statutory provision), or

   (b) Made some other arrangements, by regulations under clause [21],

(iii)   The trustees must consider from time to time whether the powers or functions which they have delegated should continue to be delegated.

8. Duty of care and extent of liability

When exercising any power (whether given to them by this deed, or by statute, or by any rule of law) in administering or managing the charity, each of the trustees must use the level of care and skill that is reasonable in the circumstances, taking into account any special knowledge or experience that he or she has or claims to have ('the duty of care'). No trustee, and no one exercising powers or responsibilities that have been delegated by the trustees, shall be liable for any act or failure to act unless, in acting or in failing to act, he or she has failed to discharge the duty of care.

9. Appointment of trustees

(i)   There must be at least [three] trustees. Apart from the first trustees, every trustee must be appointed [for a term of ....years] by a resolution of the trustees passed at a special meeting called under clause [15] of this deed.

(ii)   In selecting individuals for appointment as trustees, the trustees must have regard to the skills, knowledge and experience needed for the effective administration of the charity.

(iii)   The trustees must keep a record of the name and address and the dates of appointment, re-appointment and retirement of each trustee.

(iv)   The trustees must make available to each new trustee, on his or her first appointment:

(a)   a copy of this deed and any amendments made to it;

(b)   a copy of the charity's latest report and statement of accounts;

(v)   The first trustees shall hold office for the following periods respectively: [If the trustees are to have definite periods of appointment these should be described here]

10. Eligibility for trusteeship

(i)   No one shall be appointed as a trustee:

(a)   if he or she is under the age of 18 years; or

(b)   if he or she would at once be disqualified from office under the provisions of clause [11] of this deed.

(ii)   No one shall be entitled to act as a trustee whether on appointment or on any re-appointment as trustee until he or she has expressly acknowledged, in whatever way the trustees decide, his or her acceptance of the office of trustee of the charity.

11. Termination of trusteeship

A trustee shall cease to hold office if he or she:

(i)   is disqualified from acting as a trustee by virtue of section 72 of the Charities Act 1993 or any statutory re-enactment or modification of that provision;

(ii)   becomes incapable by reason of mental disorder, illness or injury of managing his or her own affairs;

(iii)   is absent without the permission of the trustees from all their meetings held within a period of six months and the trustees resolve that his or her office be vacated; or

(iv)   notifies to the trustees a wish to resign (but only if enough trustees will remain in office when the notice of resignation takes effect to form a quorum for meetings).

12. Vacancies

If a vacancy occurs the trustees must note the fact in the minutes of their next meeting. Any eligible trustee may be re-appointed. So long as there are fewer than three trustees, none of the powers or discretions conferred by this deed or by law on the trustees shall be exercisable by the remaining trustees except the power to appoint new trustees.

13. Ordinary meetings

The trustees must hold at least two ordinary meetings each year. One such meeting in each year must involve the physical presence of those trustees who attend the meeting. Other meetings may take such form, including videoconferencing, as the trustees decide provided that the form chosen enables the trustees both to see and to hear each other.

14. Calling meetings

The trustees must arrange at each of their meetings the date, time and place of their next meeting, unless such arrangements have already been made. Ordinary meetings may also be called at any time by the person elected to chair meetings of the trustees or by any two trustees. In that case not less than ten days' clear notice must be given to the other trustees. The first meeting of the trustees must be called by [*names of trustees to call first meeting*] or, if no meeting has been called within three months after the date of this deed, by any two of the trustees.

15. Special meetings

A special meeting may be called at any time by the person elected to chair meetings of the trustees or by any two trustees. Not less than four days' clear notice must be given to the other trustees of the matters to be discussed at the meeting. However, if those matters include the appointment of a trustee or a proposal to amend any of the trusts of this deed, not less than 21 days' notice must be given. A special meeting may be called to take place immediately after or before an ordinary meeting.

16. Chairing of meetings

The trustees at their first ordinary meeting in each year must elect one of their number to chair their meetings. The person elected shall always be eligible for re-election. If that person is not present within ten minutes after the time appointed for holding a meeting, or if no one has been elected, or if the person elected has ceased to be a trustee, the trustees present must choose one of their number to chair the meeting. The person elected to chair meetings of the trustees shall have no other additional functions or powers except those conferred by this deed or delegated to him or her by the trustees.

17. Quorum

(i) Subject to the following provision of this clause, no business shall be conducted at a meeting of the trustees unless at least one third of the total number of trustees at the time, or two trustees (whichever is the greater) are present throughout the meeting.

(ii) The trustees may make regulations specifying different quorums for meetings dealing with different types of business.

18. Voting

At meetings, decisions must be made by a majority of the trustees present and voting on the question. The person chairing the meeting shall have a casting vote whether or not he or she has voted previously on the same question but no trustee in any other circumstances shall have more than one vote.

19. Conflict of interest

A trustee must absent himself or herself from any discussions of the trustees in which it is possible that a conflict will arise between his or her duty to act solely in the interests of the charity and any personal interest (including but not limited to any personal financial interest).

20. Minutes

The trustees must keep minutes, in books kept for the purpose or by such other means as the trustees decide, of the proceedings at their meetings. In the minutes the trustees must record their decisions and, where appropriate, the reasons for those decisions. The trustees must approve the minutes in accordance with the procedures, laid down in regulations made under clause [21] of this deed.

21. General power to make regulations

The trustees may from time to time make regulations for the management of the charity and for the conduct of their business, including:

(i) the calling of meetings;

(ii) methods of making decisions in order to deal with cases or urgency when a meeting is impracticable;

(iii) the deposit of money at a bank;

(iv) the custody of documents; and

(v) the keeping and authenticating of records. (If regulations made under this clause permit records of the charity to be kept in electronic form and requires a trustee to sign the record, the regulations must specify a method of recording the signature that enables it to be properly authenticated.) The trustees must not make regulations which are inconsistent with anything in this deed.

22. Accounts, annual report and annual return

The trustees must comply with their obligations under the Charities Act 1993 with regard to:

  (i)   the keeping of accounting records for the charity;

 (ii)   the preparation of annual statements of account for the charity;

(iii)   the auditing or independent examination of the statements of account of the charity; and

(iv)   the transmission of the statements of account of the charity to the Commission.

 (v)   the preparation of an annual report and its transmission to the Commission.

(vi)   the preparation of an annual return and its transmission to the Commission.

23. Registered particulars

The trustees must notify the Commission promptly of any changes to the charity's entry on the Central Register of Charities.

24. Bank account

Any bank or building society account in which any of the funds of the charity are deposited must be operated by the trustees and held in the name of the charity. Unless the regulations of the trustees make other provision, all cheques and orders for the payment of money from such an account shall be signed by at least two trustees.

25. Trustees not to benefit financially from their trusteeship

Option 1

Unless expressly authorised by the Commission to do so, no trustee may buy goods or services from the charity, or sell goods or services to the charity or receive remuneration, or receive any other financial benefit from the charity or from any trading company owned by the charity.

or

Option 2

  (i)   Subject to sub-clause (ii) of this clause, no trustee may receive remuneration for any service provided to the charity and no trustee may acquire any interest in property belonging to the charity or be interested in any contract entered into by the trustee otherwise than as a trustee of the charity.

(ii)   Any trustee who is a solicitor, accountant or engaged in any profession may charge and be paid all the usual professional charges for business done by him or her or his or her firm, when instructed by the other trustees to act in a professional capacity on behalf of the charity. However, at no time may a majority of the trustees benefit under this provision and a trustee must withdraw from any meeting of the trustees at which his or her own instruction or remuneration or performance, or that of his or her firm, is under discussion.

or

Option 3

(i)   No trustee may buy goods or services from the charity, or sell goods or services to the charity, or receive remuneration, or receive any other financial benefit from the charity or from any trading company owned by the charity, except in accordance with this deed.

(ii)   The trustees may employ, or enter into a contract for the supply of goods or services with, one of their number. Before doing so, the trustees must be satisfied that it is in the best interests of the charity to employ, or contract with, that trustee rather than someone who has no connection with the charity. In reaching that decision, they must balance the advantage of employing a trustee against the disadvantages of doing so (especially the loss of the trustee's services as a result of dealing with the trustee's conflict of interest as required by the next subclause). The remuneration or other sums paid to the trustee must not exceed an amount that is reasonable in all the circumstances. The trustees must record the reason for their decision in their minute book.

(iii)   A trustee must be absent from the part of any meeting at which his or her employment or remuneration, or any matter concerning the contract, are discussed. He or she must also be absent from the part of any meeting at which his or her performance in that employment, or his or her performance of the contract, is considered. He or she must not vote on any matter relating to his employment or the contract and must not be counted when calculating whether a quorum of trustees is present at the meeting.

(iv)   This clause applies to a firm of which a trustee is a partner as it applies to a trustee personally.

26. Repair and insurance

The trustees must keep in repair and insure to their full value against fire and other usual risks all the buildings of the charity (except those buildings that are required to be kept in repair and insured by a tenant). They must also insure suitably in respect of public liability and employer's liability.

27. Expenses

The trustees may use the charity's funds to meet any necessary and reasonable expenses which they incur in the course of carrying out their responsibilities as trustees of the charity.

28. Amendment of trust deed

(i) The trustees may amend the provisions of this deed, provided that:

    (a) no amendment may be made to clause 3 (Application of Income), clause 8 (Duty of care), clause [25] (Trustees not to benefit financially from their trusteeship), clause [29] (Dissolution) or this clause without the prior consent in writing of the Commission; and

    (b) no amendment may be made whose effect is that the charity ceases to be a charity at law.

(ii) Any amendment of this deed must be made by deed following a decision of the trustees made at a special meeting.

(iii) The trustees must send to the Commission a certified copy of the deed effecting any amendment made under this clause within three months of it being made.

29. Dissolution

The trustees may dissolve the charity if they decide that it is necessary or desirable to do so. To be effective, a proposal to dissolve the charity must be passed at a special meeting by a two-thirds' majority of the trustees. Any assets of the charity that are left after the charity's debts have been paid ('the net assets') must be given:

(i) to another charity (or other charities) with objects that are no wider than the charity's own, for the general purposes of the recipient charity (or charities); or

(ii) to any charity for use for particular purposes which fall within the charity's objects.

The Commission must be notified promptly that the charity has been dissolved and, if the trustees were obliged to send the charity's accounts to the Commission for the accounting period which ended before its dissolution, they must send the Commission the charity's final accounts.

30. Interpretation

In this deed, all references to particular legislation are to be understood as references to legislation in force at the date of this deed and also to any subsequent legislation that adds to, modifies or replaces that legislation.

IN WITNESS of this deed the parties to it have signed below.

Signed as a deed etc.

Precedent for standard settlement administrative powers

A1.12

(Administrative Powers of Trustees)

To accept additions

(1)   Power to accept additions to the Trust Fund and if they think fit to administer them as one fund therewith for all purposes

To retain investments without need to diversify

(2)   Power at the absolute discretion of the Trustees to retain all or any part of the Trust Fund (including uninvested money) in its existing state of investment for any period and to vary and transpose investments within the range authorised below without in either case being under any obligation to diversify the investment of the Trust Fund

Wide power of investment

(3)   Power to invest or apply trust moneys on the security or in the acquisition of any shares stocks funds securities or other investments or property (movable or immovable) or rights or interests of whatsoever kind in any part of the world whether or not producing income or involving liability (including power to lend the same whether or not at interest and with or without security and power to acquire any property movable or immovable including chattels for the beneficial occupation use or enjoyment of any beneficiary or beneficiaries hereunder) to the intent that the Trustees shall have all the powers of investment and applying trust moneys available to an absolute beneficial owner

To borrow

(4)   (i)   Power to borrow money for any purpose (including investment and the payment of any tax or duty) whether on the security of the Trust Fund or otherwise and to mortgage or charge any property which (or the future proceeds of sale of which) is subject to the trusts hereof to secure repayment of any such borrowing

(ii)   Power to enter into borrowing arrangements jointly with other persons [other than the Excluded Persons]* whether involving joint or several liability

To lend

(5)   Without prejudice to the generality of the powers of investment and application hereinbefore contained power for the Trustees to lend trust money whether or not at interest and with or without security to any person who is for the time being a beneficiary of the trusts hereof and to charge any part or share of the Trust Fund as security for any debt or other liability of such person

To appropriate

(6)   Power to allot appropriate partition or apportion any property which (or the future proceeds of sale of which) is subject to the trusts hereof in or

towards the satisfaction of any share or interest in the capital or income of the Trust Fund in such manner as the Trustees (without the necessity of obtaining any consent) consider just according to the respective rights of the persons interested

To allow enjoyment in kind by beneficiary

(7) Power to permit any property (movable or immovable) which (or the future proceeds of sale of which) is subject to the trusts hereof to be occupied used or enjoyed by any beneficiary hereunder and so that the Trustees shall not be liable for any loss or damage to such property but shall have power to take any steps they think fit for its insurance repair renewal or custody

Life insurance

(8) (i) Power to effect or acquire or join in effecting or acquiring and to maintain at the expense of capital any policy or policies of insurance on the life of any person or persons

(ii) In relation to any such policy or policies all the powers of sale surrender exchange conversion into a fully paid policy or policies and of exercising options available to an absolute beneficial owner

Delegation

(9) Power to delegate their powers of investment and management of trust property to an agent (including one of their number) on such terms including terms enabling the agent to charge remuneration, to appoint a substitute, to limit liability and to act in circumstances giving rise to a conflict of interest as the Trustees think fit.

To appoint nominees

(10) Power to appoint any person (including one of their number or a beneficiary) to act as their nominee and to take such steps as are necessary to vest any property in such person on such terms including terms enabling the agent to charge remuneration, to appoint a substitute, to limit liability and to act in circumstances giving rise to a conflict of interest as the Trustees think fit.

To take or defend proceedings

(11) Power to institute or defend proceedings in any part of the world at the expense of the Trust Fund without the necessity of obtaining directions from any Court or authority from the beneficiaries of this Settlement

To pay duty

(12) Power to pay any taxes duties or other fiscal impositions for which the Trustees may become liable in any part of the world notwithstanding that such liability may not be enforceable through the Courts of the place where this Settlement is for the time being administered

To take receipts from parents, guardians and minors**

(13) Power where any income or capital is payable to or applicable for the maintenance education or benefit of any minor to accept the receipt of his

or her parent or guardian for such income or capital without being bound to see to its further application and to accept the receipt of the minor personally after he or she has attained the age of 16 years

To effect variations

(14) Power (without prejudice to or being limited by any of the other provisions of this Clause) to effect any such disposition or transaction as is mentioned in Section 57 of the Trustee Act 1925 which the Trustees consider to be expedient without the necessity of obtaining an order of any Court

*   Do not include these words if the Settlement does not define Excluded Persons.

**   This power might be excluded in the case of a bare trust where section 31 of the Trustee Act 1925 is excluded and the relationship between settlor and beneficiary is not that of parent and child.

Precedent for recital where trust property includes land

A1.13

'WHEREAS:–

(1) The Settlor wishes to make this irrevocable settlement for the benefit of the [*identify beneficiaries eg: discretionary beneficiaries*] hereinafter mentioned and by a transfer of even date (executed contemporaneously with) and made between the same parties as this settlement ('the Transfer') the Settlor has transferred to the Original Trustees the [*leasehold/freehold*] property specified in the First Schedule hereto upon the trusts and with and subject to the powers and provisions declared and contained concerning the same in a settlement referred to in the Transfer (meaning this settlement)'

NOTE: the definitions used in this recital should be consistent with those used throughout the remainder of the instrument and the property in question ought to be described in the First Schedule to the instrument. If it is intended that a beneficiary is to occupy the property the subject of such a settlement it should be remembered that the Revenue may regard him as acquiring an interest in possession in the property for inheritance tax purposes: Inland Revenue Statement of Practice SP10/79; *IRC v Lloyds Private Banking [1998] STC 559.*

The substance of the Land Registry Transfer should read:

'The Trustees hold the land upon the trusts declared by a deed of even date made between the same parties as this transfer and accordingly apply to the Registrar for entry of the following restriction on the register:

No disposition by a sole proprietor of the land (not being a trust corporation) under which capital money arises is to be registered except under an order of the Registrar or of the court.'

Precedent for administrative powers relating to land

A1.14

Special Administrative Powers of Trustees relating to Land

Powers of absolute owner

(1)   All the powers of an absolute owner in relation to any land held by the Trustees

Purchasing land abroad

(2)   Power to purchase land anywhere in the world

Undivided shares in land

(3)   Power to join with any person in the purchase an undivided share in land on such terms as the Trustees think fit

Power to improve land

(4)   Power at any time or times to apply any money subject to the trusts hereof in making improvements to or otherwise developing repairing or maintaining land held by the Trustees

To lease and repair

(5)   In relation to any land subject to the trusts hereof all the powers of leasing and alienation generally (upon and subject to any terms and conditions whatsoever) and of management exploitation insurance protection maintenance repair cultivation and improvement which are available to an absolute beneficial owner

To allow enjoyment in kind by beneficiary

(6)   Power to permit any beneficiary to have the beneficial occupation use or enjoyment in kind of any land subject to the trusts hereof on such terms as to repair insurance or payment of outgoings by the beneficiary or otherwise howsoever as the Trustees think fit Provided that the foregoing power shall only be exercisable and such permission to occupy or enjoy in kind may only continue if the occupation thereof by such beneficiary is compatible with any statutory rights of occupation of any other beneficiary or beneficiaries and the income (if any) of the land is payable to such beneficiary or capable of being paid or applied to him or for his benefit in exercise of a discretion

Precedent for administrative powers relating to business property

A1.15

Special Administrative Powers of Trustees relating to Business Property

To hold shares in a private company

(1) Without prejudice to the generality of the foregoing power to hold retain and acquire any shares or other securities in [*NAME OF COMPANY*] (or any company which is a successor to or associated with the said company) notwithstanding that such shares or securities represent the whole or the greater part of the Trust Fund

To trade

(2) Power to carry on any trade or business whether alone or in partnership or any other form of joint venture with others and to assist or finance to any extent the carrying on of any trade or business by others on such terms as the Trustees think fit Provided that in the absence of dishonesty none of the Trustees shall be liable for any loss to the Trust Fund incurred as a result of any trade carried on by them

To farm

(3) Power upon or in any land and buildings which are held upon any of the trusts hereof to carry on the business (whether alone or in partnership with any other person [other than an Excluded Person]*) of farming forestry or any other business of an agricultural nature or of any other nature and to employ in it all or any part of any assets subject to the same trusts and to finance such business out of those trust assets with full power to engage remunerate and dismiss any managers bailiffs servants and agents and to appoint regulate and change their respective duties

To employ in the course of business

(4) Power to employ and engage any persons (including independent contractors) upon any terms and to purchase any plant or machinery in connection with any trade or business

To incorporate

(5) Power to incorporate any company or other corporation in any part of the world with limited or unlimited liability for any purpose including the acquisition of the whole or any part of the Trust Fund or any other property or the carrying on of any trade or business (and so that any consideration for the acquisition of the Trust Fund or any part thereof by any company incorporated pursuant to this Clause may consist wholly or partly of fully paid debentures debenture stock shares or other securities of the company allotted to or otherwise vested in the Trustees so as to be capital in the hands of the Trustees)

*   Include only if the Settlement defines Excluded persons.

Precedent for a gift on discretionary trust of amount of inheritance tax nil-rate band for benefit of spouse and issue

A1.16

1. If [my [husband]/[wife] the said ....] shall survive me for a period of at least thirty days I give the amount which at my death equals the maximum which can be given to them on these trusts without inheritance tax becoming payable in respect of this gift to my Trustees on the following trusts:

2. In this clause:

    (1) 'the Nil-Rate Legacy Fund' means the assets at any particular time held by my Trustees on the trusts of this clause;

    (2) 'my Beneficiaries' means my [wife]/[husband] and issue.

3. For not more than 80 years after my death (which is the perpetuity period applicable to these trusts) my Trustees shall hold the Nil-Rate Legacy Fund:

    (1) to apply the capital of the Nil-Rate Legacy Fund for the maintenance education or benefit of such of my Beneficiaries on such trusts (including protective and discretionary trusts) and with and subject to such dispositive and administrative powers and provisions as my Trustees (being at least two in number or a trust corporation) may in their absolute discretion (but having regard to the rules relating to remoteness) by any deed or deeds revocable or irrevocable appoint PROVIDED THAT my Trustees shall not make any payment or application of more than one half of the capital of the Nil-Rate Legacy Fund during the lifetime of my said [husband]/[wife] and whilst [he]/[she] remains mentally capable of managing [his]/[her] affairs without the consent in writing of my said [husband]/[wife] and in the event of any doubt arising concerning the mental capacity or otherwise of my said [husband]/[wife] then my Trustees shall be entitled to rely on a letter from the then current general medical practitioner of my said [husband]/[wife] confirming his or her opinion of such mental capacity or otherwise and such opinion shall be final and binding upon all persons;

    (2) to apply the income of the Nil-Rate Legacy Fund for the benefit of such of my Beneficiaries as my Trustees think fit; or

        (a) (for not more than 21 years from my death) to accumulate all or any part of it; and

        (b) add accumulations to capital or apply previous accumulations or part of them as though they were the current tax year's income.

(3) not later than 80 years after my death to end these trusts by distributing the Trust Fund among such of my Beneficiaries as are then alive in equal shares or if these trusts fail for whichever charity my Trustees think fit.

4. My Trustees may:

(1) invest or otherwise apply any part of the Nil-Rate Legacy Fund in such manner and on such terms as this will or the or the general law may permit;

(2) make retentions to meet any taxes for which they may be liable and pay those taxes and any other expenses of the administration of the Nil-Rate Legacy Fund out of capital or income;

(3) lend with or without security all or any part or parts of the capital of the Nil-Rate Legacy Fund to all or any one or more of the Beneficiaries upon such conditions as to interest (if any) and repayment thereof and for such period and generally upon such terms as my Trustees in their absolute discretion think fit;

(4) not except under subclause 3(1) or on a distribution of the Nil-Rate Legacy Fund exercise their powers under this sub-clause so as to create an interest in possession for a beneficiary.

Precedent for a full discretionary trust of residue

A1.17

(1)   IN this Clause where the context so admits:

    (a)   'the Trust Fund' means my residuary estate.

    (b)   'the Trustees' shall mean my Trustees or other the trustee or trustees for the time being of the Trust Fund.

    (c)   'the Discretionary Beneficiaries' means the following:

        [specify the discretionary beneficiaries]. Eg, [my wife]/[my husband], my children and remoter issue whenever born, the husbands wives widows and widowers of my children and remoter issue and charity

(2)   For not more than 80 years after my death (which is the perpetuity period applicable to these trusts) the Trustees shall hold the Trust Fund:

    (a)   To apply the capital of the Trust Fund for the maintenance education or benefit of such of the Discretionary Beneficiaries on such trusts (including protective and discretionary trusts) and with and subject to such dispositive and administrative powers and provisions as my Trustees (being at least two in number or a trust corporation) may in their absolute discretion (but having regard to the rules relating to remoteness) by any deed or deeds revocable or irrevocable appoint;

    (b)   To apply the income of the Trust Fund for the benefit of such of the Discretionary Beneficiaries as my Trustees think fit; or

        (i)   (for not more than 21 years from my death) to accumulate all or any part of it; and

        (ii)   add accumulations to capital or apply previous accumulations or part of them as though they were the current tax year's income.

    (c)   Not later than 80 years after my death to end these trusts by distributing the Trust Fund among such of the Discretionary Beneficiaries as are then alive in equal shares or if these trusts fail for whichever charity my Trustees think fit.

    (d)   To exercise their discretionary powers over capital or income when and how they think fit without having to make payments to or for the benefit of all my Beneficiaries or to ensure equality among those who have benefited.

(3)   The Trustees shall have the following powers:

    (a)   To retain or sell any of the assets constituting the Trust Fund.

(b) To invest or otherwise apply any part of the Trust Fund in such manner and on such terms as this will or the or the general law may permit and this power includes the right to invest:

  (i) in unsecured interest free loans to any of the Discretionary Beneficiaries;

  (ii) in non-income producing assets including policies of life assurance (with power to pay premiums out of income or capital);

  (iii) in property for the occupation of any of the Discretionary Beneficiaries.

(c) To use the income or capital of the Trust Fund for or towards the cost of maintaining or improving any property forming part of the Trust Fund.

(d) To make loans which may be interest free.

(e) To insure any asset of the Trust Fund on such terms as they think fit and:

  (i) to pay premiums out of income or capital, and

  (ii) to use any insurance money received to restore the asset or to apply it as if it were the proceeds of its sale.

(f) To borrow money on such terms as they think fit (including the giving of security) and to use it for any purpose for which the capital of the Trust Fund may be used.

(g) In exercising the statutory power of appointing new trustees to appoint a professional person and give him the right to charge for work done by himself or his firm.

(4) [If the above trusts fail to divide my residuary estate equally among the following charities:

      ]

Precedent for half secret trust for chattels

A1.18

IF my [husband]/[wife] the said [.............] shall predecease me then but not otherwise I give (free of all duties and taxes payable in consequence of my death) my wearing apparel and my personal chattels (as defined in Section 55(1)(x) of the Administration of Estates Act 1925) otherwise than as specifically disposed of by any codicil hereto to my Trustees and I request my Trustees to distribute the same in accordance with the memorandum of my wishes left by me and signed by me, the terms of which have been communicated to and accepted by my Trustees and that in default or in respect of any such items not mentioned in any such memorandum my Trustees will hold the same as an accretion to my residuary estate (as hereinafter defined).

Precedent for standard testamentary administrative powers

A1.19

1. My Trustees shall have power:

    (1) to apply for the benefit of any beneficiary who is has a contingent interest the whole or any part of the income from any capital to which he may become entitled;

    (2) to pay or apply for the benefit of any beneficiary who has a contingent interest the whole or any part of the capital to which he may become entitled;

    (3) to pay any money to which a beneficiary under eighteen is entitled to his parent or guardian for his benefit or to the beneficiary himself once he has attained sixteen and to rely upon the receipt then given by the parent or guardian or the minor himself.

2. My Trustees shall have the following powers in addition to their powers under the general law:

    (1) Power to invest as if they were beneficially entitled and this power includes the right:

        (a) to invest in unsecured loans;

        (b) to invest in other non-income producing assets including policies of life assurance;

        (c) to purchase land anywhere in the world;

        (d) to purchase an undivided share in land;

        (e) to invest in land for the occupation or enjoyment of any beneficiary.

    (2) Power to delegate their powers of investment and management of trust property to an agent (including one of their number) on such terms including terms enabling the agent to charge remuneration, to appoint a substitute, to limit liability and to act in circumstances giving rise to a conflict of interest as my Trustees think fit.

    (3) Power to appoint any person (including one of their number or a beneficiary) to act as their nominee and to take such steps as are necessary to vest any property in such person on such terms including terms enabling the agent to charge remuneration, to appoint a substitute, to limit liability and to act in circumstances giving rise to a conflict of interest as my Trustees think fit.

    (4) Power to make loans of capital to a beneficiary which may be interest free, repayable on demand or repayable at a rate below the market rate.

    (5) Power to borrow money on such terms as they think fit including the giving of security and to use it for any purpose for which the capital of my estate may be used.

    (6) Power without the restrictions imposed by section 41 of the Administration of Estates Act 1925:

(a) To appropriate to any beneficiary in satisfaction or partial satisfaction of the gift to him any asset forming part of my residuary estate and not subject to a specific gift.

(b) To appropriate as the assets or part of the assets of any trust created by this Will any asset forming part of my residuary estate and not subject to a specific gift.

3.   Any of my Trustees who is a professional, including a sole trustee, may charge fees for work done by him or his firm (whether or not the work is of a professional nature) on the same basis as if he were not one of the Trustees but employed to carry out the work on their behalf and a trust corporation may charge and be paid fees according to the scale fees which it charges from time to time.

4.   (1) All income received after my death shall be treated as income of my estate regardless of the period to which it relates and the statutory rules concerning apportionment and the rules in *Howe v Dartmouth* and *Allhusen v Whittell* [*and Re Chesterfield's Trusts*] shall not apply.

(2) My Trustees shall exercise their powers of investment and carry out their duties as trustees without regard to the statutory duty of care and Trustee Act 2000 s 1 shall not apply to the trusts of my Will.

(3) My Trustees shall be under no duty to review the acts of agents, nominees and custodians appointed by them and Trustee Act 2000 s 22 shall not apply to the trusts of my Will.

(4) Section 11 Trusts of Land and Appointment of Trustees Act 1996 (consultation with beneficiaries) shall not apply.

(5) In the absence of proof of dishonesty or the wilful commission of an act known to be a breach of trust none of my Trustees shall be liable for any loss or bound to take proceedings against a co-trustee for any breach of trust.

(6) My Trustees shall be entitled to be indemnified out of the assets of my estate against all liabilities incurred in connection with the bona fide execution of their duties and powers.

(7) None of my Trustees shall be accountable for any remuneration or other benefit gained as an officer employee agent or adviser of any company body or firm in any way connected with the Trust Fund notwithstanding that his situation or office may have been obtained by reason of his position as one of the Trustees.

(8) My Trustees may enter into any transaction notwithstanding that one or more of their number may have some other interest therein whether in a personal or in a fiduciary capacity provided that at least one of their number has no such other interest.

Precedent for testamentary right of occupation creating a life interest

A1.20

(1) **I GIVE** my [freehold]/[leasehold] property known as [.............] or such other the freehold or leasehold dwellinghouse (if any) as I may own at the date of my death as my principal residence (my said property or dwelling-house being hereinafter called 'the Property' which expression shall include where the context so admits any other property or dwellinghouse purchased in substitution therefor in accordance with the provisions of this Clause) to my Trustees free of all taxes and duties payable in conse-quence of my death to hold the same on trust for [*name of life tenant*] 'the Life Tenant' during [*his*]/[*her*] life and subject to the Life Tenant's interest on trust for [*name of remainderman*].

(2) I intend the Property to be available for occupation by the Life Tenant free of any occupation rent but that my trustees should during the period of such occupation require [*him*]/[*her*] to pay all council tax and other outgoings payable in respect of the same and keep the said property in good repair and condition and refund to my trustees the cost of keeping the same insured. My Trustees shall not be liable to see to such repair or the effecting or keeping up of such insurance or for any breach of the obligations hereby imposed on the Life Tenant.

(3) My Trustees shall have power at the written request of the Life Tenant but not otherwise to sell the Property and with the net proceeds of sale purchase any other dwellinghouse designated by the Life Tenant and shall hold such other dwellinghouse in accordance with the provisions of this Clause (including this sub-clause hereof) and in addition my Trustees shall have power to join with any other person in the purchase an undivided share in such dwellinghouse and may apply any surplus moneys in their hands in the improvement or repair of such dwellinghouse.

(4) My trustees may exercise their powers hereunder in favour of or for the benefit of the Life Tenant notwithstanding that the Life Tenant is one of my trustees provided that the Life Tenant is not my sole trustee.

Precedent for testamentary right of occupation without creating a life interest

A1.21

I GIVE my house known as [postal address] ('the House') to my Trustees on trust on the following terms:

(1)   My Trustees shall permit [*Name of beneficiary*] ('the Occupant') to live in the House without payment to them so long as [she]/[he] wishes and so long as he keeps the House in repair, insures it and pays all outgoings relating to it.

(2)   While the Occupant is living in the House my Trustees shall not sell it without the Occupant's consent.

(3)   When the Occupant has ceased to live in the House my Trustees shall hold it [as part of my residuary estate] or [appropriate gift over].

(4)   At the Occupant's request my Trustees may sell the House and buy another to be held on trust on the same terms as the House.

(5)   In purchasing a replacement in accordance with the previous power my Trustees may join with any person in purchasing an undivided share of land.

(6)   Any surplus arising from the sale and purchase shall [form part of my residuary estate] or [as in (3)].

Precedent for memorandum of wishes to accompany a nil-rate band discretionary legacy trust in a will

A1.22

MEMORANDUM OF WISHES

To the Executors and Trustees of my Will dated [*date of will*] ('my Will')

Dear Trustees,

I am writing this letter to you in strict confidence in your capacity as Trustees of the Nil-Rate Legacy Fund. Although, as a matter of law, it is for you to decide how to exercise your discretion in respect of both the income and capital of the Nil-Rate Legacy Fund, I feel that you might like some guidance from me as to how I envisage you exercising your discretion in ordinary circumstances. I make this memorandum as a statement of my wishes and without wishing to create any binding trust or obligation upon you.

It is my wish that my [widow]/[widower] should be regarded as the primary beneficiary as regards both the capital and income of the Nil-Rate Legacy Fund and you should provide [her]/[him] with sufficient income and capital to enable [her]/[him] to live in full comfort for the rest of [her]/[his] life. If she/he does not require all of the income this should be accumulated and retained within the trust for use later. No capital should be paid out of the Legacy Fund for any beneficiary other than my [wife]/[husband] apart from in exceptional circumstances (for example urgent medical treatment being required). Following [her]/[his] death or to the extent that my [widow]/[widower] does not require the Legacy Fund in whole or in part, I would like you to regard the Legacy Fund as being notionally divided into equal shares between each of my children. If any of my children shall die then I would expect his or her children (ie my grandchildren) to take, and if more than one, equally between them, the share which his or her parent would otherwise have taken.

Although I have indicated that I would like my children to benefit from the capital and income of the trust, I would be happy for you to benefit my grandchildren, during the lives of my children, if appropriate, after consultation with my children.

Subject to any legal limitations on the accumulation of income, whilst my children or grandchildren are under the age of twenty-one, I would envisage you applying the income in the Nil-Rate Legacy Fund for their maintenance, education or benefit. Once a child or grandchild attains the age of twenty-one, I would be happy for you to release the income from a particular child's or grandchild's share at their request unless you consider that there are good reasons to accumulate the income.

I would not envisage any distributions of capital being made to any of my children or grandchildren whilst they are under the age of twenty-one unless you feel that there is a good reason to do so. Once a child or grandchild has attained the age of twenty-one then I would be happy for distributions of capital to be made if it is appropriate to do so after consultation between you and the relevant beneficiary and bearing in mind family, financial and fiscal considerations. I am aware that my children or grandchildren may prefer to keep the assets in trust.

[In the event that assets have been retained in the trust and my [widow]/ [widower], my children and remoter issue have not survived then I would envisage that you will distribute the trust assets to such of the Beneficiaries as defined in my Will as are alive at that time in equal shares absolutely.]

These are my wishes as I see them at the present time. I cannot, of course, predict what actual circumstances will face you when you come to exercise your discretions. If, in those circumstances, you feel that I would have expressed any different wishes had I been alive to do so, then the decision to ignore my wishes is open to you.

Please note that the contents of this letter are confidential and should not be released to anyone, other than your successor or other Trustees.

Yours sincerely

....

[Testator/Testatrix]

Dated .... day of .... 20..

Precedent for deed of variation

A1.23

THIS DEED OF VARIATION is made the [*date in the month*] day of [*month*] Two Thousand and [*Four*] BY

[*names and addresses of executors*] ('the Executors')

[*name and address of Original Beneficiary*] ('the Donor')

[*name and address of donee*] ('the Donee')

WHEREAS:

(1)   [*Name of testator*] late of [*address*] ('the Testator') died on [*date of death*] having made his last Will dated [*date of will*] ('the Will') by which he appointed the Executors to be his Executors and Trustees.

(2)   The Executors obtained a grant of Probate out of the [Principal]/[......] District] Registry on [date of grant].

(3)   By clause [*number of clause containing gift*] of the Will the Testator gave the whole of his residuary estate to the Donor absolutely.

(4)   The Donor has a daughter ('the Donee') [*name and address of daughter*].

(5)   The Donor and the Executors desire that the disposition of the Testator's estate effected by his Will be varied for the benefit of the Donee in the following manner.

NOW THIS DEED made by way of variation of the Testator's will in pursuance of the parties' desire **WITNESSES:**

1.   The Will shall be varied and the Testator's estate administered as if from the death of the Testator clause [*number of clause containing gift*] of the Will had provided that the Testator's residuary estate should be held by the Executors on trust for the Donee in equal shares absolutely.

2.   In accordance with section 142(2) of the Inheritance Tax Act 1984 and Section 62(7) of the Taxation of Chargeable Gains Act 1992 the parties hereto make a statement that they intend that the provisions of Section 142(1) of the Inheritance Tax Act 1984 and of Section 62(6) of the Taxation of Chargeable Gains Act 1992 shall apply in relation to the variation effected by this deed to the intent that such variation shall be treated as if it were made by the Testator for the purposes of inheritance tax and capital gains tax

IN WITNESS whereof the parties hereto have executed these presents as their deed the day and year first above written

SIGNED and DELIVERED as a deed etc.

Precedent for deed of appointment

A1.24

THIS DEED OF APPOINTMENT is made the [*date in the month*] day of [*month*] Two Thousand and [*Four*] BY

[*Name of First Trustee*] of [*Address of First Trustee*] and

[*Name of Second Trustee*] of [*Address of Second Trustee*] (hereinafter called 'the Nil-Rate Trustees')

SUPPLEMENTAL TO the Will (hereinafter called 'the Will') dated [*date of will*] of [*Name of Testator*] who died on [*date of death*] and whose said will was on [*date of grant*] duly proved by the Nil-Rate Trustees who are the executors therein named

WHEREAS:

(1)   The property now subject to the trusts of the will includes the investments set out in the schedule hereto

(2)   The Nil-Rate Trustees desire by this deed to exercise the power of appointment given to them by Clause [*effective clause*] of the Will

NOW THIS DEED WITNESSETH that the Nil-Rate Trustees in exercise of their said power of appointment under the will hereby irrevocably appoint the property set out in the said Schedule upon trust as to both capital and income for [*Name of Appointee*] absolutely and declares that all income of the said property shall be treated as accruing on the date on which it becomes payable regardless of the period in respect of which it shall have accrued and shall not be subject to statutory apportionment.

IN WITNESS whereof the parties hereto have executed these presents as their deed the day and year first above written

THE SCHEDULE

[*The property subject of the appointment.*]

SIGNED and DELIVERED as a deed by the said [*NAME OF FIRST TRUSTEE*] in the presence of:–

```
W    Signature.........................................
I     Name...............................................
T     Address ...........................................
N          ..................................................
E          ..................................................
S          ..................................................
S          ..................................................
```

SIGNED and DELIVERED as a deed by the said [*NAME OF SECOND TRUSTEE*] in the presence of:–

```
W    Signature.........................................
I    Name ..............................................
T    Address ..........................................
N         ................................................
E         ................................................
S         ................................................
S         ................................................
```

Precedent for exercise of power of advancement

A1.25

THIS RESOLUTION is made on [*date in the month*] day of [*month*] Two Thousand and [*Four*] BY

[*Name of First Trustee*] of [*Address of First Trustee*] and

[*Name of Second Trustee*] of [*Address of Second Trustee*] and

[*Name of Third Trustee*] of [*Address of Third Trustee*] ('the Trustees').

WHEREAS:

(1)   By a Settlement made the [*date of settlement*] ('the Settlement') between [*name of settlor*] ('the Settlor') of the one part and the First Trustee and the Second Trustee ('the Original Trustees') of the other part the Settlor settled his one half undivided share in the property specified in the Schedule thereto upon the trusts therein declared.

(2)   By a deed of appointment made the [*date of deed*] between the Settlor of the one part and the Third Trustee of the other part the Settlor appointed the Third Trustee to be a trustee of the Settlement to act jointly with the Original Trustees.

(3)   The Trustees are the trustees for the time being of the Settlement.

(4)   The Trustees hold the property described in the Schedule hereto ('Peter's Fund') and the income thereof upon trust for the Settlor's grandson Peter Piper ('Peter') contingently on him attaining the age of 35 years.

(5)   By clause [*number of clause*] of the Settlement Trustee Act 1925 Section 32 applies to the trusts of the Settlement as if the words 'the whole' were substituted for the words 'one half' in proviso (a) to subsection (1) thereof.

(6)   The Trustees desire to exercise their power of advancement for the benefit of Peter in the manner hereinafter appearing.

THE TRUSTEES RESOLVE in exercise of the power contained in the Trustee Act 1925 Section 32 as varied by clause [*number of clause*] of the Settlement and of any and every other power them enabling to transfer the whole of Peter's Fund to Peter for his own use and benefit absolutely.

[*Signatures of trustees*]

THE SCHEDULE

[*List of assets in Peter's Fund*]

Precedent for trustee power of attorney

A1.26

THIS GENERAL TRUSTEE POWER OF ATTORNEY is made on [*date*] by [*name of one donor*] of [*address of donor*] ('the Donor') as trustee of [*name or details of one trust*].

I appoint [*name of one donee*] of [*address of donee*] to be my attorney [*if desired, the date on which the delegation commences or the period for which it continues (or both)*] in accordance with section 25(5) of the Trustee Act 1925.

IN WITNESS whereof the Donor has executed this present as his deed the [*date in the month*] day of [*month*] Two Thousand and [*Four*].

SIGNED and DELIVERED as a deed by the said [*NAME OF DONOR*] in the presence of:–

W	Signature...
I	Name..
T	Address ....
N	....
E	....
S	....
S	....

Precedent for deed of appointment and retirement of trustees

A1.27

THIS DEED OF APPOINTMENT is made the [*date in the month*] day of [*month*] Two Thousand and [*Four*] BY

[*Name of First Continuing Trustee*] of [*Address of First Continuing Trustee*] and

[*Name of Second Continuing Trustee*] of [*Address of Second Continuing Trustee*] ('the Continuing Trustees') of the First Part

[*Name of Retiring Trustee*] of [*Address of Retiring Trustee*] (hereinafter called 'the Retiring Trustee') of the Second Part and

[*Name of New Trustee*] of [*Address of New Trustee*] ('the New Trustee') of the Third Part

SUPPLEMENTAL TO a Settlement dated [*date of settlement*] ('the Settlement') made between [*name of settlor*] (the Settlor) of the First Part and the Continuing Trustees and the Retiring Trustee ('the Trustees') of the Second Part

WHEREAS:

(1)   The Continuing Trustees and the Retiring Trustee are the trustees for the time being of the Settlement

(2)   The Retiring Trustee wishes to be discharged from the trusts of the Settlement and the Continuing Trustees and the Retiring Trustee wish to appoint the New Trustee to be trustee of the Settlement in place of the Retiring Trustee and to act jointly with the Continuing Trustees

(3)   The Property subject to the trusts of the Settlement consists of the Property and the several investments described in the Schedule ('the Investments')

(4)   It is intended that the Investments shall immediately be separately transferred into the joint names of the Continuing Trustee and the New Trustee

NOW THIS DEED WITNESSETH The Continuing Trustees and the Retiring Trustee in exercise of the powers vested in them by the Trustee Act 1925 and of every or any other power enabling them in this behalf the Continuing Trustees and the Retiring Trustee appoint the New Trustee to be trustee of the Settlement in place of the Retiring Trustee and to act jointly with the Continuing Trustees

IN WITNESS whereof the parties hereto have executed these presents as their deed the day and year first above written

THE SCHEDULE

[*The property subject to the trusts of the settlement*]

SIGNED and DELIVERED as a deed by the said [*NAME OF FIRST CONTINUING TRUSTEE*] in the presence of:–

```
W    Signature.......................................
I    Name............................................
T    Address ........................................
N        ................................................
E        ................................................
S        ................................................
S        ................................................
```

SIGNED and DELIVERED as a deed by the said [*NAME OF SECOND CONTINUING TRUSTEE*] in the presence of:–

```
W    Signature.......................................
I    Name............................................
T    Address ........................................
N        ................................................
E        ................................................
S        ................................................
S        ................................................
```

SIGNED and DELIVERED as a deed by the said [*NAME OF RETIRING TRUSTEE*] in the presence of:–

```
W    Signature.......................................
I    Name............................................
T    Address ........................................
N        ................................................
E        ................................................
S        ................................................
S        ................................................
```

SIGNED and DELIVERED as a deed by the said [*NAME OF NEW TRUSTEE*] in the presence of:–

```
W    Signature.......................................
I    Name............................................
T    Address ........................................
N        ................................................
E        ................................................
S        ................................................
S        ................................................
```

Precedent alternative clause for a settlement permitting dismissal of trustees and alternative clause for appointment of trustees

A1.28

Retirement and Appointment of Trustees

(1) The statutory power to appoint new and additional trustees shall be vested in:

(a) the Settlor during [his]/[her] life; and, after [his]/[her] death

(b) such person (if any) as the Settlor shall by deed revocable or irrevocable appoint; and, in default of such appointment

(c) [*name*] during [his]/[her] life

Provided always that the statutory power of appointing new trustees shall not be exercisable by reason only that a Trustee remains out of the United Kingdom for more than twelve months but shall be exercisable notwithstanding that one of the Trustees for the time being is a Trust Corporation.

(2) A person or corporation in any part of the world may be appointed as a trustee hereof notwithstanding the lack of any connection with England and Wales and notwithstanding that none of the trustees hereof will on such appointment have any such connection.

(3) Any trustee hereof may retire at any time provided he gives 30 days' written notice to the Settlor if the Settlor is living or after the Settlor's death to the person or persons who for the time being has or have the power to appoint new trustees.

(4) A trustee retiring from the trusts hereof (whether with or without a new appointment) shall be discharged notwithstanding that there will not be either a trust corporation or at least two individuals to perform the trusts thereafter Provided that a sole trustee may not retire so as to leave no person as a trustee hereof except with the approval of the Court.

(5) The persons listed in subclause (1)(a)–(c) hereof in the order therein provided may at any time or times by deed remove any or all of the trustees hereof (but not without the appointment of a new trustee or trustees if the result of such removal would otherwise be to leave no trustee) and thereupon such trustee or trustees shall cease to be a trustee or trustees hereof except as to acts and deeds necessary for the proper vesting of the property subject to the trusts hereof in the continuing or new trustee or trustees hereof or otherwise as the circumstances may require.

Precedent for investment policy statement for a non-charitable settlement

A1.29

[*Name of trust*] TRUST

Policy Statement for the investment of the [*Name of trust*] Trust Fund

The trustees have a wide power of investment conferred upon them by clause [*number of clause*] (a copy of which is attached) of the trust deed.

By that clause and under the general law the trustees have both a general power to invest the trust fund as if they were absolutely entitled thereto and a power to delegate their asset management functions in relation to the trust fund. In exercise of their power the trustees have agreed to delegate to [*Name*] Investment Managers Limited ('the Managers') the investment of the trust fund.

The trustees have, accordingly, prepared this policy statement and the Managers have agreed to comply with this policy statement, or any revised or replacement policy statement which replaces it.

The value of the assets comprising the Trust Fund is currently [£.......]. The trust property does not include any property which cannot be sold, exchanged, transferred or partitioned and, accordingly, the Trust Fund does not include any property which limits the appropriateness of or need for diversification.

In exercising the asset management functions delegated to them by the Trustees the Managers are to have regard to the following criteria:

1.   The trustees do not wish any one investment to represent more than [...]% of the overall value of the trust fund.

2.   In managing the investments and making or varying the investments the Managers must have regard to:–

   2.1   The suitability to the Trust of investments of the same kind as any particular investment proposed to be made or retained.

   2.2   The suitability of any particular investment as an investment of that kind.

   2.3   The need for diversification of the investments of the Trust so far as may be appropriate to the circumstances of the Trust.

   2.4   The need to maintain marketable investments.

   2.5   The trustees' desire to adopt a [low] risk approach to their investment policy.

3.   The need for a balanced approach between the interests of the beneficiaries entitled or interested in the income and capital of the Trust should be adopted with the result that the Managers are to have regard to the need to achieve capital growth and income yield.

The trustees and the Managers have agreed that [*name fund*] is to be adopted as a benchmark model for the performance and investment of the Trust Fund and the Managers have agreed to inform the trustees should the [*named fund*] cease to be an appropriate model. In any event the trustees wish to meet with the Managers every [six] months, in order to review the investments comprised in the trust fund.

The current trustees' names and addresses are:–

....

....

Future trustees of the Trust will be bound by the terms of this statement unless and until it is amended or varied in writing.

Contract notes for each investment change are to be sent to the trustees at the following address, namely [....................], as soon as possible and in any event not more than [three] days after each investment change is made.

All income from the trust is to be sent on a [monthly] [quarterly] [annual] basis to [....................]

This Policy Statement will be reviewed by the trustees and the Managers at least annually and if necessary amended from time to time in writing.

....

Trustee signature

....

Trustee signature

This Policy Statement and the instructions given in it are hereby accepted by us. We confirm that we will secure compliance with the above and any revised or replacement Policy Statement.

....

Signature of [Name of Managers]

Dated..

[**Note:** Additional considerations and provisions will be required in the case of a charitable settlement. This statement is intended to be used in conjunction with a private trust.]

Appendix 2

Statutory Material

Contents

Trustee Act 1925

A2.1 *Arrangement of sections*

12   Power of trustees for sale to sell by auction, etc

(1) Where a trustee has a duty or power to sell property, he may sell or concur with any other person in selling all or any part of the property, either subject to prior charges or not, and either together or in lots, by public auction or by private contract, subject to any such conditions respecting title or evidence of title or other matter as the trustee thinks fit, with power to vary any contract for sale, and to buy in at any auction, or to rescind any contract for sale and to re-sell, without being answerable for any loss.

(2) A duty or power to sell or dispose of land includes a duty or power to sell or dispose of part thereof, whether the division is horizontal, vertical, or made in any other way.

(3) This section does not enable an express power to sell settled land to be exercised where the power is not vested in the tenant for life or statutory owner.

13   Power to sell subject to depreciatory conditions

(1) No sale made by a trustee shall be impeached by any beneficiary upon the ground that any of the conditions subject to which the sale was made may have been unnecessarily depreciatory, unless it also appears that the consideration for the sale was thereby rendered inadequate.

(2) No sale made by a trustee shall, after the execution of the conveyance, be impeached as against the purchaser upon the ground that any of the conditions subject to which the sale was made may have been unnecessarily depreciatory, unless it appears that the purchaser was acting in collusion with the trustee at the time when the contract for sale was made.

(3) No purchaser, upon any sale made by a trustee, shall be at liberty to make any objection against the title upon any of the grounds aforesaid.

(4) This section applies to sales made before or after the commencement of this Act.

14   Power of trustees to give receipts

(1) The receipt in writing of a trustee for any money, securities, investments or other personal property or effects payable, transferable, or deliverable to him under any trust or power shall be a sufficient discharge to the person

paying, transferring, or delivering the same and shall effectually exonerate him from seeing to the application or being answerable for any loss or misapplication thereof.

(2) this section does not, except where the trustee is a trust corporation, enable a sole trustee to give a valid receipt for—

(a) proceeds of sale or other capital money arising under a trust of land;

(b) capital money arising under the Settled Land Act 1925.

(3) This section applies notwithstanding anything to the contrary in the instrument, if any, creating the trust.

15 Power to compound liabilities

A personal representative, or two or more trustees acting together, or, subject to the restrictions imposed in regard to receipts by a sole trustee not being a trust corporation, a sole acting trustee where by the instrument, if any, creating the trust, or by statute, a sole trustee is authorised to execute the trusts and powers reposed in him, may, if and as he or they think fit—

(a) accept any property, real or personal, before the time at which it is made transferable or payable; or

(b) sever and apportion any blended trust funds or property; or

(c) pay or allow any debt or claim on any evidence that he or they think sufficient; or

(d) accept any composition or any security, real or personal, for any debt or for any property, real or personal, claimed; or

(e) allow any time of payment of any debt; or

(f) compromise, compound, abandon, submit to arbitration, or other-wise settle any debt, account, claim, or thing whatever relating to the testator's or intestate's estate or to the trust;

and for any of these purposes may enter into, give, execute, and do such agreements, instruments of composition or arrangement, releases, and other things as to him or them seem expedient, without being responsible for any loss occasioned by any act or thing so done by him or them if he has or they have discharged the duty of care set out in section 1(1) of the Trustee Act 2000.

16 Power to raise money by sale, mortgage, etc.

(1) Where trustees are authorised by the instrument, if any, creating the trust or by law to pay or apply capital money subject to the trust for any purpose or in any manner, they shall have and shall be deemed always to have had power

to raise the money required by sale, conversion, calling in, or mortgage of all or any part of the trust property for the time being in possession.

(2) This section applies notwithstanding anything to the contrary contained in the instrument, if any, creating the trust, but does not apply to trustees of property held for charitable purposes, or to trustees of a settlement for the purposes of the Settled Land Act 1925, not being also the statutory owners.

17   Protection to purchasers and mortgagees dealing with trustees

No purchaser or mortgagee paying or advancing money on a sale or mortgage purporting to be made under any trust or power vested in trustees, shall be concerned to see that such money is wanted; or that no more than is wanted is raised, or otherwise as to the application thereof.

18   Devolution of powers or trusts

(1) Where a power or trust is given to or imposed on two or more trustees jointly, the same may be exercised or performed by the survivors or survivor of them for the time being.

(2) Until the appointment of new trustees, the personal representatives or representative for the time being of a sole trustee, or, where there were two or more trustees of the last surviving or continuing trustee, shall be capable of exercising or performing any power or trust which was given to, or capable of being exercised by, the sole or last surviving or continuing trustee, or other the trustees or trustee for the time being of the trust.

(3) This section takes effect subject to the restrictions imposed in regard to receipts by a sole trustee, not being a trust corporation.

(4) In this section "personal representative" does not include an executor who has renounced or has not proved.

19   Power to insure

(1) A trustee may—

    (a)   insure any property which is subject to the trust against risks of loss or damage due to any event, and

    (b)   pay the premiums out of the trust funds.

(2) In the case of property held on a bare trust, the power to insure is subject to any direction given by the beneficiary or each of the beneficiaries—

    (a)   that any property specified in the direction is not to be insured;

    (b)   that any property specified in the direction is not to be insured except on such conditions as may be so specified.

(3) Property is held on a bare trust if it is held on trust for—

(a)   a beneficiary who is of full age and capacity and absolutely entitled to the property subject to the trust, or

(b)   beneficiaries each of whom is of full age and capacity and who (taken together) are absolutely entitled to the property subject to the trust.

(4) If a direction under subsection (2) of this section is given, the power to insure, so far as it is subject to the direction, ceases to be a delegable function for the purposes of section 11 of the Trustee Act 2000 (power to employ agents).

(5) In this section "trust funds" means any income or capital funds of the trust.

(This section was substituted by the Trustee Act 2000, s 34(1).)

20   Application of insurance money where policy kept up under any trust, power or obligation

(1) Money receivable by trustees or any beneficiary under a policy of insurance against the loss or damage of any property subject to a trust or to a settlement within the meaning of the Settled Land Act 1925... shall, where the policy has been kept up under any trust in that behalf or under any power statutory or otherwise, or in performance of any covenant or of any obligation statutory or otherwise, or by a tenant for life impeachable for waste, be capital money for the purposes of the trust or settlement, as the case may be.

(2) If any such money is receivable by any person, other than the trustees of the trust or settlement, that person shall use his best endeavours to recover and receive the money, and shall pay the net residue thereof, after discharging any costs of recovering and receiving it, to the trustees of the trust or settlement, or, if there are no trustees capable of giving a discharge therefor, into court.

(3) Any such money—

(a)   if it was receivable in respect of settled land within the meaning of the Settled Land Act 1925, or any building or works thereon, shall be deemed to be capital money arising under that Act from the settled land, and shall be invested or applied by the trustees, or, if in court, under the direction of the court, accordingly;

(b)   if it was receivable in respect of personal chattels settled as heirlooms within the meaning of the Settled Land Act, 1925, shall be deemed to be capital money arising under that Act; and shall be applicable by the trustees, or, if in court, under the direction of the court, in like manner as provided by that Act with respect to money arising by sale of chattels as heirlooms as aforesaid;

(c)   if it was receivable in respect of land subject to a trust of land or personal property held on trust for sale, shall be held upon the trusts and subject to the powers and provisions applicable to money arising by a sale under such trust;

(d) in any other case, shall be held upon trusts corresponding as nearly as may be with the trusts affecting the property in respect of which it was payable.

(4) Such money, or any part thereof, may also be applied by the trustees, or, if in court, under the direction of the court, in rebuilding, reinstating, replacing, or replacing the property loss or damaged, but any such application by the trustees shall be subject to the consent of any person whose consent is required by the instrument, if any, creating the trust to the investment of money subject to the trust, and, in the case of money which is deemed to be capital money arising under the Settled Land Act 1925, be subject to the provisions of that Act with respect to the application of capital money by the trustees of the settlement.

(5) Nothing contained in this section prejudices or affects the right of any person to require any such money or any part thereof to be applied in rebuilding reinstating, or repairing the property lost or damaged, or the rights of any mortgagee, lessor, or lessee, whether under any statute or otherwise.

(6) This section applies to policies effected either before or after the commencement of this Act, but only to money received after such commencement.

22 Reversionary interests, valuations, and audit

(1) Where trust property includes any share or interest in property not vested in the trustees, or the proceeds of the sale of any such property, or any other thing in action, the trustees on the same falling into possession, or becoming payable or transferable may—

(a) agree or ascertain the amount or value thereof or any part thereof in such manner as they may think fit;

(b) accept in or towards satisfaction thereof, at the market or current value, or upon any valuation or estimate of value which they may think fit, any authorised investments;

(c) allow any deductions for duties, costs, charges and expenses which they may think proper or reasonable;

(d) execute any release in respect of the premises so as effectually to discharge all accountable parties from all liability in respect of any matters coming within the scope of such release;

without being responsible in any such case for any loss occasioned by any act or thing so done by them if they have discharged the duty of care set out in section 1(1) of the Trustee Act 2000.

(2) The trustees shall not be under any obligation and shall not be chargeable with any breach of trust by reason of any omission—

    (a)   to place any distringas notice or apply for any stop or other like order upon any securities or other property out of or on which such share or interest or other thing in action as aforesaid is derived, payable or charged; or

    (b)   to take any proceedings on account of any act, default, or neglect on the part of the persons in whom such securities or other property or any of them or any part thereof are for the time being, or had at any time been, vested;

unless and until required in writing so to do by some person, or the guardian of some person, beneficially interested under the trust, and unless also due provision is made to their satisfaction for payment of the costs of any proceedings required to be taken:

Provided that nothing in this subsection shall relieve the trustees of the obligation to get in and obtain payment or transfer of such share or interest or other thing in action on the same falling into possession.

(3) Trustees may, for the purpose of giving effect to the trust, or any of the provisions of the instrument, if any, creating the trust or of any statute, from time to time (by duly qualified agents) ascertain and fix the value of any trust property in such manner as they think proper, and any valuation so made ... shall be binding upon all persons interested under the trust if the trustees have discharged the duty of care set out in section 1(1) of the Trustee Act 2000.

(4) Trustees may, in their absolute discretion, from time to time, but not more than once in every three years unless the nature of the trust or any special dealings with the trust property make a more frequent exercise of the right reasonable, cause the accounts of the trust property to be examined or audited by an independent accountant, and shall, for that purpose, produce such vouchers and give such information to him as he may require; and the costs of such examination or audit, including the fee of the auditor, shall be paid out of the capital or income of the trust property, or partly in one way and partly in the other as the trustees, in their absolute discretion, think fit, but, in default of any direction by the trustees to the contrary in any special case, costs attributable to capital shall be borne by capital and those attributable to income by income.

24   Power to concur with others

Where an undivided share in any property, is subject to a trust, or forms part of the estate of a testator or intestate, the trustees or personal representatives may (without prejudice to the trust affecting the entirety of the land and the powers of the trustees in reference thereto), execute or exercise any duty or power vested in them in relation to such share in conjunction with the persons entitled to or having power in that behalf over the other share or shares, and notwithstanding that any one or more of the trustees or personal representatives may be entitled to or interested in any such other share, either in his or their own right or in a fiduciary capacity.

25 Delegation of trustee's functions by power of attorney

(1) Notwithstanding any rule of law or equity to the contrary, a trustee may, by power of attorney, delegate the execution or exercise of all or any of the trusts, powers and discretions vested in him as trustee either alone or jointly with any other person or persons.

(2) A delegation under this section—

(a) commences as provided by the instrument creating the power or, if the instrument makes no provision as to the commencement of the delegation, with the date of the execution of the instrument by the donor; and

(b) continues for a period of twelve months or any shorter period provided by the instrument creating the power.

(3) The persons who may be donees of a power of attorney under this section include a trust corporation.

(4) Before or within seven days after giving a power of attorney under this section the donor shall give written notice of it (specifying the date on which the power comes into operation and its duration, the donee of the power, the reason why the power is given and, where some only are delegated, the trusts, powers and discretions delegated) to—

(a) each person (other than himself), if any, who under any instrument creating the trust has power (whether alone or jointly) to appoint a new trustee; and

(b) each of the other trustees, if any;

but failure to comply with this subsection shall not, in favour of a person dealing with the donee of the power, invalidate any act done or instrument executed by the donee.

(5) A power of attorney given under this section by a single donor—

(a) in the form set out in subsection (6) of this section; or

(b) in a form to the like effect but expressed to be made under this subsection,

shall operate to delegate to the person identified in the form as the single donee of the power the execution and exercise of all the trusts, powers and discretions vested in the donor as trustee (either alone or jointly with any other person or persons) under the single trust so identified.

(6) The form referred to in subsection (5) of this section is as follows—

"THIS GENERAL TRUSTEE POWER OF ATTORNEY is made on [*date*] by [*name of one donor*] of [*address of donor*] as trustee of [*name or details of one trust*].

I appoint [*name of one donee*] of [*address of donee*] to be my attorney [*if desired, the date on which the delegation commences or the period for which it continues (or both)*] in accordance with section 25(5) of the Trustee Act 1925.

[*To be executed as a deed*]".

(7) The donor of a power of attorney given under this section shall be liable for the acts or defaults of the donee in the same manner as if they were the acts or defaults of the donor.

(8) For the purpose of executing or exercising the trusts or powers delegated to him, the donee may exercise any of the powers conferred on the donor as trustee by statute or by the instrument creating the trust, including power, for the purpose of the transfer of any inscribed stock, himself to delegate to an attorney power to transfer, but not including the power of delegation conferred by this section.

(9) The fact that it appears from any power of attorney given under this section, or from any evidence required for the purposes of any such power of attorney or otherwise, that in dealing with any stock the donee of the power is acting in the execution of a trust shall not be deemed for any purpose to affect any person in whose books the stock is inscribed or registered with any notice of the trust.

(10) This section applies to a personal representative, tenant for life and statutory owner as it applies to a trustee except that subsection (4) shall apply as if it required the notice there mentioned to be given—

    (a)   in the case of a personal representative, to each of the other personal representatives, if any, except any executor who has renounced probate;

    (b)   in the case of a tenant for life, to the trustees of the settlement and to each person, if any, who together with the person giving the notice constitutes the tenant for life; and

    (c)   in the case of a statutory owner, to each of the persons, if any, who together with the person giving the notice constitute the statutory owner and, in the case of a statutory owner by virtue of section 23(1)(a) of the Settled Land Act 1925, to the trustees of the settlement.

(This section was substituted by the Trustee Delegation Act 1999, s 5.)

26   Protection against liability in respect of rents and covenants

(1) Where a personal representative or trustee liable as such for—

(a) any rent, covenant, or agreement reserved by or contained in any lease; or

(b) any rent, covenant or agreement payable under or contained in any grant made in consideration of a rentcharge; or

(c) any indemnity given in respect of any rent, covenant or agreement referred to in either of the foregoing paragraphs;

satisfies all liabilities under the lease or grant which may have accrued and been claimed up to the date of the conveyance hereinafter mentioned, and, where necessary, sets apart a sufficient fund to answer any future claim that may be made in respect of any fixed and ascertained sum which the lessee or grantee agreed to lay out on the property demised or granted, although the period for laying out the same may not have arrived, then and in any such case the personal representative or trustee may convey the property demised or granted to a purchaser, legatee, devisee, or other person entitled to call for a conveyance thereof and thereafter—

(i) he may distribute the residuary real and personal estate of the deceased testator or intestate, or, as the case may be, the trust estate (other than the fund, if any, set apart as aforesaid) to or amongst the persons entitled thereto, without appropriating any part, or any further part, as the case may be, of the estate of the deceased or of the trust estate to meet any future liability under the said lease or grant;

(ii) notwithstanding such distribution, he shall not be personally liable in respect of any subsequent claim under the said lease or grant.

(1A) Where a personal representative or trustee has as such entered into, or may as such be required to enter into, an authorised guarantee agreement with respect to any lease comprised in the estate of a deceased testator or intestate or a trust estate (and, in a case where he has entered into such an agreement, he has satisfied all liabilities under it which may have accrued and been claimed up to the date of distribution)—

(a) he may distribute the residuary real and personal estate of the deceased testator or intestate, or the trust estate, to or amongst the persons entitled thereto—

(i) without appropriating any part of the estate of the deceased, or the trust estate, to meet any future liability (or, as the case may be, any liability) under any such agreement, and

(ii) notwithstanding any potential liability of his to enter into any such agreement; and

(b) notwithstanding such distribution, he shall not be personally liable in respect of any subsequent claim (or, as the case may be, any claim) under any such agreement.

In this subsection "authorised guarantee agreement" has the same meaning as in the Landlord and Tenant (Covenants) Act 1995.

(2) This section operates without prejudice to the right of the lessor or grantor, or the persons deriving title under the lessor or grantor, to follow the assets of the deceased or the trust property into the hands of the persons amongst whom the same may have been respectively distributed, and applies notwithstanding anything to the contrary in the will or other instrument, if any, creating the trust.

(3) In this section "lease" includes an underlease and an agreement for a lease or underlease and any instrument giving any such indemnity as aforesaid or varying the liabilities under the lease; "grant" applies to a grant whether the rent is created by limitation, grant, reservation, or otherwise, and includes an agreement for a grant and any instrument giving any such indemnity as aforesaid or varying the liabilities under the grant; "lessee" and "grantee" include persons respectively deriving title under them.

27   Protection by means of advertisements

(1) With a view to the conveyance to or distribution among the persons entitled to any real or personal property, the trustees of a settlement, trustees of land, trustees for sale of personal property or personal representatives, may give notice by advertisement in the Gazette, and in a newspaper circulating in the district in which the land is situated and such other like notices, including notices elsewhere than in England and Wales, as would, in any special case, have been directed by a court of competent jurisdiction in an action for administration, of their intention to make such conveyance or distribution as aforesaid, and requiring any person interested to send to the trustees or personal representatives within the time, not being less than two months, fixed in the notice or, where more than one notice is given, in the last of the notices, particulars of his claim in respect of the property or any part thereof to which the notice relates.

(2) At the expiration of the time fixed by the notice the trustees or personal representatives may convey or distribute the property or any part thereof to which the notice relates, to or among the persons entitled thereto, having regard only to the claims, whether formal or not, of which the trustees or personal representatives then had notice and shall not, as respects the property so conveyed or distributed, be liable to any person of whose claim the trustees or personal representatives have not had notice at the time of conveyance or distribution; but nothing in this section—

(a)   prejudices the right of any person to follow the property, or any property representing the same, into the hands of any person, other than a purchaser, who may have received it; or

(b)   frees the trustees or personal representatives from any obligation to make searches or obtain official certificates of search similar to those which an intending purchaser would be advised to make or obtain.

(3) This section applies notwithstanding anything to the contrary in the will or other instrument, if any, creating the trust.

28   Protection in regard to notice

A trustee or personal representative acting for the purposes of more than one trust or estate shall not, in the absence of fraud, be affected by notice of any instrument, matter, fact or thing in relation to any particular trust or estate if he has obtained notice thereof merely by reason of his acting or having acted for the purposes of another trust or estate.

31   Power to apply income for maintenance and to accumulate surplus income during a minority

(1) Where any property is held by trustees in trust for any person for any interest whatsoever, whether vested or contingent, then, subject to any prior interests or charges affecting that property—

   (i)   during the infancy of any such person, if his interest so long continues, the trustees may, at their sole discretion, pay to his parent or guardian, if any, or otherwise apply for or towards his maintenance, education, or benefit, the whole or such part, if any, of the income of that property as may, in all the circumstances, be reasonable, whether or not there is—

   (a)   any other fund applicable to the same purpose; or

   (b)   any person bound by law to provide for his maintenance or education; and

   (ii)   if such person on attaining the age of eighteen years has not a vested interest in such income, the trustees shall thenceforth pay the income of that property and of any accretion thereto under subsection (2) of this section to him, until he either attains a vested interest therein or dies, or until failure of his interest:

Provided that, in deciding whether the whole or any part of the income of the property is during a minority to be paid or applied for the purposes aforesaid, the trustees shall have regard to the age of the infant and his requirements and generally to the circumstances of the case, and in particular to what other income, if any, is applicable for the same purposes; and where trustees have notice that the income of more than one fund is applicable for those purposes, then, so far as practicable, unless the entire income of the funds is paid or applied as aforesaid or the court otherwise directs, a proportionate part only of the income of each fund shall be so paid or applied.

(2) During the infancy of any such person, if his interest so long continues, the trustees shall accumulate all the residue of that income by investing it, and any profits from so investing it from time to time in authorised investments, and shall hold those accumulations as follows:—

(i) If any such person—

    (a) attains the age of eighteen years, or marries under that age, and his interest in such income during his infancy or until his marriage is a vested interest; or

    (b) on attaining the age of eighteen years or on marriage under that age becomes entitled to the property from which such income arose in fee simple, absolute or determinable, or absolutely, or for an entailed interest;

    the trustees shall hold the accumulations in trust for such person absolutely, but without prejudice to any provision with respect thereto contained in any settlement by him made under any statutory powers during his infancy, and so that the receipt of such person after marriage, and though still an infant, shall be a good discharge; and

(ii) In any other case the trustees shall, notwithstanding that such person had a vested interest in such income, hold the accumulations as an accretion to the capital of the property from which such accumulations arose, and as one fund with such capital for all purposes, and so that, if such property is settled land, such accumulations shall be held upon the same trusts as if the same were capital money arising therefrom;

but the trustees may, at any time during the infancy of such person if his interest so long continues, apply those accumulations, or any part thereof, as if they were income arising in the then current year.

(3) This section applies in the case of a contingent interest only if the limitation or trust carries the intermediate income of the property, but it applies to a future or contingent legacy by the parent of, or a person standing in loco parentis to, the legatee, if and for such period as, under the general law, the legacy carries interest for the maintenance of the legatee, and in any such case as last aforesaid the rate of interest shall (if the income available is sufficient, and subject to any rules of court to the contrary) be five pounds per centum per annum.

(4) This section applies to a vested annuity in like manner as if the annuity were the income of property held by trustees in trust to pay the income thereof to the annuitant for the same period for which the annuity is payable, save that in any case accumulations made during the infancy of the annuitant shall be held in trust for the annuitant or his personal representatives absolutely.

(5) This section does not apply where the instrument, if any, under which the interest arises came into operation before the commencement of this Act.

32 Power of advancement

(1) Trustees may at any time or times pay or apply any capital money subject to a trust, for the advancement or benefit, in such manner as they may, in their

absolute discretion, think fit, of any person entitled to the capital of the trust property or of any share thereof, whether absolutely or contingently on his attaining any specified age or on the occurrence of any other event, or subject to a gift over on his death under any specified age or on the occurrence of any other event, and whether in possession or in remainder or reversion, and such payment or application may be made notwithstanding that the interest of such person is liable to be defeated by the exercise of a power of appointment or revocation, or to be diminished by the increase of the class to which he belongs:

Provided that—

(a) the money so paid or applied for the advancement or benefit of any person shall not exceed altogether in amount one-half of the presumptive or vested share or interest of that person in the trust property; and

(b) if that person is or becomes absolutely and indefeasibly entitled to a share in the trust property the money so paid or applied shall be brought into account as part of such share; and

(c) no such payment or application shall be made so as to prejudice any person entitled to any prior life or other interest, whether vested or contingent, in the money paid or applied unless such person is in existence and of full age and consents in writing to such payment or application.

(2) This section does not apply to capital money arising under the Settled Land Act 1925.

(3) This section does not apply to trusts constituted or created before the commencement of this Act.

33 Protective trusts

(1) Where any income, including an annuity or other periodical income payment, is directed to be held on protective trusts for the benefit of any person (in this section called "the principal beneficiary") for the period of his life or for any less period, then, during that period (in this section called the "trust period") the said income shall, without prejudice to any prior interest, be held on the following trusts, namely:—

(i) Upon trust for the principal beneficiary during the trust period or until he, whether before or after the termination of any prior interest, does or attempts to do or suffers any act or thing, or until any event happens, other than an advance under any statutory or express power, whereby, if the said income were payable during the trust period to the principal beneficiary absolutely during that period, he would be deprived of the right to receive the same or any part thereof, in any of which cases, as well as on the termination of the trust period, whichever first happens, this trust of the said income shall fail or determine;

(ii)   If the trust aforesaid fails or determines during the subsistence of the trust period, then, during the residue of that period, the said income shall be held upon trust for the application thereof for the maintenance or support, or otherwise for the benefit, of all or any one or more exclusively of the other or others of the following persons (that is to say)—

    (a)   the principal beneficiary and his or her wife or husband, if any, and his or her children or more remote issue, if any; or

    (b)   if there is no wife or husband or issue of the principal beneficiary in existence, the principal beneficiary and the persons who would, if he were actually dead, be entitled to the trust property or the income thereof or to the annuity fund, if any, or arrears of the annuity, as the case may be;

as the trustees in their absolute discretion, without being liable to account for the exercise of such discretion, think fit.

(2) This section does not apply to trusts coming into operation before the commencement of this Act, and has effect subject to any variation of the implied trusts aforesaid contained in the instrument creating the trust.

(3) Nothing in this section operates to validate any trust which would, if contained in the instrument creating the trust, be liable to be set aside.

(4) In relation to the dispositions mentioned in section 19(1) of the Family Law Reform Act 1987, this section shall have effect as if any reference (however expressed) to any relationship between two persons were construed in accordance with section 1 of that Act.

34   Limitation of the number of trustees

(1) Where, at the commencement of this Act, there are more than four trustees of a settlement of land, or more than four trustees holding land on trust for sale, no new trustees shall (except where as a result of the appointment the number is reduced to four or less) be capable of being appointed until the number is reduced to less than four, and thereafter the number shall not be increased beyond four.

(2) In the case of settlements and dispositions creating trusts of land made or coming into operation after the commencement of this Act—

    (a)   the number of trustees thereof shall not in any case exceed four, and where more than four persons are named as such trustees, the four first named (who are able and willing to act) shall alone be the trustees, and the other persons named shall not be trustees unless appointed on the occurrence of a vacancy;

(b)   the number of the trustees shall not be increased beyond four.

(3) This section only applies to settlements and dispositions of land, and the restrictions imposed on the number of trustees do not apply—

(a)   in the case of land vested in trustees for charitable, ecclesiastical, or public purposes; or

(b)   where the net proceeds of the sale of the land are held for like purposes; or

(c)   to the trustees of a term of years absolute limited by a settlement on trusts for raising money, or of a like term created under the statutory remedies relating to annual sums charged on land.

35   Appointments of trustees of settlements and trustees of land

(1) Appointments of new trustees of land and of new trustees of any trust of the proceeds of sale of the land shall, subject to any order of the court, be effected by separate instruments, but in such manner as to secure that the same persons become trustees of land and trustees of the trust of the proceeds of sale.

(2) Where new trustees of a settlement are appointed, a memorandum of the names and addresses of the persons who are for the time being the trustees thereof for the purposes of the Settled Land Act 1925, shall be endorsed on or annexed to the last or only principal vesting instrument by or on behalf of the trustees of the settlement, and such vesting instrument shall, for that purpose, be produced by the person having the possession thereof of the trustees of the settlement when so required.

(3) Where new trustees of land are appointed, a memorandum of the persons who are for the time being the trustees of the land shall be endorsed on or annexed to the conveyance by which the land was vested in trustees of land; and that conveyance shall be produced to the persons who are for the time being the trustees of the land by the person in possession of it in order for that to be done when the trustees require its production.

(4) This section applies only to settlements and dispositions of land.

36   Power of appointing new or additional trustees

(1) Where a trustee, either original or substituted, and whether appointed by a court or otherwise, is dead, or remains out of the United Kingdom for more than twelve months, or desires to be discharged from all or any of the trusts or powers reposed in or conferred on him, or refuses or is unfit to act therein, or is incapable of acting therein, or is an infant, then, subject to the restrictions imposed by this Act on the number of trustees,—

(a)   the person or persons nominated for the purpose of appointing new trustees by the instrument, if any, creating the trust; or

(b) if there is no such person, or no such person able and willing to act, then the surviving or continuing trustees or trustee for the time being, or the personal representatives of the last surviving or continuing trustee;

may, by writing, appoint one or more other persons (whether or not being the persons exercising the power) to be a trustee or trustees in the place of the trustee so deceased remaining out of the United Kingdom, desiring to be discharged, refusing, or being unfit or being incapable, or being an infant, as aforesaid.

(2) Where a trustee has been removed under a power contained in the instrument creating the trust, a new trustee or new trustees may be appointed in the place of the trustee who is removed, as if he were dead, or, in the case of a corporation, as if the corporation desired to be discharged from the trust, and the provisions of this section shall apply accordingly, but subject to the restrictions imposed by this Act on the number of trustees.

(3) Where a corporation being a trustee is or has been dissolved, either before or after the commencement of this Act, then, for the purposes of this section and of any enactment replaced thereby, the corporation shall be deemed to be and to have been from the date of the dissolution incapable of acting in the trusts or powers reposed in or conferred on the corporation.

(4) The power of appointment given by subsection (1) of this section or any similar previous enactment to the personal representatives of a last surviving or continuing trustee shall be and shall be deemed always to have been exercisable by the executors for the time being (whether original or by representation) of such surviving or continuing trustee who have proved the will of their testator or by the administrators for the time being of such trustee without the concurrence of any executor who has renounced or has not proved.

(5) But a sole or last surviving executor intending to renounce, or all the executors where they all intend to renounce, shall have and shall be deemed always to have had power, at any time before renouncing probate, to exercise the power of appointment given by this section, or by any similar previous enactment, if willing to act for that purpose and without thereby accepting the office of executor.

(6) Where, in the case of any trust, there are not more than three trustees—

(a) the person or persons nominated for the purpose of appointing new trustees by the instrument, if any, creating the trust; or

(b) if there is no such person, or no such person able and willing to act, then the trustee or trustees for the time being;

may, by writing appoint another person or other persons to be an additional trustee or additional trustees, but it shall not be obligatory to appoint any additional trustee, unless the instrument, if any, creating the trust, or any statutory enactment provides to the contrary, nor shall the number of trustees be increased beyond four by virtue of any such appointment.

(6A) A person who is either—

(a) both a trustee and attorney for the other trustee (if one other), or for both of the other trustees (if two others), under a registered power; or

(b) attorney under a registered power for the trustee (if one) or for both or each of the trustees (if two or three),

may, if subsection (6B) of this section is satisfied in relation to him, make an appointment under subsection (6)(b) of this section on behalf of the trustee or trustees.

(6B) This subsection is satisfied in relation to an attorney under a registered power for one or more trustees if (as attorney under the power)—

(a) he intends to exercise any function of the trustee or trustees by virtue of section 1(1) of the Trustee Delegation Act 1999; or

(b) he intends to exercise any function of the trustee or trustees in relation to any land, capital proceeds of a conveyance of land or income from land by virtue of its delegation to him under section 25 of this Act or the instrument (if any) creating the trust.

(6C) In subsections (6A) and (6B) of this section "registered power" means a power of attorney created by an instrument which is for the time being registered under section 6 of the Enduring Powers of Attorney Act 1985.

(6D) Subsection (6A) of this section—

(a) applies only if and so far as a contrary intention is not expressed in the instrument creating the power of attorney (or, where more than one, any of them) or the instrument (if any) creating the trust; and

(b) has effect subject to the terms of those instruments.

(7) Every new trustee appointed under this section as well before as after all the trust property becomes by law, or by assurance, or otherwise, vested in him, shall have the same powers, authorities, and discretions, and may in all respects act as if he had been originally appointed a trustee by the instrument, if any, creating the trust.

(8) The provisions of this section relating to a trustee who is dead include the case of a person nominated trustee in a will but dying before the testator, and those relative to a continuing trustee include a refusing or retiring trustee, if willing to act in the execution of the provisions of this section.

(9) Where a trustee is incapable, by reason of mental disorder within the meaning of the Mental Health Act 1983, of exercising his functions as trustee and is also entitled in possession to some beneficial interest in the trust property, no appointment of a new trustee in his place shall be made by virtue of paragraph (b) of subsection (1) of this section unless leave to make the appointment has been given by the authority having jurisdiction under Part VII of the Mental Health Act 1983.

37 Supplemental provisions as to appointment of trustees

(1) On the appointment of a trustee for the whole or any part of trust property—

    (a)   the number of trustees may, subject to the restrictions imposed by this Act on the number of trustees, be increased; and

    (b)   a separate set of trustees, not exceeding four, may be appointed for any part of the trust property held on trusts distinct from those relating to any other part or parts of the trust property, notwithstanding that no new trustees or trustee are or is to be appointed for other parts of the trust property, and any existing trustee may be appointed or remain one of such separate set of trustees, or, if only one trustee was originally appointed, then, save as hereinafter provided, one separate trustee may be so appointed; and

    (c)   it shall not be obligatory, save as hereinafter provided, to appoint more than one new trustee where only one trustee was originally appointed, or to fill up the original number of trustees where more than two trustees were originally appointed, but, except where only one trustee was originally appointed, and a sole trustee when appointed will be able to give valid receipts for all capital money, a trustee shall not be discharged from his trust unless there will be either a trust corporation or at least two persons to act as trustees to perform the trust; and

    (d)   any assurance or thing requisite for vesting the trust property, or any part thereof, in a sole trustee, or jointly in the persons who are the trustees, shall be executed or done.

(2) Nothing in this Act shall authorise the appointment of a sole trustee, not being a trust corporation, where the trustee, when appointed, would not be able to give valid receipts for all capital money arising under the trust.

38 Evidence as to a vacancy in a trust

(1) A statement, contained in any instrument coming into operation after the commencement of this Act by which a new trustee is appointed for any purpose connected with land, to the effect that a trustee has remained out of the United Kingdom for more than twelve months or refuses or is unfit to act, or is incapable of acting, or that he is not entitled to a beneficial interest in the trust property in possession, shall, in favour of a purchaser of a legal estate, be conclusive evidence of the matter stated.

(2) In favour of such purchaser any appointment of a new trustee depending on that statement, and any vesting declaration, express or implied, consequent on the appointment, shall be valid.

39 Retirement of trustee without a new appointment

(1) Where a trustee is desirous of being discharged from the trust, and after his discharge there will be either a trust corporation or at least two persons to

act as trustees to perform the trust, then, if such trustee as aforesaid by deed declares that he is desirous of being discharged from the trust, and if his co-trustees and such other person, if any, as is empowered to appoint trustees, by deed consent to the discharge of the trustee, and to the vesting in the co-trustees alone of the trust property, the trustee desirous of being discharged shall be deemed to have retired from the trust, and shall, by the deed, be discharged therefrom under this Act, without any new trustee being appointed in his place.

(2) Any assurance or thing requisite for vesting the trust property in the continuing trustees alone shall be executed or done.

40   Vesting of trust property in new or continuing trustees

(1) Where by a deed a new trustee is appointed to perform any trust, then—

(a)   if the deed contains a declaration by the appointor to the effect that any estate or interest in any land subject to the trust, or in any chattel so subject, or right to recover or receive any debt or other thing in action so subject, shall vest in the persons who by virtue of the deed become or are the trustees for performing the trust, the deed shall operate, without any conveyance or assignment, to vest in those persons as joint tenants and for the purposes of the trust the estate interest or right to which the declaration relates; and

(b)   if the deed is made after the commencement of this Act and does not contain such a declaration, the deed shall, subject to any express provision to the contrary therein contained, operate as if it had contained such a declaration by the appointor extending to all the estates interests and rights with respect to which a declaration could have been made.

(2) Where by a deed a retiring trustee is discharged under section 39 of this Act or section 19 of the Trusts of Land and Appointment of Trustees Act 1996 without a new trustee being appointed, then—

(a)   if the deed contains such a declaration as aforesaid by the retiring and continuing trustees, and by the other person, if any, empowered to appoint trustees, the deed shall, without any conveyance or assignment, operate to vest in the continuing trustees alone, as joint tenants, and for the purposes of the trust, the estate, interest, or right to which the declaration relates; and

(b)   if the deed is made after the commencement of this Act and does not contain such a declaration, the deed shall, subject to any express provision to the contrary therein contained, operate as if it had contained such a declaration by such persons as aforesaid extending to all the estates, interests and rights with respect to which a declaration could have been made.

(3) An express vesting declaration, whether made before or after the commencement of this Act, shall, notwithstanding that the estate, interest or right

to be vested is not expressly referred to, and provided that the other statutory requirements were or are complied with, operate and be deemed always to have operated (but without prejudice to any express provision to the contrary contained in the deed of appointment or discharge) to vest in the persons respectively referred to in subsections (1) and (2) of this section, as the case may require, such estates, interests and rights as are capable of being and ought to be vested in those persons.

(4) This section does not extend—

(a) to land conveyed by way of mortgage for securing money subject to the trust, except land conveyed on trust for securing debentures or debenture stock;

(b) to land held under a lease which contains any covenant, condition or agreement against assignment or disposing of the land without licence or consent, unless, prior to the execution of the deed containing expressly or impliedly the vesting declaration, the requisite licence or consent has been obtained, or unless, by virtue of any statute or rule of law, the vesting declaration, express or implied, would not operate as a breach of covenant or give rise to a forfeiture;

(c) to any share, stock, annuity or property which is only transferable in books kept by a company or other body, or in manner directed by or under an Act of Parliament.

In this subsection "lease" includes an underlease and an agreement for a lease or underlease.

(5) For purposes of registration of the deed in any registry, the person or persons making the declaration expressly or impliedly, shall be deemed the conveying party or parties, and the conveyance shall be deemed to be made by him or them under a power conferred by this Act.

(6) This section applies to deeds of appointment or discharge executed on or after the first day of January, eighteen hundred and eighty-two.

41 Power of court to appoint new trustees

(1) The court may, whenever it is expedient to appoint a new trustee or new trustees, and it is found inexpedient difficult or impracticable so to do without the assistance of the court, make an order appointing a new trustee or new trustees either in substitution for or in addition to any existing trustee or trustees, or although there is no existing trustee.

In particular and without prejudice to the generality of the foregoing provision, the court may make an order appointing a new trustee in substitution for a trustee who ... is incapable, by reason of mental disorder within the meaning of the Mental Health Act 1983, of exercising his functions as trustee, or is a bankrupt, or is a corporation which is in liquidation or has been dissolved.

(2) The power conferred by this section may, in the case of a deed of arrangement within the meaning of the Deeds of Arrangement Act 1914, be exercised either by the High Court or by the court having jurisdiction in bankruptcy in the district in which the debtor resided or carried on business at the date of the execution of the deed.

(3) An order under this section, and any consequential vesting order or conveyance, shall not operate further or otherwise as a discharge to any former or continuing trustee than an appointment of new trustees under any power for that purpose contained in any instrument would have operated.

(4) Nothing in this section gives power to appoint an executor or administrator.

42   Power to authorise remuneration

Where the court appoints a corporation, other than the Public Trustee, to be a trustee either solely or jointly with another person, the court may authorise the corporation to charge such remuneration for its services as trustee as the court may think fit.

43   Powers of new trustee appointed by the Court

Every trustee appointed by a court of competent jurisdiction shall, as well before as after the trust property becomes by law, or by assurance, or otherwise, vested in him, have the same powers, authorities, and discretions, and may in all respects act as if he had been originally appointed a trustee by the instrument, if any, creating the trust.

57   Power of court to authorise dealings with trust property

(1) Where in the management or administration of any property vested in trustees, any sale, lease, mortgage, surrender, release, or other disposition, or any purchase, investment, acquisition, expenditure, or other transaction, is in the opinion of the court expedient, but the same cannot be effected by reason of the absence of any power for that purpose vested in the trustees by the trust instrument, if any, or by law, the court may by order confer upon the trustees, either generally or in any particular instance, the necessary power for the purpose, on such terms, and subject to such provisions and conditions, if any, as the court may think fit and may direct in what manner any money authorised to be expended, and the costs of any transaction, are to be paid or borne as between capital and income.

(2) The court may, from time to time, rescind or vary any order made under this section, or may make any new or further order.

(3) An application to the court under this section may be made by the trustees, or by any of them, or by any person beneficially interested under the trust.

(4) This section does not apply to trustees of a settlement for the purposes of the Settled Land Act 1925.

61   Power to relieve trustee from personal liability

If it appears to the court that a trustee, whether appointed by the court or otherwise, is or may be personally liable for any breach of trust, whether the transaction alleged to be a breach of trust occurred before or after the commencement of this Act, but has acted honestly and reasonably, and ought fairly to be excused for the breach of trust and for omitting to obtain the directions of the court in the matter in which he committed such breach, then the court may relieve him either wholly or partly from personal liability for the same.

68   Definitions

(1) In this Act, unless the context otherwise requires, the following expressions have the meanings hereby assigned to them respectively, that is to say:—

(1)   "Authorised investments" mean investments authorised by the instrument, if any, creating the trust for the investment of money subject to the trust, or by law;

…

(11)   "Property" includes real and personal property, and any estate share and interest in any property, real or personal, and any debt, and any thing in action, and any other right or interest, whether in possession or not;

(12)   "Rights" include estates and interests;

(13)   "Securities" include stocks, funds, and shares; … and "securities payable to bearer" include securities transferable by delivery or by delivery and endorsement;

…

(17)   "Trust" does not include the duties incident to an estate conveyed by way of mortgage, but with this exception the expressions "trust" and "trustee" extend to implied and constructive trusts, and to cases where the trustee has a beneficial interest in the trust property, and to the duties incident to the office of a personal representative, and "trustee" where the context admits, includes a personal representative, and "new trustee" includes an additional trustee;

(18)   "Trust corporation" means the Public Trustee or a corporation either appointed by the court in any particular case to be a trustee, or entitled by rules made under subsection (3) of section four of the Public Trustee Act 1906, to act as custodian trustee;

...

(20)   "United Kingdom" means Great Britain and Northern Ireland.

69   Application of Act

(1) This Act, except where otherwise expressly provided, applies to trusts including, so far as this Act applies thereto, executorships and administratorships constituted or created either before or after the commencement of this Act.

(2) The powers conferred by this Act on trustees are in addition to the powers conferred by the instrument, if any, creating the trust, but those powers, unless otherwise stated, apply if and so far only as a contrary intention is not expressed in the instrument, if any, creating the trust, and have effect subject to the terms of that instrument.

Trusts of Land and Appointment of Trustees Act 1996

A2.2   *Arrangement of sections*

Schedules

Schedule 1   Provisions consequential on section 2.

PART I
TRUSTS OF LAND

Introductory

1   Meaning of "trust of land"

(1) In this Act—

   (a)   "trust of land" means (subject to subsection (3)) any trust of property which consists of or includes land, and

   (b)   "trustees of land" means trustees of a trust of land.

(2) The reference in subsection (1)(a) to a trust—

   (a)   is to any description of trust (whether express, implied, resulting or constructive), including a trust for sale and a bare trust, and

   (b)   includes a trust created, or arising, before the commencement of this Act.

(3) The reference to land in subsection (1)(a) does not include land which (despite section 2) is settled land or which is land to which the Universities and College Estates Act 1925 applies.

Settlements and trusts for sale as trusts of land

2   Trusts in place of settlements

(1) No settlement created after the commencement of this Act is a settlement for the purposes of the Settled Land Act 1925; and no settlement shall be deemed to be made under that Act after that commencement.

(2) Subsection (1) does not apply to a settlement created on the occasion of an alteration in any interest in, or of a person becoming entitled under, a settlement which—

   (a)   is in existence at the commencement of this Act, or

   (b)   derives from a settlement within paragraph (a) or this paragraph.

(3) But a settlement created as mentioned in subsection (2) is not a settlement for the purposes of the Settled Land Act 1925 if provision to the effect that it is not is made in the instrument, or any of the instruments, by which it is created.

(4) Where at any time after the commencement of this Act there is in the case of any settlement which is a settlement for the purposes of the Settled Land Act 1925 no relevant property which is, or is deemed to be, subject to the settlement, the settlement permanently ceases at that time to be a settlement for the purposes of that Act.

In this subsection "relevant property" means land and personal chattels to which section 67(1) of the Settled Land Act 1925 (heirlooms) applies.

(5) No land held on charitable, ecclesiastical or public trusts shall be or be deemed to be settled land after the commencement of this Act, even if it was or was deemed to be settled land before that commencement.

(6) Schedule 1 has effect to make provision consequential on this section (including provision to impose a trust in circumstances in which, apart from this section, there would be a settlement for the purposes of the Settled Land Act 1925 (and there would not otherwise be a trust)).

3   Abolition of doctrine of conversion

(1) Where land is held by trustees subject to a trust for sale, the land is not to be regarded as personal property; and where personal property is subject to a trust for sale in order that the trustees may acquire land, the personal property is not to be regarded as land.

(2) Subsection (1) does not apply to a trust created by a will if the testator died before the commencement of this Act.

(3) Subject to that, subsection (1) applies to a trust whether it is created, or arises, before or after that commencement.

4   Express trusts for sale as trusts of land

(1) In the case of every trust for sale of land created by a disposition there is to be implied, despite any provision to the contrary made by the disposition, a power for the trustees to postpone sale of the land; and the trustees are not liable in any way for postponing sale of the land, in the exercise of their discretion, for an indefinite period.

(2) Subsection (1) applies to a trust whether it is created, or arises, before or after the commencement of this Act.

(3) Subsection (1) does not affect any liability incurred by trustees before that commencement.

5   Implied trusts for sale as trusts of land

(1) Schedule 2 has effect in relation to statutory provisions which impose a trust for sale of land in certain circumstances so that in those circumstances there is instead a trust of the land (without a duty to sell).

(2) Section 1 of the Settled Land Act 1925 does not apply to land held on any trust arising by virtue of that Schedule (so that any such land is subject to a trust of land).

Functions of trustees of land

6   General powers of trustees

(1) For the purpose of exercising their functions as trustees, the trustees of land have in relation to the land subject to the trust all the powers of an absolute owner.

(2) Where in the case of any land subject to a trust of land each of the beneficiaries interested in the land is a person of full age and capacity who is absolutely entitled to the land, the powers conferred on the trustees by subsection (1) include the power to convey the land to the beneficiaries even though they have not required the trustees to do so; and where land is conveyed by virtue of this subsection—

> (a)   the beneficiaries shall do whatever is necessary to secure that it vests in them, and
>
> (b)   if they fail to do so, the court may make an order requiring them to do so.

(3) The trustees of land have power to acquire land under the power conferred by section 8 of the Trustee Act 2000.

(4) …

(5) In exercising the powers conferred by this section trustees shall have regard to the rights of the beneficiaries.

(6) The powers conferred by this section shall not be exercised in contravention of, or of any order made in pursuance of, any other enactment or any rule of law or equity.

(7) The reference in subsection (6) to an order includes an order of any court or of the Charity Commissioners.

(8) Where any enactment other than this section confers on trustees authority to act subject to any restriction, limitation or condition, trustees of land may not exercise the powers conferred by this section to do any act which they are prevented from doing under the other enactment by reason of the restriction, limitation or condition.

(9) The duty of care under section 1 of the Trustee Act 2000 applies to trustees of land when exercising the powers conferred by this section.

7   Partition by trustees

(1) The trustees of land may, where beneficiaries of full age are absolutely entitled in undivided shares to land subject to the trust, partition the land, or any part of it, and provide (by way of mortgage or otherwise) for the payment of any equality money.

(2) The trustees shall give effect to any such partition by conveying the partitioned land in severalty (whether or not subject to any legal mortgage created for raising equality money), either absolutely or in trust, in accordance with the rights of those beneficiaries.

(3) Before exercising their powers under subsection (2) the trustees shall obtain the consent of each of those beneficiaries.

(4) Where a share in the land is affected by an incumbrance, the trustees may either give effect to it or provide for its discharge from the property allotted to that share as they think fit.

(5) If a share in the land is absolutely vested in a minor, subsections (1) to (4) apply as if he were of full age, except that the trustees may act on his behalf and retain land or other property representing his share in trust for him.

(6) Subsection (1) is subject to sections 21 (part-unit: interests) and 22 (part-unit: charging) of the Commonhold and Leasehold Reform Act 2002.

8   Exclusion and restriction of powers

(1) Sections 6 and 7 do not apply in the case of a trust of land created by a disposition in so far as provision to the effect that they do not apply is made by the disposition.

(2) If the disposition creating such a trust makes provision requiring any consent to be obtained to the exercise of any power conferred by section 6 or 7, the power may not be exercised without that consent.

(3) Subsection (1) does not apply in the case of charitable, ecclesiastical or public trusts.

(4) Subsections (1) and (2) have effect subject to any enactment which prohibits or restricts the effect of provision of the description mentioned in them.

9   Delegation by trustees

(1) The trustees of land may, by power of attorney, delegate to any beneficiary or beneficiaries of full age and beneficially entitled to an interest in possession in land subject to the trust any of their functions as trustees which relate to the land.

(2) Where trustees purport to delegate to a person by a power of attorney under subsection (1) functions relating to any land and another person in good faith deals with him in relation to the land, he shall be presumed in favour of that other person to have been a person to whom the functions could be delegated unless that other person has knowledge at the time of the transaction that he was not such a person.

And it shall be conclusively presumed in favour of any purchaser whose interest depends on the validity of that transaction that that other person dealt in good faith and did not have such knowledge if that other person makes a statutory declaration to that effect before or within three months after the completion of the purchase.

(3) A power of attorney under subsection (1) shall be given by all the trustees jointly and (unless expressed to be irrevocable and to be given by way of security) may be revoked by any one or more of them; and such a power is revoked by the appointment as a trustee of a person other than those by whom it is given (though not by any of those persons dying or otherwise ceasing to be a trustee).

(4) Where a beneficiary to whom functions are delegated by a power of attorney under subsection (1) ceases to be a person beneficially entitled to an interest in possession in land subject to the trust—

   (a)   if the functions are delegated to him alone, the power is revoked,

   (b)   if the functions are delegated to him and to other beneficiaries to be exercised by them jointly (but not separately), the power is revoked if each of the other beneficiaries ceases to be so entitled (but otherwise functions exercisable in accordance with the power are so exercisable by the remaining beneficiary or beneficiaries), and

   (c)   if the functions are delegated to him and to other beneficiaries to be exercised by them separately (or either separately or jointly), the power is revoked in so far as it relates to him.

(5) A delegation under subsection (1) may be for any period or indefinite.

(6) A power of attorney under subsection (1) cannot be an enduring power within the meaning of the Enduring Powers of Attorney Act 1985.

(7) Beneficiaries to whom functions have been delegated under subsection (1) are, in relation to the exercise of the functions, in the same position as trustees (with the same duties and liabilities); but such beneficiaries shall not be regarded as trustees for any other purposes (including, in particular, the purposes of any enactment permitting the delegation of functions by trustees or imposing requirements relating to the payment of capital money).

(8) …

(9) Neither this section nor the repeal by this Act of section 29 of the Law of Property Act 1925 (which is superseded by this section) affects the operation after the commencement of this Act of any delegation effected before that commencement.

9A   Duties of trustees in connection with delegation etc

(1) The duty of care under section 1 of the Trustee Act 2000 applies to trustees of land in deciding whether to delegate any of their functions under section 9.

(2) Subsection (3) applies if the trustees of land—

    (a)   delegate any of their functions under section 9, and

    (b)   the delegation is not irrevocable.

(3) While the delegation continues, the trustees—

    (a)   must keep the delegation under review,

    (b)   if circumstances make it appropriate to do so, must consider whether there is a need to exercise any power of intervention that they have, and

    (c)   if they consider that there is a need to exercise such a power, must do so.

(4) "Power of intervention" includes—

    (a)   a power to give directions to the beneficiary;

    (b)   a power to revoke the delegation.

(5) The duty of care under section 1 of the 2000 Act applies to trustees in carrying out any duty under subsection (3).

(6) A trustee of land is not liable for any act or default of the beneficiary, or beneficiaries, unless the trustee fails to comply with the duty of care in deciding to delegate any of the trustees' functions under section 9 or in carrying out any duty under subsection (3).

(7) Neither this section nor the repeal of section 9(8) by the Trustee Act 2000 affects the operation after the commencement of this section of any delegation effected before that commencement.

Consents and consultation

10   Consents

(1) If a disposition creating a trust of land requires the consent of more than two persons to the exercise by the trustees of any function relating to the land, the consent of any two of them to the exercise of the function is sufficient in favour of a purchaser.

(2) Subsection (1) does not apply to the exercise of a function by trustees of land held on charitable, ecclesiastical or public trusts.

(3) Where at any time a person whose consent is expressed by a disposition creating a trust of land to be required to the exercise by the trustees of any function relating to the land is not of full age—

    (a)   his consent is not, in favour of a purchaser, required to the exercise of the function, but

(b)   the trustees shall obtain the consent of a parent who has parental responsibility for him (within the meaning of the Children Act 1989) or of a guardian of his.

11   Consultation with beneficiaries

(1) The trustees of land shall in the exercise of any function relating to land subject to the trust—

(a)   so far as practicable, consult the beneficiaries of full age and beneficially entitled to an interest in possession in the land, and

(b)   so far as consistent with the general interest of the trust, give effect to the wishes of those beneficiaries, or (in case of dispute) of the majority (according to the value of their combined interests).

(2) Subsection (1) does not apply—

(a)   in relation to a trust created by a disposition in so far as provision that it does not apply is made by the disposition,

(b)   in relation to a trust created or arising under a will made before the commencement of this Act, or

(c)   in relation to the exercise of the power mentioned in section 6(2).

(3) Subsection (1) does not apply to a trust created before the commencement of this Act by a disposition, or a trust created after that commencement by reference to such a trust, unless provision to the effect that it is to apply is made by a deed executed—

(a)   in a case in which the trust was created by one person and he is of full capacity, by that person, or

(b)   in a case in which the trust was created by more than one person, by such of the persons who created the trust as are alive and of full capacity.

(4) A deed executed for the purposes of subsection (3) is irrevocable.

Right of beneficiaries to occupy trust land

12   The right to occupy

(1) A beneficiary who is beneficially entitled to an interest in possession in land subject to a trust of land is entitled by reason of his interest to occupy the land at any time if at that time—

(a)   the purposes of the trust include making the land available for his occupation (or for the occupation of beneficiaries of a class of which he is a member or of beneficiaries in general), or

(b)   the land is held by the trustees so as to be so available.

(2) Subsection (1) does not confer on a beneficiary a right to occupy land if it is either unavailable or unsuitable for occupation by him.

(3) This section is subject to section 13.

13   Exclusion and restriction of right to occupy

(1) Where two or more beneficiaries are (or apart from this subsection would be) entitled under section 12 to occupy land, the trustees of land may exclude or restrict the entitlement of any one or more (but not all) of them.

(2) Trustees may not under subsection (1)—

(a)   unreasonably exclude any beneficiary's entitlement to occupy land, or

(b)   restrict any such entitlement to an unreasonable extent.

(3) The trustees of land may from time to time impose reasonable conditions on any beneficiary in relation to his occupation of land by reason of his entitlement under section 12.

(4) The matters to which trustees are to have regard in exercising the powers conferred by this section include—

(a)   the intentions of the person or persons (if any) who created the trust,

(b)   the purposes for which the land is held, and

(c)   the circumstances and wishes of each of the beneficiaries who is (or apart from any previous exercise by the trustees of those powers would be) entitled to occupy the land under section 12.

(5) The conditions which may be imposed on a beneficiary under subsection (3) include, in particular, conditions requiring him—

(a)   to pay any outgoings or expenses in respect of the land, or

(b)   to assume any other obligation in relation to the land or to any activity which is or is proposed to be conducted there.

(6) Where the entitlement of any beneficiary to occupy land under section 12 has been excluded or restricted, the conditions which may be imposed on any other beneficiary under subsection (3) include, in particular, conditions requiring him to—

(a)   make payments by way of compensation to the beneficiary whose entitlement has been excluded or restricted, or

(b)   forgo any payment or other benefit to which he would otherwise be entitled under the trust so as to benefit that beneficiary.

(7) The powers conferred on trustees by this section may not be exercised—

(a)   so as prevent any person who is in occupation of land (whether or not by reason of an entitlement under section 12) from continuing to occupy the land, or

(b)   in a manner likely to result in any such person ceasing to occupy the land,

unless he consents or the court has given approval.

(8) The matters to which the court is to have regard in determining whether to give approval under subsection (7) include the matters mentioned in subsection (4)(a) to (c).

Powers of court

14   Applications for order

(1) Any person who is a trustee of land or has an interest in a property subject to a trust of land may make an application to the court for an order under this section.

(2) On an application for an order under this section the court may make any such order—

(a)   relating to the exercise by the trustees of any of their functions (including an order relieving them of any obligation to obtain the consent of, or to consult, any person in connection with the exercise of any of their functions), or

(b)   declaring the nature or extent of a person's interest in property subject to the trust,

as the court thinks fit.

(3) The court may not under this section make any order as to the appointment or removal of trustees.

(4) The powers conferred on the court by this section are exercisable on an application whether it is made before or after the commencement of this Act.

15   Matters relevant in determining applications

(1) The matters to which the court is to have regard in determining an application for an order under section 14 include—

(a)   the intentions of the person or persons (if any) who created the trust,

(b)   the purposes for which the property subject to the trust is held,

(c)   the welfare of any minor who occupies or might reasonably be expected to occupy any land subject to the trust as his home, and

(d)   the interests of any secured creditor of any beneficiary.

(2) In the case of an application relating to the exercise in relation to any land of the powers conferred on the trustees by section 13, the matters to which the court is to have regard also include the circumstances and wishes of each of the beneficiaries who is (or apart from any previous exercise by the trustees of those powers would be) entitled to occupy the land under section 12.

(3) In the case of any other application, other than one relating to the exercise of the power mentioned in section 6(2), the matters to which the court is to have regard also include the circumstances and wishes of any beneficiaries of full age and entitled to an interest in possession in property subject to the trust or (in case of dispute) of the majority (according to the value of their combined interests).

(4) This section does not apply to an application if section 335A of the Insolvency Act 1986 (which is inserted by Schedule 3 and relates to applications by a trustee of a bankrupt) applies to it.

Purchaser protection

16   Protection of purchasers

(1) A purchaser of land which is or has been subject to a trust need not be concerned to see that any requirement imposed on the trustees by section 6(5), 7(3) or 11(1) has been complied with.

(2) Where—

  (a)   trustees of land who convey land which (immediately before it is conveyed) is subject to the trust contravene section 6(6) or (8), but

  (b)   the purchaser of the land from the trustees has no actual notice of the contravention,

the contravention does not invalidate the conveyance.

(3) Where the powers of trustees of land are limited by virtue of section 8—

  (a)   the trustees shall take all reasonable steps to bring the limitation to the notice of any purchaser of the land from them, but

  (b)   the limitation does not invalidate any conveyance by the trustees to a purchaser who has no actual notice of the limitation.

(4) Where trustees of land convey land which (immediately before it is conveyed) is subject to the trust to persons believed by them to be beneficiaries absolutely entitled to the land under the trust and of full age and capacity—

  (a)   the trustees shall execute a deed declaring that they are discharged from the trust in relation to that land, and

  (b)   if they fail to do so, the court may make an order requiring them to do so.

(5) A purchaser of land to which a deed under subsection (4) relates is entitled to assume that, as from the date of the deed, the land is not subject to the trust unless he has actual notice that the trustees were mistaken in their belief that the land was conveyed to beneficiaries absolutely entitled to the land under the trust and of full age and capacity.

(6) Subsections (2) and (3) do not apply to land held on charitable, ecclesiastical or public trusts.

(7) This section does not apply to registered land.

Supplementary

17 Application of provisions to trusts of proceeds of sale

(1) ...

(2) Section 14 applies in relation to a trust of proceeds of sale of land and trustees of such a trust as in relation to a trust of land and trustees of land.

(3) In this section "trust of proceeds of sale of land" means (subject to subsection (5)) any trust of property (other than a trust of land) which consists of or includes—

    (a)   any proceeds of a disposition of land held in trust (including settled land), or

    (b)   any property representing any such proceeds.

(4) The references in subsection (3) to a trust—

    (a)   are to any description of trust (whether express, implied, resulting or constructive), including a trust for sale and a bare trust, and

    (b)   include a trust created, or arising, before the commencement of this Act.

(5) A trust which (despite section 2) is a settlement for the purposes of the Settled Land Act 1925 cannot be a trust of proceeds of sale of land.

(6) In subsection (3)—

    (a)   "disposition" includes any disposition made, or coming into operation, before the commencement of this Act, and

    (b)   the reference to settled land includes personal chattels to which section 67(1) of the Settled Land Act 1925 (heirlooms) applies.

18 Application of Part to personal representatives

(1) The provisions of this Part relating to trustees, other than sections 10, 11 and 14, apply to personal representatives, but with appropriate modifications and without prejudice to the functions of personal representatives for the purposes of administration.

(2) The appropriate modifications include—

    (a)   the substitution of references to persons interested in the due administration of the estate for references to beneficiaries, and

    (b)   the substitution of references to the will for references to the disposition creating the trust.

(3) Section 3(1) does not apply to personal representatives if the death occurs before the commencement of this Act.

PART II
APPOINTMENT AND RETIREMENT OF TRUSTEES

19   Appointment and retirement of trustee at instance of beneficiaries

(1) This section applies in the case of a trust where—

    (a)   there is no person nominated for the purpose of appointing new trustees by the instrument, if any, creating the trust, and

    (b)   the beneficiaries under the trust are of full age and capacity and (taken together) are absolutely entitled to the property subject to the trust.

(2) The beneficiaries may give a direction or directions of either or both of the following descriptions—

    (a)   a written direction to a trustee or trustees to retire from the trust, and

    (b)   a written direction to the trustees or trustee for the time being (or, if there are none, to the personal representative of the last person who was a trustee) to appoint by writing to be a trustee or trustees the person or persons specified in the direction.

(3) Where—

    (a)   a trustee has been given a direction under subsection (2)(a),

    (b)   reasonable arrangements have been made for the protection of any rights of his in connection with the trust,

    (c)   after he has retired there will be either a trust corporation or at least two persons to act as trustees to perform the trust, and

    (d)   either another person is to be appointed to be a new trustee on his retirement (whether in compliance with a direction under subsection (2)(b) or otherwise) or the continuing trustees by deed consent to his retirement,

he shall make a deed declaring his retirement and shall be deemed to have retired and be discharged from the trust.

(4) Where a trustee retires under subsection (3) he and the continuing trustees (together with any new trustee) shall (subject to any arrangements for the protection of his rights) do anything necessary to vest the trust property in the continuing trustees (or the continuing and new trustees).

(5) This section has effect subject to the restrictions imposed by the Trustee Act 1925 on the number of trustees.

20   Appointment of substitute for incapable trustee

(1) This section applies where—

    (a)   a trustee is incapable by reason of mental disorder of exercising his functions as trustee,

    (b)   there is no person who is both entitled and willing and able to appoint a trustee in place of him under section 36(1) of the Trustee Act 1925, and

    (c)   the beneficiaries under the trust are of full age and capacity and (taken together) are absolutely entitled to the property subject to the trust.

(2) The beneficiaries may give to—

    (a)   a receiver of the trustee,

    (b)   an attorney acting for him under the authority of a power of attorney created by an instrument which is registered under section 6 of the Enduring Powers of Attorney Act 1985, or

    (c)   a person authorised for the purpose by the authority having jurisdiction under Part VII of the Mental Health Act 1983,

a written direction to appoint by writing the person or persons specified in the direction to be a trustee or trustees in place of the incapable trustee.

21   Supplementary

(1) For the purposes of section 19 or 20 a direction is given by beneficiaries if—

    (a)   a single direction is jointly given by all of them, or

    (b)   (subject to subsection (2)) a direction is given by each of them (whether solely or jointly with one or more, but not all, of the others),

and none of them by writing withdraws the direction given by him before it has been complied with.

(2) Where more than one direction is given each must specify for appointment or retirement the same person or persons.

(3) Subsection (7) of section 36 of the Trustee Act 1925 (powers of trustees appointed under that section) applies to a trustee appointed under section 19 or 20 as if he were appointed under that section.

(4) A direction under section 19 or 20 must not specify a person or persons for appointment if the appointment of that person or those persons would be in contravention of section 35(1) of the Trustee Act 1925 or section 24(1) of the Law of Property Act 1925 (requirements as to identity of trustees).

(5) Sections 19 and 20 do not apply in relation to a trust created by a disposition in so far as provision that they do not apply is made by the disposition.

(6) Sections 19 and 20 do not apply in relation to a trust created before the commencement of this Act by a disposition in so far as provision to the effect that they do not apply is made by a deed executed—

    (a)   in a case in which the trust was created by one person and he is of full capacity, by that person, or

    (b)   in a case in which the trust was created by more than one person, by such of the persons who created the trust as are alive and of full capacity.

(7) A deed executed for the purposes of subsection (6) is irrevocable.

(8) Where a deed is executed for the purposes of subsection (6)—

    (a)   it does not affect anything done before its execution to comply with a direction under section 19 or 20, but

    (b)   a direction under section 19 or 20 which has been given but not complied with before its execution shall cease to have effect.

PART III
SUPPLEMENTARY

22   Meaning of "beneficiary"

(1) In this Act "beneficiary", in relation to a trust, means any person who under the trust has an interest in property subject to the trust (including a person who has such an interest as a trustee or a personal representative).

(2) In this Act references to a beneficiary who is beneficially entitled do not include a beneficiary who has an interest in property subject to the trust only by reason of being a trustee or personal representative.

(3) For the purposes of this Act a person who is a beneficiary only by reason of being an annuitant is not to be regarded as entitled to an interest in possession in land subject to the trust.

23 Other interpretation provisions

(1) In this Act "purchaser" has the same meaning as in Part I of the Law of Property Act 1925.

(2) Subject to that, where an expression used in this Act is given a meaning by the Law of Property Act 1925 it has the same meaning as in that Act unless the context otherwise requires.

(3) In this Act "the court" means—

    (a)   the High Court, or

    (b)   a county court.

24 Application to Crown

(1) Subject to subsection (2), this Act binds the Crown.

(2) This Act (except so far as it relates to undivided shares and joint ownership) does not affect or alter the descent, devolution or nature of the estates and interests of or in—

    (a)   land for the time being vested in Her Majesty in right of the Crown or of the Duchy of Lancaster, or

    (b)   land for the time being belonging to the Duchy of Cornwall and held in right or respect of the Duchy.

25 Amendments, repeals etc

(1) The enactments mentioned in Schedule 3 have effect subject to the amendments specified in that Schedule (which are minor or consequential on other provisions of this Act).

(2) The enactments mentioned in Schedule 4 are repealed to the extent specified in the third column of that Schedule.

(3) Neither section 2(5) nor the repeal by this Act of section 29 of the Settled Land Act 1925 applies in relation to the deed of settlement set out in the Schedule to the Chequers Estate Act 1917 or the trust instrument set out in the Schedule to the Chevening Estate Act 1959.

(4) The amendments and repeals made by this Act do not affect any entailed interest created before the commencement of this Act.

(5) The amendments and repeals made by this Act in consequence of section 3—

    (a)   do not affect a trust created by a will if the testator died before the commencement of this Act, and

(b)   do not affect personal representatives of a person who died before that commencement;

and the repeal of section 22 of the Partnership Act 1890 does not apply in any circumstances involving the personal representatives of a partner who died before that commencement.

26   Power to make consequential provision

(1) The Lord Chancellor may by order made by statutory instrument make any such supplementary, transitional or incidental provision as appears to him to be appropriate for any of the purposes of this Act or in consequence of any of the provisions of this Act.

(2) An order under subsection (1) may, in particular, include provision modifying any enactment contained in a public general or local Act which is passed before, or in the same Session as, this Act.

(3) A statutory instrument made in the exercise of the power conferred by this section is subject to annulment in pursuance of a resolution of either House of Parliament.

27   Short title, commencement and extent

(1) This Act may be cited as the Trusts of Land and Appointment of Trustees Act 1996.

(2) This Act comes into force on such day as the Lord Chancellor appoints by order made by statutory instrument.

(3) Subject to subsection (4), the provisions of this Act extend only to England and Wales.

(4) The repeal in section 30(2) of the Agriculture Act 1970 extends only to Northern Ireland.

SCHEDULE 1
PROVISIONS CONSEQUENTIAL ON SECTION 2

Section 2

Minors

1   (1) Where after the commencement of this Act a person purports to convey a legal estate in land to a minor, or two or more minors, alone, the conveyance—

(a)   is not effective to pass the legal estate, but

(b)   operates as a declaration that the land is held in trust for the minor or minors (or if he purports to convey it to the minor or minors in trust for any persons, for those persons).

(2) Where after the commencement of this Act a person purports to convey a legal estate in land to—

(a)   a minor or two or more minors, and

(b)   another person who is, or other persons who are, of full age,

the conveyance operates to vest the land in the other person or persons in trust for the minor or minors and the other person or persons (or if he purports to convey it to them in trust for any persons, for those persons).

(3) Where immediately before the commencement of this Act a conveyance is operating (by virtue of section 27 of the Settled Land Act 1925) as an agreement to execute a settlement in favour of a minor or minors—

(a)   the agreement ceases to have effect on the commencement of this Act, and

(b)   the conveyance subsequently operates instead as a declaration that the land is held in trust for the minor or minors.

2   Where after the commencement of this Act a legal estate in land would, by reason of intestacy or in any other circumstances not dealt with in paragraph 1, vest in a person who is a minor if he were a person of full age, the land is held in trust for the minor.

Family charges

3   Where, by virtue of an instrument coming into operation after the commencement of this Act, land becomes charged voluntarily (or in consideration of marriage) or by way of family arrangement, whether immediately or after an interval, with the payment of—

(a)   a rentcharge for the life of a person or a shorter period, or

(b)   capital, annual or periodical sums for the benefit of a person,

the instrument operates as a declaration that the land is held in trust for giving effect to the charge.

Charitable, ecclesiastical and public trusts

4   (1) This paragraph applies in the case of land held on charitable, ecclesiastical or public trusts (other than land to which the Universities and College Estates Act 1925 applies).

(2) Where there is a conveyance of such land—

(a)   if neither section 37(1) nor section 39(1) of the Charities Act 1993 applies to the conveyance, it shall state that the land is held on such trusts, and

(b)   if neither section 37(2) nor section 39(2) of that Act has been complied with in relation to the conveyance and a purchaser has notice that the land is held on such trusts, he must see that any consents or orders necessary to authorise the transaction have been obtained.

(3) Where any trustees or the majority of any set of trustees have power to transfer or create any legal estate in the land, the estate shall be transferred or created by them in the names and on behalf of the persons in whom it is vested.

Entailed interests

5   (1) Where a person purports by an instrument coming into operation after the commencement of this Act to grant to another person an entailed interest in real or personal property, the instrument—

    (a)   is not effective to grant an entailed interest, but

    (b)   operates instead as a declaration that the property is held in trust absolutely for the person to whom an entailed interest in the property was purportedly granted.

(2) Where a person purports by an instrument coming into operation after the commencement of this Act to declare himself a tenant in tail of real or personal property, the instrument is not effective to create an entailed interest.

Property held on settlement ceasing to exist

6   Where a settlement ceases to be a settlement for the purposes of the Settled Land Act 1925 because no relevant property (within the meaning of section 2(4)) is, or is deemed to be, subject to the settlement, any property which is or later becomes subject to the settlement is held in trust for the persons interested under the settlement.

Trustee Act 2000

A2.3   *Arrangement of sections*

PART I
THE DUTY OF CARE

1   The duty of care

(1) Whenever the duty under this subsection applies to a trustee, he must exercise such care and skill as is reasonable in the circumstances, having regard in particular—

   (a)   to any special knowledge or experience that he has or holds himself out as having, and

(b)   if he acts as trustee in the course of a business or profession, to any special knowledge or experience that it is reasonable to expect of a person acting in the course of that kind of business or profession.

(2) In this Act the duty under subsection (1) is called "the duty of care".

2   Application of duty of care

Schedule 1 makes provision about when the duty of care applies to a trustee.

PART II
INVESTMENT

3   General power of investment

(1) Subject to the provisions of this Part, a trustee may make any kind of investment that he could make if he were absolutely entitled to the assets of the trust.

(2) In this Act the power under subsection (1) is called "the general power of investment".

(3) The general power of investment does not permit a trustee to make investments in land other than in loans secured on land (but see also section 8).

(4) A person invests in a loan secured on land if he has rights under any contract under which—

(a)   one person provides another with credit, and

(b)   the obligation of the borrower to repay is secured on land.

(5) "Credit" includes any cash loan or other financial accommodation.

(6) "Cash" includes money in any form.

4   Standard investment criteria

(1) In exercising any power of investment, whether arising under this Part or otherwise, a trustee must have regard to the standard investment criteria.

(2) A trustee must from time to time review the investments of the trust and consider whether, having regard to the standard investment criteria, they should be varied.

(3) The standard investment criteria, in relation to a trust, are—

(a) the suitability to the trust of investments of the same kind as any particular investment proposed to be made or retained and of that particular investment as an investment of that kind, and

(b) the need for diversification of investments of the trust, in so far as is appropriate to the circumstances of the trust.

5 Advice

(1) Before exercising any power of investment, whether arising under this Part or otherwise, a trustee must (unless the exception applies) obtain and consider proper advice about the way in which, having regard to the standard investment criteria, the power should be exercised.

(2) When reviewing the investments of the trust, a trustee must (unless the exception applies) obtain and consider proper advice about whether, having regard to the standard investment criteria, the investments should be varied.

(3) The exception is that a trustee need not obtain such advice if he reasonably concludes that in all the circumstances it is unnecessary or inappropriate to do so.

(4) Proper advice is the advice of a person who is reasonably believed by the trustee to be qualified to give it by his ability in and practical experience of financial and other matters relating to the proposed investment.

6 Restriction or exclusion of this Part etc

(1) The general power of investment is—

(a) in addition to powers conferred on trustees otherwise than by this Act, but

(b) subject to any restriction or exclusion imposed by the trust instrument or by any enactment or any provision of subordinate legislation.

(2) For the purposes of this Act, an enactment or a provision of subordinate legislation is not to be regarded as being, or as being part of, a trust instrument.

(3) In this Act "subordinate legislation" has the same meaning as in the Interpretation Act 1978.

7 Existing trusts

(1) This Part applies in relation to trusts whether created before or after its commencement.

(2) No provision relating to the powers of a trustee contained in a trust instrument made before 3rd August 1961 is to be treated (for the purposes of section 6(1)(b)) as restricting or excluding the general power of investment.

(3) A provision contained in a trust instrument made before the commencement of this Part which—

    (a)   has effect under section 3(2) of the Trustee Investments Act 1961 as a power to invest under that Act, or

    (b)   confers power to invest under that Act,

is to be treated as conferring the general power of investment on a trustee.

PART III
ACQUISITION OF LAND

8   Power to acquire freehold and leasehold land

(1) A trustee may acquire freehold or leasehold land in the United Kingdom—

    (a)   as an investment,

    (b)   for occupation by a beneficiary, or

    (c)   for any other reason.

(2) "Freehold or leasehold land" means—

    (a)   in relation to England and Wales, a legal estate in land,

    (b)   in relation to Scotland—

        (i)   the estate or interest of the proprietor of the dominium utile or, in the case of land not held on feudal tenure, the estate or interest of the owner, or

        (ii)   a tenancy, and

    (c)   in relation to Northern Ireland, a legal estate in land, including land held under a fee farm grant.

(3) For the purpose of exercising his functions as a trustee, a trustee who acquires land under this section has all the powers of an absolute owner in relation to the land.

9   Restriction or exclusion of this Part etc

The powers conferred by this Part are—

(a) in addition to powers conferred on trustees otherwise than by this Part, but

(b) subject to any restriction or exclusion imposed by the trust instrument or by any enactment or any provision of subordinate legislation.

10 Existing trusts

(1) This Part does not apply in relation to—

(a) a trust of property which consists of or includes land which (despite section 2 of the Trusts of Land and Appointment of Trustees Act 1996) is settled land, or

(b) a trust to which the Universities and College Estates Act 1925 applies.

(2) Subject to subsection (1), this Part applies in relation to trusts whether created before or after its commencement.

PART IV
AGENTS, NOMINEES AND CUSTODIANS

Agents

11 Power to employ agents

(1) Subject to the provisions of this Part, the trustees of a trust may authorise any person to exercise any or all of their delegable functions as their agent.

(2) In the case of a trust other than a charitable trust, the trustees' delegable functions consist of any function other than—

(a) any function relating to whether or in what way any assets of the trust should be distributed,

(b) any power to decide whether any fees or other payment due to be made out of the trust funds should be made out of income or capital,

(c) any power to appoint a person to be a trustee of the trust, or

(d) any power conferred by any other enactment or the trust instrument which permits the trustees to delegate any of their functions or to appoint a person to act as a nominee or custodian.

(3) In the case of a charitable trust, the trustees' delegable functions are—

(a) any function consisting of carrying out a decision that the trustees have taken;

(b)   any function relating to the investment of assets subject to the trust (including, in the case of land held as an investment, managing the land and creating or disposing of an interest in the land);

(c)   any function relating to the raising of funds for the trust otherwise than by means of profits of a trade which is an integral part of carrying out the trust's charitable purpose;

(d)   any other function prescribed by an order made by the Secretary of State.

(4) For the purposes of subsection (3)(c) a trade is an integral part of carrying out a trust's charitable purpose if, whether carried on in the United Kingdom or elsewhere, the profits are applied solely to the purposes of the trust and either—

(a)   the trade is exercised in the course of the actual carrying out of a primary purpose of the trust, or

(b)   the work in connection with the trade is mainly carried out by beneficiaries of the trust.

(5) The power to make an order under subsection (3)(d) is exercisable by statutory instrument which shall be subject to annulment in pursuance of a resolution of either House of Parliament.

12   Persons who may act as agents

(1) Subject to subsection (2), the persons whom the trustees may under section 11 authorise to exercise functions as their agent include one or more of their number.

(2) The trustees may not authorise two (or more) persons to exercise the same function unless they are to exercise the function jointly.

(3) The trustees may not under section 11 authorise a beneficiary to exercise any function as their agent (even if the beneficiary is also a trustee).

(4) The trustees may under section 11 authorise a person to exercise functions as their agent even though he is also appointed to act as their nominee or custodian (whether under section 16, 17 or 18 or any other power).

13   Linked functions etc

(1) Subject to subsections (2) and (5), a person who is authorised under section 11 to exercise a function is (whatever the terms of the agency) subject to any specific duties or restrictions attached to the function.

For example, a person who is authorised under section 11 to exercise the general power of investment is subject to the duties under section 4 in relation to that power.

(2) A person who is authorised under section 11 to exercise a power which is subject to a requirement to obtain advice is not subject to the requirement if he is the kind of person from whom it would have been proper for the trustees, in compliance with the requirement, to obtain advice.

(3) Subsections (4) and (5) apply to a trust to which section 11(1) of the Trusts of Land and Appointment of Trustees Act 1996 (duties to consult beneficiaries and give effect to their wishes) applies.

(4) The trustees may not under section 11 authorise a person to exercise any of their functions on terms that prevent them from complying with section 11(1) of the 1996 Act.

(5) A person who is authorised under section 11 to exercise any function relating to land subject to the trust is not subject to section 11(1) of the 1996 Act.

14   Terms of agency

(1) Subject to subsection (2) and sections 15(2) and 29 to 32, the trustees may authorise a person to exercise functions as their agent on such terms as to remuneration and other matters as they may determine.

(2) The trustees may not authorise a person to exercise functions as their agent on any of the terms mentioned in subsection (3) unless it is reasonably necessary for them to do so.

(3) The terms are—

(a)   a term permitting the agent to appoint a substitute;

(b)   a term restricting the liability of the agent or his substitute to the trustees or any beneficiary;

(c)   a term permitting the agent to act in circumstances capable of giving rise to a conflict of interest.

15   Asset management: special restrictions

(1) The trustees may not authorise a person to exercise any of their asset management functions as their agent except by an agreement which is in or evidenced in writing.

(2) The trustees may not authorise a person to exercise any of their asset management functions as their agent unless—

(a)   they have prepared a statement that gives guidance as to how the functions should be exercised ("a policy statement"), and

(b)   the agreement under which the agent is to act includes a term to the effect that he will secure compliance with—

      (i)   the policy statement, or

     (ii)   if the policy statement is revised or replaced under section 22, the revised or replacement policy statement.

(3) The trustees must formulate any guidance given in the policy statement with a view to ensuring that the functions will be exercised in the best interests of the trust.

(4) The policy statement must be in or evidenced in writing.

(5) The asset management functions of trustees are their functions relating to—

    (a)   the investment of assets subject to the trust,

    (b)   the acquisition of property which is to be subject to the trust, and

    (c)   managing property which is subject to the trust and disposing of, or creating or disposing of an interest in, such property.

Nominees and custodians

16   Power to appoint nominees

(1) Subject to the provisions of this Part, the trustees of a trust may—

    (a)   appoint a person to act as their nominee in relation to such of the assets of the trust as they determine (other than settled land), and

    (b)   take such steps as are necessary to secure that those assets are vested in a person so appointed.

(2) An appointment under this section must be in or evidenced in writing.

(3) This section does not apply to any trust having a custodian trustee or in relation to any assets vested in the official custodian for charities.

17   Power to appoint custodians

(1) Subject to the provisions of this Part, the trustees of a trust may appoint a person to act as a custodian in relation to such of the assets of the trust as they may determine.

(2) For the purposes of this Act a person is a custodian in relation to assets if he undertakes the safe custody of the assets or of any documents or records concerning the assets.

(3) An appointment under this section must be in or evidenced in writing.

(4) This section does not apply to any trust having a custodian trustee or in relation to any assets vested in the official custodian for charities.

18 Investment in bearer securities

(1) If trustees retain or invest in securities payable to bearer, they must appoint a person to act as a custodian of the securities.

(2) Subsection (1) does not apply if the trust instrument or any enactment or provision of subordinate legislation contains provision which (however expressed) permits the trustees to retain or invest in securities payable to bearer without appointing a person to act as a custodian.

(3) An appointment under this section must be in or evidenced in writing.

(4) This section does not apply to any trust having a custodian trustee or in relation to any securities vested in the official custodian for charities.

19 Persons who may be appointed as nominees or custodians

(1) A person may not be appointed under section 16, 17 or 18 as a nominee or custodian unless one of the relevant conditions is satisfied.

(2) The relevant conditions are that—

> (a) the person carries on a business which consists of or includes acting as a nominee or custodian;
>
> (b) the person is a body corporate which is controlled by the trustees;
>
> (c) the person is a body corporate recognised under section 9 of the Administration of Justice Act 1985.

(3) The question whether a body corporate is controlled by trustees is to be determined in accordance with section 840 of the Income and Corporation Taxes Act 1988.

(4) The trustees of a charitable trust which is not an exempt charity must act in accordance with any guidance given by the Charity Commissioners concerning the selection of a person for appointment as a nominee or custodian under section 16, 17 or 18.

(5) Subject to subsections (1) and (4), the persons whom the trustees may under section 16, 17 or 18 appoint as a nominee or custodian include—

> (a) one of their number, if that one is a trust corporation, or
>
> (b) two (or more) of their number, if they are to act as joint nominees or joint custodians.

(6) The trustees may under section 16 appoint a person to act as their nominee even though he is also—

> (a) appointed to act as their custodian (whether under section 17 or 18 or any other power), or
>
> (b) authorised to exercise functions as their agent (whether under section 11 or any other power).

(7) Likewise, the trustees may under section 17 or 18 appoint a person to act as their custodian even though he is also—

> (a)   appointed to act as their nominee (whether under section 16 or any other power), or

> (b)   authorised to exercise functions as their agent (whether under section 11 or any other power).

20   Terms of appointment of nominees and custodians

(1) Subject to subsection (2) and sections 29 to 32, the trustees may under section 16, 17 or 18 appoint a person to act as a nominee or custodian on such terms as to remuneration and other matters as they may determine.

(2) The trustees may not under section 16, 17 or 18 appoint a person to act as a nominee or custodian on any of the terms mentioned in subsection (3) unless it is reasonably necessary for them to do so.

(3) The terms are—

> (a)   a term permitting the nominee or custodian to appoint a substitute;

> (b)   a term restricting the liability of the nominee or custodian or his substitute to the trustees or to any beneficiary;

> (c)   a term permitting the nominee or custodian to act in circumstances capable of giving rise to a conflict of interest.

Review of and liability for agents, nominees and custodians etc

21   Application of sections 22 and 23

(1) Sections 22 and 23 apply in a case where trustees have, under section 11, 16, 17 or 18—

> (a)   authorised a person to exercise functions as their agent, or

> (b)   appointed a person to act as a nominee or custodian.

(2) Subject to subsection (3), sections 22 and 23 also apply in a case where trustees have, under any power conferred on them by the trust instrument or by any enactment or any provision of subordinate legislation—

> (a)   authorised a person to exercise functions as their agent, or

> (b)   appointed a person to act as a nominee or custodian.

(3) If the application of section 22 or 23 is inconsistent with the terms of the trust instrument or the enactment or provision of subordinate legislation, the section in question does not apply.

22   Review of agents, nominees and custodians etc

(1) While the agent, nominee or custodian continues to act for the trust, the trustees—

   (a)   must keep under review the arrangements under which the agent, nominee or custodian acts and how those arrangements are being put into effect,

   (b)   if circumstances make it appropriate to do so, must consider whether there is a need to exercise any power of intervention that they have, and

   (c)   if they consider that there is a need to exercise such a power, must do so.

(2) If the agent has been authorised to exercise asset management functions, the duty under subsection (1) includes, in particular—

   (a)   a duty to consider whether there is any need to revise or replace the policy statement made for the purposes of section 15,

   (b)   if they consider that there is a need to revise or replace the policy statement, a duty to do so, and

   (c)   a duty to assess whether the policy statement (as it has effect for the time being) is being complied with.

(3) Subsections (3) and (4) of section 15 apply to the revision or replacement of a policy statement under this section as they apply to the making of a policy statement under that section.

(4) "Power of intervention" includes—

   (a)   a power to give directions to the agent, nominee or custodian;

   (b)   a power to revoke the authorisation or appointment.

23   Liability for agents, nominees and custodians etc

(1) A trustee is not liable for any act or default of the agent, nominee or custodian unless he has failed to comply with the duty of care applicable to him, under paragraph 3 of Schedule 1—

   (a)   when entering into the arrangements under which the person acts as agent, nominee or custodian, or

   (b)   when carrying out his duties under section 22.

(2) If a trustee has agreed a term under which the agent, nominee or custodian is permitted to appoint a substitute, the trustee is not liable for any act or default of the substitute unless he has failed to comply with the duty of care applicable to him, under paragraph 3 of Schedule 1—

   (a)   when agreeing that term, or

(b)   when carrying out his duties under section 22 in so far as they relate to the use of the substitute.

Supplementary

24   Effect of trustees exceeding their powers

A failure by the trustees to act within the limits of the powers conferred by this Part—

(a)   in authorising a person to exercise a function of theirs as an agent, or

(b)   in appointing a person to act as a nominee or custodian,

does not invalidate the authorisation or appointment.

25   Sole trustees

(1) Subject to subsection (2), this Part applies in relation to a trust having a sole trustee as it applies in relation to other trusts (and references in this Part to trustees—except in sections 12(1) and (3) and 19(5)—are to be read accordingly).

(2) Section 18 does not impose a duty on a sole trustee if that trustee is a trust corporation.

26   Restriction or exclusion of this Part etc

The powers conferred by this Part are—

(a)   in addition to powers conferred on trustees otherwise than by this Act, but

(b)   subject to any restriction or exclusion imposed by the trust instrument or by any enactment or any provision of subordinate legislation.

27   Existing trusts

This Part applies in relation to trusts whether created before or after its commencement.

PART V
REMUNERATION

28 Trustee's entitlement to payment under trust instrument

(1) Except to the extent (if any) to which the trust instrument makes inconsistent provision, subsections (2) to (4) apply to a trustee if—

    (a)   there is a provision in the trust instrument entitling him to receive payment out of trust funds in respect of services provided by him to or on behalf of the trust, and

    (b)   the trustee is a trust corporation or is acting in a professional capacity.

(2) The trustee is to be treated as entitled under the trust instrument to receive payment in respect of services even if they are services which are capable of being provided by a lay trustee.

(3) Subsection (2) applies to a trustee of a charitable trust who is not a trust corporation only—

    (a)   if he is not a sole trustee, and

    (b)   to the extent that a majority of the other trustees have agreed that it should apply to him.

(4) Any payments to which the trustee is entitled in respect of services are to be treated as remuneration for services (and not as a gift) for the purposes of—

    (a)   section 15 of the Wills Act 1837 (gifts to an attesting witness to be void), and

    (b)   section 34(3) of the Administration of Estates Act 1925 (order in which estate to be paid out).

(5) For the purposes of this Part, a trustee acts in a professional capacity if he acts in the course of a profession or business which consists of or includes the provision of services in connection with –

    (a)   the management or administration of trusts generally or a particular kind of trust, or

    (b)   any particular aspect of the management or administration of trusts generally or a particular kind of trust,

and the services he provides to or on behalf of the trust fall within that description.

(6) For the purposes of this Part, a person acts as a lay trustee if he—

    (a)   is not a trust corporation, and

    (b)   does not act in a professional capacity.

29 Remuneration of certain trustees

(1) Subject to subsection (5), a trustee who—

    (a)   is a trust corporation, but

    (b)   is not a trustee of a charitable trust,

is entitled to receive reasonable remuneration out of the trust funds for any services that the trust corporation provides to or on behalf of the trust.

(2) Subject to subsection (5), a trustee who—

    (a)   acts in a professional capacity, but

    (b)   is not a trust corporation, a trustee of a charitable trust or a sole trustee,

is entitled to receive reasonable remuneration out of the trust funds for any services that he provides to or on behalf of the trust if each other trustee has agreed in writing that he may be remunerated for the services.

(3) "Reasonable remuneration" means, in relation to the provision of services by a trustee, such remuneration as is reasonable in the circumstances for the provision of those services to or on behalf of that trust by that trustee and for the purposes of subsection (1) includes, in relation to the provision of services by a trustee who is an authorised institution under the Banking Act 1987 and provides the services in that capacity, the institution's reasonable charges for the provision of such services.

(4) A trustee is entitled to remuneration under this section even if the services in question are capable of being provided by a lay trustee.

(5) A trustee is not entitled to remuneration under this section if any provision about his entitlement to remuneration has been made—

    (a)   by the trust instrument, or

    (b)   by any enactment or any provision of subordinate legislation.

(6) This section applies to a trustee who has been authorised under a power conferred by Part IV or the trust instrument—

    (a)   to exercise functions as an agent of the trustees, or

    (b)   to act as a nominee or custodian,

as it applies to any other trustee.

30 Remuneration of trustees of charitable trusts

(1) The Secretary of State may by regulations make provision for the remuneration of trustees of charitable trusts who are trust corporations or act in a professional capacity.

(2) The power under subsection (1) includes power to make provision for the remuneration of a trustee who has been authorised under a power conferred by Part IV or any other enactment or any provision of subordinate legislation, or by the trust instrument—

(a)   to exercise functions as an agent of the trustees, or

(b)   to act as a nominee or custodian.

(3) Regulations under this section may—

(a)   make different provision for different cases;

(b)   contain such supplemental, incidental, consequential and transitional provision as the Secretary of State considers appropriate.

(4) The power to make regulations under this section is exercisable by statutory instrument, but no such instrument shall be made unless a draft of it has been laid before Parliament and approved by a resolution of each House of Parliament.

31   Trustees' expenses

(1) A trustee—

(a)   is entitled to be reimbursed from the trust funds, or

(b)   may pay out of the trust funds,

expenses properly incurred by him when acting on behalf of the trust.

(2) This section applies to a trustee who has been authorised under a power conferred by Part IV or any other enactment or any provision of subordinate legislation, or by the trust instrument—

(a)   to exercise functions as an agent of the trustees, or

(b)   to act as a nominee or custodian,

as it applies to any other trustee.

32   Remuneration and expenses of agents, nominees and custodians

(1) This section applies if, under a power conferred by Part IV or any other enactment or any provision of subordinate legislation, or by the trust instrument, a person other than a trustee has been—

(a)   authorised to exercise functions as an agent of the trustees, or

(b)   appointed to act as a nominee or custodian.

(2) The trustees may remunerate the agent, nominee or custodian out of the trust funds for services if—

(a) he is engaged on terms entitling him to be remunerated for those services, and

(b) the amount does not exceed such remuneration as is reasonable in the circumstances for the provision of those services by him to or on behalf of that trust.

(3) The trustees may reimburse the agent, nominee or custodian out of the trust funds for any expenses properly incurred by him in exercising functions as an agent, nominee or custodian.

33   Application

(1) Subject to subsection (2), sections 28, 29, 31 and 32 apply in relation to services provided to or on behalf of, or (as the case may be) expenses incurred on or after their commencement on behalf of, trusts whenever created.

(2) Nothing in section 28 or 29 is to be treated as affecting the operation of—

(a) section 15 of the Wills Act 1837, or

(b) section 34(3) of the Administration of Estates Act 1925,

in relation to any death occurring before the commencement of section 28 or (as the case may be) section 29.

PART VI
MISCELLANEOUS AND SUPPLEMENTARY

34   Power to insure

(1) For section 19 of the Trustee Act 1925 (power to insure) substitute—

(The words substituted are set out in Appendix 2.1.)

(2) . . .

(3) The amendments made by this section apply in relation to trusts whether created before or after its commencement.

35   Personal representatives

(1) Subject to the following provisions of this section, this Act applies in relation to a personal representative administering an estate according to the law as it applies to a trustee carrying out a trust for beneficiaries.

(2) For this purpose this Act is to be read with the appropriate modifications and in particular—

(a) references to the trust instrument are to be read as references to the will,

(b) references to a beneficiary or to beneficiaries, apart from the reference to a beneficiary in section 8(1)(b), are to be read as references to a person or the persons interested in the due administration of the estate, and

(c) the reference to a beneficiary in section 8(1)(b) is to be read as a reference to a person who under the will of the deceased or under the law relating to intestacy is beneficially interested in the estate.

(3) Remuneration to which a personal representative is entitled under section 28 or 29 is to be treated as an administration expense for the purposes of—

(a) section 34(3) of the Administration of Estates Act 1925 (order in which estate to be paid out), and

(b) any provision giving reasonable administration expenses priority over the preferential debts listed in Schedule 6 to the Insolvency Act 1986.

(4) Nothing in subsection (3) is to be treated as affecting the operation of the provisions mentioned in paragraphs (a) and (b) of that subsection in relation to any death occurring before the commencement of this section.

36   Pension schemes

(1) In this section "pension scheme" means an occupational pension scheme (within the meaning of the Pension Schemes Act 1993) established under a trust and subject to the law of England and Wales.

(2) Part I does not apply in so far as it imposes a duty of care in relation to—

(a) the functions described in paragraphs 1 and 2 of Schedule 1, or

(b) the functions described in paragraph 3 of that Schedule to the extent that they relate to trustees—

(i) authorising a person to exercise their functions with respect to investment, or

(ii) appointing a person to act as their nominee or custodian.

(3) Nothing in Part II or III applies to the trustees of any pension scheme.

(4) Part IV applies to the trustees of a pension scheme subject to the restrictions in subsections (5) to (8).

(5) The trustees of a pension scheme may not under Part IV authorise any person to exercise any functions relating to investment as their agent.

(6) The trustees of a pension scheme may not under Part IV authorise a person who is—

(a)   an employer in relation to the scheme, or

(b)   connected with or an associate of such an employer,

to exercise any of their functions as their agent.

(7) For the purposes of subsection (6)—

(a)   "employer", in relation to a scheme, has the same meaning as in the Pensions Act 1995;

(b)   sections 249 and 435 of the Insolvency Act 1986 apply for the purpose of determining whether a person is connected with or an associate of an employer.

(8) Sections 16 to 20 (powers to appoint nominees and custodians) do not apply to the trustees of a pension scheme.

37   Authorised unit trusts

(1) Parts II to IV do not apply to trustees of authorised unit trusts.

(2) "Authorised unit trust" means a unit trust scheme in the case of which an order under section 78 of the Financial Services Act 1986 is in force.

38   Common investment schemes for charities etc

Parts II to IV do not apply to—

(a)   trustees managing a fund under a common investment scheme made, or having effect as if made, under section 24 of the Charities Act 1993, other than such a fund the trusts of which provide that property is not to be transferred to the fund except by or on behalf of a charity the trustees of which are the trustees appointed to manage the fund, or

(b)   trustees managing a fund under a common deposit scheme made, or having effect as if made, under section 25 of that Act.

39   Interpretation

(1) In this Act—

"asset" includes any right or interest;

"charitable trust" means a trust under which property is held for charitable purposes and "charitable purposes" has the same meaning as in the Charities Act 1993;

"custodian trustee" has the same meaning as in the Public Trustee Act 1906;

"enactment" includes any provision of a Measure of the Church Assembly or of the General Synod of the Church of England;

"exempt charity" has the same meaning as in the Charities Act 1993;

"functions" includes powers and duties;

"legal mortgage" has the same meaning as in the Law of Property Act 1925;

"personal representative" has the same meaning as in the Trustee Act 1925;

"settled land" has the same meaning as in the Settled Land Act 1925;

"trust corporation" has the same meaning as in the Trustee Act 1925;

"trust funds" means income or capital funds of the trust.

(2) In this Act the expressions listed below are defined or otherwise explained by the provisions indicated—

asset management functions	section 15(5)
custodian	section 17(2)
the duty of care	section 1(2)
the general power of investment	section 3(2)
lay trustee	section 28(6)
power of intervention	section 22(4)
the standard investment criteria	section 4(3)
subordinate legislation	section 6(3)
trustee acting in a professional capacity	section 28(5)
trust instrument	sections 6(2) and 35(2)(a)

SCHEDULE 1
APPLICATION OF DUTY OF CARE

Section 2

Investment

1 The duty of care applies to a trustee—

(a) when exercising the general power of investment or any other power of investment, however conferred;

(b) when carrying out a duty to which he is subject under section 4 or 5 (duties relating to the exercise of a power of investment or to the review of investments).

Acquisition of land

2 The duty of care applies to a trustee—

(a) when exercising the power under section 8 to acquire land;

(b) when exercising any other power to acquire land, however conferred;

(c) when exercising any power in relation to land acquired under a power mentioned in sub-paragraph (a) or (b).

Agents, nominees and custodians

3 (1) The duty of care applies to a trustee—

(a) when entering into arrangements under which a person is authorised under section 11 to exercise functions as an agent;

(b) when entering into arrangements under which a person is appointed under section 16 to act as a nominee;

(c) when entering into arrangements under which a person is appointed under section 17 or 18 to act as a custodian;

(d) when entering into arrangements under which, under any other power, however conferred, a person is authorised to exercise functions as an agent or is appointed to act as a nominee or custodian;

(e) when carrying out his duties under section 22 (review of agent, nominee or custodian, etc).

(2) For the purposes of sub-paragraph (1), entering into arrangements under which a person is authorised to exercise functions or is appointed to act as a nominee or custodian includes, in particular—

(a) selecting the person who is to act,

(b) determining any terms on which he is to act, and

(c) if the person is being authorised to exercise asset management functions, the preparation of a policy statement under section 15.

Compounding of liabilities

4 The duty of care applies to a trustee—

(a) when exercising the power under section 15 of the Trustee Act 1925 to do any of the things referred to in that section;

(b) when exercising any corresponding power, however conferred.

Insurance

5 The duty of care applies to a trustee—

(a) when exercising the power under section 19 of the Trustee Act 1925 to insure property;

(b) when exercising any corresponding power, however conferred.

Reversionary interests, valuations and audit

6   The duty of care applies to a trustee—

(a)   when exercising the power under section 22(1) or (3) of the Trustee Act 1925 to do any of the things referred to there;

(b)   when exercising any corresponding power, however conferred.

Exclusion of duty of care

7   The duty of care does not apply if or in so far as it appears from the trust instrument that the duty is not meant to apply.

Trustee Delegation Act 1999

A2.4 *Arrangement of sections*

s 1   Exercise of trustee functions by attorney.

s 2   Evidence of beneficial interest.

s 3   General powers in specified form.

s 4   Enduring powers.

s 5   Delegation under section 25 of the Trustee Act 1925.

s 6   Section 25 powers as enduring powers.

s 7   Two-trustee rules.

s 8   Appointment of additional trustee by attorney.

s 9   Attorney acting for incapable trustee.

s 10   Extent of attorney's authority to act in relation to land.

s 11   Interpretation.

Attorney of trustee with beneficial interest in land

1   Exercise of trustee functions by attorney

(1) The donee of a power of attorney is not prevented from doing an act in relation to—

    (a)   land,

    (b)   capital proceeds of a conveyance of land, or

    (c)   income from land,

by reason only that the act involves the exercise of a trustee function of the donor if, at the time when the act is done, the donor has a beneficial interest in the land, proceeds or income.

(2) In this section—

    (a)   "conveyance" has the same meaning as in the Law of Property Act 1925, and

    (b)   references to a trustee function of the donor are to a function which the donor has as trustee (either alone or jointly with any other person or persons).

(3) Subsection (1) above—

    (a)   applies only if and so far as a contrary intention is not expressed in the instrument creating the power of attorney, and

    (b)   has effect subject to the terms of that instrument.

(4) The donor of the power of attorney—

    (a)   is liable for the acts or defaults of the donee in exercising any function by virtue of subsection (1) above in the same manner as if they were acts or defaults of the donor, but

    (b)   is not liable by reason only that a function is exercised by the donee by virtue of that subsection.

(5) Subsections (1) and (4) above—

    (a)   apply only if and so far as a contrary intention is not expressed in the instrument (if any) creating the trust, and

    (b)   have effect subject to the terms of such an instrument.

(6) The fact that it appears that, in dealing with any shares or stock, the donee of the power of attorney is exercising a function by virtue of subsection (1) above does not affect with any notice of any trust a person in whose books the shares are, or stock is, registered or inscribed.

(7) In any case where (by way of exception to section 3(1) of the Trusts of Land and Appointment of Trustees Act 1996) the doctrine of conversion continues to operate, any person who, by reason of the continuing operation of that doctrine, has a beneficial interest in the proceeds of sale of land shall be treated for the purposes of this section and section 2 below as having a beneficial interest in the land.

(8) The donee of a power of attorney is not to be regarded as exercising a trustee function by virtue of subsection (1) above if he is acting under a trustee delegation power; and for this purpose a trustee delegation power is a power of attorney given under—

    (a)   a statutory provision, or

    (b)   a provision of the instrument (if any) creating a trust,

under which the donor of the power is expressly authorised to delegate the exercise of all or any of his trustee functions by power of attorney.

(9) Subject to section 4(6) below, this section applies only to powers of attorney created after the commencement of this Act.

2 Evidence of beneficial interest

(1) This section applies where the interest of a purchaser depends on the donee of a power of attorney having power to do an act in relation to any property by virtue of section 1(1) above.

In this subsection "purchaser" has the same meaning as in Part I of the Law of Property Act 1925.

(2) Where this section applies an appropriate statement is, in favour of the purchaser, conclusive evidence of the donor of the power having a beneficial interest in the property at the time of the doing of the act.

(3) In this section "an appropriate statement" means a signed statement made by the donee—

(a) when doing the act in question, or

(b) at any other time within the period of three months beginning with the day on which the act is done,

that the donor has a beneficial interest in the property at the time of the donee doing the act.

(4) If an appropriate statement is false, the donee is liable in the same way as he would be if the statement were contained in a statutory declaration.

3   General powers in specified form

In section 10(2) of the Powers of Attorney Act 1971 (which provides that a general power of attorney in the form set out in Schedule 1 to that Act, or a similar form, does not confer on the donee of the power any authority to exercise functions of the donor as trustee etc), for the words "This section" substitute "Subject to section 1 of the Trustee Delegation Act 1999, this section".

4   Enduring powers

(1) Section 3(3) of the Enduring Powers of Attorney Act 1985 (which entitles the donee of an enduring power to exercise any of the donor's functions as trustee and to give receipt for capital money etc) does not apply to enduring powers created after the commencement of this Act.

(2) Section 3(3) of the Enduring Powers of Attorney Act 1985 ceases to apply to enduring powers created before the commencement of this Act—

(a) where subsection (3) below applies, in accordance with that subsection, and

(b) otherwise, at the end of the period of one year from that commencement.

(3) Where an application for the registration of the instrument creating such an enduring power is made before the commencement of this Act, or during the period of one year from that commencement, section 3(3) of the Enduring Powers of Attorney Act 1985 ceases to apply to the power—

(a) if the instrument is registered pursuant to the application (whether before commencement or during or after that period), when the registration of the instrument is cancelled, and

(b)   if the application is finally refused during or after that period, when the application is finally refused.

(4) In subsection (3) above—

(a)   "registration" and "registered" mean registration and registered under section 6 of the Enduring Powers of Attorney Act 1985, and

(b)   "cancelled" means cancelled under section 8(4) of that Act.

(5) For the purposes of subsection (3)(b) above an application is finally refused—

(a)   if the application is withdrawn or any appeal is abandoned, when the application is withdrawn or the appeal is abandoned, and

(b)   otherwise, when proceedings on the application (including any proceedings on, or in consequence of, an appeal) have been determined and any time for appealing or further appealing has expired.

(6) Section 1 above applies to an enduring power created before the commencement of this Act from the time when (in accordance with subsections (2) to (5) above) section 3(3) of the Enduring Powers of Attorney Act 1985 ceases to apply to it.

Trustee delegation under section 25 of the Trustee Act 1925

5   Delegation under section 25 of the Trustee Act 1925

(1) For section 25 of the Trustee Act 1925 substitute—

(The words substituted appear in Appendix 2.1.)

(2) Subsection (1) above has effect in relation to powers of attorney created after the commencement of this Act.

(3) In section 34(2)(b) of the Pensions Act 1995 (delegation by trustees of trustee scheme under section 25 of the Trustee Act 1925), for "during absence abroad" substitute "for period not exceeding twelve months".

6   Section 25 powers as enduring powers

Section 2(8) of the Enduring Powers of Attorney Act 1985 (which prevents a power of attorney under section 25 of the Trustee Act 1925 from being an enduring power) does not apply to powers of attorney created after the commencement of this Act.

Miscellaneous provisions about attorney acting for trustee

7   Two-trustee rules

(1) A requirement imposed by an enactment—

(a) that capital money be paid to, or dealt with as directed by, at least two trustees or that a valid receipt for capital money be given otherwise than by a sole trustee, or

(b) that, in order for an interest or power to be overreached, a conveyance or deed be executed by at least two trustees,

is not satisfied by money being paid to or dealt with as directed by, or a receipt for money being given by, a relevant attorney or by a conveyance or deed being executed by such an attorney.

(2) In this section "relevant attorney" means a person (other than a trust corporation within the meaning of the Trustee Act 1925) who is acting either—

(a) both as a trustee and as attorney for one or more other trustees, or

(b) as attorney for two or more trustees,

and who is not acting together with any other person or persons.

(3) This section applies whether a relevant attorney is acting under a power created before or after the commencement of this Act (but in the case of such an attorney acting under an enduring power created before that commencement is without prejudice to any continuing application of section 3(3) of the Enduring Powers of Attorney Act 1985 to the enduring power after that commencement in accordance with section 4 above).

8   Appointment of additional trustee by attorney

(1) In section 36 of the Trustee Act 1925 (appointment of trustees), after subsection (6) (additional trustees) insert—

(The words substituted appear in Appendix 2.1.)

(2) The amendment made by subsection (1) above has effect only where the power, or (where more than one) each of them, is created after the commencement of this Act.

9   Attorney acting for incapable trustee

(1) In section 22 of the Law of Property Act 1925 (requirement, before dealing with legal estate vested in trustee who is incapable by reason of mental disorder, to appoint new trustee or discharge incapable trustee), after subsection (2) insert—

"(3) Subsection (2) of this section does not prevent a legal estate being dealt with without the appointment of a new trustee, or the discharge of the incapable trustee, at a time when the donee of an enduring power (within the meaning of the Enduring Powers of Attorney Act 1985) is entitled to act for the incapable trustee in the dealing."

(2) The amendment made by subsection (1) above has effect whether the enduring power was created before or after the commencement of this Act.

Authority of attorney to act in relation to land

10   Extent of attorney's authority to act in relation to land

(1) Where the donee of a power of attorney is authorised by the power to do an act of any description in relation to any land, his authority to do an act of that description at any time includes authority to do it with respect to any estate or interest in the land which is held at that time by the donor (whether alone or jointly with any other person or persons).

(2) Subsection (1) above—

    (a)   applies only if and so far as a contrary intention is not expressed in the instrument creating the power of attorney, and

    (b)   has effect subject to the terms of that instrument.

(3) This section applies only to powers of attorney created after the commencement of this Act.

Supplementary

11   Interpretation

(1) In this Act—

"land" has the same meaning as in the Trustee Act 1925, and

"enduring power" has the same meaning as in the Enduring Powers of Attorney Act 1985.

(2) References in this Act to the creation of a power of attorney are to the execution by the donor of the instrument creating it.

Wills Act 1837

A2.5   *Arrangement of sections*

s 7   No will of a person under age valid.

s 9   Signing and attestation of wills.

s 15   Gifts to an attesting witness, or his or her wife or husband, to be void.

s 18   Will to be revoked by marriage.

s 18A Effect of dissolution or annulment of marriage on wills.

s 20   No will to be revoked otherwise than as aforesaid or by another will or codicil, or by destruction thereof.

s 21   No alteration in a will after execution except in certain cases, shall have any effect unless executed as a will.

s 22   No revoked will shall be revived otherwise than by re-execution or a codicil, etc.

s 24   Wills shall be construed, as to the estate comprised, to speak from the death of the testator.

s 29   The words 'die without issue', or 'die without leaving issue', shall mean a want or failure of issue in the lifetime or at the death of the person, except in certain cases.

s 33   Gifts to children or other issue who leave issue living at the testator's death shall not lapse.

7   No will of a person under age valid

… no will made by any person under the age of eighteen years shall be valid.

9   Signing and attestation of wills

No will shall be valid unless—

(a)   it is in writing, and signed by the testator, or by some other person in his presence and by his direction; and

(b)   it appears that the testator intended by his signature to give effect to the will; and

(c)   the signature is made or acknowledged by the testator in the presence of two or more witnesses present at the same time; and

(d)   each witness either—

(i)   attests and signs the will; or

(ii)   acknowledges his signature,

in the presence of the testator (but not necessarily in the presence of any other witness),

but no form of attestation shall be necessary.

15   Gifts to an attesting witness, or his or her wife or husband, to be void

… if any person shall attest the execution of any will to whom or to whose wife or husband any beneficial devise, legacy, estate, interest, gift, or appointment, of or affecting any real or personal estate (other than and except charges and directions for the payment of any debt or debts), shall be thereby given or made, such devise, legacy, estate, interest, gift, or appointment shall, so far only as concerns such person attesting the execution of such will, or the wife or husband of such person, or any person claiming under such person or wife or husband, be utterly null and void, and such person so attesting shall be admitted as a witness to prove the execution of such will, or to prove the validity or invalidity thereof, notwithstanding such devise, legacy, estate, interest, gift, or appointment mentioned in such will.

18   Will to be revoked by marriage

(1) Subject to subsections (2) to (4) below, a will shall be revoked by the testator's marriage.

(2) A disposition in a will in exercise of a power of appointment shall take effect notwithstanding the testator's subsequent marriage unless the property so appointed would in default of appointment pass to his personal representatives.

(3) Where it appears from a will that at the time it was made the testator was expecting to be married to a particular person and that he intended that the will should not be revoked by the marriage, the will shall not be revoked by his marriage to that person.

(4) Where it appears from a will that at the time it was made the testator was expecting to be married to a particular person and that he intended that a disposition in the will should not be revoked by his marriage to that person,—

(a)   that disposition shall take effect notwithstanding the marriage; and

(b)   any other disposition in the will shall take effect also, unless it appears from the will that the testator intended the disposition to be revoked by the marriage.

18A Effect of dissolution or annulment of marriage on wills

(1) Where, after a testator has made a will, an order or decree of a court of civil jurisdiction in England and Wales dissolves or annuls his marriages or his marriage is dissolved or annulled and the divorce or annulment is entitled to recognition in England and Wales by virtue of Part II of the Family Law Act 1986,—

(a)   provisions of the will appointing executors or trustees or conferring a power of appointment, if they appoint or confer the power on the former spouse, shall take effect as if the former spouse had died on the date on which the marriage is dissolved or annulled, and

(b)   any property which, or an interest in which, is devised or bequeathed to the former spouse shall pass as if the former spouse had died on that date,

except in so far as a contrary intention appears by the will.

(2) Subsection (1)(b) above is without prejudice to any right of the former spouse to apply for financial provision under the Inheritance (Provision for Family and Dependants) Act 1975.

(3) ...

20 No will to be revoked otherwise than as aforesaid or by another will or codicil, or by destruction thereof

... no will or codicil, or any part thereof, shall be revoked otherwise than as aforesaid, or by another will or codicil executed in manner herein-before required, or by some writing declaring an intention to revoke the same and executed in the manner in which a will is herein-before required to be executed, or by the burning, tearing, or otherwise destroying the same by the testator, or by some person in his presence and by his direction, with the intention of revoking the same.

21 No alteration in a will after execution except in certain cases, shall have any effect unless executed as a will

... no obliteration, interlineation, or other alteration made in any will after the execution thereof shall be valid or have any effect, except so far as the words or effect of the will before such alteration shall not be apparent, unless such alteration shall be executed in like manner as herein-before is required for the execution of the will; but the will, with such alteration as part thereof, shall be deemed to be duly executed if the signature of the testator and the subscription of the witnesses be made in the margin or on some other part of the will opposite or near to such alteration, or at the foot or end of or opposite to a memorandum referring to such alteration, and written at the end of some other part of the will.

22 No revoked will shall be revived otherwise than by re-execution or a codicil, &c

… no will or codicil, or any part thereof, which shall be in any manner revoked, shall be revived otherwise than by the re-execution thereof or by a codicil executed in manner herein-before required and showing an intention to revive the same; and when any will or codicil which shall be partly revoked, and afterwards wholly revoked, shall be revived, such revival shall not extend to so much thereof as shall have been revoked before the revocation of the whole thereof, unless an intention to the contrary shall be shown.

24 Wills shall be construed, as to the estate comprised, to speak from the death of the testator

… every will shall be construed, with reference to the real estate and personal estate comprised in it, to speak and take effect as if it had been executed immediately before the death of the testator, unless a contrary intention shall appear by the will.

29 The words "die without issue," or "die without leaving issue," &c shall mean a want or failure of issue in the lifetime or at the death of the person, except in certain cases

… in any devise or bequest of real or personal estate the words "die without issue" or "die without leaving issue," or "have no issue," or any other words which may import either a want or failure of issue of any person in his lifetime or at the time of his death, or an indefinite failure of his issue, shall be construed to mean a want or failure of issue in the lifetime or at the time of the death of such person, and not an indefinite failure of his issue, unless a contrary intention shall appear by the will, by reason of such person having a prior estate tail, or of a preceding gift, being, without any implication arising from such words, a limitation of an estate tail to such person or issue, or otherwise: Provided, that this Act shall not extend to cases where such words as aforesaid import if no issue described in a preceding gift shall be born, or if there shall be no issue who shall live to attain the age or otherwise answer the description required for obtaining a vested estate by a preceding gift to such issue.

33 Gifts to children or other issue who leave issue living at the testator's death shall not lapse

(1) Where—

    (a)   a will contains a devise or bequest to a child or remoter descendant of the testator; and

(b)   the intended beneficiary dies before the testator, leaving issue; and

(c)   issue of the intended beneficiary are living at the testator's death,

then, unless a contrary intention appears by the will, the devise or bequest shall take effect as a devise or bequest to the issue living at the testator's death.

(2) Where—

(a)   a will contains a devise or bequest to a class of person consisting of children or remoter descendants of the testator; and

(b)   a member of the class dies before the testator, leaving issue, and

(c)   issue of that member are living at the testator's death,

then, unless a contrary intention appears by the will, the devise or bequest shall take effect as if the class included the issue of its deceased member living at the testator's death.

(3) Issue shall take under this section through all degrees, according to their stock, in equal shares if more than one, any gift or share which their parent would have taken and so that no issue shall take whose parent is living at the testator's death and that no issue shall take whose parent is living at the testator's death and so capable of taking.

(4) For the purposes of this section—

(a)   the illegitimacy of any person is to be disregarded; and

(b)   a person conceived before the testator's death and born living thereafter is to be taken to have been living at the testator's death.

Wills Act 1968

A2.6 *Arrangement of sections*

s 1   Restriction of operation of Wills Act 1837, s 15.

1   Restriction of operation of Wills Act 1837, s 15

(1) For the purposes of section 15 of the Wills Act 1837 (avoidance of gifts to attesting witnesses and their spouses) the attestation of a will by a person to whom or to whose spouse there is given or made any such disposition as is described in that section shall be disregarded if the will is duly executed without his attestation and without that of any other such person.

(2) This section applies to the will of any person dying after the passing of this Act, whether executed before or after the passing of this Act.

Administration of Estates Act 1925

A2.7   *Arrangement of sections*

46   Succession to real and personal estate on intestacy

(1) The residuary estate of an intestate shall be distributed in the manner or be held on the trusts mentioned in this section, namely:—

(i)   If the intestate leaves a husband or wife, then in accordance with the following Table:

If the intestate—

(1) leaves— (a) no issue, and (b) no parent, or brother or sister of the whole blood, or issue of a brother or sister of the whole blood	the residuary estate shall be held in trust for the surviving husband or wife absolutely.
(2) leaves issue (whether or not persons mentioned in subparagraph (b) above also survive)	the surviving husband or wife shall take the personal chattels absolutely and, in addition, the residuary estate of the intestate (other than the personal chattels) shall stand charged with the payment of a fixed net sum, free of death duties and costs, to the surviving husband or wife with interest thereon from the date of the death at such rate as the Lord Chancellor may specify by order until paid or appropriated, and, subject to providing for that sum and the interest thereon, the residuary estate (other than the personal chattels) shall be held—
	(a) as to one half upon trust for the surviving husband or wife during his or her life, and, subject to such life interest, on the statutory trusts for the issue of the intestate, and
	(b) as to the other half, on the statutory trusts for the issue of the intestate.

(3) leaves one or more of the following, that is to say, a parent, a brother or sister of the whole blood, or issue of a brother or sister of the whole blood, but leaves no issue

the surviving husband or wife shall take the personal chattels absolutely and, in addition, the residuary estate of the intestate (other than the personal chattels) shall stand charged with the payment of a fixed net sum, free of death duties and costs, to the surviving husband or wife with interest thereon from the date of the death at such rate as the Lord Chancellor may specify by order until paid or appropriated, and, subject to providing for that sum and the interest thereon, the residuary estate (other than the personal chattels) shall be held—

(a) as to one half in trust for the surviving husband or wife absolutely, and

(b) as to the other half—

(i)   where the intestate leaves one parent or both parents (whether or not brothers or sisters of the intestate or their issue also survive) in trust for the parent absolutely or, as the case may be, for the two parents in equal shares absolutely

(ii)   where the intestate leaves no parent, on the statutory trusts for the brothers and sisters of the whole blood of the intestate.

The fixed net sums referred to in paragraphs (2) and (3) of this Table shall be of the amounts provided by or under section 1 of the Family Provision Act 1966

(ii)   If the intestate leaves issue but no husband or wife, the residuary estate of the intestate shall be held on the statutory trusts for the issue of the intestate;

(iii) If the intestate leaves no husband or wife and no issue but both parents, then ... the residuary estate of the intestate shall be held in trust for the father and mother in equal shares absolutely;

(iv)   If the intestate leaves no husband or wife and no issue but one parent, then ... the residuary estate of the intestate shall be held in trust for the surviving father or mother absolutely;

(v)   If the intestate leaves no husband or wife and no issue and no parent, then ... the residuary estate of the intestate shall be held in trust for the following persons living at the death of the intestate, and in the following order and manner, namely:—

First, on the statutory trusts for the brothers and sisters of the whole blood of the intestate; but if no person takes an absolutely vested interest under such trusts; then

Secondly, on the statutory trusts for the brothers and sisters of the half blood of the intestate; but if no person takes an absolutely vested interest under such trusts; then

Thirdly, for the grandparents of the intestate and, if more than one survive the intestate, in equal shares; but if there is no member of this class; then

Fourthly, on the statutory trusts for the uncles and aunts of the intestate (being brothers or sisters of the whole blood of a parent of the intestate); but if no person takes an absolutely vested interest under such trusts; then

Fifthly, on the statutory trusts for the uncles and aunts of the intestate (being brothers or sisters of the half blood of a parent of the intestate) ...

(vi) In default of any person taking an absolute interest under the foregoing provisions, the residuary estate of the intestate shall belong to the Crown or to the Duchy of Lancaster or to the Duke of Cornwall for the time being, as the case may be, as bona vacantia, and in lieu of any right to escheat.

The Crown or the said Duchy or the said Duke may (without prejudice to the powers reserved by section nine of the Civil List Act 1910, or any other powers), out of the whole or any part of the property devolving on them respectively, provide, in accordance with the existing practice, for dependents, whether kindred or not, of the intestate, and other persons for whom the intestate might reasonably have been expected to make provision.

(1A) The power to make orders under subsection (1) above shall be exercisable by statutory instrument subject to annulment in pursuance of a resolution of either House of Parliament; and any such order may be varied or revoked by a subsequent order made under the power.

(2) A husband and wife shall for all purposes of distribution or division under the foregoing provisions of this section be treated as two persons.

(2A) Where the intestate's husband or wife survived the intestate but died before the end of the period of 28 days beginning with the day on which the intestate died, this section shall have effect as respects the intestate as if the husband or wife had not survived the intestate.

(3) Where the intestate and the intestate's husband or wife have died in circumstances rendering it uncertain which of them survived the other and the intestate's husband or wife is by virtue of section one hundred and eighty-four of the Law of Property Act 1925, deemed to have survived the intestate, this section shall, nevertheless, have effect as respects the intestate as if the husband or wife had not survived the intestate.

(4) The interest payable on the fixed net sum payable to a surviving husband or wife shall be primarily payable out of income.

47 Statutory trusts in favour of issue and other classes of relatives of intestate

(1) Where under this Part of this Act the residuary estate of an intestate, or any part thereof, is directed to be held on the statutory trusts for the issue of the intestate, the same shall be held upon the following trusts, namely:—

  (i)   In trust, in equal shares if more than one, for all or any the children or child of the intestate, living at the death of the intestate, who attain the age of eighteen years or marry under that age, and for all or any of the issue living at the death of the intestate who attain the age of eighteen years or marry under that age of any child of the intestate who predeceases the intestate, such issue to take through all degrees, according to their stocks, in equal shares if more than one, the share which their parent would have taken if living at the death of the intestate, and so that no issue shall take whose parent is living at the death of the intestate and so capable of taking;

  (ii) The statutory power of advancement, and the statutory provisions which relate to maintenance and accumulation of surplus income, shall apply, but when an infant marries such infant shall be entitled to give valid receipts for the income of the infant's share or interest;

  (iii) …

  (iv) The personal representatives may permit any infant contingently interested to have the use and enjoyment of any personal chattels in such manner and subject to such conditions (if any) as the personal representatives may consider reasonable, and without being liable to account for any consequential loss.

(2) If the trusts in favour of the issue of the intestate fail by reason of no child or other issue attaining an absolutely vested interest—

  (a) the residuary estate of the intestate and the income thereof and all statutory accumulations, if any, of the income thereof, or so much thereof as may not have been paid or applied under any power affecting the same, shall go, devolve and be held under the provisions of this Part of this Act as if the intestate had died without leaving issue living at the death of the intestate;

  (b) references in this Part of this Act to the intestate "leaving no issue" shall be construed as "leaving no issue who attain an absolutely vested interest";

  (c) references in this Part of this Act to the intestate "leaving issue" or "leaving a child or other issue" shall be construed as "leaving issue who attain an absolutely vested interest."

(3) Where under this Part of this Act the residuary estate of an intestate or any part thereof is directed to be held on the statutory trusts for any class of relatives of the intestate, other than issue of the intestate, the same shall be held on trusts corresponding to the statutory trusts for the issue of the intestate (other than the provision for bringing any money or property into account) as if such trusts (other than as aforesaid) were repeated with the substitution of references to the members or member of that class for references to the children or child of the intestate.

(4) References in paragraph (i) of subsection (1) of the last foregoing section to the intestate leaving, or not leaving, a member of the class consisting of brothers or sisters of the whole blood of the intestate and issue of brothers or sisters of the whole blood of the intestate shall be construed as references to the intestate leaving, or not leaving, a member of that class who attains an absolutely vested interest.

(5) …

47A Right of surviving spouse to have his own life interest redeemed

(1) Where a surviving husband or wife is entitled to the interest in part of the residuary estate, and so elects, the personal representative shall purchase or redeem the life interest by paying the capital value thereof to the tenant for life, or the persons deriving title under the tenant for life, and the costs of the transaction; and thereupon the residuary estate of the intestate may be dealt with and distributed free from the life interest.

(2) …

(3) An election under this section shall only be exercisable if at the time of the election the whole of the said part of the residuary estate consists of property in possession, but, for the purposes of this section, a life interest in property partly in possession and partly not in possession shall be treated as consisting of two separate life interests in those respective parts of the property.

(3A) The capital value shall be reckoned in such manner as the Lord Chancellor may by order direct, and an order under this subsection may include transitional provisions.

(3B) The power to make orders under subsection (3A) above shall be exercisable by statutory instrument subject to annulment in pursuance of a resolution of either House of Parliament; and any such order may be varied or revoked by a subsequent order made under the power.

(4) …

(5) An election under this section shall be exercisable only within the period of twelve months from the date on which representation with respect to the estate of the intestate is first taken out:

Provided that if the surviving husband or wife satisfies the court that the limitation to the said period of twelve months will operate unfairly—

(a)   in consequence of the representation first taken out being probate of a will subsequently revoked on the ground that the will was invalid, or

(b)   in consequence of a question whether a person had an interest in the estate, or as to the nature of an interest in the estate, not having been determined at the time when representation was first taken out, or

(c)   in consequence of some other circumstances affecting the administration or distribution of the estate,

the court may extend the said period.

(6) An election under this section shall be exercisable, except where the tenant for life is the sole personal representative, by notifying the personal representative (or, where there are two or more personal representatives of whom one is the tenant for life, all of them except the tenant for life) in writing; and a notification in writing under this subsection shall not be revocable except with the consent of the personal representative.

(7) Where the tenant for life is the sole personal representative an election under this section shall not be effective unless written notice thereof is given to the Senior Registrar of the Family Division of the High Court within the period within which it must be made; and provision may be made by probate rules for keeping a record of such notices and making that record available to the public.

In this subsection the expression "probate rules" means rules of court made under section 127 of the Supreme Court Act 1981.

(8) An election under this section by a tenant for life who is an infant shall be as valid and binding as it would be if the tenant for life were of age; but the personal representative shall, instead of paying the capital value of the life interest to the tenant for life, deal with it in the same manner as with any other part of the residuary estate to which the tenant for life is absolutely entitled.

(9) In considering for the purposes of the foregoing provisions of this section the question when representation was first taken out, a grant limited to settled land or to trust property shall be left out of account and a grant limited to real estate or to personal estate shall be left out of account unless a grant limited to the remainder of the estate has previously been made or is made at the same time.

Administration of Estates Act 1925

A2.8   *Arrangement of sections*

s 41   Powers of personal representative as to appropriation.

41   Powers of personal representative as to appropriation

(1) The personal representative may appropriate any part of the real or personal estate, including things in action, of the deceased in the actual condition or state of investment thereof at the time of appropriation in or towards satisfaction of any legacy bequeathed by the deceased, or of any other interest or share in his property, whether settled or not, as to the personal representative may seem just and reasonable, according to the respective rights of the persons interested in the property of the deceased:

Provided that—

    (i) an appropriation shall not be made under this section so as to affect prejudicially any specific devise or bequest;

    (ii) an appropriation of property, whether or not being an investment authorised by law or by the will, if any, of the deceased for the investment of money subject to the trust, shall not (save as hereinafter mentioned) be made under this section except with the following consents:—

        (a) when made for the benefit of a person absolutely and beneficially entitled in possession, the consent of that person;

        (b) when made in respect of any settled legacy share or interest, the consent of either the trustee thereof, if any (not being also the personal representative), or the person who may for the time being be entitled to the income:

        If the person whose consent is so required as aforesaid is an infant or is incapable by reason of mental disorder within the meaning of the Mental Health Act 1983, of managing and administering his property and affairs the consent shall be given on his behalf by his parents or parent, testamentary or other guardian ... or receiver, or if, in the case of an infant, there is no such parent or guardian, by the court on the application of his next friend;

    (iii) no consent (save of such trustee as aforesaid) shall be required on behalf of a person who may come into existence after the time of appropriation, or who cannot be found or ascertained at that time;

(iv)   if no receiver is acting for a person suffering from mental disorder then, if the appropriation is of an investment authorised by law or by the will, if any, of the deceased for the investment of money subject to the trust, no consent shall be required on behalf of the said person;

(v)   if, independently of the personal representative, there is no trustee of a settled legacy share or interest, and no person of full age and capacity entitled to the income thereof, no consent shall be required to an appropriation in respect of such legacy share or interest, provided that the appropriation is of an investment authorised as aforesaid.

(1A) The county court has jurisdiction under proviso (ii) to subsection (1) of this section where the estate in respect of which the application is made does not exceed in amount or value the county court limit.

(2) Any property duly appropriated under the powers conferred by this section shall thereafter be treated as an authorised investment, and may be retained or dealt with accordingly.

(3) For the purposes of such appropriation, the personal representative may ascertain and fix the value of the respective parts of the real and personal estate and the liabilities of the deceased as he may think fit, and shall for that purpose employ a duly qualified valuer in any case where such employment may be necessary; and may make any conveyance (including an assent) which may be requisite for giving effect to the appropriation.

(4) An appropriation made pursuant to this section shall bind all persons interested in the property of the deceased whose consent is not hereby made requisite.

(5) The personal representative shall, in making the appropriation, have regard to the rights of any person who may thereafter come into existence, or who cannot be found or ascertained at the time of appropriation, and of any other person whose consent is not required by this section.

(6) This section does not prejudice any other power of appropriation conferred by law or by the will (if any) of the deceased, and takes effect with any extended powers conferred by the will (if any) of the deceased, and where an appropriation is made under this section, in respect of a settled legacy, share or interest, the property appropriated shall remain subject to all trusts and powers of leasing, disposition, and management or varying investments which would have been applicable thereto or to the legacy, share or interest in respect of which the appropriation is made, if no such appropriation had been made.

(7) If after any real estate has been appropriated in purported exercise of the powers conferred by this section, the person to whom it was conveyed disposes of it or any interest therein, then, in favour of a purchaser, the appropriation shall be deemed to have been made in accordance with the requirements of this section and after all requisite consents, if any, had been given.

(8) In this section, a settled legacy, share or interest includes any legacy, share or interest to which a person is not absolutely entitled in possession at the date of the appropriation, also an annuity, and "purchaser" means a purchaser for money or money's worth.

(9) This section applies whether the deceased died intestate or not, and whether before or after the commencement of this Act, and extends to property over which a testator exercises a general power of appointment, including the statutory power to dispose of entailed interests, and authorises the setting apart of a fund to answer an annuity by means of the income of that fund or otherwise.

Law of Property Act 1925

164   General restrictions on accumulation of income

(1) No person may by any instrument or otherwise settle or dispose of any property in such manner that the income thereof shall, save as hereinafter mentioned, be wholly or partially accumulated for any longer period than one of the following, namely:—

   (a)   the life of the grantor or settlor; or

   (b)   a term of twenty-one years from the death of the grantor, settlor or testator; or

   (c)   the duration of the minority or respective minorities of any person or persons living or en ventre sa mere at the death of the grantor, settlor or testator; or

   (d)   the duration of the minority or respective minorities only of any person or persons who under the limitations of the instrument directing the accumulations would, for the time being, if of full age, be entitled to the income directed to be accumulated.

In every case where any accumulation is directed otherwise than as aforesaid, the direction shall (save as hereinafter mentioned) be void; and the income of the property directed to be accumulated shall, so long as the same is directed to be accumulated contrary to this section, go to and be received by the person or persons who would have been entitled thereto if such accumulation had not been directed.

(2) This section does not extend to any provision—

   (i)   for payment of the debts of any grantor, settlor, testator or other person;

   (ii)   for raising portions for—

      (a)   any child, children or remoter issue of any grantor, settlor or testator; or

      (b)   any child, children or remoter issue of a person taking any interest under any settlement or other disposition directing the accumulations or to whom any interest is thereby limited;

   (iii) respecting the accumulation of the produce of timber or wood;

and accordingly such provisions may be made as if no statutory restrictions on accumulation of income had been imposed.

(3) The restrictions imposed by this section apply to instruments made on or after the twenty-eighth day of July, eighteen hundred, but in the case of wills only where the testator was living and of testamentary capacity after the end of one year from that date.

Law of Property (Amendment) Act 1926

3   Meaning of 'trust corporation'

(1) For the purposes of the Law of Property Act 1925, the Settled Land Act 1925, the Trustee Act 1925, the Administration of Estates Act 1925, and the Supreme Court Act 1981, the expression "Trust Corporation" includes the Treasury Solicitor, the Official Solicitor and any person holding any other official position prescribed by the Lord Chancellor, and, in relation to the property of a bankrupt and property subject to a deed of arrangement, includes the trustee in bankruptcy and the trustee under the deed respectively, and, in relation to charitable ecclesiastical and public trusts, also includes any local or public authority so prescribed, and any other corporation constituted under the laws of the United Kingdom or any part thereof which satisfies the Lord Chancellor that it undertakes the administration of any such trusts without remuneration, or that by its constitution it is required to apply the whole of its net income after payment of outgoings for charitable ecclesiastical or public purposes, and is prohibited from distributing, directly or indirectly, any part thereof by way of profits amongst any of its members, and is authorised by him to act in relation to such trusts as a trust corporation.

(2) For the purposes of this provision, the expression "Treasury Solicitor" means the solicitor for the affairs of His Majesty's Treasury, and includes the solicitor for the affairs of the Duchy of Lancaster.

Variation of Trusts Act 1958

A2.11 *Arrangement of sections*

s 1   Jurisdiction of courts to vary trusts.

1   Jurisdiction of courts to vary trusts

(1) Where property, whether real or personal, is held on trusts arising, whether before or after the passing of this Act, under any will, settlement or other disposition, the court may if it thinks fit by order approve on behalf of—

(a)   any person having, directly or indirectly, an interest, whether vested or contingent, under the trusts who by reason of infancy or other incapacity is incapable of assenting, or

(b)   any person (whether ascertained or not) who may become entitled, directly or indirectly, to an interest under the trusts as being at a future date or on the happening of a future event a person of any specified description or a member of any specified class of persons, so however that this paragraph shall not include any person who would be of that description, or a member of that class, as the case may be, if the said date had fallen or the said event had happened at the date of the application to the court, or

(c)   any person unborn, or

(d)   any person in respect of any discretionary interest of his under protective trusts where the interest of the principal beneficiary has not failed or determined,

any arrangement (by whomsoever proposed, and whether or not there is any other person beneficially interested who is capable of assenting thereto) varying or revoking all or any of the trusts, or enlarging the powers of the trustees of managing or administering any of the property subject to the trusts:

Provided that except by virtue of paragraph (d) of this subsection the court shall not approve an arrangement on behalf of any person unless the carrying out thereof would be for the benefit of that person.

(2) In the foregoing subsection "protective trusts" means the trusts specified in paragraphs (i) and (ii) of subsection (1) of section thirty-three of the Trustee Act 1925, or any like trusts, "the principal beneficiary" has the same meaning as in the said subsection (1) and "discretionary interest" means an interest arising under the trust specified in paragraph (ii) of the said subsection (1) or any like trust.

(3) ... the jurisdiction conferred by subsection (1) of this section shall be exercisable by the High Court, except that the question whether the carrying out of any arrangement would be for the benefit of a person falling within paragraph (a) of the said subsection (1) shall be determined by order of the

authority having jurisdiction under Part VII of the Mental Health Act 1983, if that person is a patient within the meaning of the said Part VII.

(4) …

(5) Nothing in the foregoing provisions of this section shall apply to trusts affecting property settled by Act of Parliament.

(6) Nothing in this section shall be taken to limit the powers conferred by section sixty-four of the Settled Land Act 1925, section fifty-seven of the Trustee Act 1925, or the powers of the authority having jurisdiction under Part VII of the Mental Health Act 1983.

Perpetuities and Accumulations Act 1964

A2.12 *Arrangement of sections*

1   Power to specify perpetuity period

(1) Subject to section 9 (2) of this Act and subsection (2) below, where the instrument by which any disposition is made so provides, the perpetuity period applicable to the disposition under the rule against perpetuities, instead of being of any other duration, shall be of a duration equal to such number of years not exceeding eighty as is specified in that behalf in the instrument.

(2) Subsection (1) above shall not have effect where the disposition is made in exercise of a special power of appointment, but where a period is specified under that subsection in the instrument creating such a power the period shall apply in relation to any disposition under the power as it applies in relation to the power itself.

2   Presumptions and evidence as to future parenthood

(1) Where in any proceedings there arises on the rule against perpetuities a question which turns on the ability of a person to have a child at some future time, then—

(a) subject to paragraph (b) below, it shall be presumed that a male can have a child at the age of fourteen years or over, but not under that age, and that a female can have a child at the age of twelve years or over, but not under that age or over the age of fifty-five years; but

(b) in the case of a living person evidence may be given to show that he or she will or will not be able to have a child at the time in question.

(2) Where any such question is decided by treating a person as unable to have a child at a particular time, and he or she does so, the High Court may make such order as it thinks fit for placing the persons interested in the property comprised in the disposition, so far as may be just, in the position they would have held if the question had not been so decided.

(3) Subject to subsection (2) above, where any such question is decided in relation to a disposition by treating a person as able or unable to have a child at a particular time, then he or she shall be so treated for the purpose of any question which may arise on the rule against perpetuities in relation to the same disposition in any subsequent proceedings.

(4) In the foregoing provisions of this section references to having a child are references to begetting or giving birth to a child, but those provisions (except subsection (1)(b)) shall apply in relation to the possibility that a person will at any time have a child by adoption, legitimation or other means as they apply to his or her ability at that time to beget or give birth to a child.

3 Uncertainty as to remoteness

(1) Where, apart from the provisions of this section and sections 4 and 5 of this Act, a disposition would be void on the ground that the interest disposed of might not become vested until too remote a time, the disposition shall be treated, until such time (if any) as it becomes established that the vesting must occur, if at all, after the end of the perpetuity period, as if the disposition were not subject to the rule against perpetuities; and its becoming so established shall not affect the validity of anything previously done in relation to the interest disposed of by way of advancement, application of intermediate income or otherwise.

(2) Where, apart from the said provisions, a disposition consisting of the conferring of a general power of appointment would be void on the ground that the power might not become exercisable until too remote a time, the disposition shall be treated, until such time (if any) as it becomes established that the power will not be exercisable within the perpetuity period, as if the disposition were not subject to the rule against perpetuities.

(3) Where, apart from the said provisions, a disposition consisting of the conferring of any power, option or other right would be void on the ground that the right might be exercised at too remote a time, the disposition shall be treated as regards any exercise of the right within the perpetuity period as if it

were not subject to the rule against perpetuities and, subject to the said provisions, shall be treated as void for remoteness only if, and so far as, the right is not fully exercised within that period.

(4) Where this section applies to a disposition and the duration of the perpetuity period is not determined by virtue of section 1 or 9(2) of this Act, it shall be determined as follows:—

    (a)   where any persons falling within subsection (5) below are individuals in being and ascertainable at the commencement of the perpetuity period the duration of the period shall be determined by reference to their lives and no others, but so that the lives of any description of persons falling within paragraph (b) or (c) of that subsection shall be disregarded if the number of persons of that description is such as to render it impracticable to ascertain the date of death of the survivor;

    (b)   where there are no lives under paragraph (a) above the period shall be twenty-one years.

(5) The said persons are as follows:—

    (a)   the person by whom the disposition was made;

    (b)   a person to whom or in whose favour the disposition was made, that is to say—

        (i)   in the case of a disposition to a class of persons, any member or potential member of the class;

        (ii)   in the case of an individual disposition to a person taking only on certain conditions being satisfied, any person as to whom some of the conditions are satisfied and the remainder may in time be satisfied;

        (iii)   in the case of a special power of appointment exercisable in favour of members of a class, any member or potential member of the class;

        (iv)   in the case of a special power of appointment exercisable in favour of one person only, that person or, where the object of the power is ascertainable only on certain conditions being satisfied, any person as to whom some of the conditions are satisfied and the remainder may in time be satisfied;

        (v)   in the case of any power, option or other right, the person on whom the right is conferred;

    (c)   a person having a child or grandchild within sub-paragraphs (i) to (iv) of paragraph (b) above, or any of whose children or grandchildren, if subsequently born, would by virtue of his or her descent fall within those sub-paragraphs;

    (d)   any person on the failure or determination of whose prior interest the disposition is limited to take effect.

4   Reduction of age and exclusion of class members to avoid remoteness

(1) Where a disposition is limited by reference to the attainment by any person or persons of a specified age exceeding twenty-one years, and it is apparent at the time the disposition is made or becomes apparent at a subsequent time—

    (a)   that the disposition would, apart from this section, be void for remoteness, but

    (b)   that it would not be so void if the specified age had been twenty-one years,

the disposition shall be treated for all purposes as if, instead of being limited by reference to the age in fact specified, it had been limited by reference to the age nearest to that age which would, if specified instead, have prevented the disposition from being so void.

(2) Where in the case of any disposition different ages exceeding twenty-one years are specified in relation to different persons—

    (a)   the reference in paragraph (b) of subsection (1) above to the specified age shall be construed as a reference to all the specified ages, and

    (b)   that subsection shall operate to reduce each such age so far as is necessary to save the disposition from being void for remoteness.

(3) Where the inclusion of any persons, being potential members of a class or unborn persons who at birth would become members or potential members of the class, prevents the foregoing provisions of this section from operating to save a disposition from being void for remoteness, those persons shall thenceforth be deemed for all the purposes of the disposition to be excluded from the class, and the said provisions shall thereupon have effect accordingly.

(4) Where, in the case of a disposition to which subsection (3) above does not apply, it is apparent at the time the disposition is made or becomes apparent at a subsequent time that, apart from this subsection, the inclusion of any persons, being potential members of a class or unborn persons who at birth would become members or potential members of the class, would cause the disposition to be treated as void for remoteness, those persons shall, unless their exclusion would exhaust the class, thenceforth be deemed for all the purposes of the disposition to be excluded from the class.

(5) Where this section has effect in relation to a disposition to which section 3 above applies, the operation of this section shall not affect the validity of anything previously done in relation to the interest disposed of by way of advancement, application of intermediate income or otherwise.

(6) …

(7) For the avoidance of doubt it is hereby declared that a question arising under section 3 of this Act or subsection (1)(a) above of whether a disposition would be void apart from this section is to be determined as if subsection (6) above had been a separate section of this Act.

5   Condition relating to death of surviving spouse

Where a disposition is limited by reference to the time of death of the survivor of a person in being at the commencement of the perpetuity period and any spouse of that person, and that time has not arrived at the end of the perpetuity period, the disposition shall be treated for all purposes, where to do so would save it from being void for remoteness, as if it had instead been limited by reference to the time immediately before the end of that period.

6   Saving and acceleration of expectant interests

A disposition shall not be treated as void for remoteness by reason only that the interest disposed of is ulterior to and dependent upon an interest under a disposition which is so void, and the vesting of an interest shall not be prevented from being accelerated on the failure of a prior interest by reason only that the failure arises because of remoteness.

7   Powers of appointment

For the purposes of the rule against perpetuities, a power of appointment shall be treated as a special power unless—

(a)   in the instrument creating the power it is expressed to be exercisable by one person only, and

(b)   it could, at all times during its currency when that person is of full age and capacity, be exercised by him so as immediately to transfer to himself the whole of the interest governed by the power without the consent of any other person or compliance with any other condition, not being a formal condition relating only to the mode of exercise of the power:

Provided that for the purpose of determining whether a disposition made under a power of appointment exercisable by will only is void for remoteness, the power shall be treated as a general power where it would have fallen to be so treated if exercisable by deed.

8   Administrative powers of trustees

(1) The rule against perpetuities shall not operate to invalidate a power conferred on trustees or other persons to sell, lease, exchange or otherwise

dispose of any property for full consideration, or to do any other act in the administration (as opposed to the distribution) of any property, and shall not prevent the payment to trustees or other persons of reasonable remuneration for their services.

(2) Subsection (1) above shall apply for the purpose of enabling a power to be exercised at any time after the commencement of this Act notwithstanding that the power is conferred by an instrument which took effect before that commencement.

9 Options relating to land

(1) The rule against perpetuities shall not apply to a disposition consisting of the conferring of an option to acquire for valuable consideration an interest reversionary (whether directly or indirectly) on the term of a lease if—

  (a)   the option is exercisable only by the lessee or his successors in title, and

  (b)   it ceases to be exercisable at or before the expiration of one year following the determination of the lease.

This subsection shall apply in relation to an agreement for a lease as it applies in relation to a lease, and "lessee" shall be construed accordingly.

(2) In the case of a disposition consisting of the conferring of an option to acquire for valuable consideration any interest in land, the perpetuity period under the rule against perpetuities shall be twenty-one years, and section 1 of this Act shall not apply:

Provided that this subsection shall not apply to a right of pre-emption conferred on a public or local authority in respect of land used or to be used for religious purposes where the right becomes exercisable only if the land ceases to be used for such purposes.

10 Avoidance of contractual and other rights in cases of remoteness

Where a disposition inter vivos would fall to be treated as void for remoteness if the rights and duties thereunder were capable of transmission to persons other than the original parties and had been so transmitted, it shall be treated as void as between the person by whom it was made and the person to whom or in whose favour it was made or any successor of his, and no remedy shall lie in contract or otherwise for giving effect to it or making restitution for its lack of effect.

11 Rights for enforcement of rentcharges

(1) The rule against perpetuities shall not apply to any powers or remedies for recovering or compelling the payment of an annual sum to which section 121

or 122 of the Law of Property Act 1925 applies, or otherwise becoming exercisable or enforceable on the breach of any condition or other requirement relating to that sum.

(2) ...

12   Possibilities of reverter, conditions subsequent, exceptions and reservations

(1) In the case of—

    (a)   a possibility of reverter on the determination of a determinable fee simple, or

    (b)   a possibility of a resulting trust on the determination of any other determinable interest in property,

the rule against perpetuities shall apply in relation to the provision causing the interest to be determinable as it would apply if that provision were expressed in the form of a condition subsequent giving rise, on breach thereof, to a right of re-entry or an equivalent right in the case of property other than land, and where the provision falls to be treated as void for remoteness the determinable interest shall become an absolute interest.

(2) Where a disposition is subject to any such provision, or to any such condition subsequent, or to any exception or reservation, the disposition shall be treated for the purposes of this Act as including a separate disposition of any rights arising by virtue of the provision, condition subsequent, exception or reservation.

Accumulations

13   Amendment of s 164 of Law of Property Act 1925

(1) The periods for which accumulations of income under a settlement or other disposition are permitted by section 164 of the Law of Property Act 1925 shall include—

    (a)   a term of twenty-one years from the date of the making of the disposition, and

    (b)   the duration of the minority or respective minorities of any person or persons in being at that date.

(2) It is hereby declared that the restrictions imposed by the said section 164 apply in relation to a power to accumulate income whether or not there is a duty to exercise that power, and that they apply whether or not the power to accumulate extends to income produced by the investment of income previously accumulated.

14   Right to stop accumulations

Section 2 above shall apply to any question as to the right of beneficiaries to put an end to accumulations of income under any disposition as it applies to questions arising on the rule against perpetuities.

Supplemental

15   Short title, interpretation and extent

(1) This Act may be cited as the Perpetuities and Accumulations Act 1964.

(2) In this Act—

"disposition" includes the conferring of a power of appointment and any other disposition of an interest in or right over property, and references to the interest disposed of shall be construed accordingly;

"in being" means living or en ventre sa mere;

"power of appointment" includes any discretionary power to transfer a beneficial interest in property without the furnishing of valuable consideration;

"will" includes a codicil;

and for the purposes of this Act a disposition contained in a will shall be deemed to be made at the death of the testator.

(3) For the purposes of this Act a person shall be treated as a member of a class if in his case all the conditions identifying a member of the class are satisfied, and shall be treated as a potential member if in his case some only of those conditions are satisfied but there is a possibility that the remainder will in time be satisfied.

(4) Nothing in this Act shall affect the operation of the rule of law rendering void for remoteness certain dispositions under which property is limited to be applied for purposes other than the benefit of any person or class of persons in cases where the property may be so applied after the end of the perpetuity period.

(5) The foregoing sections of this Act shall apply (except as provided in section 8(2) above) only in relation to instruments taking effect after the commencement of this Act, and in the case of an instrument made in the exercise of a special power of appointment shall apply only where the instrument creating the power takes effect after that commencement;

Provided that section 7 above shall apply in all cases for construing the foregoing reference to a special power of appointment.

(6) This Act shall apply in relation to a disposition made otherwise than by an instrument as if the disposition had been contained in an instrument taking effect when the disposition was made.

(7) This Act binds the Crown.

Enduring Powers of Attorney Act 1985

A2.13   *Arrangement of sections*

s 3   Scope of authority etc of attorney under enduring power.

3   Scope of authority etc of attorney under enduring power

(1) An enduring power may confer general authority (as defined in subsection (2) below) on the attorney to act on the donor's behalf in relation to all or a specified part of the property and affairs of the donor or may confer on him authority to do specified things on the donor's behalf and the authority may, in either case, be conferred subject to conditions and restrictions.

(2) Where an instrument is expressed to confer general authority on the attorney it operates to confer, subject to the restriction imposed by subsection (5) below and to any conditions or restrictions contained in the instrument, authority to do on behalf of the donor anything which the donor can lawfully do by an attorney.

(3) …

(4) Subject to any conditions or restrictions contained in the instrument, an attorney under an enduring power, whether general or limited, may (without obtaining any consent) act under the power so as to benefit himself or other persons than the donor to the following extent but no further, that is to say—

    (a)   he may so act in relation to himself or in relation to any other person if the donor might be expected to provide for his or that person's needs respectively; and

    (b)   he may do whatever the donor might be expected to do to meet those needs.

(5) Without prejudice to subsection (4) above but subject to any conditions or restrictions contained in the instrument, an attorney under an enduring power, whether general or limited, may (without obtaining any consent) dispose of the property of the donor by way of gift to the following extent but no further, that is to say—

    (a)   he may make gifts of a seasonal nature or at a time, or on an anniversary, of a birth or marriage, to persons (including himself) who are related to or connected with the donor, and

    (b)   he may make gifts to any charity to whom the donor made or might be expected to make gifts,

provided that the value of each such gift is not unreasonable having regard to all the circumstances and in particular the size of the donor's estate.

Children Act 1989

3   Meaning of 'parental responsibility'

(1) In this Act "parental responsibility" means all the rights, duties, powers, responsibilities and authority which by law a parent of a child has in relation to the child and his property.

(2) It also includes the rights, powers and duties which a guardian of the child's estate (appointed, before the commencement of section 5, to act generally) would have had in relation to the child and his property.

(3) The rights referred to in subsection (2) include, in particular, the right of the guardian to receive or recover in his own name, for the benefit of the child, property of whatever description and wherever situated which the child is entitled to receive or recover.

(4) The fact that a person has, or does not have, parental responsibility for a child shall not affect—

    (a)   any obligation which he may have in relation to the child (such as a statutory duty to maintain the child); or

    (b)   any rights which, in the event of the child's death, he (or any other person) may have in relation to the child's property.

(5) A person who—

    (a)   does not have parental responsibility for a particular child; but

    (b)   has care of the child,

may (subject to the provisions of this Act) do what is reasonable in all the circumstances of the case for the purpose of safeguarding or promoting the child's welfare.

Law of Property (Miscellaneous Provisions) Act 1989

A2.15   *Arrangement of sections*

s 1   Deeds and their execution.

1   Deeds and their execution

(1) Any rule of law which—

    (a)   restricts the substances on which a deed may be written;

    (b)   requires a seal for the valid execution of an instrument as a deed by an individual; or

    (c)   requires authority by one person to another to deliver an instrument as a deed on his behalf to be given by deed,

is abolished.

(2) An instrument shall not be a deed unless—

    (a)   it makes it clear on its face that it is intended to be a deed by the person making it or, as the case may be, by the parties to it (whether by describing itself as a deed or expressing itself to be executed or signed as a deed or otherwise); and

    (b)   it is validly executed as a deed by that person or, as the case may be, one or more of those parties.

(3) An instrument is validly executed as a deed by an individual if, and only if—

    (a)   it is signed—

        (i)   by him in the presence of a witness who attests the signature; or

        (ii)   at his direction and in his presence and the presence of two witnesses who each attest the signature; and

    (b)   it is delivered as a deed by him or a person authorised to do so on his behalf.

(4) In subsections (2) and (3) above "sign", in relation to an instrument, includes making one's mark on the instrument and "signature" is to be construed accordingly.

(5) Where a solicitor, duly certificated notary public or licensed conveyancer, or an agent or employee of a solicitor, duly certificated notary public or licensed conveyancer, in the course of or in connection with a transaction involving the disposition or creation of an interest in land, purports to deliver

an instrument as a deed on behalf of a party to the instrument, it shall be conclusively presumed in favour of a purchaser that he is authorised so to deliver the instrument.

(6) In subsection (5) above—

"disposition" and "purchaser" have the same meanings as in the Law of Property Act 1925;

"duly certificated notary public" has the same meaning as it has in the Solicitors Act 1974 by virtue of section 87 of that Act; and

"interest in land" means any estate, interest or charge in or over land …

(7) Where an instrument under seal that constitutes a deed is required for the purposes of an Act passed before this section comes into force, this section shall have effect as to signing, sealing or delivery of an instrument by an individual in place of any provision of that Act as to signing, sealing or delivery.

(8) The enactments mentioned in Schedule 1 to this Act (which in consequence of this section require amendments other than those provided by subsection (7) above) shall have effect with the amendments specified in that Schedule.

(9) Nothing in subsection (1)(b), (2), (3), (7) or (8) above applies in relation to deeds required or authorised to be made under—

(a) the seal of the county palatine of Lancaster;

(b) the seal of the Duchy of Lancaster; or

(c) the seal of the Duchy of Cornwall.

(10) The references in this section to the execution of a deed by an individual do not include execution by a corporation sole and the reference in subsection (7) above to signing, sealing or delivery by an individual does not include signing, sealing or delivery by such a corporation.

(11) Nothing in this section applies in relation to instruments delivered as deeds before this section comes into force.

Charities Act 1993

A2.16 *Arrangement of sections*

36 Restrictions on dispositions

(1) Subject to the following provisions of this section and section 40 below, no land held by or in trust for a charity shall be sold, leased or otherwise disposed of without an order of the court or of the Commissioners.

(2) Subsection (1) above shall not apply to a disposition of such land if—

    (a) the disposition is made to a person who is not—

        (i) a connected person (as defined in Schedule 5 to this Act), or

        (ii) a trustee for, or nominee of, a connected person; and

    (b) the requirements of subsection (3) or (5) below have been complied with in relation to it.

(3) Except where the proposed disposition is the granting of such a lease as is mentioned in subsection (5) below, the charity trustees must, before entering into an agreement for the sale, or (as the case may be) for a lease or other disposition, of the land—

    (a) obtain and consider a written report on the proposed disposition from a qualified surveyor instructed by the trustees and acting exclusively for the charity;

    (b) advertise the proposed disposition for such period and in such manner as the surveyor has advised in his report (unless he has there advised that it would not be in the best interests of the charity to advertise the proposed disposition); and

    (c) decide that they are satisfied, having considered the surveyor's report, that the terms on which the disposition is proposed to be made are the best that can reasonably be obtained for the charity.

(4) For the purposes of subsection (3) above a person is a qualified surveyor if—

(a) he is a fellow or professional associate of the Royal Institution of Chartered Surveyors or of the Incorporated Society of Valuers and Auctioneers or satisfies such other requirement or requirements as may be prescribed by regulations made by the Secretary of State; and

(b) he is reasonably believed by the charity trustees to have ability in, and experience of, the valuation of land of the particular kind, and in the particular area, in question;

and any report prepared for the purposes of that subsection shall contain such information, and deal with such matters, as may be prescribed by regulations so made.

(5) Where the proposed disposition is the granting of a lease for a term ending not more than seven years after it is granted (other than one granted wholly or partly in consideration of a fine), the charity trustees must, before entering into an agreement for the lease—

(a) obtain and consider the advice on the proposed disposition of a person who is reasonably believed by the trustees to have the requisite ability and practical experience to provide them with competent advice on the proposed disposition; and

(b) decide that they are satisfied, having considered that person's advice, that the terms on which the disposition is proposed to be made are the best that can reasonably be obtained for the charity.

(6) Where—

(a) any land is held by or in trust for a charity, and

(b) the trusts on which it is so held stipulate that it is to be used for the purposes, or any particular purposes, of the charity,

then (subject to subsections (7) and (8) below and without prejudice to the operation of the preceding provisions of this section) the land shall not be sold, leased or otherwise disposed of unless the charity trustees have previously—

(i) given public notice of the proposed disposition, inviting representations to be made to them within a time specified in the notice, being not less than one month from the date of the notice; and

(ii) taken into consideration any representations made to them within that time about the proposed disposition.

(7) Subsection (6) above shall not apply to any such disposition of land as is there mentioned if—

(a) the disposition is to be effected with a view to acquiring by way of replacement other property which is to be held on the trusts referred to in paragraph (b) of that subsection; or

(b) the disposition is the granting of a lease for a term ending not more than two years after it is granted (other than one granted wholly or partly in consideration of a fine).

(8) The Commissioners may direct—

    (a)   that subsection (6) above shall not apply to dispositions of land held by or in trust for a charity or class of charities (whether generally or only in the case of a specified class of dispositions or land, or otherwise as may be provided in the direction), or

    (b)   that that subsection shall not apply to a particular disposition of land held by or in trust for a charity,

if, on an application made to them in writing by or on behalf of the charity or charities in question, the Commissioners are satisfied that it would be in the interests of the charity or charities for them to give the direction.

(9) The restrictions on disposition imposed by this section apply notwithstanding anything in the trusts of a charity; but nothing in this section applies—

    (a)   to any disposition for which general or special authority is expressly given (without the authority being made subject to the sanction of an order of the court) by any statutory provision contained in or having effect under an Act of Parliament or by any scheme legally established; or

    (b)   to any disposition of land held by or in trust for a charity which—

        (i)   is made to another charity otherwise than for the best price that can reasonably be obtained, and

        (ii)   is authorised to be so made by the trusts of the first-mentioned charity; or

    (c)   to the granting, by or on behalf of a charity and in accordance with its trusts, of a lease to any beneficiary under those trusts where the lease—

        (i)   is granted otherwise than for the best rent that can reasonably be obtained; and

        (ii)   is intended to enable the demised premises to be occupied for the purposes, or any particular purposes, of the charity.

(10) Nothing in this section applies—

    (a)   to any disposition of land held by or in trust for an exempt charity;

    (b)   to any disposition of land by way of mortgage or other security; or

    (c)   to any disposition of an advowson.

(11) In this section "land" means land in England or Wales.

37 Supplementary provisions relating to dispositions

(1) Any of the following instruments, namely—

    (a)   any contract for the sale, or for a lease or other disposition, of land which is held by or in trust for a charity, and

    (b)   any conveyance, transfer, lease or other instrument effecting a disposition of such land,

shall state—

    (i)   that the land is held by or in trust for a charity,

    (ii)   whether the charity is an exempt charity and whether the disposition is one falling within paragraph (a), (b) or (c) of subsection (9) of section 36 above, and

    (iii)   if it is not an exempt charity and the disposition is not one falling within any of those paragraphs, that the land is land to which the restrictions on disposition imposed by that section apply.

(2) Where any land held by or in trust for a charity is sold, leased or otherwise disposed of by a disposition to which subsection (1) or (2) of section 36 above applies, the charity trustees shall certify in the instrument by which the disposition is effected—

    (a)   (where subsection (1) of that section applies) that the disposition has been sanctioned by an order of the court or of the Commissioners (as the case may be), or

    (b)   (where subsection (2) of that section applies) that the charity trustees have power under the trusts of the charity to effect the disposition, and that they have complied with the provisions of that section so far as applicable to it.

(3) Where subsection (2) above has been complied with in relation to any disposition of land, then in favour of a person who (whether under the disposition or afterwards) acquires an interest in the land for money or money's worth, it shall be conclusively presumed that the facts were as stated in the certificate.

(4) Where—

    (a)   any land held by or in trust for a charity is sold, leased or otherwise disposed of by a disposition to which subsection (1) or (2) of section 36 above applies, but

    (b)   subsection (2) above has not been complied with in relation to the disposition,

then in favour of a person who (whether under the disposition or afterwards) in good faith acquires an interest in the land for money or money's worth, the disposition shall be valid whether or not—

(i)   the disposition has been sanctioned by an order of the court or of the Commissioners, or

(ii) the charity trustees have power under the trusts of the charity to effect the disposition and have complied with the provisions of that section so far as applicable to it.

(5) Any of the following instruments, namely—

(a)   any contract for the sale, or for a lease or other disposition, of land which will, as a result of the disposition, be held by or in trust for a charity, and

(b)   any conveyance, transfer, lease or other instrument effecting a disposition of such land,

shall state—

(i)   that the land will, as a result of the disposition, be held by or in trust for a charity,

(ii) whether the charity is an exempt charity, and

(iii) if it is not an exempt charity, that the restrictions on disposition imposed by section 36 above will apply to the land (subject to subsection (9) of that section).

(6) ...

(7) Where the disposition to be effected by any such instrument as is mentioned in subsection (1)(b) or (5)(b) above will be—

(a)   a registrable disposition, or

(b)   a disposition which triggers the requirement of registration,

the statement which, by virtue of subsection (1) or (5) above, is to be contained in the instrument shall be in such form as may be prescribed by land registration rules.

(8) Where the registrar approves an application for registration of—

(a)   a disposition of registered land, or

(b)   a person's title under a disposition of unregistered land,

and the instrument effecting the disposition contains a statement complying with subsections (5) and (7) above, he shall enter in the register a restriction reflecting the limitation under section 36 above on subsequent disposal.

(9) Where—

(a)   any such restriction is entered in the register in respect of any land, and

(b)   the charity by or in trust for which the land is held becomes an exempt charity, the charity trustees shall apply to the registrar for the removal of the entry; and on receiving any application duly made under this subsection the registrar shall remove the entry.

(10) Where—

(a) any registered land is held by or in trust for an exempt charity and the charity ceases to be an exempt charity, or

(b) any registered land becomes, as a result of a declaration of trust by the registered proprietor, land held in trust for a charity (other than an exempt charity),

the charity trustees shall apply to the registrar for such a restriction as is mentioned in subsection (8) above to be entered in the register in respect of the land; and on receiving any application duly made under this subsection the registrar shall enter such a restriction in the register in respect of the land.

(11) In this section—

(a) references to a disposition of land do not include references to—

(i) a disposition of land by way of mortgage or other security,

(ii) any disposition of an advowson, or

(iii) any release of a rentcharge failing within section 40(1) below; and

(b) "land" means land in England or Wales;

and subsections (7) to (10) above shall be construed as one with the Land Registration Act 2002.

38   Restrictions on mortgaging

(1) Subject to subsection (2) below, no mortgage of land held by or in trust for a charity shall be granted without an order of the court or of the Commissioners.

(2) Subsection (1) above shall not apply to a mortgage of any such land by way of security for the repayment of a loan where the charity trustees have, before executing the mortgage, obtained and considered proper advice, given to them in writing, on the matters mentioned in subsection (3) below.

(3) Those matters are—

(a) whether the proposed loan is necessary in order for the charity trustees to be able to pursue the particular course of action in connection with which the loan is sought by them;

(b) whether the terms of the proposed loan are reasonable having regard to the status of the charity as a prospective borrower; and

(c)   the ability of the charity to repay on those terms the sum proposed to be borrowed.

(4) For the purposes of subsection (2) above proper advice is the advice of a person—

(a)   who is reasonably believed by the charity trustees to be qualified by his ability in and practical experience of financial matters; and

(b)   who has no financial interest in the making of the loan in question;

and such advice may constitute proper advice for those purposes notwithstanding that the person giving it does so in the course of his employment as an officer or employee of the charity or of the charity trustees.

(5) This section applies notwithstanding anything in the trusts of a charity; but nothing in this section applies to any mortgage for which general or special authority is given as mentioned in section 36(9)(a) above.

(6) In this section—

"land" means land in England or Wales;

"mortgage" includes a charge.

(7) Nothing in this section applies to an exempt charity.

39   Supplementary provisions relating to mortgaging

(1) Any mortgage of land held by or in trust for a charity shall state—

(a)   that the land is held by or in trust for a charity,

(b)   whether the charity is an exempt charity and whether the mortgage is one falling within subsection (5) of section 38 above, and

(c)   if it is not an exempt charity and the mortgage is not one falling within that subsection, that the mortgage is one to which the restrictions imposed by that section apply;

and where the mortgage will be a registered disposition any such statement shall be in such form as may be prescribed by land registration rules.

(1A) Where any such mortgage will be one to which section 4(1)(g) of the Land Registration Act 2002 applies—

(a)   the statement required by subsection (1) above shall be in such form as may be prescribed by land registration rules; and

(b)   if the charity is not an exempt charity, the mortgage shall also contain a statement, in such form as may be prescribed by land registration rules, that the restrictions on disposition imposed by section 36 above apply to the land (subject to subsection (9) of that section).

(1B) Where—

> (a)   the registrar approves an application for registration of a person's title to land in connection with such a mortgage as is mentioned in subsection (1A) above,

> (b)   the mortgage contains statements complying with subsections (1) and (1A) above, and

> (c)   the charity is not an exempt charity,

the registrar shall enter in the register a restriction reflecting the limitation under section 36 above on subsequent disposal.

(1C) Section 37(9) above shall apply in relation to any restriction entered under subsection (1B) as it applies in relation to any restriction entered under section 37(8).

(2) Where subsection (1) or (2) of section 38 above applies to any mortgage of land held by or in trust for a charity, the charity trustees shall certify in the mortgage—

> (a)   (where subsection (1) of that section applies) that the mortgage has been sanctioned by an order of the court or of the Commissioners (as the case may be), or

> (b)   (where subsection (2) of that section applies) that the charity trustees have power under the trusts of the charity to grant the mortgage, and that they have obtained and considered such advice as is mentioned in that subsection.

(3) Where subsection (2) above has been complied with in relation to any mortgage, then in favour of a person who (whether under the mortgage or afterwards) acquires an interest in the land in question for money or money's worth, it shall be conclusively presumed that the facts were as stated in the certificate.

(4) Where—

> (a)   subsection (1) or (2) of section 38 above applies to any mortgage of land held by or in trust for a charity, but

> (b)   subsection (2) above has not been complied with in relation to the mortgage,

then in favour of a person who (whether under the mortgage or afterwards) in good faith acquires an interest in the land for money or money's worth, the mortgage shall be valid whether or not—

> (i)   the mortgage has been sanctioned by an order of the court or of the Commissioners, or

> (ii)   the charity trustees have power under the trusts of the charity to grant the mortgage and have obtained and considered such advice as is mentioned in subsection (2) of that section.

(5) ...

(6) In this section—

"mortgage" includes a charge, and "mortgagee" shall be construed accordingly;

"land" means land in England or Wales;

and subsections (1) to (1B) above shall be construed as one with the Land Registration Act 2002.

40   Release of charity rentcharges

(1) Section 36(1) above shall not apply to the release by a charity of a rentcharge which it is entitled to receive if the release is given in consideration of the payment of an amount which is not less than ten times the annual amount of the rentcharge.

(2) Where a charity which is entitled to receive a rentcharge releases it in consideration of the payment of an amount not exceeding £500, any costs incurred by the charity in connection with proving its title to the rentcharge shall be recoverable by the charity from the person or persons in whose favour the rentcharge is being released.

(3) Neither section 36(1) nor subsection (2) above applies where a rentcharge which a charity is entitled to receive is redeemed under sections 8 to 10 of the Rentcharges Act 1977.

(4) The Secretary of State may by order amend subsection (2) above by substituting a different sum for the sum for the time being specified there.

72   Persons disqualified for being trustees of a charity

(1) Subject to the following provisions of this section, a person shall be disqualified for being a charity trustee or trustee for a charity if—

    (a)   he has been convicted of any offence involving dishonesty or deception;

    (b)   he has been adjudged bankrupt or sequestration of his estate has been awarded and (in either case) he has not been discharged;

    (c)   he has made a composition or arrangement with, or granted a trust deed for, his creditors and has not been discharged in respect of it;

    (d)   he has been removed from the office of charity trustee or trustee for a charity by an order made—

        (i)   by the Commissioners under section 18(2)(i) above, or

        (ii)   by the Commissioners under section 20(1A)(i) of the Charities Act 1960 (power to act for protection of charities) or under section 20(1)(i) of that Act (as in force before the commencement of section 8 of the Charities Act 1992), or

(iii) by the High Court,

on the grounds of any misconduct or mismanagement in the administration of the charity for which he was responsible or to which he was privy, or which he by his conduct contributed to or facilitated;

(e) he has been removed, under section 7 of the Law Reform (Miscellaneous Provisions) (Scotland) Act 1990 (powers of Court of Session to deal with management of charities), from being concerned in the management or control of any body;

(f) he is subject to a disqualification order under the Company Directors Disqualification Act 1986 or to an order made under section 429(2)(b) of the Insolvency Act 1986 (failure to pay under county court administration order).

(2) In subsection (1) above—

(a) paragraph (a) applies whether the conviction occurred before or after the commencement of that subsection, but does not apply in relation to any conviction which is a spent conviction for the purposes of the Rehabilitation of Offenders Act 1974;

(b) paragraph (b) applies whether the adjudication of bankruptcy or the sequestration occurred before or after the commencement of that subsection;

(c) paragraph (c) applies whether the composition or arrangement was made, or the trust deed was granted, before or after the commencement of that subsection; and

(d) paragraphs (d) to (f) apply in relation to orders made and removals effected before or after the commencement of that subsection.

(3) Where (apart from this subsection) a person is disqualified under subsection (1)(b) above for being a charity trustee or trustee for any charity which is a company, he shall not be so disqualified if leave has been granted under section 11 of the Company Directors Disqualification Act 1986 (undischarged bankrupts) for him to act as director of the charity; and similarly a person shall not be disqualified under subsection (1)(f) above for being a charity trustee or trustee for such a charity if—

(a) in the case of a person subject to a disqualification order or disqualification undertaking under the Company Directors Disqualification Act 1986, leave for the purposes of section 1(1)(a) or 1A(1)(a) of that Act has been granted for him to act as director of the charity,

(aa) in the case of a person subject to a disqualification order under

Part II of the Companies (Northern Ireland) Order 1989, leave has been granted by the High Court in Northern Ireland for him to act as director of the charity

(b) in the case of a person subject to an order under section 429(2)(b) of the Insolvency Act 1986, leave has been granted by the court which made the order for him to so act.

(4) The Commissioners may, on the application of any person disqualified under subsection (1) above, waive his disqualification either generally or in relation to a particular charity or a particular class of charities; but no such waiver may be granted in relation to any charity which is a company if—

(a) the person concerned is for the time being prohibited, by virtue of—

(i) a disqualification order or disqualification undertaking under the Company Directors Disqualification Act 1986, or

(ii) section 11(1), 12(2) or 12A of that Act (undischarged bankrupts; failure to pay under county court administration order; Northern Irish disqualification orders),

from acting as director of the charity; and

(b) leave has not been granted for him to act as director of any other company.

(5) Any waiver under subsection (4) above shall be notified in writing to the person concerned.

(6) For the purposes of this section the Commissioners shall keep, in such manner as they think fit, a register of all persons who have been removed from office as mentioned in subsection (1)(d) above either—

(a) by an order of the Commissioners made before or after the commencement of subsection (1) above, or

(b) by an order of the High Court made after the commencement of section 45(1) of the Charities Act 1992;

and, where any person is so removed from office by an order of the High Court, the court shall notify the Commissioners of his removal.

(7) The entries in the register kept under subsection (6) above shall be available for public inspection in legible form at all reasonable times.

73 Persons acting as charity trustee while disqualified

(1) Subject to subsection (2) below, any person who acts as a charity trustee or trustee for a charity while he is disqualified for being such a trustee by virtue of section 72 above shall be guilty of an offence and liable—

    (a)   on summary conviction, to imprisonment for a term not exceeding six months or to a fine not exceeding the statutory maximum, or both;

    (b)   on conviction on indictment, to imprisonment for a term not exceeding two years or to a fine, or both.

(2) Subsection (1) above shall not apply where—

    (a)   the charity concerned is a company; and

    (b)   the disqualified person is disqualified by virtue only of paragraph (b) or (f) of section 72(1) above.

(3) Any acts done as charity trustee or trustee for a charity by a person disqualified for being such a trustee by virtue of section 72 above shall not be invalid by reason only of that disqualification.

(4) Where the Commissioners are satisfied—

    (a)   that any person has acted as charity trustee or trustee for a charity (other than an exempt charity) while disqualified for being such a trustee by virtue of section 72 above, and

    (b)   that, while so acting, he has received from the charity any sums by way of remuneration or expenses, or any benefit in kind, in connection with his acting as charity trustee or trustee for the charity,

they may by order direct him to repay to the charity the whole or part of any such sums, or (as the case may be) to pay to the charity the whole or part of the monetary value (as determined by them) of any such benefit.

(5) Subsection (4) above does not apply to any sums received by way of remuneration or expenses in respect of any time when the person concerned was not disqualified for being a charity trustee or trustee for the charity.

Index